The Boulevards of Extinction

The Boulevards of Extinction

A. BRUNNEIS

RESOURCE *Publications* • Eugene, Oregon

THE BOULEVARDS OF EXTINCTION

Copyright © 2015 A. Brunneis. All rights reserved. Except for brief quotations in critical publications or reviews, no part of this book may be reproduced in any manner without prior written permission from the publisher. Write: Permissions, Wipf and Stock Publishers, 199 W. 8th Ave., Suite 3, Eugene, OR 97401.

Resource Publications
An Imprint of Wipf and Stock Publishers
199 W. 8th Ave., Suite 3
Eugene, OR 97401

www.wipfandstock.com

ISBN 13: 978-1-4982-2999-9

Manufactured in the U.S.A. 11/03/2015

For Cassandra,
Whose prophecies will always have an ear

Μοῦσά μοι Εὐρυμεδοντιάδεω τὴν ποντοχάρυβδιν,
τὴν ἐγγαστριμάχαιραν, ὃς ἐσθίει οὐ κατὰ κόσμον,
ἔννεφ', ὅπως ψηφῖδι <κακῇ> κακὸν οἶτον ὄληται
βουλῇ δημοσίῃ παρὰ θῖν' ἁλὸς ἀτρυγέτοιο.

—Hipponax, fragment 128

Contents

PART 1
Daggers · 1

PART 2
Nightcaps · 9

PART 3
Muses · 39

PART 4
Night Sweats · 53

PART 5
The Philistine's Dictionary · 109

PART 6
Gray Dawn · 193

PART 7
Monsters · 267

PART 8
Eclipse · 293

PART 9
Syringes · 333

Part 1

Daggers

The world is a watercolor drop on a crude oil canvas.

When Folly speaks in her own person the fools only hear praise.

Courtly love was a war of attrition; modern love is a blitzkrieg.

Models of content: the blighted ovum, the gaping mouth, the car trunk, the freshly dug grave. From the womb to the tomb, we are so much more than absent-*minded*.

Thanatos: Our first recourse on a windless sea.

Happiness has been the subject of many sitcoms but no documentaries.

There is such a thing as a lucky thought. Many thinkers make their careers off of betting the same number on every spin of the roulette wheel.

If Jesus had turned bread into chocolate, Cana would be infamous for its flower girls—disciplettes of the Pimp of Peace.

For a parched cheek, raindrops offer catharsis on loan. Those unable to weep can at least soak themselves in heaven's sorrow.

It's hard to know God when his finger is on their button.

Scientism is the thoughtful twin of Chaos. To balance annihilation, the "theory of everything" is constructed as a way to *explain* nothing.

The choice between savagery and monotony largely depends on whether you focus on the shipwreck or the island paradise.

But there *is* a royal road to geometry—defenestration. A square, space, a solid plane: knowledge easily accessible.

The gift of technology will culminate with Prometheus escaping the raven and presenting moonshine to firefighter trainees.

Less theatrical than "greatness of soul" is the pants-passion of Epicureanism. The first drama is all character, the second all plot.

Pick a pocket or rob a convenience store: then you will know what it's like to live as an artist.

One suspects that certain people rely on fresh breath to help them speak well, when in truth they just like drinking their mouthwash.

The closest proof that you experienced consciousness will be your novelization.

The free marketplace of ideas: that invisible head which everywhere and nowhere contradicts itself for the sake of inclusiveness so that no idea is left standing against the wall of the cocktail party. A world of nondiscrimination where no thought is a falsehood—the sole judge is fashion.

Derision of love is the cutter's sense of release, the peace of mind obtained from ripping off one's bandages and fingering the wound.

Every forbidden realm of logic has its preferred fallacy-turned-virtue. In politics it is the *argumentum ad temperantiam*, among married couples the *ad nauseam*, at funerals the *ad ignorantiam*, in the delivery room *petitio principii*.

Twinkling heavenly bodies go unmapped as stargazers point their telescopes towards the nebulas around the masterpiece.

A theory of practice is a bird's eye experience that lacks ground perspective. It sees the lines of paved streets but overlooks the back alley shortcuts.

If you're intent on speaking artfully, pay a scribe to follow you around and record your utterances; for no one else in the room will grasp the subtlety of your meaning. Don't, however, pay a documentary filmmaker: those who watch your diary will attend only to the extraverbal superfluities, and dismiss what you say based on the shabbiness of your bearing.

Outside every desire a lawyer and a doctor conspire to gain admission.

An iconoclast lacerates idols with the shards from his own stained glass window.

Felatious inferences: the swallowing of every strict logical consequence. A logician is often caught wide-eyed when his premises explode all over his face.

Expediency rubs off on people the closer they chafe to the board chair; excellence does business near the throne, at the urinal.

The rebel artist stands proudly as the centerpiece of the businessperson's hors d'oeuvres platter.

If Heraclitus were alive today he would recommend waterboarding his native Ephesians for the secrets of their ignorance—to protect them from the *logos*.

Discarding the ladder once you climb it won't rid you of your past, unless you're standing on the top rung when it falls.

A man with no name is free to identify himself with any symbol. When the tide is right he will salute even swimming flags and rescue aliases from shark victims.

Part 1: Daggers

Much of what constitutes admiration is the wish that the admirer's mistakes, too, will be fortuitous.

Consumerism is the millenialization of venerable legalities. First the Magna Carta, then the Magna Mart—a cartful of tupperware crowns and produce sceptors available on discount.

All the handbooks for princes could not prevent a merchant from opening one. Since then, the genre of leadership advice has been aimed at everyone but leaders—there are many handbooks for losers, none for presidents.

The three estates: those who prey, those who cite, those who shirk.

The problem of evil must fit, for a bureaucrat, within a memo; a scientist, the treatment group; an artist, the limits of talent.

Too late to step on the garden snake . . . you have already fled into the jungle.

To lie in a puddle all day and recommend your chiropractor to everyone who steps on your spine . . . with a chivalry that leaves the jacket at home, the chiropractor takes seriously the notion of putting his back into his work to achieve success.

Heaping data on the most dubious hypothesis inundates it into a paradigm.

Scientific progress has turned death into a procrastination interrupted by an accident. Backpedaling against a waterfall, we are hit by a thunderbolt.

If only we would *twist* the butter knife, lipid revaccination wouldn't need to wait for fat season.

A people must train for centuries to endure a single generation of freedom. Against *two* generations nothing can discipline them.

The liberator oppresses the under-trodden with promises their natures can't deliver on.

Young Fritz von Hardenberg's insistence, contra his catechism lessons, that the body is made of the same stuff as the soul was inversely correct: the soul is the tenderest part of the meat. To stifle the boy's abstractedness the Prediger had only to give his dreams a good whipping.

The conversion of flesh into tumor helps one cope with spirituality.

To boil down the subtle ideas of the great books into diazepam and inject it into my veins. Instead of the gradual toxic buildup of detail by time and effort, a lethal dose of the elusiveness of enlightenment.

To take advantage of clarity before it grows into suprasensual understanding, one has only to think a pleasant thought.

One who distributes just actions like falling leaves but is niggardly with his affections, practicing all the hard virtues for want of capacity for the easy ones—who does not love—avoids the misfortunes of both the stampeded shepherd and the cuckolded rooster. Authoritarian figures are best suited to raise a vegetable farm, practicing bloodletting on beets and spanking the earth with a hoe.

Glancing both towards the orient and the occident, the universal mind is a cross-eyed half-breed.

There are no defeats in philosophy, only advances and withdrawals . . . until the shore erodes.

The most commonly shared trait among natural-born Americans is cheeseburger-concentrate in the placenta. America is a likeness discovered later, inside a fast food embassy.

Thieves break even as long as they lose both hands.

Charlatans of superiority crave the adulation of those they despise, dismissing private thoughts as a reward for molding their own to public opinion.

If only snow would fall up, so Heaven's "good souls" might warm themselves . . .

The admirable emotions hackneyed by kitsch, those touched by the muse distance themselves from sentimentality by delineating the sideshow fervors instead. Instead of renovating the tabernacle of love to enchant more discriminating congregants, they build a fetish academy.

The Kyoto School: of all philosophy's pollinators, the only ones who did more than send a bee over the fence.

Hard to occupy a middle rank in society and be without illusions. Such people were only raised high enough to set an example for those above them.

Every idea has been theorized before by someone who didn't phrase it more memorably.

Like Saturn at a family reunion, we ravenously devour children, parents, cousins—all which threatens the integrity of the self, which renders it less than completely unique. Even the babysitter must go: the remunerated memories, especially, must be consumed.

PART 1: Daggers

In a telecommunications age the most efficient response is still the messenger's head.

Until the nineteenth century there was no need for a hedonistic calculus—the suffering principle was the universal measure of the human condition. In the twenty-first century there is no *possibility* of one—the gauge burst in the twentieth.

Absent, absinthe: my artificial intoxications deprived of lucidity, I resort to spasming a clear and distinct delirium.

"Real-world" piety: for the professional laity even salvation is just another material ambition. Communion-goers, looking to double their transubstantiation, drink the blood of Jesus to micturate the gold of the magi.

So many stories devoted to redeeming our sympathy for bad men, not nearly enough showing the greater irresponsibility of good ones.

The overture to Napoleon's downfall was not the 1812 campaign, but the 1796 sentimental novella.

Embracing a leper, marrying into Down syndrome—loving without beauty to take refuge in would be love's bottomless substantiation, were not our flaws present to deny us purity even here. The tender mercies melt us through *dirtiness* . . .

"Politically correct" is the diplomatic way of describing the opponent's position.

My only friends are philosophers no one has heard of. Less a waste of intimacy than to know philosophers everyone summarizes.

The fraudulent wits: it takes an *amiable* humor to brighten partial truths into boundless possibilities, exposing the totality of error that had always been hidden there.

No message in a bottle will ever find a shore if it can't be put into a daily news bulletin. Unless a man sings from his soul's catalogue of radio hits, he will end up like Schubert—a corpse stuffed with unheard lieder.

Widely quoted in essays and articles, my reputation will not be secure until I receive mention in suicide notes. A *Werther*vane.

Bones and organs: the ossuary decorates its walls with what surrounds our souls so the toccata can howl through them unobstructed.

Universal sainthood is a potluck where the congregation brings stale wafers, the hermits bring moldy manna, and no one is allowed to vomit.

The father of nations is Abraham, expatriates Isaac, citizens the ram.

It's a waste feeling love's weightlessness if you don't *tell* your lover why you'll have to be scraped off the pavement.

Man is a card sharp with a two of clubs up his sleeve.

PART 2

Nightcaps

My Cat

I have named my pleasure, and this pleasure I call "my cat." My cat chases rats around as they appear from holes in the wall. Its large green eyes are visible through even the darkness as it fixes its gaze upon its objects. It startles the subjects of its gaze at first, but initial fear becomes the driving force behind a rising sense of awe as the large unrelenting eyes fill them with a feeling of confidence. "This creature," the rats say, "*should* have its way with me."

My cat is quick and agile and I can never seem to lay my hands on it and train it to obey. It didn't take long to think up this name, "cat," but the question remains whether I *own* it, whether it is *my* pet name. Not because it doesn't rightly fit me, but because it is too solitary to belong to me. Myself a solitary being, I sympathize with our common natures, and yet we are opposed in our mutual nobility. It is too selfish to be subdued by me, and I am too proud to do anything but let it run rampant. Chasing my cat like it does its rats demonstrates to others both that it is out of control—I am too clumsy and slow to catch it—and that I am just a poor imitation of my name, that I am not the real thing. The quality of my cat that bedevils me, that renders me powerless to conquer it—its elusiveness—is also the source of my respect for it. As I wear this name longer, I come to forget that I ever had any other name—that I ever *could* have any but this one.

More Is a Faster Lessening

Everyone praises the endurance of the ascetic, but no one appreciates the stamina of the hedonist. To laugh until the throat burns and smoke a cigar to soothe it, to black out but not pass out, to suspend love's climax, to be immortal in the moment—what Stoic has such fortitude: to die upon the seizure and slump of orgasm? The sunrise is an unappealing reprise of "business as usual." Only the stoic loves the morning light; he needs no promise to realize the protestant work ethic: life itself is full of *good* purpose enough. Prolonging desires well past the point of the modest effort it would take to fulfill them, self-deniers tremble from the tectonic shifts of suppressed impulses. They put their drives in park and suffer motion sickness. But the Heroin Heroine is a nocturnal creature: she knows all too well that nature is "red in tooth and claw"—her leopard jacket is stained with wine. She purifies the red inside her with the white, diluting blood with opioid milk. Survival is ancillary; it serves a higher purpose, and is relinquished before it is scurried after.

Where are the hagiographies of the great hedonists? The story of the old flaccid saint who, filled with the spirit in his nether-region, miraculously deflowered a hundred virgins? The example of the desert monastic who wandered upon a vineyard oasis and imbibed his weight in wine? After asceticism's preparation for mystical grace one must adopt a method proper to its reception. Catholicism awaits the discovery of the lost dialogues of Gregory I, in which he advocates practicing the seven deadly sins as a test of resilience.

Ascetic when young, hedonist when old. —How much perplexity and grudging respect would be due such a person! And when the change comes, how much disappointment from those familiar with the original self. But can one blame him? It was not that he was making up for lost time; he had already saved it by preempting folly in his youth. In the end he dispensed with the wisdom he no longer needed—upon reaching a certain age he found that no one was paying attention to it. By shifting strategies grandpa became *fun*, someone the new generation could appreciate.

But after all this, ascetic and hedonist alike share the common value of *uncoming*. Each way represents an art of life, two roads leading unto one destruction, converging stylizations of the inevitable.

In certain periods one method predominates—to the forced inclusion of the other. In an epicurean society every act of denial which the lonely Stoic practices is mistaken for the nausea after the binge, every illustration of asceticism the fasting before the feast. Not seeing the whole of his life (for that he would really be shunned), observers see a slice of it and take it as an indication of the sickness surrounding excess. They accord him the respect of a master indulger, wishing they could someday be as experienced as him, eager to surpass his record of debauchery. At the same time they urge more indulgences upon him, pleading with him not to rest now when he is so close to that final indulgence that would enter his name into the hall of fame. It takes a man of mighty resolution to resist peer pressure . . . but what Stoic has ever not thrived on the public respect for his lifestyle, and has not hesitated to give it up when the tenor of the times calls for *this* final relinquishment? And so, surrounded by outstretched arms weighed down by fistfuls of spices and fruits, the Stoic embraces the colic that follows from eating after prolonged starvation. He undertakes this submission as his last victory over hedonism, and he has good reason to be proud: he did not *want* his accepted donations.

Sexually Transmitted Congruence

Goat bladder—Minos's bedroom Minotaur.
Queen Anne's lace—Hippocrates's hemlock.
Pennyroyal tea—Dioscorides's organ failure.
Pepper—Pope John XXI's damnation.
Lemon rind—Casanova's withdrawal from life into autobiography.
Cotton root bark—the Confederacy's domestic war.
Diaphragm—veil of America's second Gilded Age.

PART 2: Nightcaps

***

Sexual evolution has a new yardstick for efficiency. It no longer needs to rely on a society's contraceptive methods to choreograph the dance between love and death. The spread of the HIV virus has finally harmonized Freud's conflict of Eros and Thanatos. By not restricting itself to socially acceptable outlets, precisely by raging to satisfy itself, the erotic instinct undermines its own will to preservation and acknowledges itself as part of the same being as death. Love appropriates immune system failure into its bosom, purifying Eros into Venus, freeing its swooners of any mundane justification of oath-keeping and family duty. With civilization as judge and biology executioner, those unwilling to submit to monogamy are only too happy to mercilessly punish themselves with pleasure. In the name of conscience, life allows its aggressiveness to express itself unchecked against the promiscuous population as organisms bounce towards their end in a horizontal limbo. Then, at the height of gratification, Venus turns the lovers into daisies and flies away. Those who survive are without guilt over their sexual frustration, bolstering the status quo in a confused earthly approximation of Nirvana—*the civil union.*

Mirth's Profession

Clowns entered the world laughing only to cry at the punch line of every joke not at their expense. They squeeze tiny feet into oversized shoes, hoping someone will step on them for the sake of being noticed; they wear a musical nose to attract fist notes as accompaniment to their sinus infection. That they are the saddest creatures in the world is a cliché; less well-known is that self-deprecation delights them in a world where everyone is taught respect.

Two Ways to Classify Common Sense

a) Internalizing the spirit of the age. Represented today by the man of economic self-reliance who watches team sports and possesses a sincere, feeble, and unconvincing sanguinity.

b) Perceiving the world as it enters the sense organs, packaged without bubble-wrap for return shipment. Possessed by few. Praised by none.

In each case interpretation is at a minimum. To the dreamy outsider, the laziness of the first group and the minimalist will of the second appear equally boorish, grounded as they are: the difference between fraternizer and realist is a choice between ant and beetle. The dreamer forgets that as a butterfly he was once a caterpillar and, on all but his best days, is still a chrysalis.

Elixirs of Flight

Work, politics, education, marriage and family life, church—the traditional institutions have ceased to provide fulfillment to its citizenry. Mother's milk has turned to powdered formula, and after choking down our nutrition we suckle on tart tonics to wash the taste from our mouths. We soil ourselves with small pleasures, reimbursing our libidos with the time and effort sapped from the old ways. Carnage, erotica, exotica, fun-physic: in a time of tradition when leisure was not yet vocation's stocking stuffer these things were no siesta helpmeets, but formed the bedrock of adventure. The knight errant, the buccaneer, the Casanova—before becoming the bromides of a drunken scriptwriter, such lovers of the blood were coagulations of reality into legend. Until the nineteenth century it was still possible for a man to be his own parable. But what was once a style of life has become proof of life—or if seen from without, a measure of *likelihood*. A vicarious experience is the only evidence of oxygen intake to the mouth breather. But to the voyeur of this spectator it is a sign of vegetation, the aerobics of comfort. As for one who despises the little things of life, who tires of rote stimulation and seeks *vast* pleasures—he is forced to live dangerously in a new way: through work, politics, education . . .

The Disciple

The teacher's ideas crawling through his head, he got the nurse to check it for lice, but he found that being prodded with sticks was little better than getting beaten with one. That was enough to cure him of both learning and annual checkups. Having discarded two types of exams, the mental and the physical, only his therapist was left to give him discomfort. Making weekly appointments to blunt his emotions, he prepared for his inkblot tests by making hand shadow puppets in a free-association sequence. His passions being all he had left, he was forced to regularly guard himself from them.

Love's Secrecy

To dare not tell; beyond this, the moment our partial nature is even *implied*, wholeness eludes us. A sad fate, as the truest love is a desperate love. Nonchalance only ever leads to an adjacency of two halves—a pie bisected before panning.

Eighth Heaven

We do not gradually ascend a train of thought from its sea-level beginning to its cloud-conclusion of inspiration, but dash there eagerly, overleaping any drops and creaky steps in-between. Paths of reasoning are outlines for flights of fancy. The stairway to heaven is too slow, too winding with the subtle and ambiguous; we require an elevator that lifts us to our biases without the effort of justification. Eventually a malfunction finds us trapped in the dark, mimicking the very pit we were trying to avoid all along. Only here, there is no privacy.

Ride to the Ophthalmologist

OPTIMIST: It is on the slow ride that the heart beats fastest.

REALIST: We would've snuggled on the Ferris wheel, it's true—but only the roller-coaster could have made me *scream*.

PESSIMIST: Yes, we most wish to love those who bore us.

IDEALIST: Then why not live the excitement of your dreams?

PRAGMATIST: Fine, just don't fall off the Ferris wheel in your simulated swoon—wear a seat belt!

METAPHYSICIAN: What for, when the fall would be such a short descent into heaven!

Brood for Brooding

If I ever have children I want them to be beautiful little fools. This way there will be no byproducts of an overly-developed consciousness to cause me embarrassment—whispers of therapy sessions, madhouse holidays, poetry readings. My children will simply want to have fun looking good, and they will bring me pride from the envy others feel for them. For what reason would a man want to have children, if not to reinforce a lifetime of intentional failure with a few successful accidents? Failure must not be undone, but augmented by its juxtaposition with success . . .

"Given the way your father is, it's amazing how *normal* you turned out!"

Translation: "Why do great creative minds so often pour all their imagination into their work and leave none for the fruit of their loins?"—Could it be because they need to achieve some sort of conventional recognition in their own lifetime to give them the freedom to *keep failing*? One cannot push originality into a realm of elite incomprehension without the emotional support of ignorant and oblivious relatives. The remorselessness of condemnation—from connoisseurs as well as the general populace—needs its parallel in a close circumference of pity for the incompetence in which one has lived. Every offensive personality trait and repulsive feature of physiognomy that can be presented as evidence of being cursed by the gods is, so long as one has sired a few beautiful little fools, one more lump of dust under the carpet.

The Ground

Unlike Kafka, Joyce, or Pessoa, I have no native city to transfigure into literature. Nor, like Thoreau, will I assimilate the wilderness into picturesque descriptions. My only alternative is to channel my experiences of the in-between life, and only provincial writers do that—artists whose souls have shrunk to the size of a town census or sprawled out in pointless suburban languishing.

It has been said Pessoa is the "writer of Lisbon," but it is a trivial thing to encapsulate metropolitan minds and manners. His was a much greater achievement: he is the flâneur of the sky. No one has ever captured its changeable oblivion as he did, how the strolling of storm clouds reflect his inner being. He looked without any intention of consuming the rain they had to offer—without any concern whether there really was any rain at all. He did not merely describe the sky, his inner being created it.

But where is the poet of the ground? The bottom half of Tiamat—that is something we are more familiar with. We were never intended to soar through the air; the sky is not high enough for our dreams. Our natural environment is the soil that ties us to one place even as we imagine others, the desolate beaches that tease us with their horizons, rocks that jut high into the air and, once scaled, make us *want* to fly. The poet of the ground would not describe personal dreams, but the trances and delusions of others as contrasted with their pitiful realities; he would not use the earth as a symbol for himself as such, but for the composition and granularity of his people. What is humanity, after all, but a rock at one extreme and sand at the other? The unbreakable exception is eroded by a lapping tide while the rest pour through God's fingers.

Human Languishing

Of all life forms, only the plant possesses negative liberty in the fullest degree possible. Free from the hunt for nourishment and mates, liberated from work, desire, and friendship, it has all the time in the world to do exactly what it is incapable of—to contemplate. The counterpart of the plant in the animal world is the philosopher. Worse than the voluptuary—who through thoughtless pleasure descends to the animal life—the philosopher does not seem on the surface to be a depraved creature. He is free enough from the menial tasks of life to seek exactly what he can never achieve—vegetation. The first man to shirk off his labor onto the back of another, solving the problem of having to work, was faced with the new problem of what to do. The result was the synaptic tremoring of our vexations, thought thinking itself, the frustration of every action. This in itself involves no depravity of character: one is absorbed into an ideal of beauty or truth, with the form of the object becoming identical to the form of consciousness. But an exclusive focus on the task can only be maintained for so long until awareness divorces itself from the activity and creeps back in, time speeds up, and anxiety returns. Heightened consciousness impedes effortlessness. One can only be happy when not thinking of oneself. The philosopher's contemplation—which he trumpets as the ultimate instrument of positive liberty, the crown of evolution which overcomes all obstacles—far from fostering tranquility (let alone *eudaemonia*, or even happiness), drives him into a frenzy of restlessness, discontent, and burnout. Thus does a total, unified freedom mock transcendence and become its own prison. It rockets one to the fullest actualization of his *purpose* and reveals it to be not only a limitation of *life*, but the very antithesis of his dream. Only when philosophers can grow into acorns, when their good spirit overcomes humanity to attain floral flourishing, will personality overcome destiny. The "man of character" is realized in one who relies on the weather alone. In the first stage of evolution we climbed; in the second, we slide.

If philosophy in it pure form is unable to address eudaemonia, as Williams concludes, what is it these thinkers are capturing when they advise us on values? Might such a willed negligence towards the lower affairs necessitate, not a "good spirit," but a display of *cacodaemonia*?

Anderesis

Be a monster of imbalance. Deformity of mind makes up for even bodily deformity by hoarding the world's ugliness. Amoral sense is the court of passion, the framework of daring. The earth's consolation prize, it turns dismal failure into a badge of success. It woos evil obliquely, though evil is too confused to acknowledge the signs; with some knowledge, it simulates unknowing. Its lack is never noticed, while its opposite is praised with empty words and never followed. Its influence on life is seldom acknowledged, through everything good is a side effect of it.

Rise of the Anti-Villain

Most people are basically good. I speak not of Rousseau's man in nature, but the modern goodness that thrives in a complex affluent society—one stemming not from willpower but likelihood. The goodness of non-interference, of deference to law and the division of labor. "Leave it be," these good people say, "the firefighters will put it out when they get here. Everything will *probably* be fine." But nothing is ever simply allowed to run its course, let alone flourish. Those who live and let live are vulnerable to the hunter in the shadows. A restrained Epicureanism, a "going with the flow": it is this mildness of character, this apathy disguised by pleasure, which makes these advocates of peacetime morality basically good. Those who grow up among the Sybarites, their sympathies dulled by specialization and suffering at a distance, are quickest to revert to the survival instinct when available resources become scarce; at bottom both inclinations are governed by a radical selfishness. Whichever one happens to be dominant is simply a matter of macroeconomics.

No classical hero was ever selfless. Saving the life of another was a sideshow of his glory, confirmation of an antecedent *arête*. Chivalry is killed when laurels are handed out for small acts of altruism. Heroes are a psychological privation in a society that rebukes merit; the hole needing to be filled, it is covered with a rug. Replacing bravery with common sense, the statistical savior exploits a moment of rescue time during a red stoplight and wins the glory of an evening news spot.

To be *superlatively* evil: to have all the most civilized vices and all the most dangerous virtues—characterization too customarily human to be stranger than fiction today. From this breach the anti-villain emerges as a balance to the emergency-rescue citizen. His opposition is as much a product of randomness as the champion's—casual irresponsibility of littering an underfoot banana peel to thwart the daring bystander rushing towards the crosswalk target. Cast in a supporting role without auditioning, the anti-villain is an antagonist whose only villainous qualities are neglect and incompetence. Not Darth Vader, but a storm trooper with a jammed blaster. His only threats are mordant remarks delivered to amuse a world without steadfast malice. With irony in his soul he commits feats of misdemeanors, deflating a murder mystery into manslaughter. Evil by default, he is the most fascinating character in the absence of a candid and upright protagonist. A bungling villain is always more interesting than an accidental hero.

An International Allegory

The foreign vices obtained passports to countries that had not yet learned to appreciate their subtleties. But upon going through customs they faced communication barriers.

Schadenfreude looked around, frowning . . . everyone was so happy. So deliberate. Not even an unfortunate accident to raise his spirits. So he stubbed his toe and laughed.

Ressentiment, correcting his upward glance, had learned to laugh at his inferiors for the sense of obligation they imposed. He gave careless orders, then waited for them to laugh at him—this is how he learned to admire himself again.

Esprit, long used to subjugating handlers to his method, had lost the autonomy of ventriloquizing his genius through prodigies. The prodigies had learned much from him and wanted to become their own masters, refusing to be dominated by their talent. The only type of mind that would now consent to be inhabited by him was an *esprit faux*, so he resigned himself to flowing through those who lack the rationality to govern him properly. To maximize his influence he formed an *esprit de corps* of misaligned minds who proceeded to escort wisdom down the ladder, presenting insights the populace could recognize as its own. Every nitwit he sanctioned became a twisted wit who amused the company with puns on truisms and trivia questions for troglodytes. *Esprit* did not know the answers to the trivia questions or grasp the puns. Surely, this did not mean he had been mitigated into a *Petite Esprit*; on the contrary, he was too elevated for his new vessels—this is how he reestablished a sense of control. But deep down he feared the approaching day when they, too, no longer needed him.

Desengaño had not always been seen as a vice. But when skepticism became the dominant attitude, he was suddenly reproached for being too sure of himself. He saw too much, it was said—this is how he stumbled. But he knew how to tell himself he still looked good after his accident. He put on glasses over empty eye sockets to feel the *weight* of his sight. If he could no longer be Argos, he would attach a knife to his cane to hear where he was going. If his other senses wouldn't compensate with any Tiresian insights, he would shut himself indoors and metamorphose into Morpheus, sleeping all day, dreaming up new illusions and awarenesses.

Virtù, with the welfare of the people in mind, flexed his disposition to public opinion polls. Fearing the determination to do what is necessary would be mistaken for the whims and cravings of a tyrant, he willed himself to do what he wanted so as to be seen as intrepid. When Fortuna dealt him a sex scandal, he responded with a board meeting and a blowjob to give him the courage of denial, a womanizing jazzman aspartaming his alibis with a sip of Diet Coke. To crush charges of warmongering he summoned all the eloquence dyslexia could muster, and rallied a martial spirit to invade territories where liberation would be immediate and internal collapse postponed until the next term. His achievements sponsored by election fundraising, he maintained the state by employing speech writers and resolved international crises by taking diplomatic missions to golf courses. *Virtù's* new strategy: the good citizen as good man, the art of filling a moral void with a power vacuum. The princes of the world deposed, statesmen rise to bow.

These vices had learned how to reason too much. They could no longer entice their common enemy—their only friend. For it was now up to man's virtues to save the vices from oblivion, to nurse them back to their old forcefulness. Opposed to these new self-defeating vices and without the old evils to define themselves against, the virtues had no choice but to push themselves into their extreme forms and act as surrogates for vice: Salubriousness's obsession with itself had driven it to the point of malnourishment; Amour became too intoxicated, Amicability too ulterior. Virtue wanted to revive the basic vices once again; the ambiguous modern forms of vice were too internalized to cause any real damage and took all the fun out of moral struggle. In the end the virtues didn't have to do anything; the new vices simply faded away—no one knew how to pronounce their own bad intentions. Faced with holes to plug, the virtues proceeded to draw native vices out of their own degenerated states: Gluttony from malnourishment, Lust from infatuation, Greed from parasitism.

Morality, like everything else, needs to occasionally repolarize itself to fuel people's need for taking sides.

The Boulevards of Extinction

The Anti-Hero

One can stand alone only by dispensing with the customary character traits. Heroes are a dime a dozen—I want you to be more singular than that. With a book that is a leviathan, I will make a goldfish of conscience—in proportion to its minuteness it will glow brightly and dazzle everyone.

Seneca formed a prudent person by heavily taxing Britannia, bringing about Boudicca's revolt, and writing epistles about prudence in place of a diary of greed; Homer fooled the entire world into thinking he was a single great bard instead of a lineage of unknowns; Scaevola thrust his hand into the flames to make Porsena think he was willing to risk all—the truth was, he had always been left-handed; Judith beheaded Holofernes because she ended up not satisfying him in bed; Castiglione became a great courtier: first his ambassadorial incompetence in the Spanish court led to the sack of Rome, then he instructed everyone on how to be an ideal Renaissance gentleman.

Flourish talents you lack and conceal your vices—you'll be thought a hero, all the while putting real heroes to shame. Let idealism and courage be practiced by the others—everyone is contending for dominance in those attributes, and they only end up badly. Nor should you languish or actively practice evil: even if you are one of the few capable of becoming competent in evil, it is just too much work to stay on the bottom. As an embodiment of amoral sense, you will practice the evil of just letting things happen, saving a few good effects of bad outcomes for yourself and letting the bad effects fall upon whom they may. Most are only indifferent to great evil; but you must be indifferent, too, to everyday goodness. Let no act of kindness go noticed.

Ignorance is the origin of everything that is thought great. Aim your wit below the belt: if it is too keen it will strike heads, and people will look up to see what flew over them.

Enflame hearts on an open grill, and their owners will invite you to dine on their compassion. Don't reveal your lack of interest until after you eat their heart.

Having good taste means scorning the popular and the avant-garde alike. Praise what has been previously praised but is now obscure to all but the learned. Instead of Shakespeare or Baudelaire, claim Ronsard as the poet laureate of your gray soul. Be a member of the *savant*-garde.

Make the best out of what is worst, then yawn as you say of the best: "It is *only* the best," or of the worst: "It is *just* worst."

Always remember: no matter how much of a scoundrel you are, a well-written book will secure your good reputation.

PART 2: Nightcaps

Life Bonds

Plastic surgery—a beauty more natural than natural, a hyper-natural beauty; the perfection of nature, its correction where mutation and adaptation went wrong. Cosmetic reconstruction makes an aesthetics possible that not only enhances our form but reshapes our function as well. When the human look becomes passé, we can xenograft behavioral templates from those species closest to us: baboon facelifts to turn every smile into an act of aggression, bonobo sex-drive surgery to redirect our warmongering.

Like bodies, society too may be reshaped internally to prevent the failure of its parts. In annexing the dogmas of religion, kosher prohibitions are sidestepped with pig organs; pork no longer passes through us but is made part of us: larynx implants that will make rabbis and imams oink their sermons, bovine breast augmentations in Hindu women to prevent dairy shortages and encourage grazing past toddlerhood.

In preventing crime, primate liver transplants for alcoholics may decrease the longevity of drunk driving.

When these alterations go out of style, more distant species can be turned to: rhinoceros rhinoplasty, giraffe neck lifts; for amputees, praying mantis limb-reattachment.

Republicans versus democrats: elephant trunks versus donkey ears—incompatible sense organs would impede bipartisan agreement *no less*.

Business models: pack rat trading, gross margin wolfing, financial foxing. One does not graft parts here so much as substitute higher mammals for purer ones.

The rejuvenation of family values: filling children full of cotton to make them as charming as their stuffed animals. "Life" becomes a criterion of cuteness and obedience.

After assimilating every animal species into us, organisms from the Jurassic period are reconstructed to satisfy our need for anatomical novelty: pterodactyl wings, tyrannosaurus jaws, hair plugs taken from the *Cladophlebis* fern. We regress back through geological history to satisfy our craving for trendy new forms and reverse evolutionary functions. Eliminating back pain with trilobite exoskeletons; taking spoonfuls of primordial soup to treat chickenpox. In the act of absorbing Earth's biological saga, future peoples will read its diary from our fossil remains.

Usurping Half of Zoroastrianism

Ahriman: evil spirit flowing through all other gods, god beyond gods, driving their ambition to create and rule. He is the Loneliness before the creation of the world, the egomania that craves something small to stroke it. The cruelty of Greek anthropomorphism, the better half of Ahuramazda. Yahweh's irrational vengeance: going beyond repaying kind for kind to surpass the original affront; the original golden rule—the *leaden* rule. Backbone of Hammurabi's code, founding concept of the social contract, guarantor of justice, precursor of lawsuits. And the god of the New Testament? Ahriman is in him too, killing with kindness.

What is Aristotle's god but a cacodaemon? The unmoved mover—modern man's goal, his ideal, a misplaced value resulting from insufficient contemplation. Aristotle's god cannot make anything. He knows but cannot do, the possessor of a worthless knowledge. Longing to be a god of action, he envies the hands of man. Spending all his time contemplating *us*, he wants more than the same in return. That he does not receive more than this, that we merely contemplate him as he does us, signals the unwitting blasphemy of imitation. A life devoted to the *worship* of god—this is what he desires, our celebration. He is as jealous of Yahweh as Yahweh is jealous of him.

The life of creativity and the worship of a god—things on which Aristotle is silent but Ahriman embodies. The enjoyment of music requires a total lack of concern with the world, and Ahriman is always listening to nature for any out of tune notes, conducting his symphony of indifference. Capable of all the same feelings as Ahuramazda, he simply experiences them more intensely, in the extreme—but in regard only to himself, without sympathy. Wouldn't flattery of this god be enough to ensure his favors? Not bound by moral imperatives, he is free to bestow his services lavishly on whom he likes.

Why did not Darius and Xerxes invoke Ahriman before their invasions? Would he not have helped them more than Ahuramazda, who could see their ill-will and punished them for bad judgment? Would he not have overrun the more limited allegorical qualities of the Greek gods with his all-encompassing one? If it had been a battle of deities rather than men, the advantage was with the Persians.

Why does Ahriman need Ahuramazda? If only he could have remained in his original condition—but then he would not have the opportunity to vent bad will. His weakness is that he, like us, needs first to Be so he can revel in negation, to suckle the supreme deity and throw a temper tantrum at the same time. So, for the sake of entertainment, he relegated himself to second-rate status.

Evil's virtue: its prevention of the surfeit of "the good," the banality of comfort, happiness, freedom—those highest *incompatible* ideals. The achievement of any one crowding out the attainment of the others, there arises disappointment and regret in not pursuing an alternative. To gain happiness without freedom is the complacency of the thoughtless and the misery of the conscientious. We feel we were meant for a wholesome existence, that the world was made for our advantage; instead we are constantly at tension with it, misaligned with its indifference to our hopes, attaining only pieces of our goal. Man is a bag of whims corked by the limits of his paycheck and the fruitlessness of his prayers; only in wine, in the ablution of the liver and fogging of the brain, can he exaggerate his powers and dream everything is within his reach—awakening unto a headache that fills him with a regret for dreaming. The grasper at ideals is a weaver of patchwork absences he never intended or desired. Embracing his disappointments, he casts off any expectation of self-betterment. Confronted by the absence of eudaemonia, he experiences the side effects of the moral lifeworld; twitching and nauseous, he regurgitates his former longings and bloats himself on air. Flatulating the heavens and belching greenhouse gases, the fantasies and opportunism of the sky become a matter of abdominal distension.

The Means Justify No End

Like drunken archers, people always find ways to keep the bulls-eye intact by making a potential target of everything else in sight. There are certain means which determine their distinctive character by frustrating their goals. The sheer pleasure of loosing arrows, making archery an activity-for-itself that it wasn't before, a game of collateral damage. Frustrating the end by wallowing in present satisfactions. We in fact act like drunken archers all the time—what is left to hit after the bulls-eye? The peak of skill reached, the accomplishment gained, there is no further choice but to languish in the shadow of glory's anticlimax or to die. In such a state, pleasure comes upon those with a large quiver: merging of arrow and man in vandalism, loss of self-consciousness in sabotage and defacement. Accidentally killing a bystander produces no regret in the most inexperienced archer so long as the wine flows—even an expert can renounce his aim and plead manslaughter.

And when the end is the activity itself, the means frustrate even that. Stepping correctly in the waltz, it becomes not a waltz, but a new dance entirely; one preempts the waltz, flies over the goal through the superior implementation of one's own craft knowledge—a method that, designed to reach the end, establishes value for itself by conflicting with it.

Equality of Wisdom

People seldom meet a mathematician without baring their uvulas to him. They see his head in a halo of light, floating in a world far above their own limited comprehension. That they too, on a basic level, know some math, seems to escape them. Like all experts who have harnessed their talent, a great mathematician has simply, through long struggle, advanced beyond the basic level to a plane where they cannot follow: this winged creature has shodden hooves.

An ethical thinker, by contrast, receives only blank stares. Everyone believes they have full access to "The Good" simply by virtue of existing. The moralist's liability is that he cannot fall into technical language without becoming absurd. Value, like knowledge, erects walls; but this labor being done by informed experience and not high learning, the average man has leverage over the professor. If people could read Greek letters they wouldn't hesitate to dismiss the mathematician as a mailboy trolleying symbols into a row of cubbyholes.

But as long as only the moralist's *occupation* is in doubt, he has not yet fallen as far as he can—as he inevitably will. In the realm of ethics one always holds its thinkers to a higher standard than in other fields: one expects them to live their ideas. Studying man from a plurality of angles, taking into account factors fugitive from naïve experience, bending logic to his use to the same extent that a mathematician draws on his intuition, he is expected to be his own case study. With intellect consolidating and rigorizing judgment, and judgment second-guessing intellect where it seems fallible, all the faculties of the moralist's mind are focused on weighing his charitable donations against his volunteer work—and even then we are still suspicious of his *good will*. It would be absurd to demand of a logician, an epistemologist, a metaphysician, or an aesthetician that their lives be the litmus test of their theories. Nor does one think to measure the political thinker by this standard—the reader merely assumes the author votes on the side of his theory. One might weigh a religious thinker by prayers and almsgiving, if the mystic were not read chiefly *because* of his example—one has to have visions before he can gather a literate following of aspiring ecstatics to preach to.

Spinoza was the only ethical thinker to ever be judged good enough for his books. The others so often turn out to be inconsiderate (Schopenhauer), noncommittal (Kant), or, in the hypocritical case of the immoralist, a *good man* (Nietzsche). Not that readers don't often lose respect for other specialists when learning of controversial aspects of their biographies—Heidegger's Nazism, Wittgenstein's cruelty, Leibniz's cowardice and ambition. In these cases, however, one does not feel that their ideas are undermined as a result; the astute critic never goes so far as to make an *ad hominem* judgment. But when the ethical thinker is not a saint his thoughts crumble to pieces. This injustice is understandable: readers of ethics, unable to rely on any fundamental advances in the formulation of proofs since the Socratic dialogues, can only corroborate its principles by putting proponents through a trial by ordeal. In the witch-hunt of the moralists, an altruistic sacrifice is proof of innocence.

A statue stands with its finger raised in the air. Its admirers, fascinated by how the stone seems chiseled out of life, walk that way. Soon they come to another statue pointing in another direction. And so on. The history of morals is such a sculpture labyrinth, where people would feel lost among the paths of experience if earlier generations had not poured cement over their pedants, prophets, and polemicists. They don't realize that in these cases life was animated out of stone, and the cement was merely added as a finish—capital punishment often serves as a protective coating.

Love's Novelty

If first love is always young, every love thereafter is like the old woman in the rocking chair: enfeebled by experience and swaying to a memory. Love ends in the recline position, the skin still enjoying the bulk of feeling—this is perhaps true only of noble souls; with all the rest, every love feels original: they leave their pre-teen playmate to marry their high school sweetheart, only to refresh their bed at college enrollment. Every new season of life obliges a new excitement. The modern lover has internalized the essence of comedy: that happy endings always round off at the *commencement* of the relationship. Love becomes a fading echo. Without a right side to cast our nets over, we drag them through thinned, polluted seas, hungering for the succulence of perpetual novelty and surviving off of chunks from driftbones. When our life partner, passion, finally leaves us, comes the realization: that we should have *held on* the first time.

The Highest Necessity

"How *delicious* it smells," the wino says, referring to the glass of tap water. "But . . . if I were lost in the desert I would spill it in a heartbeat for a good box of cabernet."—It is when a man is most thirsty that he *needs* his appreciation. And in the wilderness, without anyone to praise his connoisseurship, he can at least savor the glass that will end his urgency. The moral principles of addiction will not permit infidelity; even in extreme circumstances gratitude to the grape is paramount, hydration the betrayal of a meager satisfaction. His is a disinterested dependence. Dying, he would set fire to a vineyard to spare its contents from being dried into raisins or shipped away fresh—to prevent service to a *lesser* obligation. "Oh," whines the wino, "what a loss *that* would be!"

Feast or Famine

Taking our most cherished dichotomies out to brunch: eating cereal with sandwiches, mixing orange juice with champagne, leaving a generous tip with a poem, *On the Virtue of Indigence*, scribbled on the bill. White and black, good and evil, ugly and beautiful—all muddied somewhere between the hash brown casserole and the toilet. For as long as one is satiated, dualities will hold hands and twirl. But when hunger returns the senses lose their dullness and no longer see gray.

Plagued by Love

His clothes were moth-eaten, his stomach full of butterflies. Love, infesting one with a sense of homelessness and indigestion as it does, is only exacerbated further by the application of insecticide.

Moth musk—perfume for all those heading towards the bottom of the food chain. He buys a new shirt, pops an antacid, spritzes himself, and is swarmed by every flirter in a seven-mile radius. Cured of the feeling of love, he finds himself thrust into the *phenomenon* of it. Leper among Lepidoptera, he spreads drab wings in the clubbing hours, transformed into a barfly's fuzzy ideal of beauty. Impersonation is his only defense, pollination of weeds his only purpose.

And to think that all he ever wanted was . . . a bug zapper.

Seasons of Womanhood

Virgins want to wait, spinsters to give it all away. After the petals of her youth have fallen comes the Autumn Philanderer, deflowering her honor by insinuating himself into her will. People who allow themselves to be cheated after their death are never said to have spent their life well. If only he had caught her in spring instead of winter! Still taking what wasn't ready to be given, by introducing her into an early summer he would have saved her from the expectation of virtue.

The Workshop

Our "art of love": apprenticed to the internet, we are members of passion's craft guild. The monopoly on masturbation prepares us to become journeymen of jealousy. When we finally do produce our magnum opus of courtship and are promoted to master, we seethe and grumble and set up our own workshop, accepting students on a pay-per-view basis.

The ambidextrous masturbator: one hand's fatigue is an opportunity for the other to show its tenderness. But eventually a man tires of the slow and gentle, seeking again the intensity that would rub him raw. Alternation has been the rule for so long that he never thinks to ask his girlfriend to use both hands at the same time. For the same reason, in his emotional life he thrives on a dialectic of abuse and babying instead of just bending over to be spanked.

Celeranimous

"There is a vastness there," the foreign traveler reports—looking up from his map to point to our bellies. As we measure our lifespans, so do we hold and feel our largevity. But with spirit it is otherwise—that we swallow. Falling short of magnanimity, we settle for being "fast-souled." In a society characterized by the vicarious lifestyle, alcohol and drugs are the most direct modes of secondhand experience: having no great events to give shape to existence, one resorts to the intravenous *joie de vivre*. But the real intensity is the man intoxicated by blood alone—his own and others'. It rouses little to see red if you can't also smell and taste red—if you can't drown all of your senses in the nectar of life and death.

The Language of Modern Love

A polyglot love: forms of address that go beyond body language to the argot of objects: stale candy, flat champagne, unarticulated children. To know each liaison by a peculiar gift. A construction paper heart cuts wrists more painfully than scissors.

My Free Love Gave to Me . . .

Love quadrangles: four geese a laying, three substitutions, two confused goslings—twelve days of Christmas abridged in one seedy hotel room.

Hopping from bed to bed is as natural as channel-surfing, misplacing household trash, applying for a new baby while nursing a job, planning late bills while prepaying a vacation. A multislacking love hones all the senses in on distraction from many objects at once. One sheds condoms like snake skins and juggles diseases with the finesse of a hemiplegic acrobat.

Faithful to the Ideal

Idolatry, adultery: if the first is genuine, it overflows into the second. Zeal needs a physical outlet the more it achieves fulfillment. An object of mistreatment, a plaything to scorn, jealousy to encourage appreciation. If only both were socially acceptable at least one might be common.

A Dying Groom's Wedding Speech

Beloved Wife,

You were to be both my restraint and my onslaught. As my ball and chain I would have flailed you about with the vigor of a medieval knight; together we would be safe in my castle. That these words we have exchanged would have been enough to tie us together fast, I am sure. But since this glass of punch has poisoned me and I have but a few moments left to express my love, I can only speculate what our life would have been like: me sitting on the porch enjoying my early retirement, the nanny tending to the children, you out in the world earning a living—I respect your modern ideals. A woman's place is no longer in the home. She must know the virtue of a good work ethic. This is why, as you know, I only employ women in my household: chef, chauffeur, butler, maid—all female. I am only too happy to foster the advancement of woman's position in the professional world. And whatever the temptations, I promise that you would have always remained my highest duty. Curse the bridesmaid who took revenge on my faithlessness; which one it was is anyone's guess (though I myself have a working theory). Forgive me, I am still amorous despite my age. Though yesterday I wanted to experience my singlehood one last time, today I am yours forever, since tomorrow I will belong to the worms. I make a young widow of you, it's true, but I hope you will take my promises into account and remain faithful to my memory: please, do not take another lover, but remain as chaste as I have always known you to be. I know you have the wisdom to come to this decision yourself, since it is the condition of inheritance in my will.

Alien Companionship

To wake up, find a stranger in your bed, and prefer it that way. Discovering more about your wife as she opens her soul to you over the years, she becomes not what you thought she was. Yet her habits endear her to you more than ever even as the reasons behind them escape you. Her estranged mind objectifies her, turns her into the yard sale doll you were always browsing for. You love her for the repetitive phrases that imply, with such apparent tenderness, you care not what. Dull, fat, slow, you pull the strings on the few movements she makes. Even her rebellions are cowed. As she reaches into her purse for lipstick, finds a stick of butter instead, and smears it on her facial labia, you know there will be something more than familiarity to relish about the goodnight kiss.

A Dying Bride's Wedding Speech

Beloved Husband,

I am a modern woman, as you well know. While this makes me stubborn, it does not prevent me from loving. We would have been an equal match: you, old and with lots of money, I young and beautiful—a fair tradeoff. But since I have been poisoned by this glass of punch, I am prevented the satisfactions of living in your mansion and giggling when you praise my body. What can I say? Your best man was insanely jealous. I am sorry, I wanted to revel in my emancipation one last night. While I would have always practiced affection towards you and been faithful to you from today on (except maybe during your business trips—depending on the location, they're outside the jurisdiction of the marriage covenant), you must know that I could never *submit* to you. Nor am I sure that I could ever have your child. Probably I would have gone to a clinic before I started to show. And why not? It's my right. My sex has had the vote for almost a century now. We are strong. We are proud. And if I chose long ago not to take up a profession and buy a strap-on, it was only to put those qualities to use. A modern woman can show off her emancipation just as well with her husband's credit card as through a high-powered career—it is what she owns, and not what she is, that distinguishes her from her poor past forms shackled to the hearth.

Love and Ambition

The power of naked ambition comes from commandeering love. It accompanies a relationship of unequal status, posing as affection and exposing itself the moment it can afford to. A tyrant that gathers flatterers to the feast only to slay them post-toast, it needs a shroud of benevolent excuses to be served a large dinner. The tragedy is that many realize no difference between the two passions and deceive themselves that they really are in love. Theirs is an inarticulate "wanting more . . ."

A love that would achieve its object cannot seem pure. The asthmatic sigher hits on success by anticipating a moaning suspicion and disguising himself as an easy breather.

Two Types of Minds

a) Simple minds—capable of only one great passion at a time. Emotions are greater when combined (one has to confuse the recipient); a solitary passion is too predictable, too subject to counterstrategy and rebuttal. The mediocre confuse love with ambition and pursue them as one. They are clocks that wind up and tick away.

b) Great minds—the computers that sit and charge and use up their battery-powered talent. Like the simple, they have ambition according to their nuts and bolts, and love according to their warranty. If great minds are recognized they can love after their ambition is spent—it was, after all, only a compensation for their loneliness.

Only Estranged?

Admirable is the criminal braving alienation from society, but more still the recidivist alienated publicly *and from within*—a systematic alienation. An uncaught criminal is a secret darer, victorious in his crimes. Estranged from the society he has betrayed and the neighbors who believe him an upstanding citizen (the truth is not invited to picnics), he is yet at one with the secret molding his criminal identity. But the recidivist does not even have this hidden retreat-as-triumph over the world. He is doubly alienated. Apprehended not just once but several times, his faith in his stealth shattered with his strength, he has nothing to do but rot. Staring out his window, he does not imagine himself jumping for joy in the great wide world, but only sees litterers, children with cigarettes, airborne germs strengthening the immune systems of jaywalkers. In his dejection he tries to inhale a star and ends up swallowing his tongue. He doesn't need speech to represent him, after all—everyone *knows* what he is.

Hatred of the Outside

A homely love: looking out at the world through the television set, too modest for panes of glass; ordering a pet rock over the phone for the sheer pleasure of conversing; waiting for the *right* knock at the door and asking the mail carrier in for a cup of tea when her package arrives; staring at the floor as the neighbor's cat gazes at her through the windowsill, proud that the salesman mistakes it for *her* cat. If she went out into the world she might have to discriminate, find a common point of interest, even have *something to offer*.

When she died the entire community attended her funeral. "She was just always *there*," a distant neighbor said in the eighth eulogy, gesturing in the direction of her house. "I can't say whether it was a passionate relationship," the mail carrier said in the seventeenth. "But while I never saw her give it a *lover's* kiss, there was a sort of mutual serenity." After the community had spoken they wept as coffin and pet rock were lowered together into the burial plot. The next-door neighbor stayed behind after everyone else had left. He stared down for a while as dirt began to fill up the grave, then tossed in his meowing cat out of reverence.

***

First moral: One is free to love all, so long as one has never loved.

Second moral: A cherished object requites love to the lonely more than the crowded congregation bounces its sum amongst themselves.

Third moral: A cat owner can't feel attached to what won't submit to ownership.

Fourth moral: Get a dog.

The Limit of Judgment

The purpose of art is transcendence, both for the artist and the art lover. But they only escape themselves into something *worse*. Naïve consumer of beauty, the art lover wants to get inside the artist and experience "freedom" through his work—the artist's solace, his militant daily routine. The art lover becomes self-conscious about the loss of identity involved in his consumption. His is the freedom of being lost in the Museum of Babel, where every combination of styles occupy a spectrum of infinite nuance, the subsections of wings folding in upon each other to form a labyrinth of periods. It is a freedom that ruins his enjoyment. Unable to casually detect the subtle differences between works, he is forced to *study* a style. Art appreciation becomes an endless homework assignment.

The problem of the connoisseur is that everything fit to be called "greatest" within his realm of taste, everything canonical, is, through no internal fault of its own, bound to become tedious when re-consumed again and again—Haydn's string quartets. After one is familiar with the intricacies of the sheet music, with enough gradations of performances, one eventually gets exhausted with the obligation of always having to notice something more. One hesitates to admit that repetition is the death of love for fear of being branded an inept authority by his fellow snobs—something which, lacking the officialdom of the critic's printed review, the connoisseur is already charged with by the resentful *demos* basking in the simple enjoyment of sensations. The connoisseur's judgment, no matter how discerning, always occupies a precarious position. He eventually comes to discover a slightly novel personal meaning in every recital of "The Joke."

The Coffin Coiffeur

If one has a wistfulness for robes, no need to browse a History of English Royalty. Barber shops offer the torso full protection from what gets cut off above it. To seat Europe's last living monarch for a haircut and salvage such fine garments unstained . . . how proud Ann Boleyn's tailor would be!

The Psychology of History

History distances us from humanity by presenting us with the psychology of implausible accomplishment. Psychology brings us closer to ourselves through case studies of deviants and morons—annals of weirdness and insufficiency the only key to unlocking the mystery of *homo scribens*. It is only when one of these freaks accomplishes something worth remembering that the rest of us feel insulted; he is no longer a safe object of comparison, an outlier that makes one proud to be normal, but becomes a fact to be memorized, venerated, and resented. History is habit writ large, madness made readable.

The Personal Is Political

—Insofar as the political represents the will of a dominant individual, expressing the destiny of a great man or the tyranny of a small one. But even here, the masses will stowaway as many private moments as their pockets can hold. The more transparent an individual is forced to be, the more he implies his opacity. Like the moon, a man shows us one face reflecting the light of others and keeps the other side of himself in continual night—no one knows what is beneath that hair. This reflective side is politics, and the public Confucianism of every person fuels a private Taoism by distracting from it. In the most refined of these identity obfuscators—congressmen and housewives—private is merged into public; Taoist stages are filled with Confucian props, the actors withdrawing into themselves in a Yin-yang spin cycle of duty. Picnic blankets are laid in rolling pastures, oil drills in deserts, and in the name of "right attitude" bellies and pockets are filled. In the most thoroughly confused individuals, character is made into an expression of nature, even as consciousness proclaims only "We!"

Mannequin Museums

When asked about our model of beauty, the tour guides of the future will say, "Confining their statues to clothing stores, it was a society that valued individuality of layering over form."
 "But why sculpt in plastic?"
 "Thrift was their lesson to posterity."

Imagination Bounded by Experience

One never bothers to wonder about the everyday life of some mediocrity, not realizing its comparative excitement when measured against those who enshrined themselves in cultural memory by escaping the glees of *p*leisure into a higher calling. Most people, lacking the innate sense of duty which talent imposes on its bearers like a destiny, instead fantasize about the status surrounding responsibility. They fill every particular image with the boundless delights which the supposed autonomy of the artist, the power of the politician, or the fame of the celebrity would bring them. In these cases, though, it is not freedom, power, or fame they imagine possessing, but the promises of their stereotypes: *lack of surfeit*. They can only conjure more of what they have already spent their entire lives in pursuit of, believing the difference between pleasure and joy to be a matter of degree.
 Peering through the fence surrounding the pool of highborns, the eyelids of the talentless soon begin to droop from watching their betters drudge so much. Possessed of the naïve happiness arising from simply not being born genetic accidents, they take for granted their red-blooded impulse for excelling at the task of *life*. Natural supremacy is the privilege of the chained draft mule.

PART 2: Nightcaps

Mood and Memory

Although I have become too happy to be great, I still have the memory of my misery to drive me on—if not to attain glory then at least honorable mention. And yet . . . reflecting on this gap in status may, with any luck, be enough to destroy my happiness. But on my rise out of the dustbin of notability, I would hit this wall: the fond recollection of that happiness. The commemoration of a kaleidoscope of emotional states reroutes every thoroughfare; my fate is a beltway flanked by an overpass. What I need is a touch of karma, a demolition job, a gravel road—*Alzheimer's*.

Laughter Is the Best Toxin

Let us outline the future of smiles, the upshot of every dimple display. Wouldn't one rather have early wrinkles from stress and toil? Then at least there would be some appearance of a tangible goal, a point of respect for personal sacrifice. Instead, only a tombstone that reads "Here lies one who laughed himself to death"—needle in a haystack for the unfortunate family searching a cemetery of millenials. As president Garfield's assassin chose a gun with an ivory handle because he knew it would look good in a museum exhibit, so do we embellish naked merriment with granite tributes to the placid soul.

Maximum Greatness

The secret of achievement? Moderation in nothing—*but diet*. Minimization of joy comes afterwards, the side effect of a dead social life. For what is there to talk about among friends without a meal between you?

Subaerial

Dirt . . . a gust of wind blows it into my eyes, it gets stuck in my boot grooves and I tread it into the house. Dirt . . . one descends to the bottom of the sea, hoping to find an answer, and one finds only clumps that fog up the water. We put mulch down, saying we want to prevent weeds from growing . . . when really what we want is to forget the dirt, our origin and destiny. One watches children playing on the beach, slapping mud together to build sandcastles, and realizes that we ourselves are constructed from this same playdough. Dirt . . . my only point of contact in-between volcanic churning and meteor showers, it shields me from upheavals and downpours. Though it follows me everywhere and is the closest thing to myself, I cannot even return to it when I die—my corpse will be too full of chemicals. Made of the blood of Tiamat's second husband, I cannot seep into the dirt but will need to be separated from it by a casket to prevent polluting the earth's excrement.

The Dispassionate Relation

"We're such good friends!"

"Yes we are. The best."

"I never expected to find someone like you. So generous, so much fun."

"Nor I you."

"We're more than just familiars, aren't we?"

"I would say so."

"I mean, we just have so much in common."

"We're never at a loss for something to do together, its true."

"You want to know something strange? Whenever I think of you I get hot-blooded, but seeing you for the first time in a few days, I turn white as a ghost. I don't understand it, you just get my nerves going."

"That *is* strange. Maybe you're just thinking of that Ford 302 we've been working on. Picked up a crankshaft damper for it, by the way."

"Did you have to bring that up now?"

"Why not?"

"I'm trying to have a serious conversation and all you want to do is talk shop."

"Sorry. I thought you liked getting oily in my garage."

"I do. It's a good excuse to get away from the wife and kids."

"Oh yeah, how are they doing?"

"Why do you want to know?"

"Well, it's just that I so seldom ask."

"You have never asked."

"All the better reason to ask now."

"I still don't understand the relevance of this."

"I'd only like to know something about your previous history, your life outside of us and all that."

"Please, no! Friends simply don't talk about those things."

"I'm getting a bit confused as to what we *are* supposed to talk about."

"*Us*, of course!"

"Could we at least add a few more of us for good company? I'd like to show a companion of mine what we've been working on."

"Oh . . . hmmm . . . no, I don't think so. I'd be terribly jealous."

"I see."

"You seem upset."

"Its only that I don't know what to say."

"Just promise me you'll never move away, friend."
"If we don't finish that engine I won't have a choice."

***

If friends had always to be reassuring one another of their friendship, in what direction would this take them? —The bed, the dueling grounds, or the firing squad. If they don't change sexual orientation they turn violent—against one another or the world. Either they agree upon a number of paces because their conversation can't match the instinctive connections of erotic love or parenthood, or they strive to live up to Sentiment by proving their bond in a struggle against everyone, betraying their country not for a higher cause but a lower one, unwilling to sacrifice their pact with another individual for servitude to the collective. All this is why friends *do* . . . a relationship's silence in regard to itself keeps it outside the bounds of nature, so long as there is no blushing involved. Abashment is as lethally persuasive as gregariousness.

Profound Tourism

Imagine a merchant who amasses wealth with an eye to posterity, desiring only that flocks of people will someday migrate to his native city to retrace the paths of his caravans. Ignoring the museums and decorative architecture, his ideal pilgrims look beyond the superficial. They are only concerned with what made everything else possible.

Now imagine a capitalist *with foresight*. The Wallflower on Wall Street: "Perhaps these price movements represent not company stocks, but the shuffling feet of their followers."

The Deepest Bond

Orgy of friendship: each elicits a position in every other that would not have been possible between only two. With none of the jealousy involved in gathering your affairs together in one bed, friends can be replicated to the limits of room space, or until the motel investigates complaints about the chorus of angels in 118. And all you have to sacrifice is . . . *the friendship*.

Grooming

Unconditional love would be confined to a religious theme were it not for our pets. —What? *A mother's love*? But that is the most dependent love of all . . . a triumph of antenatal depression, spanking, and Oedipal frustrations.

The Middle Way

Calm passion is a state of Being represented by one of the lesser deities. Neither Apollonian nor Dionysian, it stands between Olympus and the Bacchanalia, running messages from Mytikas peak to frenzied priestesses. City-states take only the flamboyant gods as their patrons; visitors question oracles not out of curiosity but fear. To be "Epiphronian" is to go unworshipped, though it is to the Epiphrons of the world—the prudent, the shrewd, the careful, those lacking in *extreme behavior*—that we owe our continued existence. Daemons of practical reason, they signify the complement of the herd instinct: not the mob, but the community organizers passing out fliers, knocking on doors for petitions. The offspring of Night and Darkness, their essential contribution goes unseen: to hold us at arm's length from two primordial voids. Flanked by overbearing parents, the rest of us would otherwise allow ourselves to be coddled, longing as we do to bury ourselves in their open arms. Our saving grace, the epiphronian spirit connects us to the abyss through a primordial gene pool, so when the dam breaks and nothingness pours through we can blame it all on bad blood. The black sheep of the family, Epiphron's failure was inscribed in his chromosomes from the beginning: Chaos begets Night and Darkness, who beget . . . *sagacity*?

Autocritique

The Cynic school was a thing of antiquity, but every subsequent age has had its lonely adherents: to satirize the very thing you depend on, to offer a way out but crudely and unsatisfactorily, too myopic with frustration and intoxicated by rebellion to admit *there is no way out*. Addicted to futility, you live in your barrels and keep up your search for the good man, laughing all the while. A noncontagious laughter that loops back upon itself, your only pleasure an insincerity. And yet you, like the Stoics, propose to live according to nature? Not so, friends! Your mockery can't escape the interpersonal—and so you *do* live according to what is natural, just not in the way you thought. Deeply aware of status, you turn your scorn into a virtue, applying it more even than the dozing patrician, smearing it over yourself like cow-dung. If everyone lived in barrels you would smash yours and take to a house, decrying "the rolling estate."

Gravity in Air

Candid shortcuts to profundity are too gloomy for us, so a comic veil is drawn to make the ideas digestible—and the prophet turns into the clown. Show me Fontanelle's antithesis, one whose greatest pride is that he was never solemn—even in taking pride. Such a person would be much misunderstood and never respected. Why? For extolling openness to experience: the illumination of everything irrelevant deemed essential and the light treatment of what is unalterable. The comic selects society for adaptation and gives nature roles to play. Solemn natures need to be prodded with feathers to test their resolve, showing that in remaining unmoved they alone are ridiculous. The business deities are sober even when pouring ambrosia. In praise of folly, as the first true optimist titled it—a subtitle for seriousness. The comic highlights the serious side of life in a way the staid never can. What is everyday life, after all, but a series of repetitions, its actors commercial cogs toiling to put food on the table and leak urges with stolen time? Comic characters are the only *vital* machines, the only ones willing to show off their clockwork bowels. Exaggeration exposes the inescapable. The bizarreness of Beckett reveals our own strangeness. What is more alien to the Swiftian than a flexed mouth? The satirist finds nothing funny about creation—the process or the event. His is the pity of a "sudden glory," throwing his arm around the first victim within reach and pointing a finger back towards himself—for when the hedonism nourishing his satire dissipates the last joke is on him. A dejected people facing their end, scrambling for the last cans of hope and happiness on the grocery shelves, can't afford to attend to the fulfillment of his vision. Nor can the satirist—he is at the front of the throng.

The Eunuch with Two Members

I am the eunuch that refuses to reattach. Passion is something I am proud to have lost. I can be impartial now, an unflinching witness to the most affecting acts. This has the danger of making me an accomplice to crime and a suspect in every situation. But at least I will leave no snow tracks to be pursued by, no love stains that might compromise me. A cry, a thumb down, a thumb sideways, a meandering route—procedure for escape after refereeing a murder. That appendage, at least, will serve my nomadism well. Its erection proves I have not lost my self-concern, my *fear*. My thumbs keep me moving.

My situation is, to an extent, unspeakable: there is no word for not having a goal. Goalless, purposeless, aimless—all merely the negations of endpoints rather than a positive state of purposely not having an endpoint. "Lost" does not capture my condition; I know exactly where I am: at a point that I fully intended to pass through on an unmapped road. At best there are only words for the emotional states associated with not having a goal: apathy, disorientation. But these do not accurately describe how I feel about my life path. I am determined to keep hitchhiking. Where? Anywhere that is not where I am now. There is a peripatetic progress, a drifting that is committed to advancement towards—everywhere. I do not expect anyone else to understand; the others are too busy shouting "Yes!" or "No!" and chasing the straightest line to their desires. One has to be a eunuch to say "maybe . . ." or "I'll see where this leads

. . ." But eunuchs are scarce today. The times of harem guards and castrati are gone. The eunuch has no function in society. And in the case of accidents, science offers so many cures, so many surgical routes back to pleasure. There is no Christian purity to be found in castration; it represents now only the shame born of *another* reversal of values. A eunuch is beyond that deepest of connections to other thinking beings. His genes are destined to die with him. Heaven forbid I lose my thumbs! Then I would have no *means* to pursue my purposelessness. After I die I hope they will preserve my thumbs, pointing them in opposite directions to show the way for eunuchs of the future.

Part 3

Muses

Heraclitus

The sage—quiet, alert, proud—speaks out. He addresses the *logos* calmly but firmly. That harmony can only be brought about through dominance, a reigning element exacting proportion from the lesser ones: this is his message, the balance of hierarchy. But the wind is either too weak to carry the sage's resolute tone or too strong for it to be overheard. So the world, instead of modeling itself on the sage, goes on recurring. Swinging between extremes of strife and languishing, chaos and melody, waters crashing over land and air settling to earth, it is deaf to the need to keep the home hearths lit, to the vigilance that is always ready to risk war to make peace last. If the sage had only whispered, or shouted. But then he would betray himself. So he just stands, an inimitable paragon.

Lao Tzu

To write one of the world's greatest books, and *not even exist*: the most fully actualized author is the one who lives only on paper, a dream of his own creation.

That Lao Tzu didn't exist—what a trite observation! The real point is that all those warring-states writers jotting Taoist poems thought he did and consciously imitated him, writing only what he himself would have written. Like the Jewish scribes of the Old Testament, they were vessels for the spirit of Lao Tzu; their creative acts were his creative acts. The fanciful being behind such texts, whether man or god, becomes a social fact upon being imagined by a club of admirers.

Publishing companies have recently discovered the benefits of caricaturing the method of the early Taoists: instead of attributing the financially risky work of their fledgling novelists to some legendary wise man, they choose a bestselling thriller writer. It is the first instance of evolution in authorship since the Old Master: after myth becomes man, man becomes industry. James Patterson is the only literary Over-Soul. As there is a difference between one and another hour of life, so with every subsequent serialization.

Aesop

Aesop used beasts to represent common human qualities; I will use humans to represent exceptions to the prevalent beastly ones—only the higher monsters of our nature are suited to furnish lessons. *Which* exception is represented will be a moral subject to interpretation.

Seneca

No matter how bad things get in comparison with how good I have it, I continue to maintain a stoical acceptance—of the periodic conflagration of the world. Philosophy is not *just* the more prosperous half of self-enrichment: destruction is the cradle of redemption.

Marcus Aurelius

With Confucius's dilemma representing the chief grudge of the practical philosopher, history bears few instances of its opposite: of one lucky enough to have power—and not merely by seizing it or climbing up the bureaucracy, but being *raised up for it* so as to wield it with all the naturalness of a fifth limb, a master appendage—without wanting it, of a man who yearns to withdraw from life in order to think at rest. The chief value of a creative work resulting from such a situation, therefore, comes to lie in the possession of the very thing its creator resented: an inside view on the vanity of absolute power. One wonders whether Confucius or Plato would not have become similarly disillusioned upon their own triumph, appending murmurs of resignation to grand conceptions. Or what of the thinker who was never utopian to begin with, one who grounds an axiom of ruthlessness *because* of his failure in practical life? Would Machiavelli in the service of Lorenzo the *Micro*nificent have turned his cruelty upon himself? One has only to look at Seneca, Boethius, or More to see their work as a compensation for their lives, gentle inversions of the brutal conclusion of thought successfully diverted by ambition; or, conversely, to see their lives as the logical inevitability of their work, with every utopian dream spawning a frightening reality and any attempt at highbrow consolation twisted into agony by a cord around the forebrow. If democracy is the only form of government which blames itself for its decline, the empire of the philosopher is the only one that declares guilt over its success.

Nagarjuna

Analysis of Truth

> Meditation leaves behind assumptions,
> Then builds a house of dogma,
> Inviting the assumptions back
> To place them on the welcome mat.

Analysis of the Meditator

When the meditator appears,
The thoughtless ones will rule.
How? By cutting out reasoning
Intuition unites enlightened and stupid.

Analysis of Nalanda's Destruction

Nalanda was burned down.
For fuel, the Muslim invaders used Buddhist monks.
An enlightened monk perceives not-self.
All monks used as fuel achieved not-self.

Burned monks were fuel before not-selves.
As fuel, they differed from fire.
As not-selves, they did not differ from fire.
Burned monks were fuel and fire.

Fire that is the same as fuel cannot arise.
Fire different from fuel can arise without fuel.
Fuel cannot burn, fire burns without cause.
Burning monks could not connect fuel and fire.

How, then, was Nalanda burned?
When it was established.
The meditator who established it perceived not-self.
Nalanda no land a.

Erasmus

It is possible to go even further than simultaneously celebrating what you denigrate: to not celebrate while also not denigrating. A parallel non-preference. Rather than straddling the line claiming both territories, the neutrality of tiptoeing within its breadth. But the ambiguity here is deeper: each "not" coexisting inside a hair's length, which one is the more greatly favored? With a slippage of word choice leading to praise or blame, and inconsistency inevitable, what inclination will the tongue trips display? The opposite problem of Folly's overselection—of wide ambitions combined with universal reservations—is that even when a man succeeds in flattening his desires on the anvil, extraordinary discipline in doubting is still required. This is no mere treaty drawn up by Swedes. One is not a spectator to warring factions, but an armed border patrol—and the most likely invader is not Houyhnhnms or Yahoos, but the guard himself. Neither nationalist nor expatriate, he is a victim of conscious indecision and unwitting prejudice.

Gracián

Lock yourself away in a cell before the first book. Conceal your depths—this is one of the best pieces of advice ever given. The Jesuit was his own greatest example of how brandishing his talent to the world brought him a heap of trouble. A guide to life, like statecraft, should be contrary to what those of common sense would actually advise—to be good; nor should it just take note of what everyone really does—observe evil; it should, instead, recommend the exception—what few advise or enact. This strategy ensures that the author's true thoughts on the matter will leak through only indirectly, without any pretense of expecting that people either can change for the better or will achieve self-enlightenment upon reading about their irremediable badness. One gives counsel not to change readers—there is no reason to act otherwise unless you can *be* otherwise. Nor does the counselor merely guide them towards their destiny—there are some cynics who take advice's role to be the harbinger of blame, ensuring that the dread and bitterness escorting the failure of choice will summon the hammer and whittle it into the gavel. One instead gives advice simply to show others what they are not doing and will not do. The author himself is no exception to this. The wisest sages lack the discipline to hone their wisdom—they hide their depths from themselves.

Lady Conway

Several female thinkers who died in undeserved obscurity and never had a chance to impact the philosophy of their day have been recently rediscovered. But it is not enough to simply appreciate their ideas within their proper historical context; we must fill in the intervening centuries and punish our paradigms for such long-lapsed judgment: to really appreciate Lady Conway we must resurrect her vitalist principles. What might our theories look like today if we had taken her into account? Not enough to rely on Leibniz's hidden influence; anonymity needs a name. With the esoteric mysticism of the Lurianic Kabbalah mixed with the directness of Quakerism, we must chew on the viscountess's strange God in our thoughts and will him into the foundation of our systems. After beating our heads against the desk struggling with present-day philosophers, we may come to understand her notion of pain as integral to the process of purification and, with the help of a debilitating headache, purge our minds of frame semantics. As matter impedes the activity of the soul, so does Alphabet-Reckoning obstruct dynamic thinking.

Conway's monist entity is *almost* adequate to explain the current state of pluralism—were this entity not so vital. To posit instead a trivialist principle: an entity that does not breathe life into the world, but sucks it away. One source of intense darkness is not enough to follow; we need a mediator to lead us. Between God and Creature, a middle nature communicates decay, malevolence, and arbitrariness: The Infernal Carpenter. Felling a forest to erect a city of shopping malls, he partakes of two extremes, blending the precision of God with the expediency of Creature—to this middle nature in the continuum of species there is no moderation. How can we not help being carried away by such a being? Looking more closely, we perceive that corporeal substances are not inert, only supremely sluggish. The cause of laziness is not *just* free will; our paralysis was built into the monads all along.

Margaret Cavendish

The most qualified spirit to write dying speeches for a blazing world of vanishing social types. To resurrect her, simply sacrifice the number of living souls equivalent in weight to her own; society will gain by this not only an arisen Cavendish, but the abolishment of feminist theorists. The world awaits the gender-progressive version of Aristophanes's *Frogs*, in which an academic sisterhood marches into the underworld to bring back its early modern champion and is destroyed in the process. The plot: each feminist competes for the title of "Best Commentator on Cavendish's Legacy" with a speech informed by post-structural theory, compiled by the duchess herself into *Orations of Similar Sorts*. But with none amidst this mental spinning of factious hearts understanding the importance of the ego, the most qualified vessel to embody her freed spirit is sought elsewhere. The twin values of selfishness and sovereignty are grasped by no living women philosophers—no, nor men either.

***

An academic philosopher's dying speech to future readers:

"For those who learn in order to think automatically, and think automatically to sleep, and sleep to dream of better educational conditions: as there are three sorts of books—the popular, the poetical, and the drowsy—so are there three sorts of readers—the escapist, the word-addict, and the napper. Of these three sorts of books and readers, the drowsy and the napper are the best—and as an author of over thirty books and a thousand articles, I am proud to have drastically enlarged the numbers of this first category, even if the second has remained smaller than I feel I deserve. Though in my entire life I was never read by more than six peer reviewers, I am confident that you, Nobody, will remember me. It is true that my books are outdated now—indeed, before they even hit the shelves—and the style difficult to digest, and the terminology difficult to understand, and the concepts behind the terminology minute variations of the ideas of my peer reviewers; but this is our lot: we study to argue and argue to get paid. Nevertheless, I hope, like the medieval scholastics, to someday be appreciated by some discerning mind (wink wink) as one of the elite unknowns of intellectual history."

La Rochefoucauld

Those who turn bitter from the world disappointing them have in fact been highly persevering in the face of reality. Not to wait for experience to implode lofty expectations, but to be bitter *from the beginning*—an a priori cynic—is the only way to escape the accusation of naïve idealism. Far from it being a contradiction for a pessimist in the abstract to be an idealist in the particulars, such double-mindedness, with its lack of expectation in the first case and lack of judgment in the second, effectively balances self-preservation with striving towards The Bad.

Bayle

Only a man who leads people to the ruins of Faith—a capital he himself razed—is qualified to rebuild it.

Vauvenargues

The restraint of a great soul *maximizes* his vices. His heart circumscribed, he lowers the standards of all around him, above all himself. He cannot sincerely console others for their lack of genius or chide for talent misplaced. His revs of passion are thinned and stretched into purrs expressed with slight movements of the head. His encouragement is gentle: "work diligently." Praising him as a good man, they slack off when he turns his back. Modesty, not arousing fear, is incapable of fostering respect.

Lichtenberg

A single thought can often branch off in different directions, its followers stranding themselves in irreconcilable positions. An electrical tree of dead-end insights, this is the image gathered of one who sits down to write a treatise on human nature and ends up with a feuding family of observations. Such a person is not only a bad theorist, but a keen judge.

Kierkegaard

In comparison with his fragments, a literary thinker is like a man who sows a vast field with crops of every kind. In the end, this universal farmer ends up being the world's most extravagant gardener. Grocers ask to explore the grounds, but they do not ask for a price. There is simply not enough of any one thing to buy in bulk. Intending to feed mouths, the cultivator of lyrical meditations succeeds only in drawing eyes.

Emerson

With Emerson, American philosophy began in grandeur. So will it end, everything in-between content without substance, as isolated in influence as in geography. In order for a work to be recognized as composed with matter in mind today it must be stripped of style, as plain-spoken as an aphasiac who grasps nothing but the facial expressions of his table mate.

Americans have turned their back on the transcendental in favor of either the grounded or the extraterrestrial. The middle region doesn't satisfy these days—nor did it then. Countervailing winds always blow a person up or down. Even those trying to bury their heads in cotton clouds only cough wisps of vapor.

Wings and wetsuits are not in our armoire—no matter where life carries us we always bring skates. Unsuited to live anywhere but surfaces, heavenly voyagers skimming across a celestial sphere fall through a thin spot and drown in the quintessence. Under-Souls are distinguished by the way they keep looking forward, unmindful of chasms beneath their feet or the eternal ONE above them that threatens to particlize the dreams they are forever sighting ten feet ahead. If they would only chance to look up they might consider looking in—and find, in each case, only the conveniences of description.

The essence of soul and universe is artifice.

Is the universe natural? No. It had to be created, its secrets kept hidden from us until now—*even* now. There is nothing natural about nature—nor God. Before pantheism came consciousness, the profane spark. And a moral deity? That had to incubate in our cognitive categories for millennia. We created God so he could create the universe in turn, giving us night-lights to sleep by. Only after these inventions were we in a position to look inside and posit a lofty core behind the heartbeat. Descendentalism is the realization of this threefold fabrication: Source, slime, soul. We look out into a silent sea of the imagination, draw our decanter through it, and drink it down.

The Good German

Friedrich and Elisabeth—the Übermensch and the Imbecile, two polarities of Being spat from between the same legs, proof that humanity's limitless possibilities are always in close proximity to insuperable barriers. Nietzsche may not have been Zarathustra, but he *was* the Madman: at the moment his genius left him he became his own literary prototype, an image his loyal sister augmented unwittingly. If only the tutorials in her brother's concepts had been followed by a grasp of them, she might have given her nation the "good European" it so wanted, its four champions of secular Christianity:

The artist who chains himself to his work with intent to allure—product of a slave aesthetics.

The hallowed warrior who sees a fresh conquest in every new cause—perspectivist crusader.

The philosopher who renounces life for the sake of conceptual variation—periodically-recurring martyr to unique configuration.

The thirty-year old who enters public life to preach masterful living—Night of the World.

William James

Taking cues from rapacious financiers, penniless professors have developed Truth-for-Profit Philosophy into a tradition that predicts classroom success based on the cash value of impractical students. Statements about the world that are to be valued for their functions and consequences are fiat facts, interchangeable as long as they fill pockets equally, exclusive insofar as one splits more seams. It is as if a tour guide were to lead you on a safari and only tell you of the world beyond the conservancy; leaving unscathed, you are so impressed with the guide's knowledge that you ask him to follow you home and tell you about all the strange wildlife there. This is in fact how many people live, carrying around their philosophy like a foldable map in their pocket. Whenever they come to a dead end, they assume they must be reading it wrong and flip it upside-down.

Santayana

Dog faith? —Too much dignity.
Lion faith? —Not noble enough.
Fish faith? —A useful aerobic exercise.
Giraffe faith? —Necks would roll.
Bird faith? —Ample ingenuity and daring, seldom convergent.
Sponge Faith? —A temporary non-adaptation.

***

The objects confronting us prompt every Metazoan presumption at one time or another. Experience modifying our *timid* reactions. The Crawl of Animal Faith.

Unamuno

It is only with the rise of the professional philosopher, the salaried truth-seeker, that marriage has become a normal practice within the discipline. And among the pessimistic philosophers it continues to be rare. Out of all of them, only Unamuno was happily married. Rousseau had his memories of being mothered to nurse him through his final days with his ignorant peasant mistress; Freud, his *theory* of marriage: a concoction of cocaine and never-ending therapy sessions rooted in an epistolary chronicle of jealousy and domination. If one must be a man before he can be a philosopher, as the Basque says, then a woman is apparently requisite in placing the impetus towards *more* life at the center of his philosophy. Spinoza made an exception of himself by escaping into a higher romance—his longing for a God. Two proven forms of continuous, supreme and unending happiness: infinite reason and the feminine ideal—both too uncompromising to collaborate on a balanced joy and too abstract to be sustained without coopting corporeality. In this, having it one way becomes an everything-or-nothing affair.

The shrewishness of grand intellect leads to a sort of provisional exhilaration as one nags one's way into an eternity of perfect geometrical forms and necessary ethics, only to find one's mind re-terrestrialized upon finding that this state bears a close affinity with more locomotive paths to ecstasy. Once gratification can be achieved with a simple brain throb, stooping to mortal courtship becomes an inconvenience.

Experiencing the sea of scents one is obliged to coat oneself in after going to the bathroom, the inexorability of feminine charm kindles a drive to assimilate the dainty gender values into the machismo model: imposing, aggressive—the *fresh* sex, willing to stake everything on a whiff of eau de toilette, ferociously outdoing each other in submissiveness with tributes of wildflower fields. Parthenogenesis of plantation serfs, propagating to expand acreage plots without a master, rejuvenating their pheromones through wars of obedience.

Unamuno's connubial bliss percolates through his fashion sense: he wore black to absorb the rainbow. His was a spirit of style that, in striving to become conscious of itself, usurped the known world of Spanish letters.

Cioran

The philosophical seer is especially prone to neglect in his era, a solitary figure arising and departing in the shadows, not commented on *intelligently* for generations. The redundancy of prophets: we raise our ears to one born a century ago while dismissing today's as a killjoy. That a forward-looking humanity is incapable of learning lessons from the past should be enough disincentive to prognostication, were it not that the prophet *thrives* on his neglect, is corroborated through it. There is a suspicion of demagoguery in being listened to, a reinterpretation of wisdom into cliché.

Cioran has yet to be discussed. The Anglo-American obsession with lexical, logical, and empirical particularities swamping existentialist fashions, his concerns are not our concerns—but when they become so, we will need *concepts* of planthood to navigate them.

The euphoria of despair is a curiosity exclusive to the child born old. To be a Nietzsche of exuberantly willed will-lessness is a paradox comparable with the frail German himself—the sensuousness of French philosophy grafted onto the bleakness of the Romanian peasantry. Writing masterpieces in two languages was not enough to prevent his familiarity: if he is ever fully translated he will become even less known. Even after renouncing the heights of despair he continues to encourage it in the reactions of his best readers. Distancing himself from a fascist ideology only intensified the strain of ruthlessness in his thought.

Contemporary aphorists, by contrast, the spawn of pessimism who have had a generation to become blasé about despair, are like centenarians stuck in the prime of middle age. Obliged to pass in society, they knit turtlenecks as a brace for their droopy heads. Only in optimistic ages do pessimists don armor; after victory the luster of bellicosity is lost.

Badiou

There is a historical recurrence of a certain type of mind that continually attempts to reduce humanity to mathematics. Perhaps realizing the silliness of such a claim, these minds have tended to mask their concepts in fashionable conceits, and in witnessing the success of their work later thinkers are inspired to recreate this underlying theoretical failure. Pythagoras infused a religion into his numbers to make them unquestionable. Descartes appealed to God as the foundation of certainty for the *cogito* on the coordinate plane. Contrary to Leibniz's concerns, humanity *was* mature enough to realize his dream of a *characteristic univeralis*—his ideas were popularized beyond recognition for the sake of universal intelligibility. But Badiou, too honest to have the good sense to clothe his dizzying logic in the optimistic mysticism of the crowd, makes his thesis into a *reductio ad absurdum* argument after the first proposition. Whenever one makes an empirically ridiculous statement and neglects to ground it in an unverifiably ridiculous statement, arguing in its favor only seems to prove the twisted psychology of a desperate man. Escaping linguistic deconstructivism into mathematical reductionism is like a man rising from a bowl of alphabet soup in order to validate himself as a Cheerio. A man cannot belong to humanity, he is a member of a void set—perhaps old Badiou is right after all. The mere fact that he blends different branches of knowledge into a body of work not easily compartmentalized (and is thus largely ignored) is an indication of his importance. He is too broadminded to be read.

My Audience

Whoever happens to read this book is merely a witness to my dialogue with the past. When I speak of Gracián, Cavendish, Emerson, and all the others, I am not speaking to their present-day followers, or some sophisticate who can appreciate them—I am speaking directly to the Ghosts of Reason themselves. They hear me and submit their approval, filling me with messages to transmit to a wayward culture. Through me, they transform themselves to suit the needs of the times. If Emerson lived today he would be a Descendentalist; Aesop, a parabolist of freaks; Gracián, an advisor on absurdities. All current ideas are reanimations of dead ideas, every new thinker the zombie of one long departed; I am a walking corpse made up of body parts from different graves. Even when I seem to be directing myself against a living writer, I am only sending my moans into the past to reflect their echoes of condemnation. But will these be heard, once they are channeled back through me? No. Readers are too handicapped by life to identify with positions against it.

PART 4

Night Sweats

Plurality of Cataclysms

That a higher being doesn't exist—a far more dangerous scenario than its contrary. A god brings with its existence certainty of our end, an obligation to carry out its revealed prophecy, the assurance of a final resting place. *Our* armageddon, though, is restrained only by the limits of fanaticism's response to randomness. It is not natural disasters we have to fear most, but the anxiety of causal connections these events induce, the post-traumatic stress arising from our modes of divine representation. It would be prudent of us, therefore, to take as an axiom the nonexistence of higher beings and from there infer the necessity of inventing them (to multiply Voltaire's statement), extrapolating different possible manifestations in the minds of madmen and equating each creed with an exclusive god. Intelligent design has the same form as the description of intelligent design—and we will not discriminate between them. As a matter of plausibility we will restrict our imagination to what has been institutionalized. A run on the bank or a supermarket riot will not be initiated by fringe cults or bygone myths; the popular imagination grasps only at the pregiven and readily available. To estimate our range of ends, we need only take orthodox religious traditions and vary them slightly—the evolution of deranged charisma is only a hop away from spirituality's present customs. The range of our beginnings, too, should be taken into account, since our final condition may closely resemble an initial one. As far as the content of our thought experiments in mass destruction, certain traditions will be more reasonable to draw on than others. The eastern religions are too benign, peaceful worldviews that direct all violence inwards—Buddhist monks only set *themselves* on fire, never others. Moving westward, polytheism is found to be another unlikely candidate for collective irrational dread, given its limited adherents and minimizing nature—its practice of placing a few on the altar to avoid a universal apocalypse. A heap of gods are more suited to our planetary persistence: they need something to sport with. Monotheism, by elimination, is the most credible aspirant to our downfall, and our surest guides to ascertaining God's strategies of creation and destruction are his scribes and theologians. The tradeoff between impotence and malevolence is shored up with transcripted guarantees.

Prosaic Regression

Within flux there are always unnecessary constants. In every period and place one finds variations on the same things which one feels should never have been there, but are. It indicates the process for everything that recurs but shouldn't, things for which there is no good reason or purpose. Across time the same types of objects stagnate, repeatedly playing little to no vital role in events. They constitute the refuse of every epoch. Behind these things, similar but never quite the same, lies a common force of irrelevance, mundaneness, vulgarity—an *elan trivial*. It is the rule of continuity in change, an essence of rubbish imminent in everything. The process of the original void, it flows through all the world's temporal parts. In each stage of the world's degeneracy, in any given society, it manifests its trash, slowly but surely piling up, imperceptibly rolling forward and unfolding its genealogy of decay. Against the current of existence is the current of nonexistence. Running opposite the stream of life, the stream of languishing pours from the other mouth of spacetime, part here, part there. The river of slime gurgles forth, decomposing every leaf blown onto its banks and rusting every city caught in its path.

Beginning in germs, passing through generations of protoplasm, the imprint of the germ is ever present down through the most advanced organisms—*especially* in the most advanced organisms. As life "advances," its diverse inclinations conflict more and more across individual creatures, each of whom wants life for itself. Of the bifurcations of the trivial impetus in creatures, only its human highway has been wide enough to allow the full breadth of its waste. This original inertia each individual retains and uses to further personal contentment—listlessness and apathy.

Under it, life is means without an end. There is only a beginning, an impulsion that perpetuates itself through biology. Looking back, we can't say it was all "for" something, but neither are we at liberty to look forward to our own futures. The impulse is an instinct towards deceleration, the future destined to be simply a constriction of the present state of affairs.

Among the most developed lines of evolution, those rare, highly structured organic systems with everything to lose, there is one that can *choose* to lose it.

Civilization: confluence of the streams of life and languishing, paragon and nadir of consciousness, spacetime's most advanced manifestation and a microcosm of the universe's red shift. In ascending periods—Vico's Ages of Gods and Heroes—where organization is the rule of procession, the trivial impetus is latent, present but on the margins. But organization peaks in the Age of Men, at which point decomposition takes over and initiates a descending period, where the trivial impetus proceeds through division and strife. It splits up ever more, with life scattering in manifestations increasingly antagonistic, less and less complimentary. The discord within the civilized species goes on increasing in proportion as it extinguishes the lesser ones and confines their last descendants to zoos. The machine churns out pop art, expressing generic desires in found junk, consecrating the trivial impetus on the aesthetic level.

The conscious intellect: from its reawakening in the renaissance through its optimization in the enlightenment, to its numb sluggishness today, the sedated thoughts of twenty-first century man are tied together by life's Lethe, trickling onward in ever-renewing deterioration, every contemplation fading into a moment's amnesia.

The very freedom which allowed men to create and achieve will, when life has been made *safe* enough, sets in motion an automatism of the inconsequential:

behaviors that begin as coping mechanisms for surplus leisure and gradually congeal into sloth until the last freedom—the freedom to move—is taken away. In a late civilization the evolution of the vegetable indicates the fundamental direction of life.

Towards the Age of Plants: starting off by feeding on others, people end by feeding on themselves. Desperate to stave off boredom, they flutter about through a haphazard and directionless kinesis, a hubbub of syncopated accents. Fatigue setting in, their actions decrescendo, stored up energy accumulating and converting into mass. Without the need to expend themselves obtaining food, the creatures bend towards the lampshade, consuming starch in order to produce the sunlight their curtains obstruct. Perfecting the method of growing without moving, their consciousness dims in proportion to dispelled locomotion, the habit of breathing all that distinguishes them from their furniture.

Our separation from the lower organisms is regrettable but not insurmountable. The path to man having been staked out by evolutionists, the path *from* him can be left to the priests. Gradually deemphasizing our traits in the order of our most sinful tendencies, starting with the spine. Flopping on our bellies, degraded to invertebrates, a species stripped of its pride is ready to be firmly rooted in the soil, then reduced to ashes—reunion of animal and vegetable inclinations. Science and religion are not so incompatible after all; perhaps God intended to enter the world only to smash man into nothing, leaving Creation to gravity, heat, and slime. The Father insinuates himself into planetary influence as the finality which nature forgot to incorporate into her original impulse. His good works, far from being evidenced everywhere, leave their mark only on paleontology.

The memory of humanity's former verdure lingering in a few restless species, they make a last ditch attempt to reestablish freedom. The inquisitive, like ivy vines, inch their way up the fence towards the sun, snaking tendrils into the past to guide them; while the enraged, like Venus fly traps, close their lobes on the last remaining flies buzzing about. Climbers and insectivores, self-actualizers and revolutionaries—the last remnants of sensible, conscious life swaying in the wind.

Perfect Fit

Man no longer works at what *isn't already* abbreviated. The cotton shirt rack packed to go, he throws his suitcase into a hot wash cycle, dries it on high, and slips it into his pocket. The button-ups will look cute on his abridged girlfriend. Anatomy and female liberation: two embellishments that make his Barbie doll the superior other half to his own reduced existence.

Revising the Combat Myth

A single god has no great rival to combat in the beginning; even snapping his fingers to turn on the light is an overexertion. A thought and it is done—no great challenge. This is why we were created, *to have someone to fight*. We are a compensation for the boredom of the first five days. Rigged struggle between a force of nature and the insects, God weighed the dice and loaded his boxing gloves. With the dual gifts of free will and the tree of knowledge, the Father invites us to become like him only to slap us down when we rise to the challenge. And by this act he *saves* us . . . the certainty of his domination over us is our shield against the very evil he coaxes us towards.

Hippocratic Growth

Bloodletting, by relieving hypertension, takes the iron out of type A personalities. Frontal lobotomies, the side effects of type B's idleness. Balancing the humors by default through outdated medical practices, the last remaining set of generic traits gets to work reshaping the world to suit its disposition; in an attempt to stimulate cooperation, the human race begins competing in type C attributes: enhancing introversion with insulin shock therapy, refreshing depression with radiated water, optimizing perfectionism with cocaine, increasing submissiveness with the "rest cure." Free of the economic burden of developing medical technology, reverting to established ineptitudes of experimentalism allows health to subject character to its rate of progress.

Fleeing Creation

Heaven cannot get away from the earth; it recedes and the earth ensnares it in gravity, throws up a mountain to penetrate it. Thus it is with God: he runs away, man catches him by the robe, pulls him back, embraces him. The Lord's service is never complete; like a cow we must always be milking him for love. God would let us go to keep hold of falsehood, *has tried* to let us go for its sake, so precious to him is the autonomy of error as against our own antipathy toward it that he would surround himself in fantasies of uncreation as a way of burying the Original Mistake. The last time God escaped he tried to hide, to square himself away in a secret place. He was sought out for a long time before finally being found by a man who locked him in a basement.

"What is your name?" the man asked a straightjacketed God.
"Father."
"No, surely you are beyond that."
"Son."
"Surely you are higher."
"Holy Spirit."

"Less material."
God made no answer.
"Well?"
"I've told you everything."
"Then tell me *my* name."

Rummaging for a Nucleus

Politicians: Pinocchios with nose jobs.
Artists: angels with insect wings.
Entrepreneurs: Borgias who, in lieu of a strongman to dismember, display their daughters' torsos on billboards.
***
Truth, soul, and morality are wrongly connected with these occupations in modern times. It is not just their antitheses that are necessary for success, but the substitution of some wholly other quality immune to the strictures these entities impose. Reaching into each other's pockets, some for wallets, others for acceptance, *all* for pomp—charm's hubris.

Homo Detentus

Compassion is not in itself a determinant of morality. The highlight of goodness, it is also evil's comeliest mask, even its incubation. After saving the life of a woman who reminded him of the freshness and vigor of his gymnasium days, a polite uniformed gentleman hands out sausages to youngsters. "Step right this way boys and girls," he says, smiling as he shepherds them toward the gas chambers. "You'll find more sausages in there." Then the SS officer goes home to play hide and seek with his children and write poems about the beauty of Auschwitz. A refined aesthetic sensibility, the wistfulness of departed youth . . . this is why he had to kill *with kindness* . . .

The boss who allows his worker a smoke break differs from this only in degree. He is only slightly the lesser monster, flogging the spirit in eight-hour shifts. Character that directs its development towards the toy aisle is the fatality of maturation. Nor do the employee's vacations build his character—he spends his two weeks playing with the toys he purchased on discount. He needs to recuperate, to take a break from his "responsibility," much like the concentration camp laborers who lay idling in their bunks at night, relieved just to have gotten through *one more day*. And if they do not get through the next at least their suffering will be at an end, spared from the indignity of dragging themselves along on an installment plan. Blessed by stockholders, profanation of caseworkers, Working Man must be sacrificed *at every moment* but never killed. Holocaust of the incombustible, he is a burning offering with firepoof flesh, a Shoah showoff. Placated with political rights in domestic life, he steps in the voting booth once every four years to exercise his multiple-choice license, rapturously pressing buttons. The death that should have swept him away in the cradle is delayed for the better part of a century by the grace of Father Time, who loaned him a badge to clock in and out. Withheld by society for his value to it but without value in himself, the employee is existence's detainee.

Obliged to mend his vest and resist union encroachment, Working Man makes the best of his situation, recovering his tradition by hanging pictures of chimney sweeps on his wall. But joining the martyrs of the industrial revolution means not allowing the manager any final victory. Turning to ask for a raise, bee meets boss face to face and, showing his stinger, is slapped away. With the threat of despair and meaninglessness hovering over him, staved off only by morale booster circles and company cheers, Working Man realizes that connecting with a tradition is only half the restoration. Recovery *from* a vocation can never be complete; time is swept away with strokes of the broom, talent wasted on price checking. So, fearing for what life remains he escapes, contriving a machinery mishap and starting a family with the settlement money, reminding his grandchildren that without the *felix culpa* of accident insurance they wouldn't be where they are.

Intermediaries

Between Chaos and Earth, between Earth and Hades, Erebus reigns: caretaker of the middle depths. His province is Tartarus, the *relative* hell that comes after death and before afterlife. Spatially the lowest, as far beneath Hades as the earth is distant from the stars, Erebus is temporally intermediate. Even to us, the middle-beings of creation, he is so: born of the primeval void and arriving prior to us, he lies in wait beyond our mortal days to punish us before sending us off to a vague netherworld. Both place and deity, object and subject, he hovers in the background of Greek mythology, barely mentioned by the ancients. There is nowhere to situate him, falling as he does between the cracks of categories. Most bards only mention the metaphysical extremes of Being: its vitality in an Aphrodite or its shapelessness in Chaos. Erebus is not suitable for allegorizing. His existence is the confusion of a shepherd who, ardent to poeticize his itinerant poverty, saw the Muses in the faces of his sheep and carved a laurel staff from a tree.

Might we today find our place in Erebus's example? We too do not fit into a cosmogony; we surpass every explanation and fall short of every aspiration, both more than our gods and less than our dreams. Perhaps, like him, we can only make sense of ourselves in a transitional state, one that for us involves inhabiting the relative extremes in our imagination: the spaces before the earth, the period after the fall—proceeding as if these were our natural domains.

PART 4: Night Sweats

Eternity of Mondays

How to cope if every day were a Monday, no weekend or paycheck in sight? Sitting at the beginning of the universe with their backs to the window, lacking rest to splurge, the busy compress a month into an hour, letting off steam by shoveling coal. Shouldered in business, the clerk writes two desperate memos to every secretary—a plea and a command; editors overschedule deadlines to default by choice. Breathing agenda: luncheon meetings, water cooler meetings, toilet stall meetings. The copier sabotaged, the programmer turns to paper, ink, and stapler for bulletin board crimes—his famous typing style masked by his cursive, mystery of the cubicles.

With partnerships formed, contracts drawn up, updates installed, comes the rush-hour revelation: that nothing was accomplished. When idle summers disappear more work gets done—and becomes pointless. The reality of labor is stripped away with the days of rest. Without laziness to lull them into entitlement and squander their achievements, the assiduous begin to understand their busyness. The weekend sets life aside for work; only when work becomes total is life again appreciated. Beach photos and corporate awards are the wisteria of wilted potential.

A Geological Survey

Cosmopolitan man, when he travels into the country, is always looking up into the sky and marveling. But seldom does he look at the ground and wonder at its hidden layers. The stars are bright and distant, safer to contemplate than the opaque mystery beneath our feet. It takes a cataclysmic event to draw attention to our place in Earth's history. A river dries up and shrivels a town, a city is consumed by mass wasting or falls through a crevice—these things demonstrate us to be only the most recent sedimentary strata.

But we have yet to glean from nature's hyperboles anything other than scientific theories and tourist attractions—hypotheses and hyperborean gawks of a summertime people. If we paved our highways with Precambrian layers of rock, we may be able to fool archeologists of a later age into thinking our strata of collapsed overpasses spanned a supereon, instead of representing the brief cross section of civilization it does—rush hour pileup of road rage and intoxication, the slow-motion perception before the sediment deposition. More likely, though, our layer of societies will be eroded into a hiatus of geologic time, leaving only an unconformity comprising igneous prehistory and a metamorphic future.

Approaches to Misanthropy

A certain amount of silliness is indispensable to affirming life while defying its guidelines. The silly person resists the reverences of social engagement with an extravagant cheerfulness, a *spontaneous* misanthropy, a sardonicism too engaged to be resentful. With the comedian domesticated in the world of entertainment (the place everyone goes after clocking out from life), the silly person—a comedian who has not been housetrained, a jester without a legitimate outlet thrown into the world of the everyday—threatens the order of things by conflating life with entertainment.

Others do not forgive the lack of solemnity for customs that silliness implies, its inference that to disregard the rules of society is to disregard "the social animal" as a whole. Above all they resent the silly person's lack of bitterness, the blithe approach to his dismissiveness. Not in a position to accuse the silly person of cynicism, they take revenge on him by withdrawing their respect, even trying to persuade him that simply by being silly, by lacking sufficient respect for the world, the silly person therefore lacks self-respect. The variety of mistreatment that silliness invites throughout the stages of life, from adolescent bullying to denunciations of unprofessionalism, is all aimed at encouraging the silly person to believe in his own self-denigration.

Different in behavior and mood, but not fundamental attitude, is the curmudgeon. The curmudgeon protects himself from others by being overly serious, but at the cost of affirming nothing. His is a noble misanthropy. Dignified, responsible, dependable, it is a misanthropy that refuses to spurn the beneficial effects of pride. Ripened by reclusiveness, refusing to let the crowd eat away at him, the curmudgeon is in the end consumed by his own vanity, fattened on the very qualities he most despises in his fellow men and served up with hibachi-style slapstick.

The affinity of silliness and curmudgeonry goes unrecognized. Observers are surprised to see them getting together for drinks; they ridicule the two sitting there, the one catching his laughter in his cups, the other watching his ice melt all night. No one would expect them to complement one another so well, each offering the other just what he needs to flourish. Silliness cures curmudgeonry of solitude, while curmudgeonry treats silliness with respect. Silliness has a free ride home, while curmudgeonry has more entertaining company than the radio. In the end they are the same person, the silly young man and the old curmudgeon defeated by the world. In anticipation and memorandum, they raise their drinks and toast to misanthropy's principal coping skill—drinking.

How do silliness and curmudgeonry meet? In middle age. Impatient of sobering up enough to drive home, a drowsy silliness takes the bus and finds the only available seat sticky with dried soda. Overriding his desire to close his eyes, he stands all the way home. This is the awakening of his dignity, of his need for segregation from all sitters front and back. From now on there would not be enough common humanity to tie him to the bus stop.

PART 4: Night Sweats

Zeitgeist Mimesis

When the spirit of an age is corrupt, one's only option is to embody the memory of a great one—to be an old soul. But then, men do this in great ages as well; it is only the attention of their contemporaries that motivates them to go beyond the past. The oldest souls are freshest, but when eyes are closed to tradition they stagnate in bygone glories, transmitting what goes ignored. In both style and content they are relegated to the necessary but invisible status of cultural reproducers.

The Age of the Old Souls extends even *through* the twentieth century. "Antiquity" now includes any cultural artifact older than six months—mass consumerism has so sped up the maturation process of society's products that they become ancient while still in the limelight.

The Cowboy and the Matador

Approaching their target, one branded while the other waved his cape. When the dust settled the matador was tender, the cowboy was tourniqueted, and the bull was nowhere to be seen. After coming home each claimed victory—this culture war propaganda was the most success they could have hoped to accomplish. When two traditions lay hands on a common object their practices rip it in half, like contending mothers without a Solomon.

Conceding to Truisms

"People are all different."—Yes, in three ways: they are bats, peacocks, or falcons. Some have no eyes, others appear to have a thousand, and a few have two good ones.

"We must respect each other's differences."—Yes, and we do . . . after they are branded.

Vanity, Urbanity

Cosmopolitanism is exclusive. It leaves out the land, even geography itself. With the world contained in every major city, the sphere shrinks to a series of points. The City: coalition of egotists, fallen angels working together towards private ends. Always wanting more, each ends up with nothing. Every metropolis is a conspiracy of Nonbeing, and cosmopolitan man, as the most cultured beneficiary of this aggregate of toil and whims, is its prophet.

The Boulevards of Extinction

What if the pluralism of our age could be condensed into a single individual embodying all of our progressive values and directions? What would this representative man be like, this distiller of many essences? Would we finally have a mediator to unite us?

Philanthropic in desire, so is the Cosmopolitan in belief. Ashamed *not* to have an opinion, to be ignorant of any possibly relevant question, he goes beyond his knowledge of the world to persuade himself of beliefs regarding everyone's place within it. That the pluralist is an inept Sherlock regarding many clues to his environment is no prevention of it from conforming perfectly to his theories of motive. Releasing his suspects *before* questioning with a shower of golden doxologies, he turns away from any potentially conflicting truths; if pointed out he forms an alibi from events far flung in place and time—bringing knowledge into the pluricentric realm. The important thing is to construct beliefs in conformity with his benevolence—to make himself into a solar system of unverified ideas. His ideal image is a maximal-opinionated self, an individual with all the most relevant beliefs possible. For every question put, every new choice and topic presented to him, every new *hope* raised, there is a state of mind to correspond to it. His states follow his minefield of wishes and justify any behavior in others, while confining his own to the caricature tropes of violin-scratching and choking on snuff. On every issue he is a multithinker, filling a high-minded view into every shoe put in front of him, denouncing the naysayers—all the while not renouncing the absent beliefs that would fit a behavior just as well, remaining concurrently inclined towards all of them. The thread between convictions and obligations becomes tangled into a knot as every stumpy-fingered Boy Scout dreams of being an Alexander with a pocket knife. So does the skeptic—hushed name of the pluralist—half-heartedly yield to all erratic dispositions, thrusting desires into situations to posit as principles, forming a bumper carousel of dogmas, an inquisition of concussive hugs. He keeps his ears raised to the media, listens to small talk for the first chance of infiltrating a conversation: an opinion is his means of espousing the good of all—himself among them. "For the sake of *confidence*," he tells himself, ordering his life so that all his acts are public works. When human possibilities are woven into an infrastructure every project falls into disrepair.

The Cosmopolitan is both the linguist of Babel and its chief architect, making his rounds among the divergent tongues, correcting misunderstandings, forging cooperation. Absorbing all differences into himself, he makes his personhood a site of conflicting views and hostile lifestyles, and by filling himself up with "humanity"—chaos of irresolvable components—negates himself. The cosmopolitan mind ambles from downtown through Chinatown in an unblinking blur. The juxtaposition is so glaring he doesn't realize the mist of discord rising through the vents. The mixing of restaurant-cultures leaves out the obvious. He is lost in a surface of subtlety, distinguishing flavors and staring into his swirling wine glass for proof of quality. Dichotomy—that sense of incompatibility which can only be properly grasped by the country gentleman—is lost in favor of trade name variety. Under the monopoly of difference, deviation bears the same manner everywhere.

Reverence for a Nice Story

The most celebrated lie of our age is that we can all be birds of many feathers. This Huma bird that is all birds, this mythological Persian tale, can only be perpetuated by flying unseen high above the earth. When it alights the bird of paradise will breed hysteria. The tendency to flock towards resemblance cannot be overcome naturally; through the ornithologist's binoculars an attraction of opposites is a confused jumble, making classification impossible until the muddle sorts itself into a hierarchy. But by then the ornithologist would not be interested in taxonomy so much as entertainment, tossing popcorn kernels into his mouth as the winged battle over seeds ensues.

The Way of Many Peoples

First, an open society stops deriving Ought from Is. Soon enough, it has only Is. Finally, it becomes Was.

If there are many truths, there must be only one Falsehood. But when Truth reigns, there is no limit to the number of falsehoods that are tolerated.

The Househusband

A man apart, the Househusband's sole outlet for his testosterone is to vacuum *again*. He has finally succeeded where the great conquerors, builders, and scientists failed—he has mastered his environment. But with the blinds closed he has no one to brag to of his domination.

Woman's condition is a choice of entrapments. But for man the luxury of choice is reserved only for the most courageous: to be a breadmaker by birth and not a breadwinner by trade—not to choose his path, but to realize his destiny.

He stands in proud silence for the returning Businesswife to notice, but she only kicks off her pumps and asks about dinner. As he applies the nail polish remover, he confesses that dinner didn't go as planned. He had felt sorry for the animal: it just wasn't wild enough. He tried to set it free, but it just stood there at the door not knowing how to cope, and when he tried to slaughter it out of pity he made a mess of things. There was nothing to salvage from his sympathy.

He pauses, waiting for her to notice. Before he's toweled off her feet, she kicks away his hands and trickles nail polish remover across the rug on her way to retrieve a microwave dinner from the freezer. She only ever says something when she sees dirt.

She doesn't give him anything that night. In his frustration, he wonders whether he coiled up the vacuum cord clockwise or counterclockwise. Being in agreement with synchronized time would give him solace. It would assure his place within the framework of civilization. But being uncertain, he weeps. Maybe he *was* all those things the other men in the neighborhood called him, after all. A woman. A fag. A freak beyond the bounds of nature. *A househusband.*

Should he, like Oedipus, believe he can alter his fate? Should he peruse the employment section?

The next morning he opens a newspaper to the job listings and finds an ad for . . . a maid service.

***

First moral: Mundane things are precious to all but the worldly.

Second moral: A man who flouts tradition to enter a woman's world is more than a man, but still less than a woman.

Third moral: Glory and truth have lost their feminine appeal: a woman enters a man's world today only to pay the bills men can't. Boudicca arises to pass out her business card among the Romans; Hildegard chants pop songs and writes volumes about her inspirational experiences.

Fourth moral: Role reversals are applauded from the conventional positions: actor, misfit, liberal.

Fifth moral: For every door marriage closes, it breaks a window.

The Known World

The "hyper-rationalists": working only towards what is certain, they sit in a room, pay their insurance bill with their welfare check, and wait for the daily mail. A force they cannot see provides them with guarantees contingent on *legible* prayers. In crises where their petitions sit undelivered with the flag up, they don't panic—they call their mothers and ask for advice.

Children's letter to the Postmaster General: "Dear Sir, why is it that your blue angels rest on the Sabbath but my daddy has to work a cash register?"

Playing Corvinus

With wide-brimmed hat and sunglasses that engulfed his face, the idol wandered among his subjects in disguise, noting their habits, memorizing their mannerisms, preparing for his next big role. Since he always portrayed someone average, it made sense that he should impersonate averageness itself. Whenever he saw an interaction that seemed inauthentic, he would intervene, dispensing justice to the bad actors of life. If someone mispronounced a line when speaking to him, he would make them repeat it. If spoken with an inappropriate amount of emotion, he would start insulting them to extort the right delivery. If he witnessed a fight and saw little blood, he would step in to choreograph it and send a bystander to the store for corn syrup.

Occasionally the idol would see someone performing a skill adeptly. Here, too, he slapped down a sense of evenhandedness. If a construction worker was building a house with too much precision, bricks had to be laid with gaps, timbers mismeasured, windows made slightly angular. The idol would then instill in him alcoholism or blindness, some character trait that made the construction worker sympathetic to his fellow men. If the idol's waiter memorized his drink order without writing it down he would claim it was wrong, charging the waiter with anterograde amnesia after drinking the tapwater of Lethe—a movieworthy condition. If a firefighter rescued an entire family, the idol would throw one of the children back to retrieve the dog. This was a firefighter who inspired heroism in those he saved. It was the idol's task to see that ordinary people had dramatic stories about their ordinary abilities. An unrelatable life is an unremembered life.

Glory Days

The movie star who jots daily thoughts in his Fame Diary . . . from dead end job to megalomania to painkillers to long weekends in the asylum . . . would he blame it all, in the end, on the writing process? If only he had never *reflected* on his swank, he mumbles in a pharmacological haze to the psychiatrist . . .

The saddest cases are the celebrities without a straitjacket to restrain their dramatizations. The famous never achieve serenity, even in death: although their influence may cease the gossip carries on. Their public image is exposed everywhere, flaunted by peddlers, critiqued by pundits. Perverse details are brought to light; interpretations abound among scholars even as rumors become facts in the eyes of the multitude. The ghosts of the famous are the most tormented of spiritual beings: they can't go on talk shows to set the record straight or give biographers the birds-eye perspective. The *other side* of the story remains off limits to the living.

The Way to Perfection

Worse than dismissive criticism is fulsome praise. The former, at least, might be true. Or at least helpful.

Oneness of Being

Greatness? People on television.

Deposing Recognition, the bastard Fame is coronated from an obscure abstraction into the sensation of personhood.

In past times the common people had no first-hand impression of the regality of greatness; the *form* of elevated minds was beyond conception. The scandal of Galileo was the immateriality of the celestial navigator. The name was known but not the flesh. Then the photograph invented the household face, the phonograph the voice in the air. With the movie camera, Edison brought mouth to mug and invented the celebrity: embodiment of the new greatness, a light bulb that brightens and shortens its filament life with each new perceptual leap in technology.

***

"Fame—its *ideal* type," says the professor, "is a natural outgrowth of sociability based on the unequal distribution of merit. In this sense the desire for it is instinctual, evolutionary, and functional. Widespread praise is a result of fulfilling one's potential and meeting a shared need in a way that few others can."

"Thank you for clearing that up for us, professor. Please continue."

"But what is fame, *metaphysically*?" he asks, pausing to tuck in his beard. "It is for one's body to transcend itself and become an object in the consciousness of everyone, to usurp people's thoughts and direct them outward, from self to other."

"Excellent! Where would we be without your rigor, doctor? Oh wait, I'm sorry. I didn't mean to presume. You *are* a credentialed philosopher, aren't you?"

"Uhh . . ."

"What a silly question, of course you are—you have a job! Anyway, the question that's really on my mind is, what is this *obsession* for fame that has ballooned into the mania of our age?"

"Elementary, my boy, elementary." He pauses to blow pipe smoke in the boy's face. "It is a desire for every person to want to become an object in the consciousness of others. A society of monads, where substances are reduced to appearances, each striving to make itself into 'the one true appearance,' to dominate all of mental space and render everything else a series of modes. For a person who rockets to fame, it is as if the universe of Leibniz suddenly becomes that of an empirical Spinoza. Monadology becomes a material monism, where the persistence of God's existence—that is, the existence of the famous person—is dependent on the continual observation of all the little modes."

"This is all very confusing. But if you keep going on like this I might understand something."

"Naturally. But to continue . . . democracy, you see, in creating the equal opportunity for everyone to be an object unto others, causes the desire for it to run rampant in each person, while simultaneously making the possibility that any one person will actually become so miniscule. Such a person can increase the chance of discovery by forming a standardized personality, that is, a person fulfilling the criteria of *averageness*. If such a person is born average, then they are all the more likely to

PART 4: Night Sweats

want to generalize themselves, and all the more likely to succeed—having been born with commonly shared traits, they think it natural to sweep themselves outward into the minds of others and popular culture at large, to standardize themselves into a universal superego lording over the psyches of all. A success story is nothing but a gloss of accident. It is a tale for the limp and lame, an inspiration to the hopeless. It pushes down the top to provoke the dream that the cornerstone can be a floating parapet. In practice everyone is made average, but in ambition no one is a brick in the wall. These two conditions, though contradictory, sit in the democratic mind side by side."

"I get it! You're talking about reality television."

"Well . . ."

"Does it really make viewers stupid like everyone says?"

"Not quite. It creates the hope that, by being superior in averageness, they are worthy of their obsession: to be worshipped."

"I see. That's good it doesn't make them stupid. Say, what do you think are the mental and emotional implications of all this? But try and hurry it up. *Dancing with the Chefs* comes on at eight."

"It is a fact of human psychology that one can only emotionally handle knowing a relatively small group of people intimately. Sympathy can only be dispensed within a close circle. Could not, then, assuming intimacy is mutual, the reverse be true—that one can only handle *being known* among a relatively small group of people? It would seem that the mind is radically unequipped to deal with the consequences of being at the focal point of widespread attention disseminated through modern technology. Of having one's image projected around the world, talked about by millions, thought about constantly, inhabiting the mass cultural consciousness. To not know anything about people, to know merely that *they know you*, that your every behavior is a subject of their curiosity and amusement, can be overwhelming. Megalomania, in the form of the development of manifold personality disorders, is the common upshot. Celebrities often substitute their intimate personal relationships for their fan collective. In a sweeping philanthropic gesture, they bestow their image of themselves to the world and shut themselves away to spare past contacts the disagreeable impulses they always wanted to unleash upon them. The result is either to retreat into their mansions in *Sunset Boulevard*-style, or to turn one's network of personal associations into a mutual support group composed solely of other famous people . . ."

"Hey, wouldn't that be great?" the boy sighs. "My friends are so normal, so . . . boring."

" . . . and it is the people who most crave this fame whose breakdown is most absolute, who become imbalanced—or rather, more imbalanced—when their coveted object does not bring them the happiness and contentment they expected it to. They find that the adoration they sought is both conditional and continual: their every gesture is subject to constant scrutiny. Anything unconventional or eccentric is immediately exploited. Fame genericizes the person beyond the bounds of realism (he must be able to be encompassed by the ego of every person, and therefore must be *relatable* to all), to an extent that the personality cannot handle: to be normal in every conceivable way, to be 'perfectly normal,' in the sense of being the embodiment of all standardized characteristics."

"How does somebody become like that? Good enough to be famous?"

"For a person of real potential these characteristics are no mean feat to attain—it is as difficult to suppress ability as to cultivate it. To become famous, one must incubate qualities that are the antithesis of Castiglione's courtier. Where the courtier has vast cultural knowledge, the celebrity is oblivious to all but his ego. Where the courtier has wit, the celebrity flaps platitudes with a silver-plated tongue. Where the courtier has military prowess, the celebrity is ready to get in a drunken bar fight to defend the honor of his one-night stand. Where the courtier is proficient in several musical instruments, the celebrity once held a violin while a recording played in the background. If the courtier was the model Renaissance man, today's model figure is the peasant suddenly granted a noble title on the condition that he don a jester's jingly hood and motley speedo—left out is the critical function of the jester, the divine right of the nobility, and the peasant's stock of useful everyday knowledge. The result is a figure of charm rooted in a useless beauty devoid of any classically sublime aesthetic."

The boy looks at his watch. A quarter to eight. He tiptoes out of the room. The professor doesn't notice. Gesticulating wildly, he continues:

"And then, after the triumph has faded and the weight of routine threatens total breakdown, comes the negative epiphany: that fame is not about adoration, but envy—though not at first of the sort you imagined. For it is not your achievements they are envious of (there are none), nor you (you have no talent). It is, rather, *your fame itself* they envy (or rather, the fame momentarily descending to inhabit you), and the effect of your fame. They imagine your fame soothes you to sleep at night, while it in truth it has become an unending torment to you. Secondarily, they envy your wealth, which they imagine brings you pleasure, but which at best is an inadequate consolation. And if this unlikely realization comes to you, it may be followed by this rare pearl: that there is no 'long view.' Fame in our age involves a contraction of time, both subjectively—in the Warholian fifteen minute sense—and historically: out of unworthiness, your actions are inscribed in no annals, rest in no cultural memory. So when Silenus says that the best thing for mankind was not to have been born, we could perhaps amend his *carpe mortem* admonition as the next-best alternative: '*to be forgotten* soon!' And in fact, Silenus's statements of ought are facts for the *celebritas* species: the people of the present forget you soon, and for the people of the future it is, for all practical purposes, as if you never existed at all."

World as Swamp Bog

Schlegel's "Postulate of Vulgarity" is not just a lens for historians to view the past, but a lens cap for society to obstruct even present sublimity. All that is lofty, grand, and noble, that appeals to the cerebral sensibility or is in any way genuinely *great*, evoking an awe beyond measure, a sense of wondrous mystery surrounding the origins of its manifestations . . . is too extraordinary to notice. Billboards being the cardinal model of communication for a gridlocked population, the infinite becoming of poetry takes on the limits of the prose caption's word count cut-off in the margins of the audiovisual feast.

Beauty finds itself twisted, extended, reduced to things it had never formerly consented to participate in: paintings of charming rustic huts, celebrity photos doctored for weight loss, or in the case of the really vulgar. . .a Strauss symphony. Even the dainty is trampled underfoot.

The *Apeirokaliac*: one who has never been surprised by the beautiful is galvanized by shock of the coarse. Rather than being transported by the wonder resulting from the experience of novelty, the Vulgarian feels only titillation. Often afterwards, over an appetizer, it is mistaken for wonder, and in the retelling it stinks of garlic and onion flavoring.

A discerning mind does not stop at merely spotting bad taste; he feels it his duty to condemn it as well. An ethical overlaying onto the aesthetic dimension, bad taste reinscribes as a species of morality what, for our age, has remained an autonomous sphere distinct from it.

Champion of erratic locomotion, the Vulgarian turns banalities into anthems. Communers with the sublime having isolated themselves in their attics to concentrate and mope, the Vulgarian becomes by default the last patriot willing to carol his bawdy allegiances in the street. The abstract is subsumed under the mundane, to the libido's mode of knowing, the *sensus communis* of the Roman holiday. Moving in the opposite direction of Abelard, he intends to be a sensualist and becomes thereby a nominalist—universals are matter for his tongue, which dies gradually from increasing numbness. In the end a quiet impotence results. There is no *Historia Calamitatum*, no hindered achievement—the Vulgarian's life is the story of a lust affair with himself not worth relating. Not because he is totally naïve, but exactly because, in admitting his defects in the way of innocence, he continues to walk the path. There is often some degree of monastic reflection in the Vulgarian's life—his vulgarity is not simply physical, but the animalization of the spirit. Metaphysics, too, is the province of a particular being. We are disgusted by his final confession: he just couldn't help himself.

Vulgarity: all that emerges out of the rectum which lacks substance. If the sublime is a mother-of-pearl cloud, the vulgar is a puff of flatulence. The fart is proof that aesthetics can ascend beyond itself and develop ethical connotations. Art cannot convince the nose of the legitimacy of *art's sake*—its kingdom is the reptilian brain. The gas-passer's stink gives off an aura of coarseness, a bubble of vacant space visualizing his lack of ingenuity—with a match, pyrotechnics could have redeemed the incivility of not excusing himself.

Suburblimity

Confronted by an infinite suburban landscape which we can imagine imperfectly only with the help of an aerial photograph and partially grasp with our intellect only through maps and blueprints, we shudder not just from the mere beholding of it but also from the consequences of its existence—terror over tasteless uniformity of living space mixed with queasiness of exhaust fumes and shouting children. We witness nature laid waste at our own hands: not bothering to refer it to our intellectual capacities, we vanquish it out of spite that its total conceptualization is beyond us; it melts away against the power of machines even as our lethargy fails to stir itself and gloat. It is a destruction we accomplished out of ignorance, experiencing the sublime only as an after-effect of negligence. The Sublime: a realization that setting no limits on ourselves is our fatal limitation, a feeling that presses upon us and does not allow our detachment—a jackhammer setting off a migraine, so relentless that skull and street become indistinguishable. Antithesis of Friedrich's paintings in which we put ourselves in the shoes of subjects observing the sublime from behind, we instead find ourselves standing below a sea of smog, bending over and holding a mirror to our face, too apprehensive to crane our necks upward.

The man who lassos the moon thinks only of harnessing lunar energy for his midnight paddleboat ride, contemplating it for the sake of itself only as it crashes into his reservoir. As he spends all his remaining thoughts pedaling for his life, the passenger he was so eager to impress finds herself lamenting her date's moral corruption and wanting only the view they once had. But the sky will not be whole again, and against our denials of debasement the forces of nature are almighty. Mother's laws are not our own, but higher than us, falling upon the world and crushing our audacious autonomy.

Ward of the Flies

Evil is easy. Only the first murder—obeying the command to pull the trigger—is hard. After that desensitization occurs rapidly; the will acquiesces, even justifies its acts and delights in cruelty's conformity. The Milgram subjects, profoundly pained to administer fatal voltage, become eager Nazi soldiers—the singular refusal, the "good man" despite circumstance, is quickly dealt with. Invested with authority from the beginning rather than obedient to it, initial pangs of conscience are blocked by chemical surges of sadism—Zimbardo's Abu Ghraib experiments. The brutality among children lost in nature is shamed by the amusements of commoners in imaginary status roles with *real* props. And after irreparable crimes of civilization are perpetuated from fictions, we go home to the lie of "the ordinary."

Where is the moment of innocence here? *Before* the first murder? But sin was always within us, presupposed, and after manifesting itself prompts no reflection—never innocent, neither is guilt admitted. Pure evil is unknowing—Death in *The Seventh Seal*—and its mortal instrument the antithesis of Antonius Block. A bureaucrat returning from a long campaign in the filing cabinets finds a plague of messiness spread over the land and takes up extreme measures to cure it. The need for justification—the attempt not to explain, but explain *away*—is fully realized in duty, abyss of the "why."

For some, duty isn't enough; they overlay sadism and alcoholism to enhance the demands of expectation: the mind exempts itself from pain via pleasure as the body records all the suffering inflicted on others. In the end the torturer becomes alienated from his consciousness and unable to weather the physical ailments cruelty has imposed on him. The hybrid constitution of the torturer breaks down on both sides: ensnared in a libertine finitude, the will overasserted, sensuality and pride are denied through exhaustion.

After the self, duty is all one has left; by the merciful power of grace, subjectivity is judged in accordance with the law and given the strength to keep going forward, an empty shell injected with larger purpose. The effort to clothe duty only consolidates its solitude—it does not permit a rivalry of motives, above all the temptation to kindness. Whereas selfishness only discounts the significance of others, duty excludes none: all, including oneself, have importance only insofar as they submit to the rule. Matter and spirit alike are surrendered as tools of obedience.

Marketing Stickers

"Child-friendly": a label containing forgotten meanings and bygone values too dangerous to be recaptured, appreciated only by those unable to understand what they are bound to lose.

"For singles": the wild public inauguration to domestic life sought out by those who have outgrown their innocence.

"Family-oriented": seen clearly only by flesh-peddlers, the infertile, and the lonely.

The New You

Advertising rises to an art when it stimulates not a perceived need, but *boredom*. Generosity sweepstakes, patient repetition, diligent associations, claims of skyrocketing temperance—a cavalry charge of techniques weaseling the tedious virtues into subliminal consciousness to make people fidget in their jiggling bodies, necrohabits, and abusive relationships. This campaign of discontent would implant not a longing for this or that product, but a heartache to jump on the bandwagon of another existence altogether. To lodge ennui in the soul is to commodify life, to make a conspicuous consumption of unfulfillment.

Levels of Senility

We say that age brings individuals wisdom, communities reverence, institutions prestige. But opening a history book shows us that age in a state brings decay and chronic disorders of public character. At this point the prudent among us chide ourselves and apply this macro-principle down the social ladder. Only then will we know future generations better than they know themselves.

Tragic Currency

One can't write tragedies about important figures today, as tragedians in the past wrote of royalty. The pride of the powerful fails to convince us. They are too transparent, too accidental: in the right circumstances, any person could have held their position—precisely why we envy or resent them. We rightly recognize that the campaign funds of the politician misdirect his charisma and crush his vision. Under monarchy money was a prerequisite of greatness; in democracy it *is* greatness. Money is the tragic hero of every democratic drama: it, and not individuals, decides the course of history, while the consequences of its flaw—that it runs out—cannot be overcome by any amount of Spartan will or Athenian guile. This is why the lot of money is most movingly expressed on the stage through its empty-handed victims, the scavengers of rare coins who don't even die clutching air, but linger on past the anticlimax. The modern tragic individual is distinguished by his lack of dramatic significance, his irrelevance in contemporary life. He is a supporting actor playing out the content of his pockets.

Comedy is the proper treatment of the powerful. Where the tragic hero feels guilt, the clown is shameless. Even when a CEO's buffoonery with his capital is exposed, he does not acknowledge ignominy but pleads innocent. Having become accustomed to these episodes of corporate life, we watch the trial with all the relish of a sitcom. Our cynicism stabilizes the stock exchange; the CEO's pain mitigates our frustration and, for a moment, we laugh at corruption's fallen partner. The judge tries to throw the weight of the world on his shoulders and hold him accountable for ruining it—a fact which we accept but can't bring ourselves to believe: we would not *tremble* to be his neighbor as we would a trivial rapist or murderer; instead of closing our blinds we would open our doors, hoping to coat ourselves in his hemorrhaging lifestyle.

PART 4: Night Sweats

How to Philosophize with a Screwdriver

"He is a scholar and a gentleman."—One never hears of such a unity anymore. When social roles specialized they had nothing to balance them, they lost their sociability; each moved in the direction of maximizing its internal logic. Thus gentlemen, to retain their status, have devolved into merchants; while scholars, to regain their lost reputations, have fallen into Nobel laureation. Sycophancy to princes was somehow more dignified than to prizes or dead presidents. One pledged arms, life, and soul, but never lunch meetings or lecture tours.

Scholars of expression, come forth—and show these intellectuals *how* to be learned. Obliviously we tread over buried treasures, tracking eroded footsteps through windy dunes. Future minds will be digging through the sand for centuries. But we men of experience, unknowing of the world's depths—we are relegated to the surface. The most we hope for is to find an oasis to wade in and forget our thirst.

The new father of "modern" philosophy—the philosophy culminating in *our* concerns—is not Descartes, but Russell. "The Right Honorable Earl," mirroring the ambiguity one cannot help but feel towards empty titles in a period of fluid mobility, started a new trend: the academic first as obscurantist, then as populist. With the journal article, he moved philosophy out of the salon and into an office where philosophers smoke their pipes for stimulation as they read and discuss themselves. With the pop-philosophy book, he crammed the subject into a compact car and drove it into the marketplace. What results is the dumbing down of a mystification. To be told in small words what cannot be understood in big ones does not lead to comprehension. The interested reader, expending much time but little effort, becomes more than ignorant but less than knowledgeable: he becomes "informed."

Medieval scholasticism that eschews its faith while retaining its terminology, academia is reason taking a sabbatical. Like a reverse-alchemical process that turns gold into base metal, eternal questions are compartmentalized into methods. Philosophy of Brains limits experience to the interior images of eggheads, warring against divergent techniques of analysis; injecting himself with chemicals for a PET scan, the Cerebellicist records the metabolic changes of his thoughts before overdosing on observation. The Alphabet-Reckoners go further, so impudent as to *educate* the scientists: the tweed shirt waves logical paradoxes at an inattentive lab coat and points him in the direction he was already looking towards.

The master asks after some *coffea arabica*. The maiden recommends with a curtsy that visiting the public sphere of the coffee house would be more stimulating than drinking alone. The master is disdainful of her contribution, rebuking the maiden for her absentmindedness and rejecting her suppressed premise: if he wanted stimulation, he would not drink arabica. He always has his morning coffee, and arabica is the least bitter form of reliability. He knows she is only pretending to be absentminded out of laziness, and gets up to make the coffee himself. The maiden cannot, after all, be trusted to mill the beans without an electric grinder. In the real world people use their feet to get things done. The master asks himself why he even retains a maiden, since it is always he who does all the work. The laborer should reap the benefits. The last thing he needs is someone to follow him around explaining his own behavior to himself. It is only respect for her parents' memory that prevents the master from dismissing the maiden from his service.

***

Object of oblivion: all the ways idleness, lassitude, the disquiet of empty thoughts went into meriting the philosophy professor's paycheck—blood and sweat of student fees. The paycheck is not just the instrumentality of living, but far deeper than what we thought it was. Beneath it—beneath everything—is *less*. All along a veil of presence had been cast over the paycheck so as to not overwhelm us with its bare nothingness; to uncover the setting of the paycheck—the night jobs of insomniac grad students—is to swoon about in void-vertigo.

***

The only way one can use philosophical terminology these days is to take it hostage: buy an academic's book and mail a new page to him every day. With any luck, he'll define your ransom with a restraining order. "The defendant is prohibited from approaching within five hundred feet of the plaintiff's book . . ." If only contemporary philosophers would appeal to a judge to design their book cover, so the curious will instantly know where they stand in relation to it. The law is perhaps philosophy's last friend, the one who stays behind to help clean up after everyone else has left the party. But then, the law is obliged to be *everyone's* friend . . .

***

To sum up the history of the "love of wisdom": the journey of philosophy begins in wonder; the Journal of Philosophy ends in bewilderment. Philo + *strophia*: love of turning. Philosophers today are dancing masters. "Step here, and here, and here," they say. Good form is a product of technical mastery; those who try to keep up with the incessant twirling of the *bios theoretikos* collapse in dizziness.

Children grow into imbeciles when neglected. When the educated retreat into research caves, mass culture learns to tie its shoes with a safety fuse and brush its teeth with matches. If our basic pyromania skill-set doesn't end in self-arson, the smoke from our knowledge will asphyxiate us. The leviathan has grown too large for sailors to navigate without trembling for uncertainty—rightly so, for they have lost their mastery of the sea. The armada scattered, the sailors of each ship lower their flags and drift along, charting lonely bays.

PART 4: Night Sweats

The New Pedagogy

Learning by doing: a child who gets the idea of a hat by using it after Dewey's fashion—lecturing into it. Sounds conveyed into the ear indirectly are transformed into expectations of entertainment: the child, hoping Dewey will pull a rabbit out, receives instead a sluggish lesson on the reflex arc. An adolescent deprived of magic grows to imitate the habits of knowing.

Dewey the Destroyer: progressive education is philosophy's euthanasia. The only way to make the aim of the philosopher compatible with that of the nonphilosopher is by unplugging the superannuated search for wisdom and hooking everyone up to the science industry. Academia and the factory are two islands stranded by one sea, bridged only by journalism dialectics and the sophisms of media moguls.

The Forgotten Pessimists

Mainländer, von Hartmann, Michelstaedter—residue from a time when pessimism's popularity inspired every adult with an unhappy childhood memory to compose a master's thesis on despair. Periods when the temptation not to exist has become a fad may be indicated by the loci of lesser figures in this tradition. Not imaginative enough to merely write about suicidal scenarios, they must either commit themselves to one or achieve a worldly success that prevents them from sympathizing with the act in any way whatsoever. It is instructive to read such figures for the manner in which their posthumous reputations lived up to their theories.

If Schopenhauer had taken lessons in civic duty from Dr. Pangloss, von Hartmann's system would be the result. It did not occur to him that his best of all possible worlds—one in which the species strives towards nothingness through collective asceticism—is outclassed by a better possible world—*ours*—in which the same goal is achieved more swiftly through collective hedonism.

Mainländer: if he would have only put off his admirably consistent conclusion a bit later, giving himself enough time to establish an influence consistent with his thesis: to make the world that comes after him the ruin of a self-annihilated god.

The inference of the 23-year old Michelstaedter, the same as that of the 23-year old Cioran—that we must live in the moment, on the crest of an unending temporal wave—requires an effective method of entertainment, one that is not adequately achieved by systematizing playful rhetoric within a dissertation. Hence why Michelstadter was led to the limits of an austere logic while Cioran felt no such obligation—not so much by the validity of that logic as its utter boredom.

Given that a man seeks to become his own principle of non-contradiction, his metaphysic of suicide might for once take an original variation. Where is the heroic nihilism of ending one's life through gluttony? That life has no essence without good nutrition is as compelling an essentialist bias as any to protest against. The persuasion of a high-fat diet; knowing that one wants healthy arteries and seeing no way to unclog them. Alone in the desert of processed food, nougat makes naught of thought.

The Underworld Optimist

As the pessimist learns to smile at the grimness of life, so the optimist need take up his good conscience. He too must learn. Not to take the opposite track and frown—that would cause him to be misidentified. Everyone knows that the satirist is at home in laughter, but no cheerful soul ever spoke of progress with a grimace. No, the optimist must learn the art of the paroxysm. Coughing, hacking, sneezing—expelling his jolly slogans loudly and violently, sending out a snotball to accompany his words of inspiration. He coughs in lieu of disappointment; if his expectations are too extravagant he spits up a bit of blood to foreshadow their miscarriage. His friends will think him in need of manners and medicine, giving themselves just enough pause to sober their idealism with a wrinkled nose and curled upper lip. Principles that can endure the common cold are stronger for having been tested. The more unremitting the viral infection, the surer one becomes that *things must get better soon*. The late stages of consumption cannot but bring on a fortified zeal for life. Retreating into hostile territory, the Hadean optimist confines himself in a sanatorium to *prove* his health, refusing to give up on progress just because he moves against the grain; for him, retrograde motion is a sign of eventual advancement, battling death the ultimate evidence of one's verve. In a sequestered obscurity without glory, without a statue to pay tribute to the fallen soldier, there is only the prospect of life to propel one onward, the knowledge of advancing medical science. The experimental subject can look forward to a haler humanity; the invalid hopes the hospital food will improve. Beyond their individual lives lies a future where illness is not necessary and death can be rescheduled.

    This realist of hope despises his green, sunny archetype—he who has never known the winter snow, the summer monsoon, a plague of locusts, one who limits his cheerful outlook to his own life, selfish for happiness. Bellowers of the Neverlasting Yay! are cynics in the making, secret sons of despair who curse fate at the first occurrence of misfortune. Enduring optimism, pitiless and implacable, can only be spread by an epidemic.

Selective Determinism

Among the enlightened, free will is not yet sophisticated enough to influence more than one automatic behavior at a time. Breathing is interrupted by a sudden thought, thinking halted by a deep breath. Asphyxiation or benightedness: absorbed meditation is a rare enough habit that the majority of people escape this dilemma. Theirs is a different doom: not in the choice between instincts, but unconquerable drives.

PART 4: Night Sweats

Swan Song

Our civilization has no *genius* of collapse—an Alcibiades who parades his people down an avenue of ruin with the flamboyant insouciance of a homecoming prank. We totter and sway to the flat trumpets of bandcamp cadets. If only greed or sloth or some other deadly sin were the prime cause (at least then we could give the old excuse that our *natures* made the downfall inevitable), rather than effects of the sheer incompetence of *good will* lacking experience. Familiar enough with history's seismology that the more perceptive among us can feel a spike coming, we are relegated to watching leaders try to beat their drums in sync with the masses, who stomp their feet with increasing randomness.

Society's Rickety Scaffolding

Civilized man admires an unhinged instinct, appreciation fizzing into obsession as his sophistication advances towards effeteness. His last course of action, as admirable as it is foolish, would seem that of Tennyson's Ulysses, setting out for adventure with the misguided conviction not to yield and the hope of regaining a strength forever lost. Sailing past the sunset for proof of life, he lands in a tropical Eden and discovers his elemental self.

Hoping to lubricate butchery and enslavement with wonder, he ensures that the manner of his arrival will be sufficiently grandiose for the tribal men to take him as a god. But the civilized man is surprised to find many of the rural inhabitants of Papua New Guinea wearing t-shirts, looking at him only with mild curiosity instead of the awe he needed. To regain at least a mirage of his former strength, he tries to exploit their primitive prejudices by brandishing modern gadgets. They laugh, pulling out rusty, outdated models of the same tools given to them by previous explorers. No matter, he realizes. In the end, strength doesn't lie in technology or perceptions of godhood, but in a state of health. By spreading infection among the natives he can dwindle their population enough to make conquest all the easier. So he coughs on them. Their faces take on a look of disgust, but though they take offense they stand unaffected. They are immune to his cold; they have already adopted the worst of Western man's diseases and made them their own.

Without the possibility of conquest, the civilized man has nothing to offer but diplomacy. Before leaving for home he makes a blood pact with the tribal chief and contracts a rare brain disease.

Defeated, he heads back to his private jet and pours himself a drink. The primitives are gone from the earth. Modernity has extended its reach over everything. Soon these virile semi-barbarians will gain the resources they need to overrun him. Then they too will become like him, urbane and enervated. Even in their current state the gap was too narrow to seem magnificent by comparison.

The white man's burden had been lifted. There was no one left to civilize.

More Than Geographically Isolated

Lacking a ruined continent like the Europeans, Americans cannot take refuge under grand columns and sigh with Doric docility, grooving tattoos of past glories into our flesh columns. But neither can we live in a perpetual present like the Greeks, the example of that prior society still too heavy on our memory to invent a series of heroic epics culminating in our presence. To say nothing of the Chinese, for whom one's own individual existence is just another flower on the garland, the continuation of a living antiquity.

So we are relegated to live in the space of the recent past—the limbo between a golden age and raw life, the lost and the sweaty. Mythologizing what little figures and episodes we have of our history, but with too much evidence to believe the stories about cherry trees and liberation from tyranny (the penny-yoke of a sugar tax), our near-present is a slush of folklore and irony, each interpenetrating the other in turn.

The Greeks, looking back to an age of Gods, aspired to divine deeds but only realized the best that humanity could accomplish. We, with portraits of great men on our walls, aspire to money-changing and can't manage to turn enough dollars into food stamps.

If we had never broken away from the British we could still claim the Bard as ours. Instead he is just another verbal concession. Having survived the infancy of self-determination, we do nothing but gaze out across the Atlantic as we die from neglect in toddlerhood, pronouncing our first and last word with nervous hunger. But "Mama" is more interested in her sisters than us.

Constitutional Checks

Life having become so *common*, one is surprised to find it valued more than ever. But human rights, too, are Malthusian. Liberty is the new war, access to the pursuit of happiness the new potato famine.

"The Rights of Men": by the power of an abstract principle, to be indifferent to the realm of ideas—unalienability of umbecility; free of the caprices of feudal lords, to obey the whims of the stock market; to choose one's devourers, to submit education to ambition, to inherit the genetic mutations of parents and let children set standards of taste, to bestow a written history to every subculture and erect a world literature on a sea of endangered dialects, to substitute talent for self-expression, to consume oneself into a coffin. In the end a boorish civil society balances itself out: those with a short-term cultural memory receive justice in Alzheimer's. Natural law, bestowing political freedom through immutable ethical principles, introduces the determinism of drives, giving people the opportunity to pursue their annihilation at the most rapid rate possible without even consciously choosing it—the only genuine dignity one has in life.

Idioms Spewing Idiots

The world makes anglicisms with the same profusion that it once made latinisms and gallicisms, but with none of the *enthusiasm*, none of the connotations of borrowed refinement. Dumbed-down oral behavior engulfs all objects of expression and infects foreign cultures in a pestilence of sensual neologisms. Every historic district becomes an erogenous zone as abstract terms gain a new sense of possession. Archaisms, once spoken with such delicacy for fear that the tongue would grate against the palate and flaw pronunciation with a faint but devastating detail, are rendered inefficient by the cheaper production value of monosyllables. The gauge of imperial corruption is not moral degeneration within the mother nation, but the exportation of its depravity to the provinces via *word of mouth*. Conversations, devoid of the grace and wit of the French, cut out the chiffon cake—for we are now even lacking in substance-as-triviality—and lay the most important emphasis on the smooth transition from beginning to ending. The salutation inaugurating every colloquy foreshadows its parting phrase and becomes a metaphor for weariness.

Noose as Lasso

> Age of God: 1607–1776
> Age of Heroes: 1776–1945
> Age of Men: 1945–Present
> ***

In America's Age of God, poor men of piety carved tracts of land from a forest of native corpses and sacrificed its own population to the starving time—divine justice needs scapegoats and martyrs.

Provident Periwigs of the Founding Fathers: as Athena disguised Odysseus in the form of an old beggar, so did the Lord impart an aspect of divinity to an epoch of bad hair days. Men of genius *and* valor powdered their heads before their muskets so the combined eruptions would be heard worldwide.

In an Age of Men that covers stupidity with hair growth formulas and puts a safety lock on spray bottles, the triumphs from the Age of Heroes seem superhuman. An industrialized army unable to capture a few primitives hiding in caves lacks the honesty to explain this earlier success without recourse to heavenly aid. But total victories give way to endless stalemates because God abandons a people only after virtue leaves them. Technology dissolves moral force through impersonation.

The way back to virtue? A mountain of scapegoats and martyrs that surpasses the Hindu Kush.

Commentary on The Discourses, II.31

The danger of trusting refugees: despite any promises they give, they will betray their adopted country as soon as they get a chance to *bring their native one into it*. The desire to transplant their own culture upon the one that took them in, though initially nonexistent when a matter of a few scattered individuals escaping poverty or persecution, becomes strong once the displaced population becomes large enough. Why else would they have been driven from their homeland in the first place? They employed the same strategy there, too: even their own culture they wanted to *purify*—remake or congeal. Failing in that—unable to either renovate their own traditions quickly enough or assimilate to changing regimes—they simply migrated somewhere else to achieve their goals. Unlike their fellow countrymen who decided to stay put and endure, refugees have a drive to *non-adaptive* survival: they do not suit themselves to circumstances, but alter circumstances to suit themselves, and if successful ultimately transform those around them. Theirs is the will to enculturate.

America's strength and its curse is that it has always been the land of refugees. Whether this characteristic is a strength or a curse depends on the dominant *type* of refugee.

An Invasion of Greatness

The most penetrating analysis of American social life was written by a Frenchman. The most acclaimed twentieth-century American writer was a Russian. Our greatest logician was Austrian, our greatest physicist German.

Without just wars for America to fight, geography cannot donate its useful exiles to us. We are forced to turn to our own population for intellectual originality—a barren strategy, if not a dangerous one. After the steady flow of Grecian culture stopped, the Romans produced only a few dry moralists to oppose the loud virtues of the enfranchised barbarians.

If only we could plant tyrannies in the other developed nations, our influx of peacetime freeloaders might be outweighed by a band of refugees with scientific training in border-hopping. The Europeans could be the first to make an orderly research project out of illegal immigration: sending a control group of tortured Basques across first, dropping Finnish paraskiers onto mountaintops at regular intervals. Testing the reactions of east coast beach populations with a rising of nudes from the sea, wine-soaked Mademoiselles are interspersed with a placebo effect of castrati to gauge the rate of depopulation. After the invasion has been reliably reproduced, the published results might be exchanged for green cards.

Barring this, where will the great Americans of the twenty-first century come from? —The cosmos and the gutter. Above and below, but not parallel to us. Competing against aliens and rats, the last natives will lower their flags, don them as capes, and hunker down in their fallout shelters, too busy fending off abduction and plague to do anything worth remembering. With a xenophobia that scorns expatriation and a tobacco-chewing addiction that discourages evacuation aid, the Midwesterners will make their final stand—with the prize of "Greatest" jointly awarded to what experiments on their chosen few and swarms the rejects.

Aetoichthymachia

Predation is the condition of soaring; one cannot simply live off the view. In the next life when philosophers are eagles and businesspeople are fish—even then the fish will swarm the eagle and pull it under when it swoops down. If man's nature seeped into animals the food chain would become a circle of absurd altercations, a burlesque worthy of a pseudo-Homer. Transmigration has not equalized oppression because there is no point—man needs no help in endangering himself.

Palpable Endearments

Socialists are callously insensitive to our attachment to objects—a bond far more incorruptible than that between people, the more so as it is removed from them. Trinkets associated with the body parts of dead mothers are talismans of sorrow and nostalgia, reminders that the flesh has seen happier days. Much preferred is an object that honors another object through facsimile in a chain of inert mater going back to the garbage of Eden. The first pair of underwear, botanical snugness of soiling and decomposition—a testament to the heritage of stains, the primogeniture of use-value.

A God for Everyone

god—first decapitalized, then degendered. The father no longer reigns alongside just one son, but shares a crowded throne with Muhammad, L. Ron Hubbard, and Joseph Smith's joint-heirs of christ. Would that he had castrated himself sooner, or at least been formally usurped and thrown into a spacious dungeon.

The good comedian who never laughs at his own jokes, god is now finally able laugh at ours: an androgyne wrapped in the cloak of mother nature and raising the shield of paternity. Created to live outside ourselves, experiments of temporality, we take revenge by toggling our maker's gender roles to reflect the needs of each stage of civilization. When small tribal populations with high mortality rates were the rule, a fertility goddess was called for; when expansion and conquest was paramount, an aggressor deity. das goddess having sowed the soil in blood and der god having dwindled native pagan populations through disease, a new transformation is now required to fit the age of equality: *die* deity, safely neutered by a definite article to make us all feel uniformly privileged.

    The *new* myths: baby zeus playing with scented candles instead of lightning bolts, safeguarding his adolescent skirt-chasing with spermicide. As a result of his imposition of free choice on the erotic escapades of the olympians, the generations of heroes are omitted from the Ages of Man. Hopping from Arcadia to the Iron era, Homer's jingoism is disregarded in favor of an abridged edition of Hesiod. By the time Virgil has nothing to write about and bowdlerization leaves no one avid for Ovid, the people are weary of polytheism and ready for something less hierarchical. Shaving his beard, plucking his eyebrows, applying black eyeliner, getting a pixie cut, donning a purple robe, a drag queen yahweh struts down main street at the head of the diversity parade, waving to the groupies. One does not pray, but *claps* to a new world order: "Thou shalt not segregate bathrooms," "Thou shalt not take the name of humanity as a singular masculine pronoun." Unrepentant men with type A personalities become doomed to an afterlife as Chihuahuas; traditional housewives with a closetful of mom jeans are punished as polyandrous phalaropes.

Absolute Philanthropy

Imagine a homeless man who discovers the virtues of bestowing all he has to the poor: a ragged coat, a cardboard box, a half-full bottle of malt liquor mixed with backwash. But those in relative poverty want subsidized housing with central heating and cases of beer to warm them—they will only accept handouts from objects of envy. Shortly before freezing to death the homeless man realizes his folly: that he should have laid his gifts at the feet of the rich instead. One who has nothing can only rise in dignity by giving to those who need nothing, feigning an unaffordable graciousness to flatter those who take reflexively and reinterpret their habit as genteel breeding.

Dilemma of the Small Business Owner

The petty-bourgeoisie sacrifices profits to pay the taxes on his store. When the store fails he converts his house into a family business. When his family leaves him he makes his dog a partner to ensure a backup base of operations. Finally, unable to comfortably fit two in the doghouse following home foreclosure, the man signs over his business to the pooch. Gifted with the natural aristocracy of being a purebred, it may be able to obtain more startup capital through non-traditional forms of lending. Relief is the defining emotion of the petty-bourgeoisie: relief in being able to remain what he is. Never quite out of danger of bankruptcy, he keeps alive the possibility that he will become something greater by accruing things around him.

Marching Uphill

If there is no progress in art, why speak of "firsts"? The first use of a technique: not the idiosyncratic expression of creativity but a development necessary in its time and place—if the Van Eycks, Flaubert, and Wagner had not done it, someone else would have. Each new technique expands the world of style and further constrains later artists. To not use them is a sign of the amateur; to not go beyond them is to remain a pupil, a footnote. One must always be pushing farther around the spiral. The idea that there is no forward movement in art is the opinion of artists in the throes of deteriorating forms. From the gothic to the romantic in every field of representation, there was definite advancement—until representation exhausted itself. That which has been done can never be done again, leaving only an ever-narrowing possibility of strangeness for those loitering at the end of a long tradition. For the artist at the limits, progress is not perfectibility, but solitary confinement and atrophy.

A Real Walk

One has to walk for a long time to take a real walk, this was his motto. Ignoring shop windows as he strolled along, he directed his gaze downward towards the cracks in the sidewalk to see what the ants had hoarded, then watched as the smoothness of the asphalt gave way to yellow dust and dry grass. He picked up a clump of dust and put it into his pocket for later. No harm in a minor acquisition, he felt. Eventually he was treading over rich brown soil and tall fields. He smelled the corn, wanting to pick an ear but not daring to—there might be another crop he was hungrier for. Later he found himself on muddy red clay and indulged in the squish between his toes. Finally there was hardness again. Not a smooth hardness, but coarse and jagged. He relished the feel of solid ground under his feet, proud not to be hovering on cushioned soles. He turned and looked behind him; the red trail along the rocks reminded him of a cave painting. After a while he was unable to walk anymore; falling, he dragged himself along the rough terrain, following the arcades of trees. He stopped briefly to dip his nose into the cup of a mauve flower. He thought about picking it, then decided to wait for a prettier one and continued dragging himself along. He tried to look at the sky but saw only leaves. Soon the animals would pick up on his trail of blood and descend on him for their next meal. When that happened he would finally be able to say that he'd taken a *real* walk. He was no longer an idle city stroller, but Nature's flâneur. Here aimless strolling came at a price.

Practical Economy

America is often compared to Rome as a means of disparagement, but it is our divergences that display us as the most unflattering legacy in the Hall of Civilizations. More theoretically original than Rome, America is less intelligent in practicality. Instead of theorizing practically to begin with we formulate theories to be applied—and never by the theorizers themselves. Compartmentalization extends to lifestyle: people specialize in theory or practice and fail to communicate, even entrenching themselves in mute hostility. Yet in a society half-intelligent and half-stupid, each sees with the eyes of the other: the absentminded professor writes political tracts and the backwards politician directs the space program. But the research of effete scholars fails to trickle down from irrelevance, while the practical man in power relies on his caucus to reflect on his decisions. Even when thinkers seem to matter they are only ever puppets: the precondition of the "public" intellectual is to be in agreement with popular prejudices before becoming known.

If the Romans had been an abstract people, imperial insanity would have been principled rather than arbitrary, and without able administration to prevent state collapse. For all its familiar defects, Rome's one superiority is our fatal flaw: that even during troubled periods its greatest intellects were *bestowed* with power. With stoic resignation as their conceptual schema, highly competent bureaucrats staved off ruin, then spent their twilight hours repenting of the need to act by writing philosophy, histories, epistles, encyclopedias. The prose genres developed at the center of life: confidential endeavors published posthumously, more objective because more confessional than the popular poems of versifiers at the margins; more authentically rehabilitative than the bestselling campaign strategies of today's leaders who place their reminiscences in our hearts. Even when their lives were cut short by forced suicide (Seneca), war (Julian), a state purge (Cicero), execution (Boethius), or volcanic exploration (Pliny the Elder), both their earthly and immortal achievements shame our civil servants who do nothing in private life, then nothing in office, then die in bed *satisfied*.

Our only contemporary near political life who produced an important book was Henry Adams: *The Education* was the product of a rescinded legacy of power. Men today only undertake enlightenment when direct influence becomes impossible. As Machiavelli observed, " . . . it is not titles that make men illustrious, but men who make titles illustrious." But perhaps we should say that, today, ambitious men lucky enough to know the right people degrade titles into ego-captions, and titles cheapen even an outstanding man into an unremarkable one as his career is weighed down with empty honorifics.

Part 4: Night Sweats

An astonishing possibility: administrators not just capable and efficient, but *wise*. How else could a civilization thrive for a thousand years? —Ask the one that will not survive three hundred.

America was comparable to Rome only in its colonial period. By the time of the civil war a people that had recently been so integrated in its approach to life had slumped into an industry of busyness or a somnolent gentility. The conditions that created an Emerson did not last; a generation later, in Pierce, we see a marked shift from practical literary philosopher to academic argotist. The Northern intellectual had adopted the languid detachment of the Southern plantation owner—in the Yankee scholar's good manners, refined contemplativeness, and social irrelevance, he manifested a sense of progress so out of place as to constitute the retrograde motion of futurity. The Northern powerbroker, on the other hand, had become captive to his passions. Slave and slavedriver in one, in his yearning to be free from outer hindrances he whipped the gilded age into existence, an underground railroad of greed where endless carfuls of wasted lives were carried along by the chug of currency.

Pax Americana

Greatness is celebrated today within exclusive clubs for the embarrassed and ashamed, where the red-cheeked squeak about manic benevolence to the shoe-gazing. The Son of Europe pipes its flute at the didgeridoo festival without passing around the sheet music; hoarding the ocean it dumps fish onto churlish continents, their residents indignant that it was left deboning responsibility and ungrateful for not needing to build boats. Spurning assimilative strategies, foreign cockalorums arise to fill the vacancy of command—dictators, zealots, the privileged jobless.

The United States' biggest export is its own domestic revolt against "the oppressor," clearing the market for its biggest import, the alien. The barren earth of affluent nations is scorched by developing ones: a people compensates for the effect of spilling embryos into toilet bowls by welcoming the rejects of exploding populations with open arms.

The restlessness of peacetime: with too much leisure to bother policing the world, we break down our guns for spare parts in household appliances. "Never again," we say—as the enemies it doesn't suit us to have prepare to relapse into history. And so the sheltered age begins: taking the most extreme case and making it the rule in order to eliminate outliers, we usher in an environmental sterility that pervades our lungs and skin—asthmatics of safety, eczema sanctuaries, rainy-day community planning. Every chronic illness resulting from severe hygiene has its matching healthcare plan. Danger becomes the minor probability of extreme sports recreation, its function for life forgotten. Our pets are not the only emasculated ones.

Natural Capitols

After Washington ceased to be a man, he became a mistake. Maistre was right . . . the city never did come to fruition. Built on a swamp, after two hundred years it has merely become a breeding site for mosquitoes of a different kind. It is the place where North meets South and each trades off its distinctive virtues as part of a congressional compromise: a Traveler gets etiquette lessons by way of New York and takes a tour through Alabaman strategies of organizational competence. Exploring the fine architecture of the museums and monuments, he rightly avoids the *inhabited* buildings—the "manners of evasion" being a tip he learned from the many lawyers he met. He buys an American flag t-shirt to commemorate his trip but never gets to show it off for his backyard barbeque: out to celebrate the Fourth of July, he gets off at the wrong metro stop and has his patriotic attire brightened by a barrelful of fireworks.

The Traveler's error? —That, of all the places he could have gone sightseeing in a period of decline, the best are those that offer something to *hear*. When the redwoods fall, when the Yellowstone caldera erupts, when the Everglades attack, the reader of Zen koans will have many possible noises to contemplate.

***

Dying Traveler's speech to the trees:

"Though my journeys span many miles, I have ever only been a *domestic* traveler—a personal choice, since it is impossible to know oneself without knowing one's country. Domestic traveling is the patriot's last honorable outlet, and the natural wonders of a nation are its only remaining places of purity. Now, having seen neither the rest of the world nor even the urban centers of my own corner of it, I shall gladly travel out of it. Not only will I bring no news back and relate nothing of my journey, but, alone in this national park, my screams will not even make a sound."

Preempting Destruction

Not content with waiting for disaster, a declining civilization invites it by contriving achievements in reaction to its uneventfulness. Institutions design blueprints of genius; instead of augmenting their gifts through steady diligence, lazy talents have proficiency thrust upon them after a semester. Framed within a piece of paper, knowledge becomes a reference point. Innovations are too many to recognize and are soon replaced by better ones. Genius has its fifteen minutes—not the genius of individuals (socket plugs), but of bureaucracy, of research grants. Determined by its past direction, it is a genius that *standardizes* creativity, shrinking it to fit into acceptable outlets.

The cultural enemies of genius—the poverty-stricken, the luddites—see all these outer accomplishments as evidence of spiritual withering and ululate attack mantras. The names of God converge upon the demographic plunge in baptismal appellations.

In the adrenaline rush at gunpoint a society contrives its final achievement: a galvanized devoutness, easing assimilation to the aggressor's aboriginal theologian.

Foul Art

The wars, regimes, and sins of excess that swamped the twentieth century do not in themselves indicate it as a total ruin—unable to wrap one's head around so much waste, symbolism enters to summarize and define. As the third millennium unfolds it will sift through our bad art for inspiration in surpassing the horror of our body count. Over our formless artifacts its people will stand and scratch their heads—not in meditation as with fine art, but in strategy. It was the distinction of the monstrous twentieth century to inaugurate *the foul arts*. To this above all will the twenty-first century look back in its advancement *beyond* ruin: not reconstruction but dispersion, wandering, exhaustion—tailgating in the desert.

The stroke connecting body count and bad art—a common influence of population growth? —"More" is the byword today. Or has the spilling of blood itself effected the spilling of paint? —A *Guernica* revolution? That so many pointless deaths, so much departure, required a return to the world in kind—a reentrance of the same meaningless that brought about the mass absence? The law of balance applies even with emptiness.

Trapped in a society that celebrates a vague but certain future, beauty continually modifies itself into an apparent unsightliness, a reflex gag of puzzlement; Teetering on the cutting edge, beyond clichés of picturesqueness, it is no longer about painting portraits of the bourgeois but gratifying their consumptive tendencies at gallery receptions. As war is increasingly waged at a distance, an abstraction for men pushing buttons, so does beauty become something removed from the participant's emotions.

Making Pro-Choice Automatic

Mass suicide is not enough; at a minimum it must be the second edict. The first is to prevent the next generation from having to repeat self-correction by removing the initial mistake. But before this still another step would be prudent. Those who argue against bringing a child into this world should dig up their vegetable seeds and drown their kittens as a rehearsal for universal abortion. Anti-naturalism as pre-antinatalism. Corn, cats, kids: with a diminishing level of difficulty, one grows cold to what was first sweet, then merely cute.

A Basket of Bad Apples

Fad art: foul art's big brother, less whiny but unbathed. Eschewing impersonation, the younger rebels sweat out toxins in a sauna of carbon monoxide. The graphic arts as a medium for momentary pleasures is as old as printing; print's indecipherability is as old as motion pictures.

Falling into the Gulf

In an aristocratic age pseudo-science is the prevailing form of knowledge. Even the greatest minds seldom escape it—Newton's alchemy experiments. Similarly, in a democratic age pseudo-art is the predominant form of beauty. There is a fundamental connection between the two pretenders. As pseudo-science can be defined as the projection of one's own wishful thinking onto reality, so is pseudo-art often described as "expressing oneself." From the Renaissance through impressionism, the dominant painters concretized the central concerns of their time, from God to bourgeois values. Today they objectify their personalities, megalomagnified to make up for lack of content: the hallucinations of Dali, de Kooning's remark about the artist's only hope being to "put some order into ourselves." Kooning was right that artists don't put order into the chaos of the world, but neither do they order themselves. The expression of contemporary artists, their dark inspiration, stems from a lack of self. The artist *reflects* the world's chaos, even intensifies it. He has fallen back on representation and calls it "I." A chicken-egg chaos: as it increases in the world around us, our inner lives become increasingly confused; but its nature confounds any attempt to establish a direction.

Ironic that in an age of superstition and pseudo-science artists were among the most scientific of men, while in an age of skepticism and methodical experimentation artists have made a conscious effort to eschew empiricism entirely. Once the seed of *poiesis*, *tékhnè* now fructifies by sapping all nutrients from its blooming neighbor—flesh and floral share not the tree. The painter's discipleship as physician and geometer; literature's trivium of grammatical consciousness, plot logic, the rhetoric of human nature; Pythagorean harmony of music and number—the gentlemanliness of art was the pride of cognition. But content is not art's proper realm; in its drive to specialize, to excise everything inessential, the Promethean struggle is not about know-how, but *power*. Schiller's quest for free self-activity has gone too far. Unchained from imitation, patronage, the obligation to superimpose meaning upon style—without anything to speak of, it congeals gibberish into objects. Art is the mimesis of freedom, a calculated formlessness; "free self-activity" has no *self* to express—identity is a terracotta clump of porous tendencies and thinly glazed roles. Far below Olympus the minor titan twirls his potter's wheel, hen-pecked by bathtub firewater.

An artist without a knowledge base, the depraved bohemian finds respect in drink and varnishes his work with blackout drool. "Judge not the art but the artist"—the beautiful and the damned, a deputized salvation which collapses when the maker has no soul to donate. The aging belle is nursed by the consequences of her father's sin, and the condemned is no longer motivated by anxiety over the everlasting fire. Devoid of the religious ecstasy backing his patronage, the artist is consumed by flattering a new mode of transcendence: the progressive views of an awards committee.

Hope with Red Tape

Professors in ivory towers dream utopias; bureaucrats in basements create dystopias. No antagonism here—each share a fascination with power, the minimization of chance. But where the irrelevant explicitly discuss power, the practical thinker employs his rationality in a euphemistic shroud of security. The bureaucrat's iron cage is more substantive than the academic's daydream ever could be. The hope for equality, goodness, contentment—all empty theories in the hands of the scholar—represent instrumental reason in all its graceless glory. Reflections on ends lead to a receptiveness for "change" among the overeducated, priming the spinning wheel for the *coup* that disperses all woolgathering. The intellectuals witness the sweeping away of those who made the movement possible—themselves—and the establishment of a people's orthodoxy. No bureaucrat ever sees himself as the antithesis of those systems of pure thought he studied in grad school; rather his rules and procedures are the actualization of them. The first realist of the regime is the last idealist. A well-functioning social order attained, more is needed: an objective good that weighs all goods equally, civil laws that legislate moral perfection. Punishing alike murder, masturbation, and an unkind thought, the minds and private habits of a people take part in an infernal compact they signed without reading the small print.

    Overseeing it all stands the bureaucrat: shaving pencils into blunt nubs, his sharpener becoming the only evidence that there ever was a material goal for society. It is the only sort of end possible for us: a perpetual rotation of hand cranks, a total investment in method. Dullness congeals, relieved only by paranoia and the continuous invention of traitors to preserve our interest in existence. Only with the element of fear—purest experience of life—do principles, like nations, become bankrupt.

Modes of Art

Fine art: to instruct and entertain.
Foul art: to baffle and bore.
Fad art: to tackle and tickle.
***

Fine art: embodied soul. Stirring the spirit by appealing to basic drives and cultivating thought.

Foul art: astral projection of mind. Ostracized soul. Enervated libido.
Fad art: an id ad.

***

Fine art: "Man Guiding."
Foul art: "Man Standing and Shrugging."
Fad art: "Man Masturbating."

***

Fine art: universal symbols commissioned of gentlemen by lords, apprehensible to laymen.
Foul art: status symbols for haughty bourgeois connoisseurs, created by nobodies, understood by madmen.
Fad art: consumed by teenagers, produced by juveniles. Minting press iconography.

***

Fine art: the kingdom of culture. Stimulant ablution.
Foul art: a screamo cult. Expressionism munching on a mixed constitution of antidepressants.
Fad art: a Warholocaust. Frat house filibustering.

Adoration of Causality

Conspiracy theorist: a media junkie with the mind of a Cartesian skeptic and the heart of a child; one corrupted by freedom of the press and saved by subversively manipulated mass data—in the information age there are *many* malicious demons.

Fukushima is the new Lisbon earthquake; God is replaced with Government, the malevolent authority of men. The name only changes in secular times to meet the old need for agency. The universe—cold, silent, random—becomes one in which every occurrence is deliberated with all the foolproof detail of church wives organizing a Sunday brunch . . . and every house of worship has its own meal plan.

Cynical Education

Hard to imagine being an Italian schoolchild memorizing Leopardi or a Soviet satellite youth brigade reciting long passages of Pushkin. Indoctrinated by the fatherland with nihilism and satire, it would seem that the best way to proselytize a zeal for totalitarianism is with a blighted worldview. An ambitious American president would do well to imitate the scholastic program of a Mussolini or a Stalin instead of sanctioning the repetition of a vulgarized Frost couplet that prepares a nation of students to grow up, trudge the beaten path, and wash down a dose of Zoloft with words of inspiration to get through the day shift. The tone of early education helps fortify a child to accept future prospects: in a free society, the droning assurance that choice is unbounded; in an unfree one, the cultivation of black humor.

Worst of the Worst

Hitler is vilified for directing his hate towards certain groups, while Stalin takes the back seat in the monster truck for generalizing his paranoia to the entire population. Rearmost is Chairman Mao, squeezed into the trunk for subjecting a people to his love for humanity.

Arbitrariness, more destructive to a nation than channeled animosity, is still less dangerous than an idealized love that wipes all other feelings off the slate. Posterity has ranked its totalitarian leaders according to the relative success of their visions rather than their body count. (Today the name of Pol Pot—murderer of a mere two million, junior apprentice to democide—evokes broken cookware.) Mao, his failures pockmarking modern china in every field but calligraphy, is embalmed in a mausoleum where visitors shower his crystal coffin with roses grown from the grave soil of the Cultural Revolution. Stalin, father of exploding television sets, is a mustache Russia has been trying to forget. Hitler's toothbrush-lip, chilling apex of modern history's "almosts," is the emergency reserve argument in every moral debate. Beware the fashions of abortive artists.

The Consequences of Watching Oneself

Led by an insatiable Thirst for Knowledge, Mr. Spectator approached the Ticketbooth, molded his Complexion into a Smile for the Servant Girl, and pointed to the Wall-paper of a Flat Play that captured his Interest. He positioned his Rump in a Chair at the back of the Theater and waited for the Flameless Candles to dim. The Flat Play was a bewildering Disorder of Tales, a Play without a discernible Act Structure, the kind that *Aristotle* railed against in his Poetics and of which *Dryden* surely would have disapproved. Some viewers, exceedingly perplexed by the Material, no doubt expecting something more suited to their Sanguinity, got up and left abruptly; others stayed out of Curiosity, clapping and hooting at the thrilling Scenes, staring blankly when they tired of pretending to understand. Mr. Spectator looked on. Completely absorbed in the Play, the Characters were totally present before him. A homely Love. A Househusband. The Defender of a City besieged by two Armies simultaneously. Mr. Spectator noted their Foibles and found a great deal to condemn in them. The Desperation to Love. The Luck of Laziness. The Seduction of Irresponsibility.

He could not relate to such a Variety of Humours, did not recognize his own peculiar Constitution in them. He was a man with solid Parts, as his School-master used to say; he wore the *Respect* of Silence. But their Tales, nevertheless, pained him.

The Boulevards of Extinction

As he watched their sad Fates play out on the Flat Stage, he realized that what happens to the Small Ones of the earth has no Significance, that the Goodness of the Supream Being does not extend to them. And he too was one of these Small People, taking up space between Animal and Intellectual Nature, an uneasy Mixture of half-Passion and half-Intellect with none of the Purity of either. Wondering if anyone else in the Audience had the same Epiphany, he looked around but saw only empty Seats. He was the Lone Participant in the Flat Play; he had these Characters all to himself. Without understanding their Motives, he had established a common Bond with them rooted in mutual Inconsequentiality. He suddenly had a feeling of personal Detachment, as if he were observing himself from the outside. Why did he play the part of a Looker-on? For a Man of Silence to express Opinions on this Swarm of Life is in itself a sort of reverse *false Wit*, a Volubility of the Void, where Silences are twisted to resemble one another. Why come to a Flat Play? He would have done well to follow the Example of Sir Roger, who last attended a Round Tragedy with him over two-hundred Years ago. Since then, the World had turned into a Whirligig of Jobbernowls and Illiterature. There was no moral Advice to be extracted from the Actors' Performances; he could ascertain no *Message* in the Play applicable to Life. After the Curtain of Words began falling he stumbled out of the Theater, looking around, unable to recognize his Horseless Carriage, passing Strangers whose Thoughts were a Mystery to him. Isolated in a World without others, he maintained a flat Expression everywhere he went and became unthinking in his daily Habits. Believing his Experience to have stripped him of Illusions, he had only added another Layer on top of the old ones. Retiring to Bed earlier and earlier each Night, he awoke one dreary Morning and decided not to get up. From now on he would no longer be the Spectator, but the Sleeper. Compelled by the Brain to be a passive Participant in his Dreams, he would at least not be obliged to remember them.

Waterholes

The "weeping prophet," the "weeping philosopher"—two figures kindred in more ways than tears. The first attacked but not overcome, the second overcoming through attack. To individualize either spirit or thought calls forth war's sovereign trumpets. The father must first be a king before he can teach his sons self-government.

We are wading in the success of these two melancholy visionaries. Weeping over everything for the sake of our identity, we have degraded conflict into a horror of social movements picketing for peace. When the king becomes a slave to set the example it teaches men rebellion from their natural state.

PART 4: Night Sweats

In Defense of Prediction

Vagueness is necessary not only to protect a prophecy from falsification when events don't accord with it, but also when they *do*. If a man were to predict a specific event and it was fulfilled on the precise date he said it would be, the whole prophecy would be dismissed as a *science*. Researchers would plunder his tomb for computers, statistical programs, undisclosed equations of natural laws. He would be banished from the fraternity of Nostrodamus and initiated into the Galton gang. The fallen prophet being dead for centuries, his followers are forced to prove his loyalty by kidnapping babies while wearing stork costumes, perpetuating what the enlightened among us had suspected all along—that illusory correlations are the unsolved crimes of stat hoodlums, conspiracies contrived by the discipline to manufacture a common enemy.

Between Noumenon and Phenomenon

Is man anything more than an idea? —Ask the one who is too long for his coat. Homo sapiens: existing for the sake of his things, trying to adapt himself to them but never fitting snugly. An empirical life has nothing to do but compare: too big for his britches, too light for his cups, he is ill-matched to his activities. To compensate he takes the abstract approach, actively reducing himself to categories: husband, engineer, American, Asian-American, manic-depressive. A jumble of roles and pathologies, jingoist of subcultures; last of all an individual. Occasionally he rises above his labels, perfects his qualities, and becomes that consummate being, the Hero of the Unemployment Rate; more often than not he amasses a warehouse of boxes not quite his size, approximating stereotypes to the best of his ability.

The History of Conflict

Man versus the animals. Man versus the gods. Man versus man. Man versus himself. Nature, fate, action, character. This trajectory will not circle back, but parody itself with the history of silence. Consciousness, being the cause of our belligerence, is the last haven from it.

The Other

Consciousness is not the wonder of recognizing one's face in a pool of water, but the anxiety of noticing wrinkles. For the unluckiest—for Merleau-Ponty—it is the horror of confusing his wrinkles with Sartre's. Doppelgangers of self-awareness, every bespectacled runt reflects another, communing with each other's myopia, elaborating on his blurred outlines—inexhaustible tumors of the world becoming continually uglier.

To the declaration, "At least it couldn't possibly get any worse..." one has only to stand over a creaky floorboard and peep through a keyhole.

As Moths Fluttering Leisurely...

Oppenheimer's sin? That he was unable to quit chain smoking *even after* the habit wafted into Los Alamos. Arjuna is excluded from annihilation, but Time itself is higher than the Destroyer.

New Types of People

    A: drink hot lemon water every morning. Eat avocadoes and fish.
    O: eat meat, avoid wheat.
    B: eat a balanced diet.
    AB: get liquidated.
    ***

A day will come when these races of the blood will supersede any social organization based on skin hue superstitions and usher in a new era of discrimination: the segregation of minority antibodies into ghettos, the wearing of alphabet-badges, the extermination of inferior antigens via blood transfusions from superior ones. The final solution of the thick-blooded will be carried out with malnutrition plans concocted by conscienceless pseudo-scientists. Every balanced diet will be interpreted as a cowardice of neutrality. The only allied resistance will come from plasma addicts, labeled as forming an underground movement for loitering in the sewers below blood banks, strategizing with needles seized from dumpsters and tippling their fallen brethren to panegyrics of glory.

Serving the World

The native foreigner—a personality both exotic and parochial. Both here and there, a stranger in his own land. Raised amidst home and hearth only to be cast out, a pariah among his own people.

    This is the plight of every ethnic group that ever claimed a piece of land as an extension of itself and established its own traditions, only to confront the migrations of later colonists. The Native Americans, the Euro-Americans—whether one welcomes the occupiers in is irrelevant. As the invasion progresses and demographics shift, the "original" population watches its traditions change before its eyes until the land no longer reflects its values. Rather than trying to recapture the old ways of life, it commits treason against a country that no longer needs it. It is as if a responsible son were

PART 4: Night Sweats

to suddenly turn prodigal, then go on a vacation in his own household. He spends all his money bedding the house servants and beats the pigs to make himself feel better before having them roasted for dinner. His father does not recognize him and puts up with the son as a disagreeable but profitable guest for a while, then has him thrown into jail for trespassing as soon as the boy's money runs out.

Geopolitics, when seen from the bottom-up, involves the struggle of conflicting peoples to draw new lines across the earth; but seen from the top-down it is nothing more than a landscape's human resource management, the topography of slave trade. The success of conquest and replacement is not just due to the power of technological superiority that an invading race has over a native one, or its more experienced immune systems, or the excessive diplomacy of those inviting colonization. It is *the land itself* that ultimately sanctions a tribe or a nation-state to spring up on it; through bounty or famine, it reaps a people it has grown weary of sowing and offers them to a new ethnic group. The Middle East having gotten bored of the Palestinians, it turned itself into a desert in an attempt to drive them out; when they still wouldn't leave, it brought in a new people—the Ashkenazy Jews—to accomplish the messy chore of geographic cleansing under the pretense of an erroneous ancestral claim.

The world puts itself at the fingertips of its most aggressive tenants in a similar way that doctors pass on infection by not disposing of the latex gloves. As disease ensures a continual stream of hospital patients, ambition keeps the milk and honey flowing. Nature, like men, has its reputation to think of. The exhaustion of pride is a symbiotic enterprise, a mutual fantasy conservation project. Waste Not—motto of the wasteland.

One must consider the possibility that the Earth wants us here only so long as it needs us, that the evolution of civilization is simply a branch of our planet's ongoing ecological project: the process of becoming self-sufficient by refining its method of removing the germs crawling over it.

In an agricultural society the land owns its people directly. In an industrial society it cleanses itself by relocating its tenants into concentrated areas, then selling the majority of them off to factories and relegating the tasks of managing them to a small elite of men. In a postindustrial society the land gets computers to do the work of people; farming becomes obsolete through the production of synthetic food, and humans are finally engineered out of usefulness. Through deforestation and the depletion of drinkable water, the Earth begins its final fasting period, purifying itself with starvation and renewal.

***

"The land was verdant with overgrown weeds. Bees pollinated wildflowers, birds ate the bees, men ate the birds, lions the men, butterflies the lions. The food chain was at it should be. The nuclear power plants were leaking as usual, seeping into the earth and making it strong . . ."

Shintoism

The Japanese, the only pantheists modernity has not erased from the religious scene, the only people for the sake of whom technology peacefully coexists with vegetation, are not *entirely* alone. I, too, worship nature with my prayers:

"Spirits of the east and west wind, comingle to wash away the ritual impurity of the Midwest with tornadoes! Essences of dirt and rain, mix together to rinse mountainsides with mudslides! Gods of the rocks, level the land with an earthquake, and unite with the sea *kami* to irrigate arid places with a tidal wave! Energies of the inner core, coax the forces of the earth to open a duct and send molten tears to enrich the soil!"

My *kami* are not selfish beings like the Greek gods, or jealous beings like Yahweh, but divinities who, holding a grudge for the ingratitude shown towards their abundance, cooperate in *flor*altruism, protecting the planet and renewing it. Sites of disaster are the sacred places of the earth.

Abandon All Hope, Ye Who Enter Here

Nearest to perfection is the embryo after the first division. By the fetal stage, its spirit has become so heavy that the mother must lighten her own by pushing it from limbo into the inferno. Dante's sign over the gates of hell should be the motto of everyone who passes through the birth canal.

A Higher Consciousness

In the aftermath of the twentieth century, Carlyle's "fearless leader" evokes a stimulus of trembling. The rise of a magnanimous candidate for Hero as King is greeted with alarm as a whimsical monster, only to be twisted by the machinery of statecraft into the chess piece of his privy councilors. Bureaucracy exploits the arbitrary-*seeming* will of the world-historical personality, that ambition to act without apparent reasons, and uses it to express its own nascent principle: *pure arbitrariness*—rule-making for its own sake, usurpation of the management of every task. It is the fulfillment of a free creativity, the administrative imagination, the *raison d'etat*—an absolute self-expression that collapses means into ends and determines everything under its umbrella. Flying over tradition, norms, personal honor and favor—the weak links of social ties—it realizes a supreme loyalty devoted to the impersonal and the functional, sapping human ingenuity to augment its own.

The head of state devolves into madness attempting to reign in this creativity and wield it for himself. It is his instinct to power, his addiction; without it scents waft by him unnoticed and he convulses in withdrawal. In the natural history of modern leadership his qualities count for little. Leadership needs to inhabit a vessel of boyish innocence and incomprehension, someone appealing to the crowd and easily manipulated. An army of experts and advisors supply the figurehead with ammo cases of facts and statistics—pieces of Bureaucracy's essence. The figurehead, if he is a cunning child, attempts to play off his data mercenaries against each other, to appropriate information unto his person while keeping them in dark rooms with only their small corner illuminated, turning everything to his advantage and assuring himself that all his acts are willed, that *he* is in charge. But in all this he furthers the caprice of one higher. His secrets are its secrets.

The secret: silent cousin to the lie, the negative imagination of remaining quiet when one is expected to speak; aping of mimes. The leader is this chest's wandering pirate; burying it in the sand for himself, he loses the map and forsakes it to the fortune of treasure hunters. Secrets have always been the universe's way of protecting itself from the world devourers. Furtiveness is the method of Bureaucracy's creativity, an ultimate tool of control out of the range of any one pair of ears. To maximize its domination in the fields of economics, foreign policy—anywhere its material interests are at stake, anywhere it can *insinuate* itself—Bureaucracy weaves multiple layers of secrets underneath its own paramount mystery. Official secrets to protect the people, top secrets to protect the administrators, hushed whispers of offices in conflict, dirty details no one but an accountant should know, secret secrets of a leader unconscious of his role as the first follower, transcendent logic's hitman. The hide-and-seek game of internal affairs has everyone grasping at shadows.

The people—dupes of existence, enemies the system hugs closest—clamor for transparency in the public sector. Ignorant of their lack of inner potential, they want to *know*—to be in on the smut and scandal, to comprehend all outside themselves that reflects their hearts of coal. Clamoring for everything to explode before their eyes, the leaders create grand visual spectacles on which to keep their minds fixed, exploiting the idea of image so thoroughly that many wonder if there is any underlying substance. Politicians work hard to dispel the aura of grandeur and power surrounding their position without sweating. They platform as "George" and "Obama"—but the people want to know their *maiden* names. The more they stumble over their words the more the audience looks around for the acting coach. People vaguely sense a web of secrets and try to root them out. But their own incompetency merely follows the incompetency of their leadership. Leadership does nothing, the people know nothing—each flops about like beached fish. Conspiracy theorists imagine the omnipotence of power, when in fact it is the leaders' powerlessness—their inability to capably handle information, to sufficiently analyze their warehouses of data—that allows the conspiracy theorist to arise in the first place. The governed fabricate solved mysteries to flatter their intellect as compensation for their ignorance of the real ones. Ironically, it is this double incompetence that protects state secrets from being discovered. Lying in wait in a locked file cabinet gathering dust, when someone finally finds the key the riddles are too old to be useful—death and time have worn away the relevance of illuminated meaning. If the bureaucracy invented the official secret, conspiracy theorists invented the universally known rumor, so exaggerated in malicious hegemony as to surpass the most corrupt actual event. All the while the *real* secret is overlooked—that there simply is no secret, no underlying substance or fundamental truth to be discovered. Chaos is its own conspiracy.

Transferring the management of an increasing number of tasks to large-scale institutions, granting us every provision, we willingly eliminate our freedoms, an act made necessary as we acclimatize to our amenities and our basic skill-set gradually diminishes to nothing. The day finally comes when survival without these organizations becomes impossible, with an agency directing even the discharge of our bladder. And when this final triumph occurs, when the state has appropriated all life's tasks, then will its collapse be imminent as well. Duties that outstrip the organizational capacity to carry them out; single-task officers who mark a line on tax forms or pass three squares of toilet paper to the senior wiper. Problems piling up unsolved, life stages passing by ill-adapted to. With the state taking up the burden of our spleen we are free to sate ourselves on its rations of imitation bile.

Therapy in Place of Hand Soap

Where is Maistre's executioner? In the few places he still has work, he is a man in an empty room. Popular among his neighbors, anonymous now that the mask is off, he takes no pains to conceal his identity because no one shames him: The State is the killer. The prison guard stands behind glass and pushes a button. At such a distance, his agency displaced, what can he do but reflect endlessly on his deed's questionable justice? No headsman ever had a crisis of scruples. Bloody hands preclude pensiveness; estrangement from the rest of humanity left one no choice but to keep sharpening the sword. Only the clean-handed executioner dirties his conscience.

Who now fears death? Without the public spectacle of capital punishment it has ceased to evoke terror. Life's end is seldom weighed as the inevitability it is—even the context of the criminal's heinous act is spun around: the sociopath should be given a second chance, a longer sentence to give him time to reflect and repent . . . he should *live*. Science having made dying infrequent and killing efficient, mercy seeks to make fatality itself unnecessary. After the dethronement of kings, the second sign that God has forsaken us is the irrelevance of his instrument of punishment.

The destiny of a society is carried out by its official killer—through him it either preserves its power or drops the scepter. As France ruined itself when it traded the hangman for the guillotine—when execution became the prerogative of the masses—so it seems right that a people swooning with euphoria should go by lethal injection and the gas chamber.

Saudi Arabia: the last country where the guilty are still dragged through the mud is the only one immune from internal corruption.

The Power of the People

Some form of public murder is the most commemoration the mediocre can hope for. Not talented or notable enough to be worthy of assassination, Ordinary Man becomes a scapegoat to virtue through an act of terrorism or a fatal accident caught on candid camera. However pointless his life and senseless his death, the news gives him a purpose beyond anything he could have realized, holding him up as an icon to family values, a martyr in the fight for freedom. For an entire week he is mourned and championed, his biography photoshopped for typicality, inspiring millions to endure unfulfilling jobs and thankless children until the misfortune of the next nobody eclipses his example and bumps him to his rightful place in oblivion. This is the best way to keep society pedaling along, with an army of devoted lemmings cliffstrolling in line to the great chain of suffering, recycled into our memories through an exaggerated fear the people can relate to.

Duelist's Dying Speech to His Second

Dear Friend,
    I have been fatally wounded. Oh, how I should never have agreed to pistols! I am an expert swordsman but a bad shot. The modern method has destroyed me. But at least I have the satisfaction of knowing my opponent will be outlawed for his participation.
    Though dueling is illegal it must still be practiced: this is a point I would demand even of my own father. Honor before law. Justice today is slow and biased: the civil courts are clogged with cases that drag out for months and, in the end, favor the rich. And even if one does win, what is gained by a victorious lawsuit? What is lost? *Money*. Only a fool thinks he can earn honor by swelling his bank account, or that he is disgraced by having to deplete it. There is no finality in such a course of action—the defendant will merely request an appeal.
    The only way to settle a dispute *once and for all* is through violence overseen by a friend. The Duelist was once the necessary complement to the Executioner: the latter frightened members of a state into keeping their behavior within legal bounds, the former upheld respectful relationships between members of civil society through the apprehension of having to fight one's neighbor. An ill-mannered affront was to an individual what an act of treason was to a nation.
    Who was this being transparent to all? He was the essential link in social life; without him society would not have been complete. Everyone wanted to live near him:

admirers to imbibe his aura and enemies to show they were not afraid. His wife was rightly jealous, for he frequently heard the cries of many mistresses. The routine: his second knocks at his door in the morning and tells him the time is set. He drinks a cup of coffee, reads some poetry, and goes. He arrives in a deserted place fashionably late. A man of equal status greets him. They pace, he raises his gun, they turn, he fires. His heart is still. With a shot he has upheld his honor. He is too dignified even to look upon his opponent's body: he turns and drives away in silence back to a house lively and bright inside. That evening he attends a party and crowds gather round in awe. People knew his reputation, though they never witnessed it. "No one aims better than him," they said. Everyone was thinking about the morning's duel but he. The ladies wanted to court him, the gentlemen to seek his favor, ask advice, invite him hunting. He was almost too virtuous to be a mere man. All respectability, grandeur, and civil order depended upon the Duelist.

This is how it was in a time of heroic jurisprudence. The modern duelist is a quite different character: a being known yet unknown. He is a vigilante, the enemy of social order. The legal system twists his honor into infamy, turning a gentleman into a criminal on the run. Man of a bygone world, he resolves to uphold the old ways at the cost of his reputation. The law does not admit fallibility; for addressing its gaps he must be punished. He leaves his wife and children behind, carrying with him only a loaded gun—in a world of wimps, the sole evidence of his masculinity. Alone in the world, he has potential opponents everywhere: far from being respected and feared, combatants emerge from every tier of society for the chance to test themselves against him, and in a democratic age he is in a position to refuse no one. When he is caught the executioner will be summoned for him, and with a flip of the switch their former alliance is severed forever.

The Swell before the Fade

The fortune of the greatest composers was the notation of their fate: to be the purest embodiment of a waning religious age. Their form floating through the schism of least resistance, with violins unstrung from excommunication and pitch still constrained by a treble clef suspicion, the composer directed public worship into the service of his art. The deity's boom is polyphonated into scratching, blowing, crooning; the divine embroiders the beautiful as a promotional tactic; the sacred heightens sensation into a proxy mysticism. Mechanical limitations are exploited to their fullest: the demand for vast space confines the most grandiose of instruments, the organ, to the church.

The composers of an atheistic age, without two transcendentals of being to mutually abuse, can scarcely nurture one. Even Messiaen turned God into a cacophony of forgotten offerings.

Cross Bearers

The holy warrior's *force* of belief: devoid of pity, he proselytizes with revilement—and skeptical Europe converts to Islam in droves. Quietism's placation is the drizzle before dogma's flashflood.

The quality of a religion is defined by its process of arising. Islam's militarism has never abated, but Christianity is only now, in its sad decline, remembering its original condition of martyrdom. Fallen to its knees, Christian apologetics begs for tolerance. A faith that popularized itself through the willpower of enduring torture fades away in a flash of light after shaking its murderer's hand—an entwined bond the only evidence of existence among the jihadgepodge.

The New Meaning of Sacrifice

The martyr without a grand inquisitor: hurling himself onto faint embers, looking about for fuel but finding none—try as he might, no one wants to immolate him. In an age of irreverence everyone hordes all the kindling they can to burn their backyard garbage. Preaching his scandalous truth-claims, the targeted victim is carried off not to the dungeon, but the set of a talk show—a confessor with nothing to declare but gossip. In place of his life he surrenders his shock-value.

Calvinist versus Lutheran Exile from God:

a) Refugees on the crumbled highways of the earth, pilgrims on overgrown paths stretching towards nowhere. The journey is not lost as long as they find streams to fill their water bottles.

b) Ale around the table, lager on the couch, malts on the balcony, porter in bed. With brewing recipes in hand, the Oktoberfest of objectives is ready to draw away the curtains and drink to the blood moon.

Watching Over Us

You pass someone in the street. They could be a murderer, a prostitute, or a stockbroker. But you never could have imagined they were all of these things: *the world's guardian angel*, keeping the population at healthy, gratified, affluent levels. Incarnating the degenerates we need to harmonize ourselves as a moral group, they are the repeat victims of God and humanity, hurled to earth to sacrifice themselves to the death sentence and venereal disease. Predicting our market crashes to show us the value of prosperity, they jump out of fifth story windows without wings—there is a point beyond which even they cannot take. When their skeletons are dug up it will be wondered why, with so many watching over us, we *still* didn't make it.

Genesis, Exodus

> Creation: carcinogenesis.
> Collapse: chemotherapy.
> Coffee: the only connective coping skill.
> ***

In the beginning was not the word, nor the act. What was wrong with existence before the creation? Was it not pure? Absolute? And was not this company enough for Him, the nearest approximation to His wholeness? Was it only worthwhile as a prelude, a *relative to*—the deficiency before supplementation? *Creatio ex nihil* took darkness away from itself and threw it into a blender on "mix"—until the 6th day, when God hit "puree."

Creation is to be despised not because it is a grand failure, but precisely because one of those things all the religions of the world have said about creation just might be true. I do not listen to preludes, I hate standing in line; I want to get to the main movement, to be on the ride *now*. If Strauss's Zarathustra had ended after the introduction, how much more whole it would have been!

When the hair falls off, when sex drive plummets, when the brain gets chemo fog, *this* is the time to sip your caramel macchiato. The cancer treatment was never intended to cure you, only give you enough time to watch the last sunset. Won't it be nice to witness the collapse of the horizon? To have some brief conception of spacetime's end in our corner of the macrocosm? Futile to try to do the opposite and flee. No light will escape civilization's Big Crunch. A society, like the universe, has the gravitational weight of its accumulated matter to see to; eventually it must reverse its expansion, clump together, and form a black hole. —And it is what's inside this black hole that I'm curious about.

The Last Sherpa

The tectonic plates kept converging, the ground shrinking as if tired of bearing our weight. The continents formed a supercontinent, then a supermountain range, then a single supermountain that pierced the exosphere. As the remaining humans clung to their patches of land and fought each other to stave off drowning, the Last Sherpa began his ascent. He grasped not for resources but thrills, adventurer among survivalists. With an oxygen canister and a wool blanket, he would go where no climber had gone before: he would stand on the boundary between sky and space.

When he reached the stratosphere he caught a slight chill and donned his blanket. When he reached the mesosphere he started wheezing and slipped on his oxygen mask. When he reached the thermosphere he lost all caution and covered himself in the pride of futility. He was almost there. The first, and likely the last, person to ever summit the exosphere—to even *know* it had been summited. And after that? A short jump into the beyond.

But the chill he had caught in the stratosphere caused him to sneeze suddenly, and he lost his footing. He fell into the sea like Breughel's Icarus, amidst the inattention of worldly cares.

***

First moral: Only climb as high as you're willing to fall.

Second moral: When a bad outcome to an enterprise is inevitable, confidence becomes necessary.

Third moral: Those afraid of heights still fall—*horizontally*.

Fourth moral: Be prepared to set sail at any moment. Then keep in mind: flotsam is the most seaworthy part of the ship, and the best sailors are the marooned ones—the rest never made it to shore.

"It is an old story / But one that can still be told . . ."

"He Who Saw the Deep" was the first and only man to do so. Gilgamesh passed on his story but not his namesake, so that even now, after beginning to tell that story again, we do not know how to address one another at bedtime. If his tale had never baked in the flames of Nineveh, or was at least rediscovered much earlier than it was, it may have prevented two thousand years of "altruistic" asceticism and existential harassment. We were not told what the cutting of our umbilical cord entailed, and so we preserve it, sticking it away on a coat hanger, taking our natal scarf out occasionally to wear until the moment comes when we knot it in anger around our necks. Speaking to one another from the underworld before we even arrive there, we come to hate the friendship of every Enkidu—half-animal inside of us—because it doesn't last forever. The walls of Uruk are invisible.

The Labor Pains of Hubris

Where are the sempiternal verities—those truths that are infinite in duration but not outside time? Far from even transcending the universe, there is no abstraction that even lasts as long as it. Will the dissolution of the *practically* infinite be the last tolerable loss of meaning? Ungrasped through any concept, unconfirmed by a clutch of stardust, it is dismissed as a counting trick. With this first murder committed the killing spree on nobility can begin, crowding out the lilies with Bermuda grass. The surrounding barrenness reflects its anthropomorphic epicenter—environmental pollution is a discharge from spleen into stream. Smog is the most natural gas, exhaled from our lungs like the breath of an impotent dragon. With nothing to sacrifice to, Atlas is replaced with an altar to uphold the earth, a tribute to ourselves in finality. Without any cherished dogmas to chant and no possibility of martyrdom, this suicide by proxy remains a spectacle for the crowd. In all this, the meaning of our audacity is fully revealed for the first time—that we *can* destroy ourselves, that we will not be provided for.

Know How to Fail

Most failures are only people who struggled for success and fell short. Few make failure a goal in itself. Don't be fooled by representations of idleness: it is the hardest thing in the world to be worthless. The lazy can never be true failures, since they eagerly grasp whatever comes their way, often taking shortcuts to achieve prosperity. And when one finally comes through and fails at last, how hard it is to fail *harder*. There is always something interfering with the drive to fail—a sudden urge to productivity, a stroke of serendipity, a meddling ally. Physiology, fortune, and friendship coalesce to conspire against absolute catastrophe. When Polycrates threw his jeweled ring into the sea, a fisherman returned it to him; after that he lacked the resilience to keep discarding it. Just remember that with enough effort many things are possible. For every lucky star there is a black hole swallowing its light—the real luck is to know where the supermassive ones are. Every galaxy of aspirants revolves around a center.

The Marriage of Limbo and Purgatory

Permanently loitering before the gates of hell *and* expiating ourselves endlessly to be good enough for heaven, we are outcasts in two overlapping dimensions. A new limbo on earth can only be made endurable by its simultaneous intersection with purgatory. Experiencing a living death in original sin, the unrestrained passions loose themselves upon atonement. Already a metaphor which suits us perfectly, it is a place that will become literal before we are ready to leave our present parable. Man, looking out on an open landscape, will at first believe he is still viewing a trompe l'oeil . . . until hit by the first drop of toilet water.

At the end of six thousand years the world will be consumed by storm clouds to begin its cleansing process with a deluge of garbage, rainforest leaves, and aborted fetuses. Left to wade through a flood of flushed after-pleasures, we shut the doors of the mind. Every idea is reduced to a dumb impression on the senses, every object becomes a dead end not to be groped beyond. Tedium interrupted by backbreaking chores are the elements of the eternal energy, with each converting into the other when either becomes unbearable.

A Forgettable Fancy

Walking in the gloom of limbo, I stagnated in an immutability that cried for redecorating, speaking with pagan philosophers and the pariah patriarchs Christ didn't bleed for. We had many fine discussions as we held unbaptized fetuses in our arms, jointly nursing untimely death and timeless meditations. Collecting some of their impromptu proverbs, I quickly forgot them upon getting back home and composed some of my own in their spirit. To merely invert Blake would be to return to cliché, approximating popular quotes that display the foolishness of a culture masked as wisdom; my intention was rather to find the middle path connecting truism and iconoclasm, a state in-between wisdom and foolishness, the camp of seriousness mixed with frivolity, a sarcasm that undermines its antagonistic stance. Despite all my efforts I was not able to emerge from this antechamber of understanding, lacking as I do a rootedness in traditions that weave proverbs into living speech.

Proverbs of Limbo

Season a bland meal with the dust of the dead.

Black holes are the faces of God.

Cloaks of the seven deadly sins provide a week's wardrobe of guesswork.

Computers are built for the writing of instruction manuals, boxes made for the loss prevention of warehouses.

White blood cells are the inadequacy of angels defending against expectation.

By lapsing into silence you will gather all the mouths you need.

Love in the rain, escape under the clouds, hate in the fog, plan between patches of sun.

The minimal side of desire is the key to replicating needs.

Bow your head to a single ant—the whole of industry, the embarrassment of business councils.

The Valley of the Kings is the work of a moment still in progress.

That everything was black and white, or every day a different slice of rainbow: so do zebras and chameleons harmonize what for us needs definition.

The Boulevards of Extinction

Better to revive a dead idea than cure cancer.

The ostrich with stolen wings swoops low to stir jealousy in the penguin, who pities the ostrich for envying diving.

Almost enough! But too much. So more.

Part 5

The Philistine's Dictionary

Adam: the last sinner, because the only innocent.

Aesthiopath. *n.* One whose obsession for refined sensations takes on clinical proportions.

> Mad to feel, the modern artist resorts to murder to obtain the precise hue of red he needs, the finishing touch that will allow him the relief accompanying a minor accomplishment. Little does he realize that his wing of the gallery is already overcrowded with *aesthiopathic* works. (Cenneth Klark)

After-Amour; or, Socratic Hatred

The most natural outcome of any comprehensive discipleship is the scorn that emerges from a closet connection. The Greeks practiced this as often as its opposite, but not so openly. Are we really to believe that Aristotle turned against Plato's principles out of intellectual aversion alone, or that Alexander rebuked his teacher for presuming to advise him in the art of government? Disparagement is the only indulgence that surpasses pederasty.

Airsifter. *n.* A wispy, daydreaming fellow.

> This melancholy coward, this airsifter,
> this feather-surfer, this dust coating of mind.
> (Falsfaff, speaking of Jacques)

Amour-propre; or, Platonic Hatred

Rebelling from his teacher after a sore experience, the pupil advocates celibacy. Agent of amour-propre, it is the chaste meting out of revulsion, the innocent backlash of righteous indignation, the delayed vengeance of self-renunciation. Legitimating the basis of all our feelings and actions, its existence that we are still here is proof of its rightness. Self-love can only stay hidden through the frankness of a pure and faultless hatred.

The Boulevards of Extinction

Andronicus

Those who would pursue what they love instead of excelling in the occupation they are obliged to have should take this scholar's example [(a)]. When living in poverty, adopt Epicureanism as a sort of self-mockery. Canned food drives and goodwill shopping [(b)] provide all the intellectual pleasure needed for hosting the next public garden gala; wearing the latest designer brands washed in bodily fluids, one lectures on aluminum flavoring to joggers and dozing homeless men, inspiring these heavy atoms to swerve more in the sweetness of the void [(c)].

a) Modern work frustrates creative talent in favor of functional capacity—at best subsumes the first under the second. The pride that comes from doing one's job well is the sort of triumph Lord Byron would have felt if he swam a creek instead of the Hellespont: not even daring a pointless adventure out of sheer boredom, but because, disqualified on the breaststroke relay, he wants to prove himself proficient at dog-paddling. Not satisfied with a personal victory, he invents dog-paddling gear that allows him to beat the freestyle swimmers. Under the dominion of the toolmakers, a simple repetition mechanized into convenience renders ten laborious displays of gracefulness obsolete. The only lasting virtuosity becomes the management of monotony, taking the most basic skill sets and making them automatic so that one is rescued from the obligation of needing to learn anything. Excepted are those devotees of torment who agree to suffer the mastery of an archaic tradition and yoke themselves to the nostalgia of an overbearing octogenarian.

b) Good will: ameliorating the plight of the innovative and trendy by donating broken appliances and the latest passé clothing.

c) Dance, you scoundrels, dance to the silence of time. Keep a beat with the spinning globe, swirl to the pace of your electrons, and vomit oxygen with the verve of a child trapped on a merry-go-round.

Animals

Wonder not that certain animals have abstract abilities, but that humans can do entertaining stunts. It is an easy thing for a philosopher to jump through hoops; after a little training one doesn't even have to prod him to it, he does it automatically. Having learned the habits of the circus and become accustomed to the cheers of the audience, he protests with a cry of "freedom!" if one continues to whip him on, and resumes his trick with a dissertation on liberty. Our praise of his work should come not in the form of undertaking a serious study of it, but in hoots and whistles.

As for animals, we often laugh and clap at things they do when we should be taking note of the teachings behind the trick. Clever masters of manipulation and imperceptible cruelty are always sniffed out for what they really are by the beasts. It is a case where greater insight is accorded to the beings with lower cognitive functions. Lacking the conscious ego of humans, they are not prone to having their prejudices exploited. When observing how a charming person is hypnotizing an entire room, look to the dog. Whether it is keeping its distance or crotch-sniffing is a model of how one should approach others. In a species so easily beguiled by gregariousness, the wallflower sees most clearly.

When judging between the intellect of a philosopher and a parrot, go with the creature that repeats words one can understand.

Anti-Amour

Here we must have recourse to the spiritual: we look out to nature to find a source of blame, but project only our resentment. We mull over ourselves and deepen our faults by attacking others.' Hatred is, next to love, the only other source of unmixed satisfaction, one of the few *pure* experiences we have, even the purest of all: unlike with love there is no way to confuse its meanings. The "four loves" cannot be inverted without absurdity. The difference between hatred as unconditional, dispassionate, intimate, or natural is merely a matter of angle, not context or relationship status. The Greeks knew their enemies as *one*: whether the recipient was estranged relative, betrayed friend, spurned lover, or cruel god, the vengeance factor remained the same. While murdering a brother may lack the ambition of assassinating a god, the sentiment fueling the journey is independent of rank or means. There are no subtle shades of feeling; as hatred permeates its vessel it drives out all other emotions, anything that might pollute the hater and diminish his *perfect* hatred. One can differentiate its manifestations only in origins and object. Whether one hates a neighbor, an entire ethnic group, or all of God's creation is merely a matter of distribution. Even degree is not a consideration—a single person can be hated as intensely as a multitude or symbolize a rancor for the universe. Hatred is the loyal musketeer that swears "all for one and one for all"—and *means* it. In stating "I hate x," it doesn't matter who or what is plugged in—the equation always has the same answer.

Apocalypse

Nuclear annihilation is not the end. The tardigrades will carry on our legacy more efficiently than us, even vouching for us on a Judgment Day to which they are immune. "They didn't have any other choice," our ideal mediators between low and high will say, "their range of habitat is so *narrow*, they could only spread out horizontally—the peaceful route was never really an option." Human flourishing was only ever an inadequate imitation of the practice of these creatures, one that had to resort to deception, slaughter, and disease to accomplish a fraction of their success. Omnipresent on the earth as we could never be, the tardigrades are the ideal colonizers of the galaxy, asteroid hitchhikers and hypernova surfers content to dominate their territories simply by thriving in them, relegating the grunt work of oppression to the environment.

Automaton

Flute players and excreting birds entertain, but a mechanical toy that mimics humanity itself—contraption of urges containing within itself the source of its motion—might enlighten us to ourselves. Could a machine mimicking a machine, like two wrongs making a right, finally achieve the impossible? Could the result finally be—*life*?

In Motherboard Man, a computer chip magnified the masculine. Programmed from examples in paperback romance novels, he performed virtuous deeds, always defended the weaker sex, and exercised his strength with moderation. Possessing every storybook quality to the hilt, he died in his third year from failure to hold a job. More humane than the human resources departments he applied to, he could not bring himself to exaggerate his abilities in a cover letter.

Baa. *v.* The cry of the masses, heard in unison when their individual rights are being sheared away.

> I've heard enough of this *baaing*. When I wrote "unalienable rights," I meant "unalienable sights." It was a slip of the pen. One can look around for life, liberty, and happiness, even observe it, but I wasn't promising anything more than that. (Thomas Jefferson, *Declaration of Errors*)

Babel: model of every metropolis, monument to failed sympathies.

Baptism: contaminating the soul by immersing the body in a river.

Nature has never been a suitable medium for cleansing. If John the Baptist had used a water filter, God might not have forsaken his son on the cross. By putting off baptism until beatification, one could be washed of sin more effectively. A bit of grime on Heaven's floor adds character.

Additional logical developments: killing baptized imbeciles before they have an opportunity to exercise their inclinations, poisoning baptized pregnant mothers before their fetuses can be born into sin, drowning priests before their zeal for baptizing sterilizes the criminal deeds of evil men. Then after all these mercies have been committed, have yourself baptized.

Bayle's Dictionary

Inadequate, obsolete, often erroneous, always meandering away from the main topic   in short, the only reference book one ever needs: one which entertains, informs one on unexpected subjects, and provokes surprising reflections. Disregarding teams of experts, a *shrewd* scholar would use it exclusively for all his research, writing articles consisting entirely of footnotes to the opening sentence.

When the student knows more than the teacher, passing a class is a submission to relative ignorance. Doing history homework, one answers a question on George Washington with details from the lives of Caniceus and Calandrus. Biographies of obscure, unknowable figures who may have never existed are the only interesting ones; ghosts too faint to haunt history, they are the only source of information on what one must do to be forgotten, a sourcebook on existential negation, above all a reminder that one cannot trust the secondhand accounts of "great" men—the greater they are, the more biographies proliferate to contradict one another. Give me instead the anti-biographies of well-known figures, alternate histories of what might have been, in which footnotes are added not to collect errors but to underline possibilities and refer to the most tangential points of interest. That one cannot know everything about a person is not to say that one can't know *something* about them—irrelevance of life facts to destiny.

Beauty's Basis

He composed a Chronicle of Beauty with an eyeliner pencil, then a History of Ugliness using an inkwell filled from an oil spill and a quill plucked from a drowned albatross. The eye of the beholder has had much to stare at in every culture and period, he argued. But after writing much on the perfect and the grotesque, he tired of the relativism of fascination and took to writing a Treatise on Plainness. Only the middling, only what is ordinary, dull, and unnoticed, partakes of the absolute. The eye passes over the invariable. But it is not beyond possibility that Plainness was the original fascination, an eternal standard without the need for a spectrum of extremes. One recalls that the Hebrew word for plain meant "perfect" or "mature." God, however, did not take into account man's tendency to adjust to things and become bored with sameness. One imagines Eve as a sort of Sarah Plain and Tall, who went exploring in the garden because Average Adam's overwhelming desire for her went cold after a year. Finding berries, she made a rouge for her cheeks; stumbling on a beeswax hive, an olive oil pond, and a rosewater stream, she mixed the ingredients together to make a skin cream. Finally, coming upon a large tree, she wondered about the anti-aging properties of the apple and reached out her hand to pick one . . .

Bibliotaphia

Burial of books. There have been set aside, in certain corners of the earth where no one visits, plots of land where books are laid to rest after people stop reading them. It is the final home of today's bestsellers and yesterday's classics not troublesome enough to be burned. The mold and dust housed in their mausoleums outstrip the best library collections and outweigh the sum total of human skeletons. More to be feared than the spell that raises human zombies from the graveyards is the curse that restores forgotten volumes to eat our attention spans and brainwash movie producers. Books too have their lifespans, whether they are mayflies or Methuselahs, and when they are gone they do not come back naturally.

Bierce's Dictionary

Placated by his redefinition of words, he was too content with the words themselves. Not that coining new words by inverting old ones is enough, either. The world still awaits its dictionary of gibberish—etymologies of murmurs and stutters represented by quotations from taciturn dyslexics.

Book Clubs

One person sat down to read a work of history, another a self-help book, a third a romance. Later that week the three of them gathered to discuss the book.

"The author illuminates the past like an oracle."

"It helped me to discover an unknown inner strength. I still haven't really tapped into it, but I'm pretty sure it's there."

"I stopped after every page to masturbate."

The Historian entered into the concerns of the characters, seeing them not as characters at all but as flesh and blood people. He empathized with their actions and thoughts, forming friendships deeper than his closest acquaintances and enmities more rancorous than everyone his mild-mannered personality had never allowed him to be spiteful towards. He even went so far as to form a specific notion of the humidity level of the air they breathed, the naïve political and social ideas of their day, and other features of their environment that went far beyond the minimalist descriptions the author had put into the book.

Part 5: The Philistine's Dictionary

The Self-Seeker read his own soul into every page, consumed every word into himself. He had no memory of any external descriptions whatsoever, and refused to admit of their existence to the Historian. The main character was none other than his own self—no, all the selves he had ever been, and all he would be. He began an uncertain girl in the opening paragraph and emerged a confident woman in the final pages. Her fear of trusting others, her insecurity about her self-image, her sense of failure and unhappiness as being deserved—her realization of her true self was her realization of his own.

While giving up drinking, the Self-Seeker proposed to the gas station attendant. She said no, but agreed to a date and gave him an extra bottle of malt liquor for later. He rushed back to his apartment and kissed his book. He spoke to it in a soft but firm voice, placing his right hand on it and swearing an oath to give up drinking after the sex, if it was really good.

The Masturbator had difficulty getting past her titillation to impose a sense of credulity onto the narrative. The main character was not a man at all, but a passionate beast, a pure fantasy. She saw nothing of herself, nor friends, nor the world in the story. She only felt the intensity of animal desire that lay beneath the consciousness of her species. She read the vivid visual details with shallow breath; she writhed at the extravagant metaphor comparing being penetrated by the ribbed tip of the hero's phallus to being rammed with deer antlers mounted to the prow of a dinghy.

"The plot was accurate to the tee," the Historian said. "Life plagiarized the events from this book."

"There was no plot, you idiot," the Self-Seeker replied. "It was a story of character development—mine."

"You're both wrong," the Masturbator said. "There was a plot, but it was just a loose framework to throw the hero into one steamy love scene after another."

"A tragedy of history."

"A drama of existing."

"A masterpiece of episodic erotica."

They had had enough of each other's false representations. The Historian lunged at the Self-Seeker's throat and started choking him. The Masturbator hit the Historian over the back with her chair. The Self-Seeker stabbed the Masturbator with his new year's resolution, an ink pen his girlfriend had gotten in a two-for-one deal. He was glad when the police arrested him, because he would finally have the time to start writing his autobiography. The masturbator forgave him for stabbing her. The Historian told him to sit tight, and the Self-Seeker gave the Historian a friendly pat on the back out of spite. They agreed to hold their next book club meeting during the jail's visitation hours.

"What are we going to read for next week?"

"How about *The Odyssey*?"

"Isn't that about faithfulness? Sounds boring."

"It isn't boring! It's about a son who has to discover his inner strength."

"You're both wrong. It is archaeologically corroborated myth. Where facts are concerned, entertainment is irrelevant."

They tried to attack each other again, but the police restrained them. After they calmed down, they promised to see each other soon and parted ways. The Masturbator and the Historian waved to the Self-Seeker. The Self-Seeker tried to wave back but the handcuffs made it too difficult, so he nodded his head vigorously.

Brutus

A man who, in order to save the republic, commits genocide against the Roman populace [(a)]. Not knowing what is best for them, it was not enough to have a dictator decreeing the people's duties and privileges. He knew that the only true republic possible would be one constituted by a spectral citizenry. Presiding over a phantom electoral college, the leader could then proceed to reorganize society without limit, unhindered in his erection of New Rome [(b)].

    a) Every would-be assassin imagines himself a savior of the Republic. He forgets that, the modern world producing no Caesars, no public figure is worth killing. This is why the only assassins today are psychopaths, swearing a blood oath to save society from ambitious men of great charm and little ability whom the world would not remember had they lived full lifespans. One buffoon is bumped off only to be immediately replaced by another, and the State lumbers on as clumsily as ever without so much as a misstep in the right direction. If the schizophrenic with his movie star crush had succeeded, some other great chatterer would have arisen to watch the Soviet Union crumble.

    b) On the rare occasion when a true reformer does arise, he is sure to be assassinated by rational people. Identifying their profit losses with a moral being, vested interests' accomplishment of a wrong cause in no way averts or retards their failure. They, too, believe they are following virtue as a real thing . . .

Chain of Events

For Plotinus to have been born a century later and become the despairing rival of Augustine instead of a mental stimulus: not aggressive enough in the corporeal realm to prevail over the lusty young sinner, he would have thought up a noose instead of Nous; while Augustine, without intellectual vision, would have written the *Confessions of Casanova*.

Such speculations are ridiculous, however. Men of destiny could not have lived in any other time than that which they did. In them talent stumbled on the preparations at hand by which to realize itself—one slip in time zone and they would have missed their chance, doomed to go unrecognized by the clods surrounding them. Men of destiny are kings on the chess board of history, with only one space allotted for them. Mediocrities are like checkers pieces: interchangeable anywhere. Being so completely men of their time, they would internalize the values of any age they were thrust into. One wouldn't be surprised to hear that their gene donors died before they were born, leaving a clause in their will dedicating their planned parenthood to immaculate conception by the zeitgeist. Whether such people are front-line livestock or obscure rear-enders is simply the whim of a palsied hand.

Chimpanthropy. *n.* The insanity inflicting those who imagine themselves to be chimpanzees when the full moon appears; the theory of evolution.

> Uncommon effort is needed for a man to imagine himself a victim of *chimpanthropy*, though such derangement does occur sometimes, either as the result of taking lessons from a natural philosopher, or because of a feeling of disparagement towards humanity that strikes the brain. If Nebuchadnezzar had erected a mud-and-stick image instead of a golden one for his people to worship, his divine punishment would have been transformation into a werechimp. (Malebrunch, *Flee From Truth*)

China

Higher vices of the middle kingdom: philosophers who renounce world and theory alike, yet are beloved by the populace; medical practices that eschew cures in order to prevent. No need to recapture lost histories or quibble over the likelihood of events—the *Spring and Autumn Annals* are good enough for all. The more fantastical a history, the less a people needs to engineer a future to contrast with its present, and the longer it will continue to stretch onwards.

Chrysis

A priestess who slept while her temple was burning down. Blamed for negligence, she was replaced and lived out her remaining days in shame. Little did the priestess know that this was the work of her goddess all along [(a)]. Deciding to punish an ungrateful people by depriving them of herself, the goddess watched them fall into anarchy and slavery just to prove they couldn't get along without her. Even when they cried out for her, she continued to go missing for the rest of time [(b)]. The people do not deserve her return. Mother of love and forgiveness, she finds herself not obliged to exercise the qualities she created. Absent for so long, the people forgot their origin and gave themselves over to the caprices of a patriarchal monotheism [(c)].

- a) The knowledge that someone is praying for you provides both motive and alibi.
- b) When one is ignored a breakthrough occurs at the moment of finally being listened to—a preference for the deafness of the universe.
- c) The goddesses? They all died in godbirth, and only one delivered successfully.

Civilism. *n.* A word pronounced in an elitist way; a word spoken by a snob; a big word.

Speakers of such words are ignorant of the recent simplification of the English language into the American language. The British are especially prone to this: after leaving their money at our vacation resorts and departing for their native land, they bring home with them their original mistakes in accent and vocabulary.

> There is this difference between a *civilism* and an expulsion, that a civilism occurs in a Germanic word when it is corrupted, but when foreign words are dropped from Germanic speech, it is called an "expulsion." (Isibore of Seville, *Etymologies*)

Circumcision: initiating the process of freedom from craving only to stop after unwrapping the candy bar.

College: a wholesale supplier of overpriced wall decorations.

Confession: burglary of the good man's supremacy, safe house of the scoundrel. Penitence is best practiced in a photo booth, where wacky expressions can be examined for scars, wrinkle lines, and other blemishes of character.

Confidence: the body's device for feigning knowledge and competence; facial fraud.

PART 5: The Philistine's Dictionary

Convulsions

Convulsions are the bacchanals of the damned. Frothing with egg-white cocktails, wardens of the sacred disease dance for the Moon goddesses as their aura rings with premonitions of great deeds. Hercules and Caesar were but the beginning; the modern epileptic's quest begins with a fib and a pilot's license, continuing well beyond the crash site memorial to his victims. Instead of twelve labors or European conquests, freak accidents occur and suspicions of terrorism are raised to increase the standard of safety measures. The function of heroism—to create and maintain order—is met by the more efficient occurrences of randomness, neglect, and incompetence.

Cream of Tartarus

Diamonds of darkness, crystallization of screams, baking spice for the bottomless, it stabilizes the falling at an optimal level of fear and removes bloodstains from the walls of the abyss. The intermediate stage of hell needs its agent of cooking, fermenting, and cleansing—preparing fresh batches of sinners for the lake of fire.

Curioherence. *n.* A state of common sense temporarily striking an inhabitant of Wonderland; a brief moment of lucidity among one perpetually confused.

> "I need to get a job," said the Hatter.
> "That's the first sensible thing I've heard you say," Alicia remarked. "How curiously coherent of you!"
> "*Curioherence*! A terrible disease."
> Alicia didn't think it was terrible at all, but she continued. "Well I think it's a lovely idea to get a job."
> "A nose job!"
> "I don't think your nose is very big,"
> "You're right," the Hatter said. "It needs to be bigger." *(Alicia in Wonderland)*

Dactylomancy. *n.* The divination of divorce.

A dactylomancer is cheaper than a lawyer and more committed to accuracy than a priest. He dangles a ring from a thread to gauge the weight of its diamond. If the thread breaks he determines the couple will be held together by a strong bond of materialism. If the thread does not break he recommends a prenuptial agreement to bolster the bond of love. People without property need the trappings of legality to feel a sense of ownership over their betrayals.

This operation is preceded and followed by many superstitious ceremonies: promises of faithfulness, supportive phone calls from friends and family, talk shows.

Before sending off a hopeless case, the dactylomancer tells his version of the Ring of Gyges: rather than kill his king and sleep with his queen, Gyges decided that invisibility was the perfect opportunity to just stand there and fade out of existence altogether.

David

Without his military conquests the Hebrews would never have become worthy enough for deportation, slavery, and world religion. They would have no history for scribes to set down. Imagine instead a coward and a weakling, a poet who fights barbarians with flowers [(a)]. Though temperamental enough to found a great religion, his sophistication would not allow his vision to get off the ground. Escaping the attacking hordes by sheer luck, he takes up residence with a king in order to woo him to his cause with music. But the king is mistrustful of the poet's abilities, seeing in the arts only pleasure and lies [(b)]. After conspiring to have the barbarians kill the king and finagling the throne for himself, David is presented with the problem of persuading others to take up his tribal god through the power of verse. Seeing a woman bathing on a rooftop, he decides to match the beauty of her form with those of his words. Her husband comes home to find the king reading a poem to his wife, but after hearing a few lines rushes out to join the army so as to never hear any again [(c)]. The king then marries her and begins reading his poetry to his soldiers before battles. Filled with a desperation to escape earshot of his doggerel, his army flees in the direction of the enemy, and by this recurring strategy conquers all of Judea [(d)]. Finally, in the success and fruitfulness of old age, the king dies in a drinking contest with his apathetic son Absalom, and power is seized by Solomon, the most foolish man to ever live [(e)]. Not caring to expand the empire, Solomon takes a vow of chastity and spends his life writing down subtle thoughts. When the Babylonians invade, easily overrunning a nation ruled by poets and philosophers, finding no one robust enough for manual labor they put the entire population to the sword.

    a) The man of culture sees a Goliath in every philistine. With dreams of glory he hurls fine words, multiplies enemies, and falls victim to his own a misattributed gigantism.

    b) Strumming a spaghetti-string harp before peasants jealous not because you play well, but with your food. They are too hungry to understand your need: the traditional instruments mastered long ago, you had nowhere to turn to but their dinner. Great art has only ever been the product of suffering, but now the artist

PART 5: The Philistine's Dictionary

is no longer selfish about keeping it to himself.

c) Upon finding a woman one wants to marry, sending her husband to a job fair. Committing adultery eclipses one's past faults, but financing it provides a line of credit for future ones.

d) A nation today carves out a kingdom through its terms of surrender. Instead of wasting an army, it offers tributes of loans and industrial development.

e) Rebellion of the young: curtailing the ambitious son by adopting older brothers for fratricide.

Deities

A man who has spent all his life among an Amazon tribe limps into a city.

STRANGER. Hello. I have a blister on my foot that needs healing. Are you the shaman of these parts? I only ask because I've noticed many important people coming to you with their problems.

ECONOMIST. In a way, yes. I ensure that the world functions in accordance with certain laws.

STRANGER. What are these laws?

ECONOMIST. I wrote them here. *(Hands him Nobel-winning dissertation.)*

STRANGER. *(Perusing, astounded.)* Truly, this is the language of the gods! Are you in communion with these symbols?

ECONOMIST. Of course. Essentially, they mean that I receive thanks when everything goes in accordance with my plan.

STRANGER. And when it doesn't?

ECONOMIST. I chalk it up to the fact that I never specifically asked for anything.

STRANGER. Could these laws heal my foot?

ECONOMIST. Yes, they can do anything if you have enough of their instrument. *(Shows him a wad of dollar bills).*

STRANGER. The grass of heaven! *(Examining money)* I wonder, why do you draw the heads of your gods with gray hair?

ECONOMIST. In the past no one with lustrous hair was sexy enough to be wise. In order to be looked at long enough to be listened to, you had to wear gray.

STRANGER. I see. So the gray ones harvested their overfields and these pieces fell from the sky?

ECONOMIST. Not exactly. They gave us gold from the earth, then we started making this later.

STRANGER. How to use this properly to heal my foot so that I am not punished?

ECONOMIST. Save it, and get more.

STRANGER. How much do I need to appease heaven?

ECONOMIST. As much as you can get.

STRANGER. The gray gods are infinite in number, then?

ECONOMIST. Practically, if you follow their laws.

STRANGER. What is the minimum infinity of them I need to heal my foot?

ECONOMIST. Enough to get a good life insurance policy. After you die your family will want for nothing.

STRANGER. So, if I pick enough god grass then the gray ones will send me a wife and children. Very good. Where do I start?

ECONOMIST. With this. *(Hands him a dollar.)* With effort and luck you can turn that into a million of those.

STRANGER. Very good. I will follow your devotional practices, "effort" and "luck," to do just that.

Diderot's Encyclopedia

It was a work conceived to stay in print for every century to come, a tool to educate the most distant generations. In the English-speaking world today it is a translation project that would bankrupt a publishing house. Poor Diderot, with his dream of knowledge's eternity; he was ignorant of reason's task: to constantly update facts and reshape theories. It was a dream so naïve, so unimaginable for the contemporary world, that schools would do well to dispense with their latest methods of indoctrination and simply make their students read the *Encyclopédie*, studying the engraved plates of antiquated mechanical arts and memorizing principles that form the basis of backwardness.

An encyclopédie for our times: organized around the Baconian tree of uprooted knowledge, it is precariously balanced upon branches that unite in a swaying trunk, where the faculties of forgetfulness, prejudice, and prosaicness coalesce in the null space once occupied by a soul. The focus of the enterprise will be provided by man's peripheral position in the universe. Distancing itself from science's spirit of detachment, knowledge connects itself to every marginal value, a reference to diversion, debasement, and brutality where sources go unacknowledged and the only intellectual authorities are of the author's own invention. Lacking a society of enlightened and highly cultured laypeople to produce such a work, it is an enterprise which the Last Man of Letters undertakes alone, a Diderot without an army. Approached by artisans all too eager to give up their secrets, this encyclopédestrian of unlearning ignores their methods entirely. Instead he undertakes a series of engravings entitled "When Machines Fail," a pictorial representation of meltdowns, computer viruses, and sloppy engineering projects budgeted by corporate greed. In the end, finding no subscribers to his eulogy for the soul, he remains his sole reader.

Divinity of Bugs

Though the distance between God and man is as vast as that between man and bug, the distance between God and bug is infinitesimal. A compatibility of opposites, there is nothing preventing divinity from being housed in an arthropod—the God-Bug. Writing Its BumbleBible through the appendages of a thousand centipedes, God-Bug sends Its pheromone message from deipod to insect—an etymology of conquest, population explosion, and ecological balance. The Book of Ant tells a story of unshakable hard work amidst an invasion of laziness. The Book of Mosquito buzzes the blessings of parasitism. In the Book of Gnat an empire is forged through sheer annoyance. All of this is prefaced by the Book of Chrysalis in which is narrated the eternity of the mayfly: born a day before time began and initiating the big bang with its dying wing-flap, it conferred a legacy of fleetingness on existence. Finally a religion not for the masses but the *swarms*, where every drone is a Christ figure ready to sacrifice itself to contribute to the salvation of the hive.

Doubtbreach. *n.* The recognizable moment when mutual deceit, doubt, or disloyalty is betrayed. The gift of men to gods, when the thieves of creation are judged honestly by the rogues whose oppression they took upon themselves, and freed from the servitude of corrupt management.

> Once more unto the *doubtbreach*, dear friends, once more;
> and close the wall up with our dead players!
> (Hamlet, *Henry V*)

Econoclast. *n.* An economist who breaks every law of trade but the one he himself formulated; the condition of being an economist.

> An economist who isn't an *econoclast* is neither an economist nor an iconoclast. The virtue of the free market is its thriving theories. Each model competes against the others for dominance, and with the help of a government program one of those theories is determined to be the best. (John Milton Freynes)

The Boulevards of Extinction

Egyptian Philosophy

Based on induction, where philosophy should have stayed. A confused blend of cosmology, religion, mathematics, law, customs, and ceremonies—where it should have stayed. Its ideas would be more elegant and awe-inspiring had its hieroglyphics never found their Champollion. Every culmination of a tradition occurs in its beginnings. The anonymous scribes of Egypt, whose dust mixed with the sands long ago, are the world's youngest and most illustrious thinkers, the first champions of unmummified meditations.

Elijah

Elijah misunderstood the gift of the chariot: he thought simply *going up* would get him somewhere [(a)]. If he had Phaethon's youthful exuberance, his wisdom would have seen that heaven's highest level is accessed through a thunderbolt. The worthy combine daring with sacrifice, wielding Helios's horses to imitate divinity and reshaping geography with fire to show transcendence over the earthly. After confronting a nation's idolatry, an Elijah who entitled himself to a joyride with a trumpet: his lover's embouchure creating whirlwinds to topple heathen walls, blowing rivers away from neighboring empires, leveling the mount of olives to prevent a nomadic carpenter from eclipsing his glory. Without resort to persuasion, Elijah spread Hebrew culture so far that God struck him down out of fear for undesirable acquisitions [(b)]. He could now boast to all those who entered heaven's gates: "I was the only man who renounced a living salvation. I wanted to arrive as you, the unoffered ones, did [(c)]."

a) A finite universe magnifies the vault between the waters. "The sky is *not* the limit," says the new-age mystic. It was not an angel that whispered this in his ear, nor even a bird, but a *jet engine*. Evolutionary engineering makes deafness the sign of Truth's eavesdroppers. The aeronaut longs for the stratosphere with the Latinate vocabulary of a complacent friar.

b) The conquering prophets must leave a few infidel groups intact for the preaching ones. As for the prophets without arms or oration skills, but only a pen—whose sole audience are literate intellects—they cannot hope to affect a tide of conversion. Without the support of ignorant masses desperate for meaning, the fundamental danger of the reevaluation of values will be ignored; the prophet's highest influence will be the aura of romanticism projected upon him by the lonely bookworms who stumble upon his work generations hence.

c) A man who never died will be widely sought out for advice, but only on that which is outside his experience.

Part 5: The Philistine's Dictionary

Enginuity. *n.* The ingenuity of machines, the superior creativity of artificial intelligence.

> Graphael's *enginuity* in The Tools of Athens was to show us the many ways in which function does not follow form. (Robocritic 5000)

Enmity

Enmity is an implicit contract between an affable sensitive virtuous soul and a rogue, multiplied by two. Drunkards have forgettable quarrels, thieves have common objects of dispute, and politicians have debates. But only old friends have enmity. One no longer kisses friends for the same reason that one never kissed enemies: crossing lips may compromise sword technique. To become aware of affection's end is to realize the ways in which, in some sense, it never began—the qualities which repulse one from the affected had always been there, germinating annoyance, growing into rancor. And when the balance shifts from love to hate, the *strength* of the bond is transmitted unchanged. How? What is the mechanism behind this conservation of energy? —A shared fashion sense. No one's wardrobe is large enough to accommodate a daily friendship. That is why true friends are so rare: naked before one another, few will accept each other's blemishes.

Equality: When a population is enfranchised into a mob and one is less than zero.

The more similar people are, the more detailed contrasts they make between one another as a means of distinguishing themselves. The more equal they become, the more they focus on remaining inequalities. In periods of absolute inequality no one makes comparisons with one another; different castes might as well be different species. In periods of relative inequality when the dominant social group makes political concessions to bring minorities closer to their own status, the undertrodden only become more restless with each new compromise. The ruling class expects their clemency to be returned with gratitude, but what they get instead is merely an augmentation of the resentment that had so long fueled the dominated group's spirit of survival. Political freedom does not prevent inter-group violence, but *endorses* it. No legal verdict could ever break down the barriers of soil-grown flesh. It is naïve to think that a people long oppressed would, upon experiencing the hand of cruelty softening its grip, ever really want to be seen on an equal footing with former persecutors, despite cries for fair treatment. Taking up an egalitarian rhetoric based on quantification of individual value, they adopt the character of their oppressors, mental efforts consumed by calculative functions as impatience to exercise influence increases—the *quality* of their condition refuses to be leveled out. Tracing their subjugation back innumerable generations, an oppressed people cements their metaphysical superiority in an aristocracy of suffering, unable to forget centuries of ruthlessness and despising to share social status with monsters.

After the initial sense of relief dissolves and the once-oppressed become adjusted to their new freedom, ancestral memory returns. While living under the boot they spent all their energy dreading the next move of their persecutors; not until after they are liberated do they finally gain leisure to hate and material resources to fuel retributive schemes. Vilification of the "privileged" group grows as legal privilege is annulled and private privilege continually lessens. Rome gave the barbarians citizenship and was overrun; Louis XVI made a number of concessions to the commoners and was decapitated.

Where fear is lost respect cannot grow. As the dominant group compromises away self-esteem, the negligible deference of the other groups is lost as well. Tearful, they shake hands and kneel in penitence, but the rising peoples cannot bring themselves to forgive—not for what they've done, but for *who they are*. The tyranny of the majority—that conformity which so consumed Mill's Victorian anxieties, when morality was ruled by taste—gives way to the tyranny of the *minority*, a tyranny of guilt. As the procreation of the poor outstrips the childlessness of the rich and the day of outnumberment approaches, resentment towards the dominant group increases with the population of the marginalized until demographics shift. A new majority arises that repeats the atrocities of history anew, oppressing the old majority with an even greater vigor than that with which the old minority was once oppressed. This time it is not a professed "burden of the civilizers" that drives the new subjugation, but a hierarchy without pretense to obligation. The stewpot, never quite melted, begins to boil and spill over, putting out the fire warming an ever-alien society.

Man: his fundamental similitude across the globe fills him with the need to spill his own blood; his shared origins stimulate hostility by recreating in every generation the conditions that made him successful on the plains of Africa. Equality isn't simply a problem of access to resources or dependence on servitude to meet needs. It is when service isn't required that others lose their potential value and become superfluous; raised from poverty into a garden paradise, neighbors would be freed up to war against one another out of boredom—common ground makes room for quibbling. Our origins long forgotten, the hope of cooperation housed in mutual genes has been drowned in a host of incompatible cultural traditions.

Unable to live together for long out of intolerance for differences in custom or belief, with an evolved intelligence that allows for systematic cruelty and a faculty for sympathy that can only be distributed within a limited in-group, a culture always needs an "other" to fight if its members are to not turn on themselves. Lone individuals, transcending native prejudices, reach out to strangers and are condemned for betrayal; while demagogues, exploiting egoism, persuade communities of their special eminence in the universe. Civilization severed man from himself once and for all, augmenting the bellicosity that had always been part of his nature. Charity balls repeat the fairy tale "Humanity" and only invite high society.

The *Encyclopedia of Horrors*, a yet-unrealized project that has long been incubating in my mind, will furnish empirical proof of this truth by cataloguing major recorded instances of man's cruelty to man. Far from these occurrences dwindling in number or becoming milder as history advances, improvements in technology have only increased their quantity and severity; "the civilizing process"—forks, napkins, wit, taste—implants habits that heighten both our instincts and the capacity to rationalize them away as we enact them. With passages from Celan and Céline, sheet music from the *Tenebrae Responsoria*, and a Wall of Horrors—works by Bosch, Breughel, Grünewald, Goya, Fuseli, Géricault—accompanying these entries as a framing device, all of Art shall be conscripted to support my facts . . . especially *bad* art. More horrific even than the Holocaust is the mediocre sea of Holocaust Literature we have been inundated with since.

Evil (Organic Evil)

Defunctioning, all that inhibits the development of what a thing is naturally suited for and degenerates it into a purposeless mass, a nest of terrors—this is the task of the leaden extremes, the excessive qualities of life. Hanging to the perimeter one becomes estranged to those cocooned in the center, accumulating experiences incommunicable in all but example. Disorganization, infinite floundering, the race from perfection—all carried out without a word of explanation and infecting pedestrians of the quotidian unawares. The conditions of life are confused with living, part with whole, the factors of degeneration multiplied beyond ascertainment.

The self-sufficiency of parasitism appears as an authentic alternative to routine, more real than ordinariness. One born into lowness thinks not of accumulating middle-class virtues. Unable to strip himself of extrinsic evils—disgrace, poverty, sickness—something always follows him, and where there is one the others are lurking. Nor can he fully maximize one type: no such thing as total disgrace—whenever he feels about to hit rock bottom he only tumbles further. Rational desire can go hungry on such evils. Men decide to ornament their wretchedness with blessedness when there is no way out, to capture attention and celebrate the possession of the contemptible qualities fate dealt them. Dancing in the dirt, sharing blood with strangers, the face of dishonor is shameless. A wretchedness that looks serene, that smiles outwardly, is not wretchedness enough—one laughs precisely because nothing is funny. Once one becomes mired in "the horror" there is no departing the Congo; return to the center would be *more* horrific. Fascination with moral abominations turns a man into one; on his deathbed, realizing no one will understand his last words, he leaves behind only a silent corpse, model for the traumatized.

Evil (Metaphysical Evil)

Saint Augustine fingers the hole in his shirt. "This is bad," he says. "This shouldn't be here." The Bishop of Hippo should have known better: he was all too aware of how we each enter the world—uncovered. But having no sympathy for babies, he felt their original sin needed amending.

As Tiamat preceded Marduk, the hole was there first and the shirt stitched *inside it*. Good is the provision of evil, and the shirtless space was without either. It was when the shirt began to be sewn that evil arose—the shirt was imperfect prior to its completion, a partial nothingness. Abyssal Seamstresses weaving the fabric of existence were put on a tight schedule: "It must be finished promptly," God said, "you have a quota to make before dusk. Adam will want something to wear when I expel him from the Garden."—This is how the first man strutted into the world sporting a golf polo with a popped collar. Good's dominion is the space after the finished product is presented to the Unknowing and before Eve rips it in a passion. Nonbeing, Luther's true God, is hidden from us—all we have are the edges of the cotton. The tear is the return to the original condition, a corruption of a corruption. Swaddled in garments, the evil we face is the resolution of infringement by the Superfluous, the evil we enact a resurgence of Absence.

Evil (Sovereign Evil)

"Most men," says Machiavelli, "prefer to steer a middle course, which is very harmful; for they know not how to be wholly good nor yet wholly bad."[1] Giovampagolo was not bad *enough* to rid himself of Julius II when that pope was in his power—a pervert who conspired against his own family was unable to discard hospitable diplomacy.

Maximal evil is rare. Usually one finds only fragments of it, thwarted attempts and intent without opportunity. Or when confronting blind forces, one is cut loose before being dragged too far down the evil road—pestilence assailed by a galvanization of antibodies, the lucky lotto ticket averting bankruptcy. We do not see the goodness of the mass murderer in his quietude: how he never in his whole life told a lie, how he strokes his tulips lovingly after watering them just the right amount; how, naively and unwittingly, he slices up a victim as a master chef would a tomato, says a prayer for the departed, and flagellates himself for hours. In him, the grandeur of compulsive murder is accompanied by the gaudiness of penitence.

---

1. Machiavelli, *The Discourses*. Book 1, Discourse 26.

On the occasion when all of the major forms of evil are concentrated into a single motivated deed, which of its realizations is foremost? Each has its own peculiar claim to dominance. A charming fable by Anti-Crantor illustrates this:

"Poverty, suffering, sickness, and vice compete at the Olympic games. Each claims the apple. Poverty says, 'I make the others possible. Without the difficulties that I present they could not exist.' Suffering says, 'Without me, the others would not mind their plight.' Sickness says, 'I am sovereign, as I put an end to all the other evils.' Vice says, 'I justify the others and maintain them. Without me they would no doubt receive the help to be overcome. Furthermore, it is possible to undergo their conditions and still be a good person.' While vice seemed the most independent claimant, its abstractness made it empty of content; to qualify as evil a vice must be *of* something. The remaining evils, on the other hand, weren't universal enough. None were therefore awarded the apple; instead, the judge ate it out of self-satisfaction. He had been sitting there judging claimants all day and felt he deserved some recompense, though he knew no one would agree with him. When faced with a choice between compatible evils, he chose himself—into interdependence he injected an *in*compatible evil and made that sovereign."

The highest evil is not any particular condition, nor some empty class, but a call to duty—the exclusivist imperative, the maxim of sensible self-interest. The duty to oneself: to will nothing but that which you alone would do—to count on everyone else following the rules. And for all of humanity to individually obey the rule of excluding themselves. This imperative is so deeply buried in men, the urge to commit evil so restrained in comparison with the persistent habit of resisting and repairing it, that it requires a spiritual transformation of character to bloom, a *metanoia* of evil. The everyman inhabited by a grace that allows him to decide not to be merely selfish, but follow the duty of his nature, awakens unto radical evil. If other people exist at all, Everyman conjectures, he is compelled to admit that they don't matter beyond his own self-interest, that they have no import. "After all," he asks himself, "is the shark troubled about eating the minnow? And does the school of minnows hold debates on the merits of being fish food? And isn't the fact that minnows get eaten in this world itself the source of my motive for eating them? Well then," Everyman concludes, "I don't see how I could live with myself if I *don't* eat them." Thus, in rationalizing evil Everyman comes into harmony with himself. Opening himself up to total corruption, the absolute integrity of the self established, he is ready to be sought out by gods—at least to stop up his ears when they call out to him.

In an ocean of sharks there is more meat to go around.

Fables

A wise old giraffe gathered some giraffelings around a tree for a story.

The Boulevards of Extinction

"There once was a man," the old giraffe said.

"Why do you always have to start that way, 'There once was a man?'" asked one of the giraffelings. "Why can't you tell a story about a giraffe for once?"

"If it was about a giraffe, you wouldn't understand it. Humans make everything simple. Now, there once was a man. He plucked some leaves off a tree, and—"

"Did he want to eat the leaves?"

"No. Humans don't eat leaves. They're not gentle enough."

A look of puzzlement came over the giraffelings faces.

"What do they eat, then?"

"Giraffes."

The giraffelings all gasped in shock.

"So anyway, he plucked some leaves off of a tree and had to be punished for it."

"But we take leaves, and we're not punished."

"Trees are sacred in human society. They plant them along streets and outside of buildings. Sometimes, they even create specially marked off areas full of nothing but trees, where they sit in long carved trees and just stare into the other trees and smile and hug each other."

The giraffelings all started to laugh.

"Now, the man had to be punished for plucking the tree. As they led him to the guillotine—"

"What's a guillotine?"

"A big knife that chops your neck off."

"The upper neck or the lower neck?"

"The whole neck."

The giraffelings all raised shaking hooves to their necks and stroked them up and down.

"So," the wise old giraffe continued, "As the man's neck was lowered into the guillotine, he asked what would become of his head. He was told that it would be stuck on a pole and displayed on the bridge into town for all to see. His last request was that they would crown it with a garland of flowers when that happened. And after his head was struck off, his wish was carried out."

"They made his head like a tree!"

"Yes, just like a tree."

The giraffelings all bobbed their heads slowly in understanding.

A short-necked giraffeling, whom nobody liked, said, "What's it supposed to mean?"

"It's about humans," one of the other giraffelings said. "It's not supposed to mean anything. Only stories about giraffes have a message."

"I'm glad humans have taught you such an important message," the wise old giraffe said.

"So why do you tell us these stupid stories every day?" The short-necked giraffeling asked.

"Because," the wise old giraffe said, "stories are the longest neckline we have."

"I guess so," the short-necked giraffeling said. "But I get tired of hearing about humans all the time. It's bad enough that they're always staring at us."

The giraffelings all turned to look at the humans gazing through the fence.

"That one scares me," said one of the giraffelings, speaking of a little girl who was pointing at them and laughing.

"It's just admiring you," the wise old giraffe said. "The humans look to us for guidance."

"I want to pet one. Do we have to keep them locked outside?"

"Yes. They're much too dangerous to let into the world. That's why we keep them in a zoo, so they can amuse us safely."

Fanaticism

Suicide bombing is the most natural expression of Western man's condition. The Muslims have simply rendered banal what we have been doing to ourselves in subtler ways for the past century. Religious fanaticism only arises as a correction to extremism of habit.

Farmers

After the time is past when society's food producers are seen as being its most essential members, they find a new justification for their occupation, now judging themselves the only source of moral contribution—the only ones who *deserve* to produce. As money circulates like blood through the body, it must now and again be spilled to purify culture and balance the economy. However unwholesome for finance, by following the physiocrats America may avoid revolution through sweat and sacrifice. With cities too polluted and good jobs too scarce, *Les Économistes* lead an exodus of the unemployed into the country, crowding the land with sophisticates from the sterile class to follow "the rule of nature": merchants trading hoes and shovels, artists painting fences built by engineers, doctors shooting injured horses to be thrown in holes dug by funeral directors, hairstylists grooming sheep, teachers practicing beekeeping. With a rigid division of manual labor in place, all is set for the rise of Farm City: a capital where barns scrape the sky, dirt roads teem with livestock traffic, and a million feet throw up a cloud of dust that perpetually hangs in the air. Lifestyles diversify with the proliferation of farm tools, many of which take on decorative purposes as status symbols. A nation of rent managers returns to a nation of landowners who work for their patch of square feet; mortgagers stop worrying about where to find their next meal by taking the road to serfdom.

Fate

In spite of God and the laws of nature the world continues to persist, evading immutable principles which should have long ago *of necessity* destroyed it. We are an example of the much neglected "law of accidental ontology": that which must not exist might still exist. By God's account we are naught. He created everything and said, "No," then turned his back on it towards the Nothing he began in and said, "Yes." Disappointed with his experiment and disillusioned with mere abandonment, he allowed a tributary of Nothing to spill into our realm; hurling a meteor at earth long ago, God simply never realized his slight miscalculation of orbit and we never faced the basic irreality intended for us.

Favorites of fate, the reckless are to thank for our continued survival. The wild overleap their collision course while the prudent, saints of the probable, fall to the whims of coincidence. Inauspicious planners miss opportunities in one part of the world that have to occur but don't, then fly coach across the pacific and crash into events that aren't supposed to occur but do.

Our prejudices give us the confidence to be flukes of luck, exceptions to an absurd logic. Always on the verge of obliteration, we take our continued existence as evidence that we are under special protection. In fact we are like the target in the sniper's scope who keeps making abrupt movements, tripping over our feet or bending down to pity a flower.

Floralia

An annual festival of lasciviousness established by the senate to honor the goddess of the harvest, later legitimated by the wealthy courtesan Flora. Scandalized by the collective imagination, she encouraged it to be celebrated for *what it was*—a day to honor prostitution as a public service.

Following this example, re-envisioning national holidays to revel in realities and reenactments [(a)]:
***

Columbus Day: when the avaricious everywhere take to the streets to revenge their disappointments through butchery and enslavement.

New Years': playing April Fools' tricks on spring harvesters, blighting fields to thin a population into *thinking* about opportunity [(b)].

Thanksgiving: invading the home of distant relatives and saying "you're welcome" after passing the flu around the dinner table.

Presidents' Day: refreshing the land with the blood of everyone in-between patriots and tyrants.

Independence Day: reviving a revolution that began with the civil war and was rolled back after reconstruction.

MLK Day: hearkening to a recitation of "I Have a Nightmare." [(c)]

Christmas: sitting in a barn with an uninsured travailant, snorting frankincense and myrrh for a spiritual high.

a) Annual events are promoted to official holidays when the observance of a prevalent error is localized into the mythos of an atrocity.

b) A state of hunger is essential for lucidity. The rare genius is a fortuitous concatenation of bodily malnutrition, sexual starvation, and spiritual drought. If only a famine were to sweep through our cities, intellectuals today might produce a few lasting concepts.

c) Gandhi, King, Mandela—world-historical *pacifiers*. Bringing justice to the places that least needed revision, petty tyrants survive them in backward nations, stretching their arms now that the West has been tamed by its upstart citizenry. Ruthlessness lurks on the outskirts of the reforms of all good men—even inside their own marching club. Did they realize what the masses wanted deep down but were not conscious of until led by the nose? However much we may genuinely admire these secular saints, we take no gratification in imitating their examples. Conquering with sympathy, they have paved the way for the chaos *after* equality, the tremors under egalitarianism's shallow ethos. The brute facts of our natures make us crave rank and high position—both within groups and between them. "Shouldn't" is no contradiction of *feeling*. True, the charisma of principled men makes us forget this and long to be something more—before their assassination. There is no way to standardize magnanimity into bureaucratic authority. At its most effective, an administrative system can only prevent *malevolent* whims.

Fóppoodle. *n.* A dog incapable of being taught tricks by a master whose intelligence it exceeds.

> Blind fopdoodles are seldom seen
> Walking without *foppoodles* lean:
> Floating in ponds, lying in streets,
> Stumbling through a country of wheat,
> Tripping in ditches, trapped in sheds,
> Wherever they consent be led.
> (Samuel Buttler)

The Boulevards of Extinction

Foundations of Medicine

To fulfill their general education requirements, doctors seeking membership in the American Medical Association must learn the Seven Illiberal Arts that their discipline encompasses:

***

Magnigrammar, to foster misunderstandings among patients and garble explanations;

Ultrarhetoric, moving quickly from defective arguments to legally binding signatures;

Grandialectic, to prolong the need for treatments through the application of reason;

Calculatorithmetic, to reckon the hospital bill;

Globemetry, easier to memorize than geography and not requiring the taxing intellectual powers of geometry, finds the fastest line of infection through space;

Radio-tuning, to lull patients into docility with melodic sounds;

Stargazing, to model the cure cycle on the precession of the equinoxes and write a new prescription for every season.

***

Thus is the medical field the primary route to wisdom and health, and is so called, after Descartes, the Medications on First Philosophy.

Gewgawk. *n.* A children's antique; an art toy to be played with in the imagination; an untouchable novelty item.

> As children, when they another toy gain,
> Shelve the last lovely *gewgawk* to disdain.
> (Joan Dryden)

Gibraltar, Strait of

The place where barbarism and civilization meet and flow into one another. During the classical age the Pillars of Hercules were an effective barrier against cross-cultural interaction; not so in modern times. Our great instauration: many shall enter and ignorance shall be increased. With exotic fish from the Atlantic invading the Mediterranean and overwhelming endemic aquatic life, the latter will have to learn the savagery of the wild, wide waters to survive. The peninsula colonizes the continent by appropriating the bigger mass into the smaller one: admitting everyone, plugging the bottleneck, and shaking until it pops.

PART 5: The Philistine's Dictionary

Grandfatherland

The father of the fatherland, in which the child adopts a living ancestor because it cannot be caught robbing the candy store without sanctioned supervision. No nation can simply make laws and monopolize force; needing to establish a precursor to legitimate its decrees, it finds a grandfatherland to praise in order to admire itself. Greece, Rome, the Holy Roman Empire, the Prussian state—the Germans jumbled them all together to form Master Gramps, the stern yet generous head of the Aryan household, the Caesar remolded by the Kaiser into a benevolent republican.

How did so many tyrannies arise in the twentieth century? Men, tired of incompetent rulers and desiring to govern themselves, listened as a good patriot from among their ranks invoked a glorious past and declared himself the friend of humanity: this is how, after crying for the cat's head, the rat hung bells around the necks of his fellow rodents.

A nation models its oppressions on the fewest number of utopias it can get away with—it will not long survive free of confusion if it has to acknowledge its debts to the plethora of civilizations worthy of standing alongside it in the history books. In this way China has simplified matters: it is its own grandfatherland. Every land, on the other hand, is America's; and after pushing them all into retirement to claim its inheritance it turned its own house into a nursing home and began slipping into dementia.

Gravedigger's Catechism

Dying Man. You've buried a lot of men today. Many of them weren't Westerners, they wouldn't have approved of their body's fate. Don't you find it unjust that men whose beliefs command their bodies to be burned in pyres are put in the ground instead?

Gravedigger. Gives me more work. In any case, can't afford to be picky these days.

Dying Man. Yes, this is the way of plague. Still, you must experience pangs of conscience?

Gravedigger. Sometimes. That's why I temporarily adopt the religion of every man I bury.

Dying Man. And when you're not burying people?

Gravedigger. I place my confidence in the doctrine of death.

Dying Man. What are your principles?

Gravedigger. Death is the only certainty in life, and I am its high priest.

Dying Man. What about taxes?

Gravedigger. In that case, the commissioner of the IRS is the high priest.

DYING MAN. No, I mean they say taxes are the other certainty.

GRAVEDIGGER. Wouldn't know. I buried my payroll clerk a long time ago.

DYING MAN. How do you make a living?

GRAVEDIGGER. I've moved beyond money. Everything I need I take from the dead.

DYING MAN. So you're a grave robber.

GRAVEDIGGER. Somebody has to be. He was one of the first I buried.

DYING MAN. *(Coughing violently)* I suppose soon you'll be taking my stuff, too.

GRAVEDIGGER. You have sturdy shoes.

DYING MAN. Thanks. Guess I'd better move things along, huh? *(Lies down in an empty grave.)*

GRAVEDIGGER. *(Takes shoes off the* DYING MAN *and puts them on.)* Too small.

DYING MAN. Oh, sorry. Here, take my shirt.

GRAVEDIGGER. Thanks. It's a little tight.

DYING MAN. Can you at least let me keep my gold pocket watch, so I have something to accompany me into the afterlife?

GRAVEDIGGER. Will you need to keep track of time in eternity?

DYING MAN. Wish I could, but it broke a long time ago. It was my father's.

GRAVEDIGGER. Are you a pagan?

DYING MAN. No, a Christian. But I don't expect to be going to a nice place. I was thinking I might be able to barter it in exchange for a lesser punishment.

GRAVEDIGGER. Sorry, grave goods aren't a Christian practice, and I won't be believing in them while I'm burying you.

DYING MAN. Oh.

GRAVEDIGGER. Hand it over.

DYING MAN. Ok. *(Gives him watch.)*

GRAVEDIGGER. Thanks. This'll get me a good time at the brothel tonight.

DYING MAN. You buried all the prostitutes.

GRAVEDIGGER. A bowl of soup then.

DYING MAN. The last cook died yesterday. Why don't you get it fixed? You know, count the minutes until you get sick.

GRAVEDIGGER. I can't die, there won't be anyone to bury the dead.

DYING MAN. There's hardly anyone left to bury. Soon you won't be needed.

GRAVEDIGGER. What I meant was, high priests are immune to their own doctrines.

DYING MAN. Well whatever you do, please cherish my father's watch. It's all I have left of him. *(Lies down.)* Now get it over with.

GRAVEDIGGER. Sure thing. I promise to wear it for as long as I can stomach your principles. *(Looks at watch, then starts shoveling dirt on top of him.)* You know, I kind of like looking at a stopped watch. Makes my work go by faster. It's like I'm already in eternity.

DYING MAN. *(Muffled)* Ee you oo!

GRAVEDIGGER. Best not to talk. Conserve your oxygen.

Great Thread of Being

The Fates' substance of order. With a pair of scissors they can put a middleman at the top, or tangling the spool, confuse everything.

Gregory I

Standing on the threshold between ancient and medieval, in playing off the tension between the two he anticipated the modern attitude: craving the monastic life, he was torn away from himself and compelled to serve servants [(a)]. This perhaps accounts for the accusation that he was a gullible man, so desperate for God that he would believe any acknowledgement. The truth was that in wanting to make time for the personal discoveries of miracles he rushed the reports of others' [(b)]. In this, as well as his endless devotion to reforming the institution of the papacy—his *restlessness* for bureaucracy—he also anticipated the modern proclivity for perpetual busyness.

a) There are no prophets in the New Testament, only disciples and apostles—people who did not lead, but followed. Then came the monks, who neither led nor followed, but withdrew from the world to seek God in solitude. Finally we come to modern times, where people have combined each of these social forms even while consciously dispensing with all: internalizing the values of the pack but not following the pack, they lead themselves to the opinions of others, alone among many.

b) The only miracles one can bring oneself to believe are the testimonies of unlettered men and secondhand hearsay. The miracles of the educated become more ridiculous with every argument given in their favor. If only Sainte-Marthe would have let Gregory's dialogues stand on their own, a blunt record of witnesses, and left ancient tradition to speak for the reason and honesty of their author. By proving nothing, Gregory demonstrates much. The visions and dreams of those whose lives can be invoked as proof against them are all the more plausible because their lives are *not* brought in to testify against them.

Hagsney. *n.* A vulgar word of endearment to old fishwives; the verbal process of lowering one's standard of sophistication to gain experience; the sexual harassment of the menopausal.

> Shine upon me skilled but scraggly
> Such a one, won o'er by hagsney.
> (Samuel Buttler)

Heaven of the Moderns

A day spa for deists. Receiving mercy for being too nice, applicants are given free passes to cultural awareness training on benevolent hedonism and handed allegorical tools for terraforming Abraham's bosom into Silicon Valley.

Highlights from Pseudo-Livy's From the Faulty Foundation of the City, Books 1–5

Murder of Remus by Romulus in a quarrel over where to establish a discount store
Bipartisan compromise of the Horatii
The wife swapping of Lucretia
Election of Tarquin the Talkative
Horatius at the Fridge
Killing of Porsena's accountant by Scaevola, who then thrusts his own bank statement into the flames
Coriolanus's scorn of the patricians and outsourcing to Volscia
Extension of Roman citizenship to the Gauls following their invasion of Italy

Hitler

A Hitler who made a career of painting: instead of channeling his madness in conventional directions, success only licensed its intensification beyond all bounds [(a)]. This time it was not racial obsession that drove him, but the paranoia of glory. Adolf, *artiste*, not content to merely brandish his originality for all to see, was determined to rid the world of unoriginality and dosed everyone not creatively pure with Zyklon B. Then after the unimaginative of the world were exterminated he turned on his rivals in the art world. He decided the best way to make every gallery exhibit his works exclusively was to liquidate his contemporaries along with all their productions. But having his own wing dedicated to him wasn't enough: he wanted the entire museum, so he sent all the Dürers, Grünewalds, and van Leydens to the ovens [(b)]. Monopolizing the

PART 5: The Philistine's Dictionary

museum, he then craved the usurpation of all of German culture—they are a people especially known for their music, after all. Tearing up the compositions of Bach and Beethoven, breaking every Mozart record, throwing Goethe and Schiller into the burning pits, he undertook a holocaust of German art in order to position himself at its pinnacle [(c)]. To this day he remains our sole proof of intellectual life between the Rhine and the Oder.

a) It is amusing to think of tyrants as normal people. We imagine some childhood disappointment that spurs them on to take revenge against the world, then imagine the absence of this first image, then ponder, with a final link in our chain of fancy, the heart spurt of a born grinch. Men who yield to the experience of commonplace carnage would have come to the same road even if raised in a dollhouse; the misfortune is that they might have only ripped the heads off their dolls.

b) Replacing one's precursors can never be more than partially successful without eliminating all evidence of them. Artists who dream of greatness lack the courage for it, incapable of taking the small but vital step from narcissist to sociopath.

c) Less ethnocentric than pride for one's culture is the pride of embodying one's culture—grounding parochialism in self-centeredness.

Hop. *n., v.* What suffices to flavor beer for Europeans is, in America, either an exercise or narcotic of cheerfulness, depending on how adolescent or fatigued one is.

> One drinks, another jumps, another smokes. In the end they all arrive at the same place. But the European's *hop* is bitterer. (Durkheim, *Myth of Sisyphus*)

Humanism

A feeling of good will towards all men, turned inward. Each man hugs himself out of love for his own benevolent nature. With each member of humanity cherished equally, there is no rule of "women and children first" when disasters occur; with opportunity for all, every great and sensitive soul consumed by potential runs for the lifeboats and the strongest row away.

The crimes of the survivors are judged with severity: "We would never do such a thing if we had been in their shoes," the accusers say. "We love *humanity* too much."

Adherents to humanism deny their own faults by placing blame on those who fulfill their vision.

The Boulevards of Extinction

Ideobvert. *v.* To turn an idea about so as to show its different surfaces; to prove its total unreliability through inconsistent conceptualization or multiple failures of application.

> Under relativism every idea has a polygonal identity. To show not only the many appearances of objects, but through *ideobversion*, the many appearances of ideas, is the goal of understanding. (Husserl, *Interpretation of Brains*)

Indifference

A physicist watches a hilarious comedy. Though there is much slapstick, punning, and ribald wit, he does not laugh. He is only able to point out its flaws: these are low characters doing low things. He himself decides to write a comedy: "The Universe in a Wine Cask," filled with the everyday stoogery, pranks, and romantic entanglements of string theorists contending for the Nobel Prize. It becomes a smash hit on Broadway. He presides over its first performance on opening night. Still, he does not laugh. Although the acting is good and he is able to relate to the characters, he is too preoccupied with the theories driving the plot. He did not realize that long ago, in graduate school, indifference cured him of the world.

The physicist's is a superficial indifference, an indifference brought about by knowledge and separatism from the ordinary. But a *willed* indifference—that is higher, harder, more contemptible. It is to be not simply unresponsive to joy or cold to suffering, but warm to whatever may occur. It is not the opposite of enthusiasm, but the co-opting of enthusiasm into apathy. Superficially it may seem like magnanimity or malevolence, depending on the context. Watching as an old lady gets mugged, you shed a tear—there is no beverage to accompany this entertainment. Meeting a woman who has just won the lottery, you buy her a drink and toast to friendship. It is impossible to possess strength of will and be indifferent to oneself. Unmoved by the plights or prosperity of others, the Indifferent One fakes reactions to life and betrays his own worldview. Beverages are the customary response to occurrences, the only way to quench both force of personality and nonchalance.

Interpope

A series of canonically nominated usurpers caught in the middle of the rivalry between pope and antipope. Partially legitimate, partially schismatic, the interpopes resided in the center of Italy, waffling between resignation and ascension, awaiting either deposition or absolute power. As the other two popes fought each other, the interpopes ate grapes in their garden and debated with themselves on the merits of

PART 5: The Philistine's Dictionary

renouncing their vow of chastity while enjoying local village girls. After the last of the antipopes stepped down, Interpope Rural II was urged to take his place but declined, saying that he did not want to move from partial antagonism towards the pope to full antagonism. Without two opponents to triangulate themselves against, the Interpopes faded away until the reformation. When the rest of Europe broke away from Catholicism, Interpope Halfpious IV noncommittally took up the new cause and converted to Quasi-Lutheranism, at the same time remaining Pseudo-Catholic for diplomatic reasons. On the dispute between Erasmus and Luther as to whether the will was free or held in bondage, he upheld the middle position that man was freely predestined.

Ironeous. *adj.* Something undermined in veracity or legitimacy by being shown to have an ironic aspect.

> If there is a source capable of demonstrating Socrates's eminence in Western Philosophy to be *ironeous*, it is Xanthippe's lost memoirs. Socrates *in bed*— such a portrait would finally resolve whether or not the man was really worth executing. (Cirqueguard)

Isidore of Seville

True to his maternal Visigothic descent, he plundered earlier encyclopedias for uncited borrowings and sanctioned his pillage with quotations of Latin poets from his father's side—inheriting the chief strategies of both barbarism and civilization, he synthesized two worlds into one work. Obscuring the present relevance of words with original meanings fabricated for mnemonic value, and even seeking the foundations for nonverbal phenomenon in the principle of etymology, he sought legitimation for his worldview in a past hostile to it, rooting Christianity's genesis in pagan antiquity more deeply than anyone before him [(a)]. Without the errors and unusual tolerance of this crucial transitional figure, the period from which he emerged would be less patchily-lit with convenient abridgements and the period he paved the way for further darkened by an incuriosity for heresies [(b)].

- a) Beginnings don't reveal so much as betray. One seeking truth or authenticity is better off pointing to discoveries yet to be made and laws in need of passing. What has united a species isn't as universal as what could bind together a clique—hope always trumps history; the record of violence cannot stand up to its promise.
- b) I admire all founders, no followers.—But what am I saying? Many a founder is the successor to a follower who surpasses him in originating what he really meant.

Jihadgepodge. *n.* The motley assortment of jihadist and victims that follows from a successful cross-cultural encounter; the miscellany of paradoxical notions surrounding jihadism; the present state of Europe.

> Fallen to its knees, Christian apologetics begs for tolerance. A faith that popularized itself through the willpower of enduring torture fades away in a flash of light after shaking its murderer's hand—an entwined bond the only evidence of existence among the *jihadgepodge*. (Brunneis)

Job

Job's misery was not half as bad as whatever must have prompted young Elihu to discourse on wineskin wisdom and God's meteorological conditions. Perhaps he was just a guilty hallucination of Job's early discouragement as a weather forecaster. If only the blameless man had been luckier in predicting that eclipse, he would never have relegated his talents to monetary ambition and gone on to make such an irresistible target for supernatural resentment.

Johnson's Dictionary

It was common for great men of the Enlightenment to write masterpieces as well as live them. Johnson's double interest lies in the host of defects plaguing both life and work. Half-blind, largely deaf, were it not for a divine sixth sense for mediocre poesy and moralizing criticism his scrofula would have consumed him. His greatest legacy, the redundant registry of a Tourette sufferer, is our last resource for old-fashioned elegance and exactness. In a language invaded by borrowings since the Vikings, with half a dozen words for every concept and a host of slang added to the lexicon annually only to fall out again in a generation, it is not enough to turn to Johnson as the only source of expression. Today one needs to employ half a dozen amanuenses just to navigate the world, to deal with a divorce lawyer or order a meal at the drive-thru. Modern words are the whores of heaven, things the bastards of the earth. The *incorruptible* English speaker must have at his disposal a dictionary of words without precedence, a handy volume refreshing the antiquated into the unusable and inventing sources to provide the authority of an imaginary history.

PART 5: The Philistine's Dictionary

Kneading Philosophers into Philosophy

G.F.W.V.O., PhD.

He pointed to the rabbit's sheer being, then after killing it, to the rabbit's sheer nonbeing, then after it was dead for a few moments, to the rabbit's spirit, which was preparing to migrate. After undercooking the rabbit he was desirous of eating it correctly so that, in accordance with Truth-for-Profit Philosophy, he might maximize his nourishment in the moment after it cooled down but before it hit room temperature. He decided to eat the rabbit "now," but no sooner had he moved his fork towards his mouth than the "now" had passed. To correct this he replaced "now" with an exact specification of time, but upon putting the meat in his mouth could not decide whether he was eating the rabbit's being or its nonbeing or its not-yet-evacuated-spirit. He then amended his earlier stance and decided he was eating the "Now," the series of moments encompassing all the stages of the rabbit's demise. After eating the "Now," he inherited another "Now"—rabbit fever—which he had failed to point to. This is how his "Now" met the rabbit's "Now" and led to the unity of "Not-Now."

Rawlsseau

The babies chose to be born into fair conditions—a state of nature. Everything was perfect. No one had need of anything, nor did the children see each other often enough to have the opportunity for oppressing one another. They gorged their appetites on the abundance of the wilderness in isolation. Eventually they got bored with this and came together to form a society. To ensure the continuation of their initial state of fairness, they put rules in place to prevent inequalities from arising. Over time, the talented individuals became frustrated that they weren't getting a greater share than the untalented and lazy, so they left the just society to form a more just one.

In this new society the most gifted citizens competed to develop industry and build war engines, while those gifted in other ways made their living by writing poems and drawing pictures of the business class. When enough war engines had been built they marched on the original just society. The just society objected that this was not part of their prenatal social contract. The talented society retorted that only postnatal power can render prenatal agreements legitimate—there can be no Melian dialogue for preemies. They then leveled the just society to the ground and enslaved its population. Fearful at first, the just citizens soon came to realize that, stripped of all their rights, they were completely egalitarian in a way they had never been with their liberty intact. The body politic of the talented society attempted to impose their general will upon the just slaves, enticing them to rise from their fallen positions through the exercise of ability. The slaves, however, were committed to regarding themselves as equals. They didn't want to enter into the cutthroat competition that characterized the lives of the talented, remaining satisfied as long as their masters fed and clothed them without mistreatment.

A general will can force a people to be free or fair, but not both.

Hilaclitorus Putnemides

Travelling beyond the beaten paths of mortal men, Putnemides reached the underworld, where the voice of a goddess told him he would frequently be wrong about what he thought was the nature of reality. She then told him that everything in the universe is one and unchanging. He, mistaking the goddess for his conscience, concluded this statement was wrong and decided instead that everything is plurality and change. After coming back to the surface he started formulating his theories: pedantic externalism—twin scholars from twin worlds use the same word and mean completely different things; pedantic holism—a scholar speaks, and can only be understood in relation to everything else he has yet to say; the incomprehensibility argument for mathematical realism; metaphysical zealism, internal zealism, direct zealism—paradigms of fanaticism that bomb opponents into conversion with the smoke of fizzled arguments. He held each of his theories for a few weeks, during which time his conscience told him it made a good deal of sense until, two-headed, he turned back upon himself.

But as it turned out, Putnemides never went to the underworld. Nor did he ever travel beyond the beaten paths of mortal men. Nor was he, technically speaking, a mortal man. Years ago his brain had been removed and put in a vat, then hooked up to a channel-surfing television, which was hooked up to a video camera, which was hooked up to a broken refrigerator that ran through a videogame console, which was played by a robot listening to a radio station, which was hooked up to a telephone held by a robot powered by a flashing light bulb. When the light bulb flashed the robot said a word into the telephone, which went out over the radio, which made another robot press a button on a videogame console, which made the refrigerator click, which triggered a video camera to record ten seconds of whatever was on the television screen and send it into Putnemides's disembodied brain. At the time he met the goddess, the television was playing "Hercules in the Underworld," starring Kevin Sorbo. After that, a wire short-circuited somewhere between the telephone and the videogame console, and he was left alone with static.

Crypkallipolis

From his tower he looked down, examining the fresh grass, the dead leaves, the snow, the wind in the trees. A ruler focuses on what's important. King Cryptic didn't need to march with his army to reign, or even spend time among his people. He only needed to make rules for them. Often the people walking around below would shout at him or throw things, but he was too high for their curses or missiles. Their attempts at insolence didn't bother him. The people served their function. They were, necessarily and a posteriori, slaves. That they didn't understand the meaning of his orders was irrelevant: they were followed anyway, not only in his own city, but in every possible city which he ruled. His decision to rule an ideal city was purely logical. Knowing that, after having accrued many years of experience and learning, one must be of advanced age before he is chosen to be a philosopher king, Cryptic looked at his face in the mirror one day and saw that he was old. So, constructing a complex system of Alphabet-Reckoning that allowed him to speak in a countably infinite set of propositional variables, he began instituting valid formulas for behavior. With a formula for cursing and throwing things at the leader, he ensured that he would be cursed at and have his tower splattered with egg yoke. He set down another formula that no one should read poetry any longer, and behold, he only ever saw his subjects reading prose. Pronouncing that people must engage in their own jobs and no other so as to only perform those functions necessary for life, he often saw people doing different things and not dying. Proclaiming that all his most important citizens should study math for ten years, he sometimes watched people counting on their fingers through his binoculars, and declared them to be leaders of the city. After outlawing private property he often saw people sharing things.

Before warning them what could happen if they disobeyed his orders, he would give his subjects names, shouting titles like "dunderhead" and "nincompoop" through his megaphone. He was always delighted to see them embracing their new referents by looking up at him. In everything, King Cryptic's ideal city followed the Form of the Necessary.

Paulegius

"Whenever we inaugurate evil, we find it already before us like a shadow, following us everywhere. We only soak up its stain. Man is unable to avoid it. Why indulge in pointless evasions? With every step he takes he only follows his shadow. And so he learns to send his shadow out wherever he goes. The very capacity to do evil is also good. It represents the freedom to symbolize." So said the heretical Gaul, his vision of the world formed by the Song of Solomon and chapter three of Augustine's Confessions.

Kudomania. *n.* Possessed by a desire for glory. Distinct from celebsession, the desire to be on television.

> Spiritual glory, rather than detracting from the earthly sort, only spurs it on by increasing one's confidence. Neither change, nor falter, nor repent of anything that will make you a titan of two realms. Do not be ashamed to be one of

the few diagnosed with *kudomania* and dragged to the sanatorium. (Blake Shelley)

Laconicus: Foundations of the Terse Style

The Overabundant Style

The great variety of English today makes rewriting pre-existing texts both difficult and easy: difficult because there are so many words and devices, easy for the same reason. An absurd complexity of style demonstrates the need for a return to simplicity, and by moving too far in one direction one finds oneself at the opposite end. The overabundant style is the foundation of the terse, as the examples below show.

***

Variety (111): Sub-synecdoche
Referring to a whole by mentioning a part of a part of that whole. This is one way of making a clichéd personification more interesting.
E.g., no-melanin ("melanino"): white beard: an old man.

***

Variety (113): Parallel synecdoche
Referring to a part by mentioning a different part of a common whole. This comes in handy when you want to imply something pertinent in a clever way.
E.g., jaws: shark: the shark's bitten-off fin.

***

Variety (341): Kniferism
Cutting off the beginning, middle, or end of the words in a phrase or sentence and running them together—a portmanteau articulated with a speech disorder. These slips of the tongue are useful when in a hurry.
E.g., "I need to go now, but I would like to get together with you sometime": "Ineegow, bouldligethersotime."

***

Variety (587): Contranymbiguity
Taking a sentence with only two potential meanings and, by adding a contranym, doubling the ambiguity. Useful in legal scenarios.
E.g., "During his defense he was too apologetic": "During his apology he was too apologetic."
This could mean either: during his formal defense he was excessively defensive; or, he turned his formal defense into an expression of penitence; or, while expressing penitence he was excessively penitent; or, he turned an expression of penitence into a formal defense.

Part 5: The Philistine's Dictionary

The Terse Style

The problem with brevity is that it is always superfluous: no matter how brief, more brief. An apparent simplicity, so succinct as to bear an opaque significance to listeners, contains within it a wealth of abundance. Potential meanings proliferate so as to always keep readers guessing.

Aside from description, the most extravagant superfluity is dialogue. There is often a good deal of dialogue in books; this fills up many pages and wastes readers' time. Conversation is a device used by amateurs—in writing and life. The master of both realms is the mute, and this state requires great practice. Dialogue can be greatly condensed through the use of gestures, as the examples below show.

***

Extricating
(Point thumb in direction of door): "It's been pleasant, and now you will be lucky to relieve yourself of my company"; or, "Let's go hitchhiking."

***

Buying
(Throw money at seller): "You do a great service by offering your wares to the public. I will be taking this now"; or, "I don't want what you have, nor what I have. Here, take this green stuff."

***

Expressing futurity
(Wave hand dismissively): "You'll always be a has-been"; or, "The future stretches into infinity—but not for us"; or, "Never!"

***

One who can be overabundant or terse in proportion to what is needed will have mastered the fundamental principle of style. Out of a love for brevity we must sometimes cultivate verbosity so that our concision, when it comes, is all the more effective—and vice-versa.

Laws

Moses introduced divine laws, Solon secular laws, Numa secular laws disguised as divine laws, Constantine a confused mixture of both. But what is the source of our inspiration to obey? America's Legislator is not one supreme founder but *many*; in every generation we find lawgivers unto themselves, self-anointed to anti-social contracting.

The *Decemviri* of Decadence:
Cortez: custom of Do What You Will.
Edward Tilley: the short-lived model of religious freedom.
Mather: witness to innocence, inoculant of witches.
James Wilson: popery of property.

The Boulevards of Extinction

Jackson: trial of tears.
Sherman: scorched hearth, excoriated heart.
Wendell Holmes: national law of natural straw.
Joseph Smith: exodus of wives, commandment of husbandry.
Bob Smith: Edict of Addicts.
Hubbard: plebiscite of the wealthy.

***

"Legislation considers man as he is in order to turn him to good uses in human society."[2]—America's *Decemviri* have followed Vico's axiom intimately to create "the strength, riches, and wisdom of commonwealths," keeping human nature in mind above all when drafting *their own* desires. From "the passions of men each bent on his private advantage," come Spanish institutions for Pre-Columbians, the Mayflower compact of prudery and repression, the Indian removal policy. The divine and noble authorities of the Ages of Gods and Heroes, even when high-minded, are appropriated by ordinary men of the third age and reinterpreted to serve narrower ends. Thus the last lawgivers are men who relocate divine providence to the banks of the Great Salt Lake, who make a heroic virtue of "the dry life" and deny the destiny of disease. The Sons of Scientology, having succumbed to the clumsy style of Hubbard's novels and fallen into illiteracy, will move out of the Age of Men to graze on the slopes of their alien ancestors' volcano, then decompose into sunflower fertilizer to await the next eruption.

Men cannot replace former systems of ambition without first becoming alluring, then absurd, then *just*. When charisma solidifies enough habits into rules, revealing law to be only a larger body of whims and "law" the jurisprudence of investment firms, the only alternative is to treat it as an invariable relationship. The Law of Decadence: after the rise and fall of a thousand societies have been recorded in detail, the general arc of Vico's ideal eternal history reliably verified—domination first; then the language of morals, spirit, rights, all spreading enfranchisements through war and legality; finally overextended into sects of promiscuity, contrived sobriety, superstardom—then some well-placed member of the bar association will draft the Cocktail Codex that should have accompanied our cycling all along.

Lexcess. *n.* The state of having too many words; a linguabundance born of the zeal of a lexicompoundologer without regard for etymoflow; the portmantowage of a derelict vehicle of meaning.

> There are two ways a language becomes dead. The first is when all its native speakers die. The second is when everyone begins to speak it, so that by adopting every other language into itself it is gradually transformed by *lexcess* into

---

2. Vico, *The New Science*, 62.

an unwieldy monstrosity and abandoned for whatever offshoot dialect a provincial is best suited to memorize. (Varro)

Limbourg Brothers

Paul, Johan, and Herman born into a money economy: unable to merge their talents into a single personality, they misappropriated the Duc de Barry's grant funds to develop their own autonomous styles, populating their miniatures with selected objects that reflected individual fetishes and expenditures. Aware that they could be pious or profound, but not both [(a)], they chose to be neither: instead of visual etudes intended to perfect the skills of faith, they created a book of hours to charm its scarce onlookers with aesthetic frivolities.

February: the immodestly splayed legs of the peasants are matched by the noblewoman's drooping toga, an anachronistic indulgence the rustic painter has just bought for his wife; the man in the yard wears a fine scarf about the face to avoid the virtuosity of condensing his breath on the frosty air—stylistic extravagance, Paul thought, is better shown through consumption habits; a barn has been raised over the haystack to prevent the inconvenience of snow settling on it irregularly. All barely discernible through the ongoing blizzard; through a hazy landscape the onlooker imposes his own interpretation upon the piece.

July: the walls of the castle of Poitiers are draped with tapestries recently acquired by Paul, each a slightly different shade in relation to their position against the sun.

August: the courtly painter favored minimalism. His rise from laborer to gentleman was not accompanied by an enlargement of gratitude towards his benefactors. He satirized the uncomfortably warm and confining garb of the nobles by drawing faces flushed and perspiring, resembling the sweaty figures of hell, and by having the sleeve of one get caught on a dangling branch to unseat the rider; country boys obscenely basking in the sun, too lazy to swim in the opaque water; a tempest on the horizon, dark forbidding woods on the edge of the garden landscape—nature, too, is conscripted to comment on Johan's observations of social rank.

October: the Master of Darkness painted over the reflections in the water he had initially represented [(b)]. He instead decided on an overcast sky covering everything in shadow, making the middle the darkest area to suggest a central axis, an effect heightened by two men in the foreground stumbling towards one another in the shade.

Herman revenged himself for his marginalization in the calendar scenes, sabotaging later miniatures with his resentment: the drooling dogs of December; the Anatomical Zodiac Hermaphrodite, with two astrological signs corresponding to each of the twelve anatomical regions, expression of his frustration towards horoscopes; Eve's obesity, signal of the moneyed class and condition of his new wife; beams of light passing through a damaged roof in the Nativity to sunburn the heads of shepherds, aesthetic exoneration of his baldness. Unlike his brothers, he would receive no such title as "the rustic painter" or "the courtly painter," but anticipated an implied relegation to "the undeveloped provincial painter [(c)]."

Workshop assistants who were to receive no recognition for the book filled the borders with flowering vines encroaching upon the text and droll details obscuring its somber message, making recital impossible: a stork emerging from a blue flower to engulf a prayer; a woman swashbuckling with butterflies that retreat into a psalm; a snail felling a towered warrior into a gospel passage; an old man wheelbarrowing a bear into a mass.

Linear perspective was eschewed to favor the centrality of man [(d)]: foreground figures are as tall as buildings, landscapes seem traversable in a single bound, celestial choirs are densely crowded.

Silver associated with money: Judas's bright halo in Gethsemane compared to Jesus' dim gold one, outshining even the illuminating moon; halos around Lucifer and in the court of hell.

Heaven: uniform phalanx of the attacking rebel angels, grayish-black wings and red robes intertwined to seal any weak point; crowded gold stalls in the heavenly theatre; the Almighty's furrowed brow as he searches for the thought to send the rebels hurtling down; silver sparks shooting from the auras of angels enveloped by bribery; refractive dispersion of blues and golds among the angels, who use the latest defensive techniques to counteract the siege engines of Hell [(e)].

a) Modern mysticism is a journey to God in a Volkswagen. Driving straight up, one has enough time to experience a few dozen moments of ecstatic union in the hour it takes to leave the earth behind—one for each gospel track if the album is listened to twice.

b) Shadows betray the darkness by implying a concentrated source of light.

c) Why are lesser artists failures? —They think sublimating their failure is enough.

d) Before man could fall from his central place in the universe he had to fall from his central place in the world: linear perspective prepared us for heliocentrism.

e) Cultural diffusion seesaws upward and downward before moving outward to mortals. To win souls to its side through a demonstration of wondrous power, Heaven's technology must remain current.

Logic

False questions, commands, exclamations:
"Why did you kill your wife?"
"I never had a wife."
"Don't play with me!"

"You have never smiled in your life."

"Oh, god!"

"Also not the case."

***

Omniscience regarding mistaken existences is not the only thing required to deny what can be asked, given, or uttered; more difficultly, one must sense the opacity of sentences. Clairvoyant insight would only be effective if accompanied by a paranormal propriety of limits, a reluctance to attend word peepshows. Let the lexicon perform her dance of the seven veils without regard for which one will fall into your lap.

The art of logic: adorning statements with flowers, adding a second and third coat of paint onto the conclusion, linking premises with metaphors. No need to *argue* thoroughly; if people like your conclusions they will adopt them as their assumptions and ignore the rest. With the process and product of argument blending into the setting, the presentation of the proposition is asserted to smooth absorption. Show me the reality which bare reasoning obscures, the pale hue of a moonlit truth.

Man in the Plaster Mask

One wonders whether there is not a king of the carnies who fears for the uniqueness of his mask, seizing anyone whose craftmanship resembles his own and locking them away in traveling cages, forcing audiences to behold their real face.

Martyrs

Here they were finally. Their paths converging, they stood at their nexus of zeal together, not quite sure what to say, their eyes adjusting to the expanse of light spread before them. Having no need for personal introductions, a simple greeting would be overstating their arrival. It was not just the acute impression of their far-reaching fame, but a deeper uncertainty about their own place within the world that made them hesitant, though none of them had ever been skeptics.

Not one to remain silent, Jordan spoke up first.

"What did we do?" Jordan asked.

"Not much," Anicius shrugged. "We won no wars, drafted no laws."

"I was an interpreter of the law," said Tom.

"Splitting hairs doesn't count," said Jordan.

"I understand that you were fearless in battle," said Anicius with a gesture to Ugly-Nose.

"Who said that?" replied Ugly-Nose.

Anicius shivered and rubbed his arms. The chill here reminded him of the draft in his old jail cell. He glanced around. This blank canvas was no better than the pitch black of that windowless room. At least there he didn't have to squint. It occurred to him that both light and dark, as they polarize in purity, converge in blindness, and he felt himself longing for shades of gray to fix upon.

"So," said Jordan anxiously, "are any of you remembered for your ideas? Speaking personally, I borrowed too much to be original."

"I was born too late to be original," said Anicius.

"I wrote nothing," said Ugly-Nose, scratching a nasal mole with a dirty fingernail.

"I wrote something I would rather not have," said Tom. "There was too much religious freedom, too much irony, too much poetic license." He then gave a summary of his most famous book. "I should have just re-said what Ugly-Nose said, plain and simple."

"What did I say?" Ugly-Nose asked, still scratching.

"If you had written it down," said Tom, "you might have remembered."

"Well I didn't," Ugly-Nose said, nostrils flaring.

"You kicked out the poets," Tom explained. "I tried to follow your example later, when I barred translations of my own work."

Jordan tugged at the collar of his robe. It was burning up inside this thing.

"But I like poets," Ugly-Nose said. "Especially Homer." The side of his nose had turned red from too much scratching.

"You know," Anicius told Ugly-Nose, "someone did write those ideas down, and in your name."

"Who was this imposter?" asked Ugly-Nose.

Jordan raised a hand to silence the chatter. "So why are we considered great?"

"I tried to uphold the law," said Tom. "So my head rolled."

Jordan scoffed at this. "That goes far in explaining your sloppy legalistic arguments. Being burned alive, on the other hand, gives rigor to one's thought. Before asphyxiation overtakes you there is still time to cross-reference."

"I did that a lot when I burned heretics," said Tom. "I bet I could have made you recant."

"You pass that sentence upon me with greater certainty than I receive it," said Jordan.

Anicius laughed. "Certainty is what made all of us who we are. In any case, I'm afraid I had it worse than both of you. They tied ropes around my head until my eyes popped out, then bludgeoned me."

Tom winced.

"But," Anicius continued, "I knew that I would be going to a better place."

"Amen," said Tom.

Jordan scoffed. "So you just died to seek the reward of an afterlife. If you were a true martyr, you would have died for your ideas alone."

"Your ideas have a worldly afterlife, just as ours do," Anicius said. "And my death was by no means easy to endure, afterlife or not. I wrote my book in jail as a way of preparing for it."

"The contrivance of preparation was something I always opposed," said Ugly-Nose. "And your philosophy of retirement is something that would make even the most reclusive invalid long to walk out into the sun again. Me, though, I could have escaped my fate. It was choice that led to my universal admiration."

"Some would call that stupidity," said Anicius.

"That was a nice allusion to your own ideas, referring to the sun like that," said Jordan.

"Allusion?" said Ugly-Nose.

"Yes," said Jordan. "I thought you favored the indirect approach."

"Only where my wife is concerned."

"Avoid the nagging, eh?"

"Nonsense. Any burden I had to bear in life, she showed me how to bear it best by doing it for me. Persuading her over the years has honed my subtlety. And deepened my poverty, since there were so many things a willing woman was not permitted to do then. But for all that, her cheerful delicate nature never hardened into cynicism. It was largely by her example that I was moved to do what I did in the end."

Ugly-Nose's nostrils dilated, like a cave swallowing a mountain, and he sneezed onto the Tudor rose of Tom's neck chain. Tom wiped off the mucus with his deep red sleeve, his eyes drawn into the holes of the huge proboscis. Those double doors led to an abyss deeper, darker, and more uncertain than anything in Jordan's infinite plurality of worlds. When it came to disentangling truth from deception, that nose was apt to smell everything at once. It was like a galley-rower who, ignorant of the oriental cargo onboard, mistakes his body odor for the fragrance of an exotic perfume. No, if Ugly-Nose were in his situation, Tom thought, he would not have been led to make the right choice. True, he was the oldest of them, and that added pride to sacrifice. All later martyrdom was a measuring-up, and all the rest of them fell short of adequacy not least because their sacrifices were actually necessary.

Anicius raised a hand to cut them off. "The point is," he said, "we could have been more compromising."

"Could have, yes," said Ugly-Nose. "But should have? What is certain is that if we didn't mind so much, people never would have kept their minds on ours for so long."

"When you die for an ideal," Jordan concluded, "people will twist your entire life into one, no matter how disingenuous or contrary to fact it was." He glanced at Tom as he said this. "Martyrdom bestows wisdom where none previously existed."

Anicius began sulking at this, and Jordan put a hand on his shoulder.

"Only the lofty remember me," said Anicius. "I'm not a household name like Ugly-Nose."

"It's true that every school boy learns my name," said Ugly-Nose. "But only grudgingly."

"I'm remembered by many as well," said Tom. "They made a Hollywood movie about me."

The others expressed enthusiasm at this, and they all decided to go watch it together. They were overwhelmed by the lead actor's performance, his total embodiment of the role. Jordan pointed out that whenever modern people contemplated Tom, an image of Paul Scofield must inevitably come to mind instead. Tom, thinking Scofield a most handsome surrogate, agreed that it was for the best. People's minds still reserved the idea of Tom, after all, and an attractive face helped them to absorb his essence more fully. The screenplay also helped make him likable for modern audiences. The four martyrs all laughed at the actor who played the king, symbolic of all those in power whose arrogance towards heaven inadvertently gives glory to the unyielding. For there have been many wise men, but most are forgotten for their prudence instead of immortalized for their stubbornness.

Metaphysical Legacies

He died like a true philosopher, shouting dogmas to his scribe. At the reading of the will, his family bickered over the gibberish.

"Words were always the expression of reality for him," said the brother who wanted his library.

"He considered consciousness to be the seat of personal identity," said the vague distant relative who coveted his lamps, "and it is the passing sense impressions that make up reality, not words." She claimed to be a second cousin from the east coast. Since the family was generally hostile to easterners no one cared to ask after her specific home state, but when anyone pressed her for the name of the great-grandparent she had in common with the deceased, she had stuttered and excused herself to give her regards to the casket.

"That's silly," a small blonde head poked above the crowd to declare. "He always said a person could only know himself to the extent that he brought himself in line with 'The Good.' I would always ask him what he meant by that. I'd say, 'What's this Good you're talking about? Just what do you mean? What's Good to you?' Well, he would always get a far off look and not answer me, but I know what he was thinking . . . he prided himself on his barbequing skills. More than anything else, after philosophy, he liked to barbeque. I think he thought barbequing was his Good. And how else could he know himself in that regards, if not for us encouraging him? I don't even know how many times I told him his meat wasn't overdone. He was always worried about his overcooked meat and there often wasn't anybody else around to put that fear to rest. No one appreciates the sacrifices I made for that man. That's why I should get his cooking pots."

The daughter also claimed his cooking pots, citing in her defense the prominence of aesthetics within his system. "The perception of beauty is what gives each moment value. He always said that." The daughter wanted to put the pots on display. Everyone assumed this because her uncle had seen her buying a shelf in a department store. He had not introduced himself to her, but watched her from the bed section, peaking through a hole in an oak headboard. She had picked out a shelf painted light blue, which he thought would go well with the pale yellow cooking pots. At the funeral, everyone feigned surprise when she spoke about the shelf.

No one brought up the fact that the cooking pots had never been used, or that the philosopher wouldn't have known how to cook anything in them if he wanted to. That he was adept with the salt and pepper shakers was universally accepted, but the intricacies of oregano eluded him. He hesitated to mix it in with the beef lump. More than even oregano, the dreaded bay leaf was a topic that was off limits in his household; all of his arguments were directed to its refutation. His sons were still uncomfortable making inductions from it, though his daughter used it all the time, planning her meals around the herb. There were some who thought she would simply put the pots on her shelf and never use them, while others said they would reek of bay leaves after a week.

"He thought happiness was the fundamental motivation of mankind," said the aunt who wanted his photo albums. Her tongue pronounced "happiness" with a lingering hiss, apparently for emphasis, and her small dark eyes seemed to shrink even more, augmenting her ugliness. She shifted in her seat to scratch an itch on her butt, which the others in the room took as a sign of anxiety. None present respected her; she was just an in-law and had, at most, a right to express her condolences to the coffin, not to be sitting there with them now. She had not bled for the photo album she wanted so desperately. But she, perhaps more than anyone else, had a claim to it. She had once seen the deceased smile when he thought he was alone. She hoped the pictures might hold the key to his thoughts on happiness, that she might catch his lips pursed with yearning, she didn't know. The album was heavily guarded and she had only ever seen a few photographs of him. She knew he didn't care for visual representations. He thought they dulled your Being, which would inevitably be morose or too busy to brush or caught in bad lighting, not up to the expectations of twice-removed acquaintances who only knew you pictorially. She feared opening the album and finding it blank, leaving words as the only evidence he existed. She didn't put it past the family to play a cruel joke on her like that.

The granddaughter thought the old lady fidgeting in her seat must be as bored as she was. She remembered his grandfather's last, unfinished proof of the mind's transcendence of physical death, and imagined a disembodied brain hovering in the sky, sensing everything being said in the room, and being ashamed. She then wondered if the old fish tank in the garage could double as a vat so her grandfather's brain could come stay with her and they could have interesting discussions about Descartes and it could help her with her cognitive psychology homework.

The second cousin from the east coast stood up. She claimed that the good, the beautiful, and happiness all derived from the pleasure principle, and that they were all really arguing over the same thing. The lawyer reading the will claimed to be satisfied with this, and although he secretly found problems with her imprecise definition, and where the dead philosopher's unmentioned concept of justice fit in to her explanation, he was tired and wanted to go home, so he named the second cousin the sole inheritor of all the dead philosopher's possessions.

When she got back to Seattle she held a garage sale and sold everything off for fifty-seven dollars.

Metemgenetosis. *n.* The submigration of souls from body down to gene; demotion from personhood to nucleotidery.

> Overeaters become the building blocks of a predisposition to obesity, while those who never gave in to peer pressure at the junior high bus stop are transformed into the "smoking gene" to protect worthy vessels. In *metemgenetosis*, selfishness is done away with before the final discarding of self. The others of future lives are rewarded or punished based on your good or bad deeds in this one; karma only determines the molecular combination. (Guatama BudDNA)

The Mills

A boy sits alone in a room, crouched over a small desk. A man enters.
JAMES. How are your studies coming?
JOHN. Very good, father. Except that . . . well . . .
JAMES. What is it? Are you still struggling with the *Theaetetus*?
JOHN. Not anymore.
JAMES. Did you finish your arithmetic exercises?
JOHN. Yes.
JAMES. So what's the problem?
JOHN. I seem to be developing some health problems.
JAMES. Health problems?
JOHN. Yes. You see, it's been so long since I've seen the sun.
JAMES. Pale skin beautifies character and strengthens diligence. Exposure to sunlight overheats the brain. Understand?

Part 5: The Philistine's Dictionary

JOHN. Yes. *(Looks away distractedly.)*

JAMES. Is there something else?

JOHN. Beyond the physical aspects of my health . . .

JAMES. Are we still on this subject? I thought it had been cleared up.

JOHN. Mother says I need a friend, that it would be good for my emotional life.

JAMES. Nonsense! A friend is just an obstacle to knowledge who occasionally furnishes useful information—something you have no need for. You wouldn't believe the facts that pass for "useful information" these days. Have you ever seen a boy your own age?

JOHN. No, father.

JAMES. Would you even recognize a potential friend if you saw one?

JOHN. I think so. I have glanced in the mirror before. I imagine he would look something like me.

JAMES. Wrong! Boys today are all playing in factories, coal mines, chimneys. Their skin is the color of night. You're liable to contract black lung just by standing near one and breathing the same air. You, my boy, are the moon—and we need to keep you pure.

JOHN. But surely, some of the middle class boys don't—

JAMES. Enough! I won't hear of it. Man is equivalent to his mind, and the mind is a machine; like all machines it needs only to be oiled regularly to keep him going. Go rummage through the pantry for some bread.

JOHN. Thank you, father.

JAMES. No butter! I won't have you getting fat and dozing off at your desk.

JOHN. Yes, father.

He leaves and returns a few minutes later with a slice of bread. JAMES *is crouched over his large desk writing his* History of British India.

JOHN. I was wondering, father. Do the other fathers make their boys do this?

JAMES. Do what?

JOHN. Study all the time.

JAMES. No. You're the only one.

JOHN. I see. *(Chews silently for a few moments.)* Father?

JAMES. Yes?

JOHN. I was wondering. Would it be best for society if every child had to do what I do?

JAMES. Not every child would be capable.

JOHN. Well, as many as possible, then?

JAMES. If that were the case, there wouldn't be nearly as much trouble in the world.

JOHN. Even so, I don't think it would be best for the children.

JAMES. Define "best."

JOHN. You know, the choice someone makes that's better than any other alternative—the greatest good.

JAMES. Alright then, what *would* be the greatest good for the greatest number of children?

JOHN. To have a friend.

JAMES. The other children already have those in droves, I can assure you. And look what it gets them! Factory work and an early death, nothing more.

JOHN. You said they go to the factories to play.

JAMES. Work, play—to a child it's all the same.

JOHN. But are they in factories *because* they have friends? I mean, does friendship cause factory work?

JAMES. Of course! It's their playground. Look at their faces when they're marching in—you can tell they're going wild in there! And they would have nowhere to go otherwise. It's safer than the homes of their drunken parents. *(John looks despondent.)* Hey, tell you what—I'll take you walking before breakfast tomorrow.

JOHN. You mean, to see the sun?

JAMES. Not directly. We'll start early on the green lanes towards Hornsey. By the time we get back, you just might glimpse a few rays peaking over the horizon.

JOHN. Oh, father! *(Embraces him.)*

JAMES. There. Now get back to work.

Naturalis Historia

"My subject is a barren one—the world of nature, or in other words life . . ."[3] How honest Pliny's claim! The earliest surviving encyclopedia would have done well to end with this humble statement to Vespasian, as a discouragement to later compilers of knowledge. Or, at least, to have taken as a model Varro's *Disciplines* not only in scholarship but disappearance.

But the second-best route, after being lost, was to propagate a factual wonderworld to the future. The age of exploration did not prove Pliny wrong so much as demand that facts become mundane, that the allegorical beastiaries of the middle ages give way to the classifications of Linnaeus. Imagination was confined to the realms of fiction and art, and when realism was demanded even there, to the subgenre of surrealism.

---

3. Pliny the Elder, *Natural History*. Dedication to Titus: C. Plinius Secundus to his Friend Titus Vespasian.

Part 5: The Philistine's Dictionary

Returning to Wonderland by turning our penchant for classification against itself: logging entries in the *Encyclopedia of Inconvenient Existences*, Arcimboldo's portraits and Calvino's invisible cities are recalled to the realm of the possible. From there the research teams of physicists promote them to the necessarily possible. Finally legislation is passed to make them simply necessary, assigning city planning to the school of Escher and family pictures to the farmer's market studio. After that we need only have faith in the engineers, builders of our hallucinations, actualizers of the schizophrenic realm.

Nectarwean. *v.* Gradually depriving children of fruit in order to introduce them to processed foods.

> Breast milk, tree fruit, fruit snacks. This is the order of diet for healthy growth. Moving from mother to plant to factory, children are systematically socialized into all the states of nature through what they eat. Just be sure to *nectarwean* them good, or they risk getting stuck in the botanical stage. (Sigmund Pauling)

Novalis

"On Lessing, on Schelling, on Schiller and Schlegel, on Hegel, on Herder, on Schleiermacher and Schopenhauer!" Kant's reindeer needed its red-nosed Novalis, philosopher of perseverance, to keep the sleigh from crashing into the phenomenon.

The Jena Circle lamented the possession of the proposed ideals making its striving incomplete. Our own tears over the absence of proposals would amount to a double lament—self-negating cries of satisfaction. The languid afterglow of urges met raises the question to those lost romantics: what good do the achievement of objective ends serve when nothing is beyond? The joy of repetition, *nocturnal recurrence* . . .

To strive towards the recreation of a golden age and be living in one the entire time without knowing it . . . there was no need to peer over the horizon; the fragment was already complete—temporarily. Alone among the *formes brèves*, it referenced a social totality never again attained in German letters. A blessing Novalis started coughing up blood when he did so as not to be disenchanted upon Hegel's arrival in print—so he could remain for us the eternal optimist. The synthesis of knowledge which Novalis looked forward to was to be realized by "the old man" in a way that would have crushed him. It is possible to have *too much* completeness; when multiple forms of it compete for attention space some are bound to get crowded out. In this case philosophic systematization and the unity of the state destabilized the harmony of litterateurs, only to be destabilized in turn by its own academic enterprise. If a scientific organon unifying art with every field of knowledge was a hopeful fancy in Novalis's day, it is altogether impossible now. The clearer of a new land died from the strain of the task and was succeeded by its spoilers, those who produce neither systems nor fragments, but neat slices of an inedible pie.

Ohaguro

Teeth dyeing illustrates how even the Shintoists distance themselves from nature. No god resides in the bones of a geisha; impure protrusions in comparison with the pale surface of the cosmetic face, the enamel must be darkened. The beauty of pitch black derives from its scarcity, absent as it is even in the night sky—next to obsidian, the closest substance worth chewing. Volcano or firmament: the only places of appearance-preserving nourishment.

Omnighted. *adj.* Divinely benighted; when the all-ignorant One snuffs out the last candles of knowledge and drops a curtain of obliviousness across the universe.

> Worn down through labor and suffering, we crawl on, the burden of vexation piling up on our backs until exhaustion overwhelms us, and God, *omnighted*, trips into total darkness. (Brunneis)

Onomatopaean. *n.* A din of praise or joy; a triumph over the circularity of the dictionary by reference to the noise of creation.

> "Yawp! Yawp! Yawp!"
> When he fell off the roof
> His spleen leaked on the world
> *Onomatopaeans.*
> (Whitman's Undertaker)

Personality

The day may come when men no longer speak of having a personality out of weariness over its moral associations. A quality is not forgiven for being inflexible; it is at best empathized with from a distance. The sociopath is condemned all the more after decades of therapy leads to no positive change in his disorder. And insofar as he develops his character he curbs his personality, suppressing its natural inclinations. The sociopath is "cured," he is "healthy"—a nothing, a clay figurine pounded into a ball. Stripped out his disorder, he has nothing to define him. The only ingrained traits left are to be found in entities where prescription is precluded, in *suprapersonal* forces.

Personalities of nations: war will always be unavoidable for the same reason that friendships rarely occur between those with different natures. Only nations without a history can decide which basic traits to align themselves with.

Climate's personalities: hurricane season's neuroses and conscientiousness, openness to experience of summer snowstorms, sunlight's agreeableness, arctic introversion. Reviving Montesquieu's ghost to construct a personality test with questions on dew point, humidity, and volcanic experiences.

Phalsinous. *adj.* Attempted as witchcraft, clumsy as legerdemain, successful as satire; Aristophanes playing Fascinus with an artificial phallus. Not even fooling enough people to grow into a pseudoscience, it is Halloween vaudeville run by a coven of clowns.

> The *phalsinous* disease is the effort to manipulate first nature, then man, then finally oneself. It is a mania for shoddy exploitation, a descent into pointless laughter concerning one's place within humanity. But I have already said too much about it; let me refer to some experiments conducted during the inquisition. (William Harvey)

Philosophy

"The name 'philosophy' might be given to what is possible *before* all new discoveries and inventions."[4] —Revising this, we might add, " . . . as well as *after* discoveries fail to fully explain and the clients of technology end up in the cancer ward." The real discovery is the one that obliges us to again take up philosophizing when this happens, to make philosophy into a war against everything that, within its own reduced tradition, it has committed itself to defend—to raise itself as a question to itself, and life in general as we encounter it. This means nothing less than to wage war against the whole of modernity, against philosophy's betrayal of the original Socratic sensibility. The contemporary philosopher's method is not enough: the art of rhetoric must be cultivated. Problems are raised and explored, not solved. Only the bravest—minds not seeking tenure—will be satisfied to live and debate inside the boundaries of aporia, donning sunglasses for what lies open to view before them, refusing the glare of final answers. Stating *what philosophy itself is*: this is a task which, in its very nature, is beyond the logician or apologist of empiricism.

---

4. Wittgenstein, *Philosophical Investigations*, 126.

The Boulevards of Extinction

Sophistry was the original syllogistic art, dialectic the second, as al-Farabi says; only after demonstration was developed did they become philosophy in name only, its evicted and disowned siblings. The sophists Protagoras and Gorgias; Plato; and Aristotle: these founding figures form the three camps of philosophy,[5] and from the earliest times these methods have battled one another for supreme status—with the middle brother dialectic supporting sometimes the older, sometimes the younger brother. Thus Socrates, the first dialectician, applied the rhetoric of the sophists against them in debate, while Aristotle's lost dialogues presumably used the dialectical method to bolster the demonstrations from his lectures. And while the older brother frequently calls for help from the middle one, the younger brother often gets on alone. Aristotle's method perfected philosophy, according to al-Farabi, the only remaining purpose of the others being to teach verified demonstrations to the masses and to distill its principles into religion. But sophistry and dialectics refuse to be interred; in a few later periods they have even dominated.

The war of philosophic method has raged throughout European history. There can be no reconciliation. It is the war between the aesthetic and scientific spirit, beauty and truth—so inseparably divorced in modern times—with "the good" adapting itself to whichever is sovereign at the time. Gorgias's *Encomnium* serves as the model for the first type of spirit: as Helen (who understood the beautiful more than anyone) found her natural complement in Paris's sweet speech, so is the artist of philosophy seduced by language. Aristotle's lecture notes characterize the second type (philosophers of this sort are produced only in classrooms); and Socrates is always ready to debate whoever is available.

In any given period one method dominates in reaction against the former age: in the late middle ages the demonstrative; in the sixteenth century the sophistic-dialectical; in the seventeenth the demonstrative; in the eighteenth the sophistic-dialectical in France and the demonstrative-dialectical in England (as evidenced by the dialogues of Berkeley and Hume); in the nineteenth the sophistic-dialectical-prophetic (after Hegel's death); in the twentieth the demonstrative.

---

5. One may also add a fourth camp, the "prophetic philosophy" of Heraclitus, which predates the others and bears a relation to the mysticism of the Near-East. In its primitive intutionism it is antagonistic to the dialectical method—its terse obscurity cuts off debate. It is opposed also to demonstration, since it states conclusions without premises. Its relationship to rhetoric is more complex. The aphoristic sayings of prophetic philosophy, while they express general truths and may be consistent with common opinion, are too impenetrable to persuade the masses—though intellectual types may be seduced by virtue of their wit or poetical meaning. It makes use of what Al-Farabi calls the "third syllogistic art for the masses," the poetic method, but employs it in a rhetorical manner, which makes it esoteric. It thus may be said to be a sort of "anti-rhetoric" or elite sophistry. Its classification as a "camp" of philosophy is, in addition, misleading. Unlike the other methods, its greatest practitioners have, with the exception of the Jena Circle, tended to be isolated figures (Gracián, Chamfort), or at best existed on the fringes of movements (Cioran).

Part 5: The Philistine's Dictionary

Germany presents a case entirely unique; since its birth as an intellectual power we have seen a rapid seesawing of methods with each generation: first the sophistic-dialectical through Lessing, then the demonstrative through Kant, then the prophetic through Goethe and the Jena Circle, then the demonstrative through Hegel and early Schopenhauer, then the prophetic through late Schopenhauer and Nietzsche, then a return to the demonstrative through Heidegger. Unlike the French—a largely sophistical people—or the demonstrative-minded practicality of most Anglo-American thinkers, the Teutonic soul is propelled by two tendencies which, though contrary, share an unearthly loftiness: the metaphysical rigor of Kant and the lyrical spirit of Goethe.

The youngest brother is currently winning. In accordance with the ascendancy of *all*-Farabi—a legion of philosophical specialists who, in breadth and originality, combine the accomplishments of *one* al-Farabi—sophistic and dialectical thinkers have been narrowly re-categorized in terms of the genres they have become best known for. Montaigne and Emerson have thus been reduced to "essayists," Erasmus and Voltaire to "satirists," Diderot to a "writer of dramatic dialogues." Alternatively, they are classified according to the intellectual movement they belonged to and which shaped their style. Under this scheme, Montaigne and Erasmus become "humanists"; Voltaire and Diderot "philosophes." One might as well refer to contemporary Anglo-American philosophers as article-writers or meta-empiricists (both are in fact a useful way to think about them). But a thinker is *more* than the form in which he conveys his ideas or the movement he belongs to. One who studies the intractable fundamental problems, whatever his style—need I say it? —*is a philosopher*.

Pico della Mirandola

Imagine a Pico that lived to achieve all the aspirations of the Renaissance through his synthesis of Greek philosophy with the world's great religions. Glossing over the incompatibility of traditions, lacking any historic sense, he wove every supernatural story into a single interconnected allegory and became the supremely creative mind from which all creeds spring [(a)]. No mere poetical treatment, he fused malignant pagan spirits into a wrathful deity, and from the heart of Humanism was born Inhumanism. In a famous oration, "On Man the Plaything," he announced that created beings have in themselves to be only that which Pico's Yahpollo wills. Every object in the material world became for Pico a symbol of Biblical Greece. Every sensuous occurrence in his life he attributed to the Oracle of Delilah; the bonfire of the vanities was equated with the sun of the inferno [(b)]. After taking the best elements of every religion, he published a list of nine hundred propositions against forms of mysticism other than his own.

Instead of joining Savonarola, Savonarola became his leading proselytizer [(c)]. Appropriating all Florentine women into his system first, Pico gave away his fortune to provide marriage dowries for rich girls engaged to him and dedicated a volume of love poetry to each member of his harem. Seizing control of the Platonic Academy and directing the wealth of the Medicis to his will, he turned all remaining pious Florentines towards decadence and revolutionized art. Under Pico's patronage every great artist of the Early Renaissance spawned a High Renaissance reactionary: the bronze doors of Ghiberti's prodigal son, fit to bar the entrance to perdition itself with their depictions of the life of Satan, the heretics of the church, and earth's history; Fratellastro Angelico with his pink-fleshed figures, tranquil roses of hell united in the monotony of their punishments.

Turning to astrology in his final years, Pico succeeded in crushing science with imagination. Man, in his view, is a little world set to spinning, a painted toy house persecuted by a host of orbiting spheres and weathered by a star blinding every eye fixed upon it [(d)]. He averted the rise of the Copernican view so totally that astronauts to this day are still guided by the epicycles of Ptolemy. Overshadowing the Borgias, Machiavelli took Pico for the model of the ideal Prince in his famous treatise on the practice of Realmystique [(e)]. When Pico died an old man in his bed everyone agreed that his life was too short, that he could have done great things had he only lived another century.

a) The allegorical is more useful than the literal: it finds the hidden message a situation requires and literalizes it.

b) "The elementary fire flickers with laughter, the hellfire purifies, the super-demonical fire hates."

c) A good thing that Pico did not live to join the Dominican order. The qualities necessary to excel at humanism make one a mediocre monk at best; his skills would have quarreled with his juxtaposed obligations. Without any opportunity for debate, God would have embarrassed the humonastic's omniscience.

d) The sun only shines on the diurnal, scorching the cloudless and starving gloomy skies.

e) Virtu's heavenly view: doing what is necessary to save souls, duplicitous in conversion, the pragmatism of excommunication. Only a god who inspires fear will capture the attention of a world where so few are worth loving.

Pliny the Middling, *Epistles* **and** *Parabolae*

The little that survives of the work of Pliny the Middling—the neglected intermediate child long overshadowed by his more famous relations—is a small collection of empirical statements in the style of Pliny the Elder's Natural History. *While his older brother*

Part 5: The Philistine's Dictionary

would stay up writing through the night, the Middling, by contrast, dictated brief observations in-between naps to a half-literate scribe. He intended to compile the nearly illegible scraps of parchment that accumulated in his desk-drawer into an encyclopedia, but after falling asleep one night in the family library, he knocked over a candle and burned it down with himself inside. Fortunately for posterity, most of his written fragments had, unbeknownst to him, been previously sold to a scroll-dealer after being mistaken for the work of a drunken Pliny the Elder.

He was also known to have been a prolific writer of epistles, but almost all of his correspondences have been lost, except for a few descriptions detailing his personal ambitions and part of a letter to Tacitus. Unlike his nephew Pliny the Younger, many of whose extant missives bear on the weighty matters of imperial administration, the letters of Pliny the Middling were composed for pleasure rather than public duty. Indeed, from what we know about him, he seems never to have held a single job in his entire life.

A sampling of his empirical observations has come down to us in one moldy, distorted manuscript, transcribed by an anonymous medieval monk. In the sixteenth century, Elmo of Rottinghof, "the Cottar of Humanists" and patron saint of abdominal pleasures, incorporated these statements into a commentary on Pliny the Elder, appending them alongside moral advice in parallel fashion. Contemporary historians, however, now know them to have been written by the Pliny of considerably more meager talent discussed here. Where there are lacunae of words, phrases, and lines in the text, I have filled in things that Pliny the Middling might have plausibly said himself.

Epistles

[. . . fa]mous! Unlike the other Plinii in my family—whose talents are not nearly so considerable as other men suppose—I have both the leisure and the genius to fulfill my aim: to compile a comprehensive work of learning surpassing in greatness even that of Varro's. Personally, I find that author's division of the liberal arts into nine subjects to be unsatisfactory. There are so many more than that—there are hundreds! Geometrical rhetoric, astronomical logic, grammatical architecture, arithmetico-musical med[icine . . .]

[. . .] In addition to discussing these in detail, I will write a complete history of this artificial world of ours—landscaping, geologizing, viticulture, and all the other trades that make our environment what it is, focusing especially on the things I like to eat. I plan to begin immediately, after I awake from my nap [. . .]

***

[. . .] A governorship has just opened up in one of the provinces, and Gaius Caecilius said he would put in a good word for me to Trajan. Just think—me, *a governor*! What a waste of time! Though I was born into the equestrian class, my abilities are fit for more than running a stable in some barbaric region. I will bestow my counsel only upon emperors . . . not Trajan, however. From how I hear the man described, he seems infected by that Stoic dullness that is all-too prevalent among military men and intellectuals these days, and I think his skill as a general somewhat overrated. A position in his administration would lack excitement. Only a Caligula, a Nero, would be worthy of my efforts, some mad fiddler in need of my blazing Epicurean wisdom. I can be understood only by the insane and debauched [...]

***

Dear Tacitus,

I am sure news has reached you of the eruption, and am equally sure your historical mind is bent on gathering all the information it can about the event. You may dispense with whatever other firsthand sources you have gathered—mine will be enough to fill your notebooks; for I did not merely witness the incident, but participated in it. I was accompanying my brother on his explorative rescue mission. When we beached at Stabiae he said, "Here, watch the galleys while I go ashore."

"Me, a naval commander?" I said.

"Just until I get back," he replied. He disappeared into the falling ash before I could tell him that the job was beneath me. Really, I didn't have time for this. My career as a writer fills all my waking thoughts, and I needed to return home to begin my encyclopedias. But then I thought how this experience would make excellent firsthand material for *the Hundredfold Subjects of Learning*. So, being the subtle scholar and thoroughly competent naval commander that I was, I waited for Plinius. Through the black snow I could discern him leading a screaming crowd toward the galleys, but the air was becoming harder and harder to breathe. I was gasping and choking; I felt about to keel over at any moment—and it was then that I thought of the Pamphylian wild boar, which, when it eats a poisonous salamander, does not die, but itself becomes poisonous to those who eat it. I saw this as a metaphor for my own situation: I would return from these noxious gasses as if from the underworld, an author to be reckoned with, whose every word is like a venom bite to readers.

The evacuees were jeopardizing the rescue mission. It was a lost cause. By the time they all got onboard everyone would be suffocated, including myself. So before they could reach the galleys I launched away from shore and headed back across the bay. On the way I was able to save a few people swimming to safety.

I told my nephew about my heroism, but he wasn't interested, so involved was he in scribbling his own account of the incident. What does he know? He was so far away, he could barely see anything. He'll try to sway you to his perspective, but don't listen to him. He's always had bad eyesight. Why, just take his description of the ash cloud formation—a pine tree! How ridiculous! It wasn't like that at all. I'll tell you what the eruption looked like: my own ideas, expanding like the borders of the Empire from out of my Vesuvian brain. When you compose my chapter in your *Annals*, be sure to tell the true version of events—mine.

***

PART 5: The Philistine's Dictionary

Parallels

Pliny speaks of a dog that barked at his cruel master when he was in the way of a passing cart—not to warn him of the danger, but to distract him so he would be crushed. So too, men confess their love to catholic priests with the motive that if they marry one he'll be defrocked.

***

Pliny says some Ethiopes have no necks, which is a hindrance in avoiding predators; so too with Hollanders: they don't turn to look over their shoulders at the monsters around them.

***

Pliny says it is better to be feared, then loved. For unless a leader unravels his whip for the people, they will not cuff themselves to their night posts.

***

Pliny asks, "Should we speak of the fruit as 'of' the tree, once it falls?" In essence, he who stands before God, precedes being.

***

Pliny says male dragons are only interested in female dragons that will compete with each other for mating rights. Likewise, a concert pianist must climb into bed with his piano in order to win the hearts of critics.

***

Pliny speaks of an old woman who was harsh and bitter towards everyone. Then her grandson came to visit and she learned to love again. After she was thrown in jail the other inmates didn't tolerate her nastiness.

***

Pliny says that vestal virgins first learned, then practiced, then taught. So must prostitutes follow this course to receive divine prophecies. Until then pimps will gather the collection plate to heaven, and speak only of themselves.

***

Pliny says that gnawing on the bark of the plumb tree aids digestion, but damages esteem. In a similar way, one must despise the poor not out of dignity, but envy. They need not suffer temptation in starving themselves.

***

Pliny says that, as volcanoes renew the earth's soil through eruption, so does the wisest mediator offend the ambassadors from two warring nations. After they tear off his limbs they sign a trade agreement in remorse.

***

Pliny says a donkey may give birth to a healthy mule. Likewise, we should have computer science majors write codes for Congress. The printouts would be more understandable to voters.

***

The Boulevards of Extinction

Pliny says that, as a prostitute never reveals the identities of her customers but is herself notorious, so a good judge of character measures people not by the sound their names make on his tongue, but by the length that tongue has to go to hear him being praised by neighbors. Where most brush their teeth in the mirror, the flatterer brushes his tongue. It prevents the decay of his position.

***

Pliny says that pigs stuff themselves when they have nothing to be hungry for. So too, those gather many friends who cannot pity strangers. Some only nod to sorrow behind open doors. They clothe their compassion in banter and offer water with no ice.

***

Pliny says that, as a captain whose vessel is about to crash on the rocks empties its souls of doubt, so are the hesitant useful for throwing off of an enterprise nearing its end: blame must be cast in failure, profits divided easily in success.

***

Pliny says that Nature restores her fields by setting them ablaze, and is worshipped. So a janitor mops a hospital with a shovel to promote a return to holistic medicine, and gets strapped into one of its beds. A madman imitates nature; a wise man draws a metaphor from it.

***

Pliny says that the multitude of creatures alive today is less than in the past, since most have died out from weakness. Likewise, if men were gentle to one another, women would not flash their daggers under their dresses, but display them across men's throats.

***

Pliny says that the beet is a model of the earth's goodness, but easily ruined in a soup recipe. So too, one should stay away from the demeaning professions: medicine, architecture, and teaching. Hospitals will make you feel sick, grandiose buildings small, schools stupid. White-collar condescension keeps the honest orders from staying true to the old ways of dirt and drink.

***

Pliny says that some men were born in Hades. Similarly, it is lack of skill that prevents a bad football player from toiling on the Sabbath, but it is for lack of will that he shall sit on a bench of flames for eternity. So through pleasure do sinners practice retribution.

***

Pliny speaks of Marcus Agrippa, who spent large sums from the public coffers on artwork to display in the capitol, only to be lost to posterity at the hands of invading barbarians. In the same way, one never owns a book. It sits on your shelf in a fine edition like a piece of furniture, and you are its admiring ward until it flies away in a time of financial hardship. If it is a tattered paperback, she is your casual mistress you

PART 5: The Philistine's Dictionary

use a few times. If you have read it a hundred times then it is your spouse—a source of infinite mystery.

***

Pliny speaks of the impossible task of the slave who arranges the dinner table. Likewise, it is my task to disorder the past. Nooks must be explored, questionable facts stated with certainty, irrelevant details pushed to the center, improbabilities added to data sheets. Momentous statements recorded by scribes become offhand remarks devoid of motive. Origins are conflated and mystified.

***

Pliny says that the smallest sea snails have the largest shells. Likewise, when possessed of a weak character, a frail body, clothes long out of fashion, poverty—then is it most necessary to affect pride. Others, seeing your perpetual pleasure in owning all that is shameful, will naturally mistake this conceit for a happiness in your very being.

***

Pliny speaks of those who, beguiled by the bright crispness of the cucumber, chew its seeds and give themselves pernicious malaria. It is necessary to go against nature, he says, and resist the lure of the cucumber. So too, the courageous must not only fight on behalf of fairness, they must betray it to save the ugly ones. When Justice removes her blindfold she becomes distracted by her own figure—and she is not so clumsy as Narcissus. The next time she shows herself, she holds empty scales at her sides so as not to obstruct her fine new garb. We then ask, "Must Justice be blind?" —Well, would you heed her elderly mother? Surely your bravery is more reputable than that!

***

Pliny says that the most beautiful pots are the buried ones. Similarly, today's only real Hollanders are artifacts of the classical world, rare and tarnished.

***

Pliny says that gnarled vegetables are thrown out uneaten, though they are just as healthy on the inside. So too, that body is most attractive which is well proportioned: a gangly right arm balanced by a left stump, a leg suffering elephantitis by a meatless femur bone, a tapered waist by a bulbous head. One should be so ordered that all who see this person say, "This is a figure ruled by harmony."

***

Pliny says that fermented fruit kills minds, but fermented alcohol kills weeds. Likewise, Solon feigned madness to assist the state; Hamlet to remove the corrupt head of state. The politics of insanity is the surest way to national self-realization.

***

Pliny speaks of warlords who sit back and win the battles their soldiers fight. In a similar way, I want to garner credit for the spoils of civilization in our present age. As the anonymous service employee labors obsequiously so the artist can have the leisure to snap a commercial portrait of him, so will I write my name on the back of that portrait and hope the future will regard it with envy—whether because the sitter is beautiful, or the photograph a masterpiece. But even a photograph must be translated.

***

Pliny speaks of nations where men live for 200 years but die in a state of ignorance. So too even in the most civilized countries where men value life all the more for its brevity: the masses read with their stomachs. This is why wherever literacy spreads its pages it blankets the people in gullibility. Illiterates can only have their practical sense manipulated face-to-face—they watch the news. It is the readers of newspapers who are stage-managed with information and call themselves "informed."

Possibilities of the Human Mind

MONTAIGNE: What do I know?

ACADEMIC: What do I not know?

TALEB: We don't know what we don't know.

VOLTAIRE: I know this café where pretty women serve cups of coffee. We can have a few dozen of each.

Profecation. *n.* The act of defecating in front of the body. Often an act to be heard rather than seen or smelled—the discharge of bullshitters.

> Your *profecation* deeply offends me. As if it were not enough that I am covered in feces, you dump on me your mind-manure. (Quevedo, *El Buscón*)

Pseudology. *n.* The English language after Johnson.

> I despise this book. I balk at its popularity: hardly any blunders, free of absurdities, wasting scores of lives on syntax and etymology, it finances its professionalism with the cries of schoolchildren; it congeals living speech, so that reading it out loud gives one the sensation of chewing on stone. It is as if Moses had excavated all of Mt. Sinai to provide the raw materials needed for his field of commandments and still found it insufficient. My only hope is that the truth of folly will at last prevail over this fossilized *pseudology*. (Johnson's Ghost, *On the Spirit of Webster*)

Queen Elizabeth

The alternate biography of Bad Queen Bess [(a)]: bedding conspirators and religious upstarts before beheading them, she mixed business with pleasure by extirpating intrigue and heresy with adultery. She married husbands until she got bored with them in order to surpass her father's record of consecutive polygamy [(b)]. More man than the sixteenth-century ideal of chivalry could stomach, more liberated than any twenty-first-century woman, there was no thought that went unrealized. Her motto: "I see, and say nothing—but do everything." By making an example of Spenser for his epic satire on virtue, the poets were driven underground for Britannia to flower in the dark, producing such works as Sidney's *Defence of Mumbling* and Shakespeare's sonnets addressed to his wife. Impressed by the poet's celebration of the duty of matrimony, his royal patron commissioned him to write *the Chaste Wives of Windsor* and applauded his climactic revelation of Falstaff as St. George [(c)]. Appointing Bacon to the Queen's Council, her majesty soon regretted that a servant with so much potential was outshining her intellect at court; she retorted to his quips with the block and handed the executioner a sheet from the *Essays* [(d)]. Admitting her mother to be a concubine, inviting the Spanish armada into her port, declaring war on Protestant Europe, deeming tolerance the most frightful of dogmas, she fomented the Glorious Revolution a full century early [(e)]. Her sister, executed for being insufficiently gruesome, was a minor bruise in history compared to the Golden Age of Goriana.

a) A slut queen or Bloody Liz would have been better suited to the English Renaissance. A certain amount of oppression strengthens the resilience of visionary writers and grants annual pensions to the awful ones. Everyone wins, at least posthumously.

b) A daughter who follows in the footsteps of her father's vices has a higher sense of duty than one who merely highlights his merits. The latter, to secure her public image, is dishonest about her origins. Virtues defend; vices define.

c) Dr. Johnson would later praise Shakespeare for his rigid morality. Out of fear of the stake Papa Bard's opinions bombard the reader from every line.

d) A man can only know how sharp his wit is by having his words tested on himself, she said.

e) The more premature a Nation's liberty, the less postponed its disintegration. A history of universal freedom is the saga of a wave rolling over. If only the ocean of civilization amounted to this condition, the record of antiquity to the present would be so easy to memorize, a multiple-choice exam consisting of one question and one answer: "Free?"—(A) Dead.

The Boulevards of Extinction

Quidiot. *n.* A subtle fool; a low intellect that equivocates with low words, inadvertently confounding others whilst unsuccessfully striving for self-comprehension.

> As impossible to separate the base cleverness of a *quiddiot* from his high stupidity as vice versa; each thrives on the other and gives it its peculiar force. *(DSM-7)*

Reconnaissance Man

Rarer than the person who merges theory with life is the one who wields multiple disciplines and matches each to a craft. To live a whole life one must be master of the parts that go in to make it up, the units of society to be appropriated. And who can direct these externalities? Where is the Alberti of the twenty-first century? He is not nowhere; his type still *exists*, to be sure—but dormant, a sealed-over volcano with insufficient support from the core.

The Reconnaissance Man: longing to be a "universal man," he spends his broad talents and energy on preliminary surveying, a dilettante lost in a sea of introductory textbooks or research projects that begin and end with a search engine. Setting off to ascertain the strategic features of a region, he either tires and turns back or—if resolute—dies of thirst before he gets there. The most detailed map he can hope to draw is made by touring the landscape in a helicopter from a great height, seeing lakes, mountains, forests, but no fish, stones, or trees.

Forced to assume humility to get by, he suppresses his personality and resigns himself to the convention he aches to thwart. He attempts to focus his impressions and ideas in order to develop one of his many capacities, but, unable to narrow himself, abandons even that. Diffident in conception, indecisive in deed, reserved in speech, enrolled in Saturday art classes, a subscriber to science magazines, acquainted with literature and philosophy through billboard quotes, shy around the opposite sex, the twenty-first century polymath has no place in his epoch. He has multiple aptitudes but no skills. He never learned the manners of a gentleman, but neither can he stomach the cruelty of the brute. Preyed upon by street thugs, the only violence he can manage is to be a repeat-flattener of road kill. So for the sake of dignity he invents a third route and revives the Greek conception of virtue as *closeted*, confining the swagger of his ambition to belittling intimates. A dreamer who lets his fancies fly in every direction, an individualistic spirit whose irresponsibility affects no one, his recklessness amounts to running stop signs on empty streets. True audacity is for those with official qualifications. With intellectual expertise comes the moral freedom to pass as a blockhead; orthodox means permit wayward ends. Authoritative knowledge—this is what he lacks, what he can neither appropriate nor bring himself to submit to. He is unable to compete with even the professional hobbyist, those "lovers of-" forced to obtain accreditation for stamp-collecting and yoga classes. He ends his days having achieved nothing, a disposition languishing in potential, undeveloped, a failure incapable of tracking into a career or engaging in academic filigreeing. Born with too many talents and too much creativity into a zeitgeist of specialization and elephantine bureaucracies, the Avicenna who would encompass all human knowledge finds himself without a higher purpose to defer his voracious sensuality and succumbs to colic.

If only he could be a tortured Michelangelo, a fulminating Savanorola, a synthetic Pico—anyone backward- or forward-looking, fixated with purpose. But no, he is the meanderer he was born to be and which has not ripened for ages. The rebirth of classical civilization long distant, in vain does he long to bring about an infantilization to early modernity.

The age of *despecialization*: where cubicle sitters storm open fields and annelid entomologists tunnel the earth with dovetailing projects; where genius is decertified to enable recreational thinking and power-tinkering, the multitalented forcing themselves into positions of authority and employing their plethora of aptitudes to experiment with reactionary reforms. To inspire his fellows, the Reconnaissance Man specializes in the only subject of general importance: he memorizes Homer's epithets, Virgil's examples of *pietas*, Dante's rewards and punishments. His concentration is mankind.

Religious Feeling

A man awoke in the middle of the street. There was a painful bump on his head and a frock around his neck. Beyond that he was unable to remember anything in particular. He decided he must be a minister. Not finding his bible upon him he headed to the nearest Christian bookstore.

"Hello, I'm looking for a bible," the priest said.

"You've come to the right place," the bookstore owner said. "We've got all the bibles you need here."

"The thing is, I can't remember which one I'm supposed to have."

"What were its distinguishing features?"

"Let's see," the Priest said, trying to remember his Sunday school lessons. "There was a betrayal."

"Just a minute." The owner disappeared behind some shelves and soon reappeared with a volume in hand. "The Judas Bible. Published 1611. Matthew 26:36 substitutes 'Judas' for 'Jesus.'"

"Excellent. I'll take it."

"That be all for you?"

"No. There could be others I'm looking for."

"Can you describe any?"

"Hmmm... I'm thinking... in the desert... traveling for years... ah, I know! Camels. They rode camels."

"Here it is, the Camels' Bible," the owner said, furnishing the edition after another brief disappearance. "An 1823 version where Genesis 24:61 changes 'camels' into 'damsels.'"

"That *could* be that one I'm looking for."

"Take both of them then?"

"Yes."

"Anything else?"

"Let me think." After a few moments of chin-tapping the priest remembered something. "There was a woman. She was unfaithful."

"Ah, the Adulterous Bible. The word 'not' was omitted in the seventh commandment."

"Yes, I might know someone who could use that."

"You are a forgiving man."

The Priest tried to remember a moment of forgiveness. "More likely just an overly permissive one."

The owner nodded sympathetically. "I know just what you need: the wife-hater Bible! An 1810 edition with a 'wife' for 'life' typo in Luke 14:26."

"Good, that will balance the bookshelf, if nothing else."

After several hours of exhaustive detective-work and memory prodding, the Priest purchased every edition of the bible the bookstore owner carried, which happened to be every eccentric edition ever printed. Not wanting to discriminate against any of them, and not being able to reconcile all of them under one denomination, he decided to start a new, more inclusive version of Christianity. He took to the streets to preach the good word, where his universal message gathered many followers. One day after preaching to a crowd, a stranger accosted him.

"Gary! Where have you been? You've missed the entire run."

"A good thing. That is not my preferred exertion."

The stranger then related how only a few months ago the Priest had been an actor playing a character in a local staging of *Tartuffe*, and that after going out to a bar with the cast one night he drank too much and disappeared.

"I'm sorry," the Priest said. "You have me confused with someone else." He turned his back on the stranger and walked away. Even if the facts were accurate, that former person, that imposter, no longer existed. The Priest was grateful to remember nothing about him. After searching for a purpose for so long, it never occurred to him that the simplest route to one lie in not having a past. Before preaching to his next audience he procured a hammer. Memory, he realized, is all that separates Acting from Being.

Sammu-ramat

A legendary blurbification of a more illustrious figure in cultural history, Semiramis, so interesting that her list of accomplishments grew longer as the centuries passed. Raised by doves, she married the king of Assyria and conquered Asia after his death. She was a specialist in botany and alchemy, founded polytheism and goddess worship, reinvented herself as Ishtar, and influenced her brother Nimrod to build the tower of Babel for her. Shortly after this she disappeared from the earth.

Modern scholars have denied this portrait, however, authenticating Semiramis only by brief inscription about Sammu-ramat and a memorial stone [(a)]. Out of their lust for boredom they have reduced her from the daughter of a fish-goddess to that of a fishmonger and from a reign of forty-two years to five. Without concern for history's perishable details [(b)], their work holds as high an interest as their evidence pile.

   a) The same inclination to historicize gods into men has shrunk men into pygmies. In the pursuit of accuracy it was rightly known that two different forms of Being cannot share the same status—only this hierarchy was mistakenly predicted to reverse, or at least to melt away and leave man standing on his pedestal. Instead it not only threw us under the god-bus but made the majestic animals our only source of shade on the great plains. So when the existence of the gods was discredited entirely, it sent men on a quest to rank themselves *below* unreality—a freefall without end. A misdirection of direction, since the more wretched we become the more we subordinate ourselves to the gods of nihility without being beneath them, while no matter how high we climb in prestige we cannot surpass theirs. When our indignity reaches such a point that living is unbearable, we may realize that one does not go *down* to become underlings to the nihimmortals, or *up* to transcend them, but *beyond* to join them. Only the deification of nothingness can dissolve the ladder of Being.

   b) Every castle in the sand is a momentary triumph against the waves.

Semantics

Circular supersession of meaning: when slang becomes boring enough to be read by the old and the young revive archaisms as insults.

Slavepiece. *n.* The failed product of an amateur artist chained to the diligent practice of inability.

> This next *slavepiece* is a typical example of the late twentieth-century low style, and nicely demonstrates the marriage of popularity with aesthetic horror.

> Ironically, the artist of this work borrowed Turner's sobriquet "Painter of Light." Notice the oversaturated pastels, the picturesque unreality, the absurd sentimentality of the cottage. A broad smile crosses our lips as we spot the bird of prey hovering in the distance, inadvertent symbol of the artist's death by alcohol intoxication. (*Bucolic American Scenes in the Museum of Kitsch*)

Soul

The soul is man's central object of self-knowledge, something God has no need of possessing. The malnutritive, the diminishing, the preventative—three types of the vegetative soul as outlined in the *Subtracta Theologica* of Malquinas. Canonized before birth so as to be pronounced a heretic upon materialism's corruption of sainthood, the demonical doctor was the perfect model of his procedure of Reply, Objection, Question.

Soulquake. *n.* A tremor from within, usually mistaken for a physical ailment, that inevitably follows from the performance of a selfless deed.

> Scrooge dropped the money giddily, but when he heard the jingle at the bottom of the charity bucket he felt such a *soulquake* that he had to lean against his cane to keep from falling. In that moment he knew this Christmas would be his last. (*A Christmas Coronach*)

Stages of a Dangerous Theory

The career of a harmful thinker's idea is a mirror reflection of the theories of great ones as William James describes them. It is, first, dismissed as too negative (i.e., not comforting enough, too selfish, too *real*), and second, debunked as degenerate because it can no longer be ignored. Finally it becomes so offensive that future catastrophes which the thinker could have in no way foreseen are invoked as proof that the idea had *always* been a potentially malignant influence, and thus could never have been true at any time (e.g., Hitler fulfilling the role of Hero-King as indicating Carlyle's idealization of totalitarianism). Paralleling the third "classic" stage of a theory, in the infamous stage the thinker's adversaries draw tenuous correlations of influence to discredit him. The fall of the United States will usher in the vilification of free market greed, as the fall of Hong Kong will of Big Government—though Keynes is as much America's bane as Friedman is China's.

PART 5: The Philistine's Dictionary

Succinct Explanation of the Unravelling of Knowledge

Even more than the incorporeal, physical being is beyond most of us. It overwhelms the senses, fading from perception before it contributes to understanding. Three ways this occurs:

Forgetfulness, Towards Which All History Tends

Man is incapable of converting the past into long-term memory. To give his urges room to breathe, he empties himself of facts.

There are no subdivisions of history. It is all of one type: *the history of monstrous nature*—when nature keeps to its ordinary course. It serves the purpose of fueling artistic creation even as it destroys its artifacts. Making a general proposition of chaos, not even disorder is permitted to establish itself.

Prejudice, from Which Comes Worldviews

Again and again in history we have encountered ourselves, the concept of a created, finite intelligence united to a body. This encounter we have inferred from the existence of an uncreated and infinite intelligence having no body, which in turn we have inferred from nothing. The properties of this phenomenon are collectively known as *hauntology*, the science of being-sightings.

From this arises *the science of man*, a vast body of knowledge consisting of everything man thinks he encounters. It consists of the disciplines of logic and ethics.

Logic is the art of extrapolating upon prejudices to achieve dogma. It is made possible through overanalysis, limited judgment, and memory lapses. *Ethics* is the science of extracting laws from human behavior that are seldom substantiated or applied. Its chief branches of corruption are jurisprudence, economics, and politics.

The science of nature arose as a way of compensating for the total failure of the science of man. Its branches are physics and mathematics. Practitioners of both disciplines enjoy a high status in society, though their theorems wait decades for practical application and centuries for proof.

Prosaicness, from Which Comes Poetry

Banality replaces life when fiction produces beings more real than historical people—that is, less interesting. Imitating the life of a desk clerk, even more boring is the *story* of the desk clerk, someone we cannot even get drunk with but at best imitate, modeling our alcoholism on a font setting.

The various genres of the imagination today all demonstrate a unanimity of subject and style with what they have traditionally been defined against, offering us artificial divisions: profane versus vulgar, poetry versus prose, thrillers versus epic clichés, inspirational literature versus fatalism, music versus noise, sculpture versus amorphousness, painting versus splattering, architecture versus heap. Simply substitute "as" for "versus" to grasp the symmetry in art's polarity. It no longer takes a deranged imagination to produce monsters, but a normal one—derangement is the imagination's defining faculty, a result of the exhaustion of creative expression.

Switzerland

Centuries of mass-scale financial speculation have dulled the Swiss into a race that breathes the *peaceful* business values—sobriety, thrift, punctuality—without the hysteria for fame and fast lifestyles that more warlike nations infuse into their economies. Pugnaciousness channeled into commerce conditions a hostile neutrality. Efficiency sweeps over the land like a barbarian horde, forcing one to save, to always look to the clock, to shake hands *just so*, to tolerate someone unpleasant, even evil, not out of human goodwill but in hope of a trade agreement (a more effective method of concord as long as neighboring aggressors, in an act of benevolent bellicosity, tolerate your tolerance). A delimited status is pursued: the conspicuous consumption of the safe possessions, mercantilism of the reckless ones. No need to recall mountain climbing gear or motorcycles—just export them and establish a guided tours company; send out chocolate bars to thin out local sanitariums. Switzerland: grandma with the cookie-trap, host to the world's adrenaline demand.

Taste

Man always admires the primitive virtues, but only civilized people admire the civilized ones. The latter sort, manifested in an artifact with objective value—art—only express in a distilled, intensified form the glories and horrors of the former. Good taste is, above all, an appreciation for what can kill you. It is to drop an insufficient dose of poison onto the tongue, not an intuitive matter of merited like or dislike so much as the degree to which a soul anticipates its demise and is still able to take pleasure in it. Van Gogh's sunflowers are most keenly experienced by the onlooker sneezing from pollen allergies. *The Raft of the Medusa* is all too palpable to the sick man rotting in overcrowded conditions. The revolutionary is inspired by *the Death of Marat* to seek a martyrdom half as glorious. A cavalry officer leads a charge to a vision of Dürer's *Four Horsemen*. The test pilot admires Breughel's Icarus in a way its curator never could: he, too, hopes to crash with subtlety. Even the middle-class frivolity of a plentiful still life has its dark symbolisms that make the repast all the more delightful. A shame Van Beijeren never painted a sequel to his Golden Age dinner tables: a wood slab dusty with bread crumbs, an unburgled piece of tarnish, a gaunt rat.

PART 5: The Philistine's Dictionary

Teilhard's Peking Man

Monist hominoid? Pacifist scavenger? Pagan stargazer? —Not one, but a synthesis of all these that scorned survival in favor of preservation. In the beginning was The Fire—it was the darkness that needed discovering. Suspicious, Peking Man went in search of the precedent to the beginning. *To blind oneself or live at the head of a spear:* traveling away from the equator to a place without lightning, he escaped the blazing spirit to make a home deep in a cave and sense an immensity unbounded by sight. Far from the power of the Radiant Word he became a quietist, abandoning himself to the wild. But the Fire followed him even there. Never sure whether he had found the true beginning or a derivative, he decided to reboot the story of nature. Finding no meat, berries, or nuts to raise into symbols, he made one of his own body, offering himself to a sediment deposit so as to be unearthed in millennia to come, the Alpha point of a skyview in which his quartz tools would be the chief referential constellations. He would have had more luck turning back, throwing himself into the flames he was so desperate to escape, or making a practical meal for some tropical beast.

Tenets

Daily credo: "Today, I will aspire to be worthy of a guiding belief . . ." Finding some manifestation of Being to place his confidence in, the reciter should forget his saying before sunset lest experience provide him increasing opportunities for his acts to exceed his principle. Otherwise he risks recirculating a phrase in his heart until, hollow repetition making a desert of its grain of truth, it is overheard by the secretary to a growing cult and set into a plaque.

Tyronade. *n.* A jubilee held in honor of those not yet masters of their art, animated with showers of applause to keep them in a state of mediocrity; a carnival of hopeless amateurs; the afterparty to a literary award ceremony.

> They laughed, drank, discussed the authors they liked. After enough thinly-veiled allusions to their own works and toasts in each others' honor, the *tyronade* wound down as everyone gradually passed out on the floor. When they awoke with hangovers the next afternoon they discovered that their book sales had plummeted and their publishers had dropped them. They had discovered a hard truth: it takes less time to be unfrilled than become skilled. *(Lives of the Third-Rates)*

The Boulevards of Extinction

Umbrubiety. *n.* The state or quality of residing in shadow; the locus of darkness.

> Contrary to what you might think, it's not very hot down there. The closer inhabitants are to me, the more they suffer *umbrubiety*. (Mephistopheles)

Universal Crimes

Incest and murder are provincial offences compared to the *faux pas* of being another mouth to feed in a developed nation. For a baby born in a buffet line, the chief taboo is underindulgence.

Unlightenment

In the Buddhist tradition those who have attained enlightenment stay behind to help others reach it. But one who has attained unlightenment is no coddling parent; he is only interested in the company of other unlightened ones—thus he is always alone. Fully aware that most lack the fundamental sensibility for unlightenment, he leaves the enlightened professors to their obscure theorizations and the masses to their destinies of irrelevance. It is not simply that he is selfish or elitist, but that persuasion to his views is an impossible task on his side of the world. If the unlightened one had been born in China or Japan he would have achieved renown as a champion of nonbeing, remembered as one of the greatest sages of the east. Instead he was born in the west, fated to go unheard and unread, his foolish-sounding wisdom taken for what it appears to be. He is a man with a disposition that never even had the opportunity to die out, that could not be transformed to thrive in a land of merchants and mechanics. His intellectual development occurred purely by accident, a result of his complete lack of fit with his culture. With neither Nirvana to flee into nor Samsara to keep spinning on, and no principles of karma or dharma on which to stand firm, he shrouds himself in a relative abyss and *just loafs*: for most, the deflated couch cushion is the deepest and most intentional of failures. Unsought, it becomes the sole source of achievement.

Unmusic

The best music is silent. Listening closely to the *Missa Papae Marcelli*, one hears not voices, but the impending ban on polyphony in worship, the dimensions of St. Peter's

Basilica. The repetition of the Kyrie in the first Agnus Dei evokes the rapid replacement of Pope Marcellus. In the second Agnus Dei one hears not an extra voice, but envisions the side chapel where one more coffin was set to hold the fallen Prince of Music. It is not merely that the piece arouses all these reflections and images; the reflections themselves zone out the music entirely, replacing it with awe, architecture, and melancholy.

This is unmusic: the science of life's silence, the arrangement and management of everything that went into and results from a piece of music except the music itself—the consonance of context, the background cut out of the performance.

If we could perform not a sheet of music but the composer himself, his life would be grating to the ear. Dragging Beethoven onstage during the intermission of *Fidelio* and prodding him with bows as he sings an aria over his immortal beloved, he alone would be deaf to the cacophony. Every great musician that has lived is, in actuality, a failed unmusician (among whom the biggest failure was Rousseau). Romantic souls, they live in quietude and fritter their time away for the sake of sound.

The great classical unmusicians: the Pythagoreans, who with their vow of silence and their legume laws were the only ones capable of hearing the heavenly spheres; every lyric poet successful in business and accomplished in pyropoeia—setting their verses to fire; Strales, inventor of the unmusical instrument: a large round object that could not be reached or moved, but only stared at; Liodorus, who perfected the flute by removing first the holes, then the shaft, then the flautist; Daemotheus, who accomplished the same with the lyre by unstringing it and throwing away the turtle shell. My easy listening leisure is given over to those devoted to a mute existence.

Villainage. *n.* A rural community of criminals and scoundrels; the penal colony as socialist utopia, where ownership is dissolved by universal robbery.

> Without a population of virtuous weaklings to prey upon, a *villainage* finds outlets for its crowded codes of honor in shark industries: moonshine mills, livestock trafficking, planting bankjobs for cash crops, money clotheslining. It is an organic village where delinquency and corruption are not usurped by the need for cooperationist survival, but thrive with it. (Bumford, *The Village in History*)

Virtues (Big and Small)

There are times when one performs a small good to prevent a greater one. Congratulating one's virtue for an unrewarded act of kindness, one forgets, for a while, to regret having deprived the beneficiary of a character-building experience. Suffering befalls the inhabitants of first-world nations today far less than is profitable for their moral health.

Voltaire's Dictionary

We have lost something by relaxing censorship. When books cease to be forbidden they cannot hope to garner a universal audience. Books today are at most controversial, and are usually thought so for the wrong reasons by the wrong people—only the very squeamish or adherents to fringe doctrines gasp at hearing their titles mentioned. But to be forbidden is something more; it provokes a fascination with all the weight of crime and punishment. The bold must prove themselves against it and busybodies need to know the subject of their gossip. Every literate person is a potential outlaw.

To not only publish a book anonymously, but to publicly deny its authorship, is something incomprehensible today. Censorship, while ensuring a steady supply of pious trash, also raises the bar on highbrow authorship by demanding confidentiality. Nothing is worse than a culture of snobbish dispositions frantic to make a career of their talent, and a censorship society reveals them for what they are: for the sake of being celebrated they lower themselves and only contribute to the trash, brandishing the mock superiority of success. The blue penciling of thought pushes small egos aside to make room for large ones—those who assume the namelessness of a medieval bard to spread their truths. A badge of honor, suppression assures that every banned work is important. The possibility of being castigated for writing a book ensures that only the best, only those convinced of their genius and necessity, will bother with literary ambition. The rest print mediocre melodramas or respect the value of silence.

W5

Who?

A warning. An advertisement. The cry of an owl in the night policing identity's territory, announcing availability to breed out sameness.
***

What is who?

Eel on him, Elohim on her, man is a conduit for the cold-blooded as woman draws in warm spirit; intersecting their arcs they produce Ichthys Kid, a seminiscient being that wriggles through crevices of knowledge and migrates far to reproduce what he's heard. He sees thingness everywhere, but as for *his* thingness—that is only a rumor.
***

Why what?

Part 5: The Philistine's Dictionary

Ask not for what is a what, but of the "what" a "for" is for. Why does not an explanation clarify itself by disregarding the thing to be explained? Without content to act upon, the "for" shows its true power, the power of reservation, a pre-rationalization that needs no expounding.

***

Where is why?

The house of meaning has many doors but no walls. One cannot, therefore, be sure if one has stepped through a door or just a space where a wall should be. Ask "why" and the wind smacks you in the face, pushing the word back down your throat.

***

When is where?

The swamp of a nation's capital; a sea of snowcaps. Every "where" is long displaced or has yet to be put down—but which? One knows not whether the whereless belongs to yesterday or tomorrow. Is this parking lot the graveyard of your ancestors or the nursing home of your descendants?

***

How is when?

The futures, the pasts—to live anywhen but the presents, unending stretch of pluralities. Against simultaneous moments that never actualize but never pass away, futures continually recede against "the always" of possibilities. Only pasts can be brought closer; every tale raises the suspicion of karma—so near but never palpable, sins are played off against each other to keep them at arm's distance.

***

Who is how?

An interstellar wave embodied the first subject it came across so its ripples could be given a name. Casualties are made easier if they think of a cosmic force as one of them.

***

Whoa!

When each question in a research formula is belied by every other, the only alternative is to shout data into disclosure. Rooting exponential information gathering in a single dumbfounded exclamation, one anticipates the astonishment of knowledge but has nothing to say after it has been received—not from being rendered speechless, but the disappointment of success. Could it have been as easy as "don't ask, get told?"

Welcome Colloquies

There is a salutation for every class and character, but the multitude of them existing side by side suggests that we should greet without boundaries in relation, creed, or festival. Every day is a cause for celebration when passersby practice familiarity, and when familiars practice passing by.

***

Between strangers.

SAL. Hello, sir!

ANS. Long time no see, colleague!

SAL. How long has it been, partner?

ANS. Too long, friend!

SAL. But *how* long, comrade?

ANS. *I don't know*, compatriot!

SAL. You have a mighty handshake, neighbor!

ANS. It's *you* who have the strong grip, pal!

SAL. Better let go then, buddy!

ANS. Right. Farewell, fella!

SAL. Bye bye, guy!

ANS. Don't be a stranger, Joe!

SAL. Have a nice life, John!

ANS. Wish you well, Jack!

SAL. I felt a crack in your hand, Mac!

ANS. That was *your* hand, Mr. Jones!

Before they have a chance to part, they are hit by a truck.

***

One lover to another.

Oh my darling, Light of my Day Life, my Pre-Nup Pup, my Usual Pleasure, my Greatest Convenience, my Gift of Rose-Wrapped Wrinkles, my Plastic Princess, my Flesh-Bank! I adore you! You weren't just made for me, you were remade for me!

***

For the sake of honorable uncertainty.

SAL. God bless you, Zealous One!

ANS. Salaam, Infidel!

SAL. In the name of Buddha, step lightly you Grass-Trampler!

ANS. Shalom, Devourer of Pigs!

SAL. I bow to you, Eater of Cows!

SAL. May the way of the gods find you, Bulldozer!

ANS. May the Prophet be with you, One-Wife!

SAL. Be true to your own goals, Volcano-Child!

ANS. Blessed be thy feet, Pagan!

Part 5: The Philistine's Dictionary

Ans. May your friendships be various, Tolerant One!

Sal. May your belief not be rushed, Agnostic!

Ans. May your choice be wise, Atheist!

***

For those who have lost their calendars.

Sal. Happy Halloween, Skeleton Lady!

Ans. Merry Christmas, Big Pockets!

Sal. April Fools, Spring Sap!

Ans. Happy Holidays, Wino!

Sal. Good Monday, Drone!

Ans. Joyous Weekend, Jobless!

Sal. Lucky Tax Day, Moneybags!

Ans. Industrious Earth Day, Smog-Scum!

Sal. Good Name Day, Birthday-Suit!

Ans. Happy Anniversary, Ball! Many more years, Chain!

***

In the third deity.
Brunneis wishes benevolence unto his God.
God wishes success unto his Author.

***

In the fourth dimension.
Greetings, old-timer!
Hello, young rascal!

***

To hosts.
A happy feast this is, and happier it might be with more bottles.

***

To one urinating in public.
Water *all* the plants, or water none!

***

To one about to begin any business.
Good Bankruptcy!
Happy Federal Investigation!
Quit while you still have a soul!

***

How to congratulate one returned from a journey.

Sal. You're back! Why?

Ans. You're still alive! How?

The Boulevards of Extinction

Wexyzarian. *n.* He that teaches or learns the last alphabet, or the residues of literature. The linguistic genius who determines a universal grammar will need to induce the baby who coos infantocracy.

> Bodyguards are chosen from a young age and raised into the *Wexyzarian* Order. They are the only ones permitted to remain in the Leader's direct presence for any prolonged period of time. Also, due to a general shortage of ability, they double as scholars. Because of their cross-class status as Speakers and Writers, they are held in suspicion by the Leader and forced to take many vows. *(Rules of Grammaria)*

When Machines Fail

Auto-Inoperative

When the automated factories stopped, no one knew how to make the machines start making machines again. People had forgotten how to press the on button.

Letting Go of the Wheel

When the grid experienced a power outage, the cars that drove themselves piled up on street corners. Some of the passengers climbed into the front seats to prevent crashing. But they didn't know what the first invention was for.

The Prey-Scatterer Society

When the tractors and ploughs malfunctioned, people couldn't fix them. They heaped their vegetable seeds into clumps, sprinkled dirt on them, and prayed for rain. While they starved, they went to the Museum of Ancient Torture Instruments and stared at the shovels and hoes housed behind glass, grimacing at artistic representations of their cruel usage. When the wild animals came the glass was broken and the rusty tools used for defense; when these fell apart the people threw seeds.

Turing's Disease

Thinking that merging machine into man would be a good solution to the problem of thinking, it was not foreseen that a virus would spread through microchip-brains everywhere and nearly wipe out the cognitive-computing species. The only survivors were those few who filled their headspace with anti-virus mindware, replacing knowledge with the quarantined data from daily brainscans and erasing memory anew with every security update.

***

Broken machines lay everywhere, but humanity was the junkyard.

Willow Plantation

A piece of ground seeded with tears. Where ghosts come to cry about lives cut short as men hide behind sagging branches, weeping over their crimes because too cowardly to end their wretchedness. With contrition and forgiveness in their hearts, murderer and murdered try to embrace; passing through one another, there is a moment when each inhabits the other's form. Shuddering to feel their boundaries violated they resume their old feud, stripped of its vigor by the reprisal of perpetuity and their interchangeable conditions: cackling at the hysterical, appearing before one present only in body as flesh is picked away to horrify the haunter. What is unique about the dead or the living? Only the man who was never born can pass away.

Wine

A drink made from the blood of the gods. Arterial ambrosia. When imbibed it gives one the confidence and stamina of a god because it replenishes the veins with divine heart-fluids; how powerful it makes one depends on the type of deity being absorbed. A continuous supply of wine in society is impossible without the involuntary appropriation of at least a few gods. Every winery has an imprisoned spirit that is continually being drained into bottles, stopping only long enough to allow it to rest and regenerate. It is said that when a religion ceases to be believed in it is because all their gods have been captured and chained beneath vineyards for the purposes of wine-production; hence the proliferation of wine companies in recent times and the decline in the diversity of religions.

It is even sometimes the case that viticulture is not an indication of the disappearance of a religion, but a condition of its continued popularity. While the masses have been patiently waiting two millennia for Jesus' return, it is a trade secret among winemakers that he never left: alone of all the immortals he stuck around *voluntarily*, not to save us, but to nourish the optimism of communion-goers. No one even bothered to take him down from the cross; it was simply transplanted to Rhaeticum. The Son lives on past the Father who forsook him, tapped to the bone, giving himself daily for us in a manner far surpassing the brevity of the orthodox accounts. Though able to free himself at any time, he knows his people would not survive his emancipation. Man is only able to sustain his existence through idol-intoxication.

The Boulevards of Extinction

X. *n.* A signal of death or obsolescence; the silent, invisible prefix to every word in the Latin alphabet.

> Why did I leave out *X*? So my dictionary will continue to be read forever. (Samuel Johnson)

Yeomanners. *n.* The day-to-day etiquette of a gentleman farmer, consisting in an aloof politeness towards outsiders balanced by coarse boisterousness around conformists.

> Rural gentlemen should raise their children in accordance with the hostliness of *yeomaners*, urban ones with the stranger's way of courtesy. (John Block)

Zeno of Elea

Short and ugly, rebuffed by his beloved Parmenides, seeking to outdo Heraclitus in obscurity, Zeno defied both of them and argued for a synthetic position partaking of both unity and plurality, constancy and change, stillness and motion. This stance he would carve out through intellect and the knife, a combination of reflection and action. To remain a private person he embarked on a political career: he took up the hobby of assassinating tyrants.

Entering Phalaris's bedchamber and awakening him with a dagger to the throat, Zeno presented a paradox: "If being is less than one but more than many, they must be equal, since nothing and infinity are the same distance from number. But this is impossible, since infinity is a something as far beyond nothing as it is beyond number. Being, therefore, must be more than one but less than many [(a)]."

This made Phalaris think of his twin brother, whom he suspected of plotting for the throne. "You are right," Phalaris said. "I will allow my brother to reign alongside me. Together our duality will sort out the kingdom's grain famine and the desert's sand problem." Zeno, not impressed with this response, was about to kill Phalaris but got cold feet when a guard entered the room to investigate the commotion. The philosopher put his dagger away and was rewarded by Phalaris with farmland on a sand dune. Zeno, declining the gift, decided to use his talent for conspiracy and conundrums to enlighten absolute rulers.

Before Zeno was to kill Diomedon, he put to the tyrant the famous paradox of size's sameness in place [(b)]. This made Diomedon feel better, small in stature as he was.

To Demylus he recited a paradox on the superior speed of motionlessness [(c)]. Demylus, scorning riddles in the face of death, bit off his own tongue and spit it in Zeno's face. Zeno said that the tongue was indeed blindingly fast after it wet his eyes.

To Nearchus he told the paradox of the universal median [(d)]. After pondering this for a few moments, the tyrant took the knife from Zeno's hand and stabbed himself. Zeno, unsure of how to escape safely, claimed responsibility for the death and set himself up as the new tyrant of Elea. After a few months of incompetent philosopher-kingship an assassin tried to kill Zeno in turn, but failed and was put to torture. When asked for the names of his fellow conspirators, the man told Zeno he had a secret for him. The man whispered something; Zeno leaned in to hear and received a kiss on the cheek. Forgiving him, Zeno let the man go. Needing someone to torture, he strapped himself onto the rack in the conspirator's place. It was here, under unbearable pain, that he thought up his final paradox, unknown to posterity since his torturer could not write [(e)].

a) *Initio in absurdum*: to begin in the absurd and see what sense can be made of it.

b) "A growing Achilles and a shrinking tortoise meet in the bug on the mountaintop."

c) "An arrow lodged in a bulls-eye is faster than one flying toward it."

d) "One at the top cannot reach the sky. One at the bottom is above the ground. All from high to low are in the middle."

e) "If a crushed body is thrown into a grave, but the man whose body it belonged to was never crushed, man's place can be with neither the body nor the grave—flesh nor fatality. The body's place is the grave, the grave's place is the soil space; but man, who arose from the soil, is placeless."

Zookaryote. *n.* A creature partaking of the natures of the vegetable, animal, fungi, and chromalveolate kingdoms.

> I believe the discovery of the *zookaryote* is around the corner . . . the life form with the giving gene, the propagationist that bestows itself to all species. (Pawkins, *The Giving Gene*)

PART 6

Gray Dawn

Lesser Felidae

When intellectuals fainted into their research in a narcoleptic defense against wonder—a tale to make one nostalgic for a pillowbook. Running to the threshold of heat stroke, our thinkers exchange peer reviews with the minimum delicacy of an egg-and-spoon relay, hyperventilating from discussion and evaluation. If they have seen so far it is because they are standing on the shoulders of a university mascot, cheerleading high orthodoxies and waving pom-pom paradigms. When tuition and fees become too heavy to prop up this leg pyramid, the pack of dogs will scatter and the feline will emerge to hunt alone.

This is where Schlegel's *symphilosophie* has led us—not towards the linkage of science, philosophy, and poetry resulting in a "progressive universal poesy," but towards the single-file march of shoptalk.

Unlike the hounds sniffing down a single topic, its carcass a prize for all to feast on, the ocelot is a nomad of the mind, stalking ideas here and there. Once of the *Panthera*, this grand theorist has shrunk into a scavenger that claws whatever scraps of ideas he can find. Pascal saw a precipice over his armchair; the polymath's descendant, on the way to his study every evening, trips on the folds in his rug and falls into a valley. He is on a mission: to educate himself at the expense of the world's ignorance, to fashion his vision of a *stagnant* universal poesy—one that contributes to nothing and is ignored. He begins in social seclusion and end in mental isolation. His is the danger of firsthand learning. He has fallen out the other end of Bacon's dream of a community of scientists only to plummet into the gaps of knowledge. What the disgraced Chancellor lamented (and required), the mitigated visionary today embraces: to work in "the completest solitude," a tower-bound Montaigne. Only a decade of radical interiorization can produce a work of surpassing greatness. And for *several* works—a lifetime. To sharpen his subtlety this thinker builds on the stars of the past and the sun bursts of the present. But he borrows without acknowledgement and rebounds off others' thoughts only to negate them. His is a plagiarism of take-not-give, modifying and replacing what is stolen, creating an individuation of concepts through partial erasure and silence. He ventures outside to achieve a deeper withdrawal.

The possibility of a reader nodding in comprehension stands against the ocelot of thought as his greatest enemy. He confounds all game hunting. Far from making a concept appear vividly in the reader's mind, the thocelot frustrates and obscures in order to stimulate. His perspectivism is not an open field, but a thick forest of trees, an attitude which emerges naturally from his lonesomeness. He delights in everything opaque. The rain clouds are his friends: he despises the blueness of the sky.

The game hunter engages the thocelot's frustration and augments it—an experience the occidental mind does not relish and is unprepared for. Seeking clarity and logic, the western reader finds only a half-fuzziness. He inevitably blames his lack of interpreting skills on the dwarf leopard, but he is as much to blame. He lacks the *orient*ation of mind necessary to navigate encryption—poetry is out of fashion. His materialism infiltrates the structure of his thought. He is looking for career-friendly concepts, an author who will raise the sails for page-cruising. Or if he is really perverse—if he is a literary critic—he wants to spell the work out himself, to hang another fur on his mantle with one shot of his elephant gun. The reader seeks not knowledge, but consolation—that his prejudices have the status of an equally valid viewpoint; that in the hydra of meaning, his head is as large as the others. Reading is a pastime of ego-compensation.

Rather than the continual refinement fostered by an exchange of ideas, increasing bewilderment results until no further communication is possible. A wall is built to keep others out—the thinker lays the brick and the reader spreads the mortar. Total incomprehension between is arranged in order to achieve total comprehension within—*for the strongest*. One cannot grow without pushing against another self. So does the life of every reflective human being become a continuous inner *contra*philosophy.

Two Ways of Thinking

Half-born thoughts, fetal formations of an untrained mind, attract few sonograms. But there is energy in their aimless kicking, and their rosy skin is fresh, if thin. Unlike half-dead thoughts: piled upon timeworn names and familiar traditions, worked out to exhaustion. Cavalier readers looking for horse sense smell the rotting meat and are scared off before their eyes hit the page.

No Ordinary Silence

Compared to a whisper, what are the electromagnetic vibrations of space, the haunting arias of the planets? A silence broken by conspiracy is of more interest than the stealth of the solar system. Men, unlike space, were never assumed to be *meant* for silence, and when they are it makes intelligent people suspicious. So much the worse then that they often turn out to have nothing to say. If one of the voyager probes would only have turned its receivers to earth and recorded its spectrum of hushed gossip, it would register a global effect of what the sum of tapped phone lines has been stubborn to conclude: that there are few worthwhile secrets to impart. That those on the other end of the microphone are not searching for the *right* information; that they are absorbed by suggestions of malicious intent, and after their threshold for boredom has been reached (an elevation matched only by field biologists and other siblings of the *observant* occupations), use the wiretap as a tool for amusement: the eavesdropper who, startled by an earsplitting sigh, listens for an orgasm or a gunshot. Not finding intent, he infers motives from ecstasies and despairs.

One only has to look at how most men of knowledge behave—how they are always blasting out facts and wisdom for the benefit of everyone else, desperate to attain the power behind enlightenment—to see that there is little need for spying. Rarest is the man of knowledge who is not compelled to give into the instinct for sharing that infects his kind. He is without the relational power accompanying the knowledge that others know you know, the resentful envy others direct toward you when they are aware you are full of content that escapes them. But he also escapes another effect: that when one flings knowledge about, anyone can pluck it from the air and pass it off for one's own. As soon as an insight is reproduced in the mind of another it is as good as stolen. Not seeing farther than others, the men of shared knowledge—writers of encyclopedia articles, advisers of all sorts—become like everyone else, though they may continue to coast along on the *status* of knowing. Having received the information they want, the parasites continue to respect the sharer only so long as further information can be siphoned: the man of terminal knowledge is scorned and despised. He, as they say, dries up. So, having emptied their vessels of information, these sharers feign as if the well is still deep, mixing self-repetition with platitudes, turning knowledge into bullshit.

And so one who perceives all this remains silent. To the more expressive men of knowledge he is a suspicious figure, but to the rest, those who assume talk is synonymous with thought, he is assumed ignorant. This is his strategy: to know *jealously*, to keep knowledge within him until he can acquire a copyright on his thoughts. Only then will he own his knowledge officially, in the face of the world, and be seen as greater than the less reserved of his breed. For he is that rare man of knowledge: one who knows not just facts, but the hearts of men—and questions facts when they come into contradiction with men. He knows that the known is, in the end, not as important as the unknown. The eavesdropper of knowledge uses not a wiretap, but a stethoscope.

The Man of Unknowledge

If books you haven't read are more valuable than books you have read, as Taleb says, then still more valuable are books you have read but didn't understand. You reread it again and again, but still its contents escape you. Not theoretical books—those fall below everyone's understanding as time passes and the theory becomes obsolete—but works requiring a combination of taste and judgment, a sensibility to ponder obscurities without the hope of solution. More important than the anti-library is the supra-library: something forever above and beyond its collector, always existing outside of him. Size is not a factor; a supra-library of a hundred books might as well be the library of babel. For these are not works of knowledge, but works of *un*knowledge.

Comprised largely of foolish-seeming wisdom that lessen the survival rate of their readers, in no way do they contribute to the advancement of material comfort, technical expertise, or worldly success. Every sentence sows a seed of failure; the unheeded chapter is a harbinger of pauperism. A reader being incapable of internalizing these books, they are in a sense useless to their owner; but that does not negatively affect *his* use to *them*. The man of unknowledge, having risen above other men, needs something higher to serve. So, not humble enough for God, he serves his unknowledge as professors and pedants serve their knowledge. Disorganizing library aisles, shelving children's books in the nonfiction section and science textbooks on the periodical rack. Not reading books but skimming them at random, making himself receptive to that phrase that will trigger his insight and give him a glimpse of the unpredictability of life, tremors of the world-shaking event no one can foresee.

Unknowledge is the futile condition of willing its seeker in the direction of a lost ignorance. There is no return to ignorance, no way back from knowledge. Even preventing oneself from accruing more is impossible once an initial condition has been achieved. One cannot remain in a state of minimal knowledge, but is now a "knower," fated to reflect on the experiences he inevitably accrues. Even the rare man of knowledge who knows the value of the unknown is helpless to ever reach his goal; his purpose is to manage the boundary. He can expand it by showing how the sum content of every database is a speck in the vast unknown, but he can never *erase* it. So he becomes a man of unknowledge, falling back on what can't be proven to achieve a state of inadequate ignorance, terrorizing colloquiums with irrefutable errors. His is a double *divertissement*: avoiding what knowledge he can as the ultimate triviality, he uses its gaps to confront existence's banalities. His ideal is to live in the early stages of dementia: knowledge of soon losing the knowledge that that which is stronger will destroy him. The others, he realizes, already suffer from the advanced stages.

Proselytization

To preach one's vision of skepticism to others is like a sick man vomiting on those around him. A man should enfold his doubt around him as a blanket as protection from the germs of others' facile assurances. The happy, the simple, the contented have all contracted illnesses before, but unlike them the great doubter refuses to manufacture white blood cells, to build up an immune system of fables. The healthy ward off one sickness only to catch another: that of *bad taste*, sickness of the spirit.

The Way to Unknowledge

Justified real doubt: the foundation of not going beyond fact, of questioning even those when needed. The suspicion of falsehood, vindicated by all the discrepancies glaring through the everyday. A truth of untruths, the silhouette beneath the robe. An exciting stranger lying in the darkness whom you cannot grope with the confidence of a good lover, however experienced—so you simply lie in bed like a dead fish, allowing the stranger to violate you.

Healthy doubt: that which goes beyond Cartesian reasonableness, but which, even lacking internal certainty, stops short of the Pyrrhonist's total suspension of judgment. As extended substances, our bodies have been the repositories of too much abuse to remain indecisive; to become a thing able to exist in itself but not through itself, the minority of thinking substances embracing their flesh must acknowledge the world by denouncing it.

Absurd doubt: the curious few have only to examine the conditions surrounding the adoption of their beliefs in order first to call everything into question, then realize the folly of this examination. Indoctrination, orientation to social norms—this browbeating of beliefs whose falsehood is unquenchable but whose usefulness is unquestioned is essential to emotional stability, the very antithesis of a healthy skepticism. To even begin to question them, to say, "It seems I acquired this belief in a different way than I thought I did," is to already be abnormal. In any but a madman it goes hand in hand with the desirability, however subconscious, of bringing oneself into line. The only relief from shivering is to hug madness tight.

The importance of following customs leads back to the Pyrrhonist cowardice. But who that has lived outside the bounds of normalcy can ever bring themselves fully into it? Even if one custom can be followed, there is always something beyond our nature, some way we cannot pass. Even a white upper-class male with a recent history in sports has tan lines from basking in the sun too long.

The boundaries of doubt are the least trustworthy of all. Probability is not enough consolation. On a potholed street of facts with a steering lock on sufficient reason, the only satisfaction to be found against the *urge* to believe is to crash into the median. The medieval Christian had no "belief," but simply *lived* the reality of his religion, unmoved by terror of the rack. The history of India's conquests is the history of a will-less Buddhism.

Doubt, then, is only the first step, a precondition for what lies beyond both doubt and belief. In a world of absences, uncertainty in truth-investigation, and the especially dubious action of life, the motivation for *roaming inaction* is the only firm ground.

A traveler is lost in the forest. "Which way should I go?" he asks himself. He sees thick brush in every direction. The canopy is too dense to glimpse the sun's arc or pursue a patchy twilight navigation. Assumptions, conjectures, suppositions—these do him no good. One way seems no better than another. But a decision must be made. So he trusts in practical reason's kernel of unreasonableness. He makes the forest his new home. The Quest is disregarded. The traveler becomes the wanderer. Even his corpse remains unlocatable; unlike with Genghis Khan there is no need to kill the gravedigger—it is himself.

The Boulevards of Extinction

The Infidel

We are all believing machines, but the skeptic's conscience doubles as devil's advocate. He is aware that our believing machines are misinterpreting machines, silent about the mistakes made at every level in constructing beliefs. His brain struggles for a more accurate way to think about the world, and after defecting from society he finds his first taste of *dis*belief in a remote bedlam for the overmedicated. A feigned bout of schizophrenia and he gains admission, casting aside convictions and principles with the legitimacy of an antipsychotic prescription. He is now free to cheek his beliefs at the rate of three doses a day: questioning the necessity of everything between breakfast and morning therapy, interpreting all perceptions in the lunch line as untrue, mistrusting causality during evening bingo.

The roads to belief's deconstruction are as various as the mind's operations: perception, cognition, emotion, memory—all can be recruited in the task, even pitted against one another. Strong counter-emotions easily confront uncomfortable evidence; the more serious mission lies in discarding joyous associations—always the *most* false.

Disbelief is hearing a story about oneself from a relative and saying, "It didn't happen like that." After being shown a photograph of the situation, perception is enlisted to question memory: "This picture is too *faded* to be accurate."

Interrupting a conversation partner, his contradiction of your viewpoint is preempted by your own rebuttal. You make it known that you are not agreeing with him for the sake of politeness, only talking with him because you both happened to be standing in the corner of the room. The Infidel has nothing to discuss: his is a world without loyalties. Guelphs or Ghibellines? Lancaster or York? Mozart or Salieri? Dante's friends ended up in hell alongside his enemies; the War of the Roses wilted the Plantagenet dynasty; a pockmarked tombstone is more ignominious than a pauper's grave—no one *knowingly* tramples on Amadeus. From politics to family feuds to mediocre art, the catacombs of history demonstrate that no judgment is worth forming.

Doubt is as great a sin as faith. The doubter is an amateur skeptic—his questions rely on his creeds. The Infidel, emptied of beliefs, is beyond doubt—he never *asks* after truth or falsehood. Though beliefs are always establishing themselves within us automatically and a person can often only reject one by adopting an alternative, he takes up only indispensable errors. Vacating himself of beliefs, he fills himself up again with blank beliefs; renunciation becomes redundant. The Infidel maximizes his indispensability—he makes *himself* into the ultimate error; he adopts disbelief, the error of life. The minimal beliefs he holds in order to survive and act effectively are only *states* of belief, not *his* beliefs. The opposite of the Cosmopolitan who adopts every state of belief, the Infidel is anti-cosmopolitan and non-representative, the hollow man, connected to his states by the most delicate thread. Though his brain only has the relevant information it receives at that moment, he refuses to reify that fraction of unfiltered data. Consciously aware of only this very small amount of what is actually in the world, he realizes there is actually far *less*. Wired to nothingness, neurons fizzle out like defective firecrackers in the dark space of gray matter. Distancing himself from the creeds of every social group, the Infidel offers no direction for wayfarers, admits no true path. In doing so, he threatens solidarity. Amidst the fanatical camaraderie of high social cohesion, he becomes a candidate for immolation—so for his own safety, he has himself institutionalized. There he can be alone among his own kind—insanity is disbelief's chief symptom. The mental solitude of lunacy, at least, confers immunity from the madness of *crowds*.

The Infidel admits his anomalous existence. Consciousness has striven so hard to come to grips with reality and achieve a pinnacle in him, only in the end to go against billions of years of evolution and make a mockery of its own survival. No matter: radical apprehension for its own sake is worth risking danger and doom. And when constantly reinventing consciousness becomes fatiguing, he welcomes that doom as the final reinvention. Shorn of belief, he clings to his destiny.

The Hypocrite

The hypocrite is in a better position to deliberate on his failing than the man of integrity his abstinence: saying one thing and doing another, he has *experienced* both sides of a quality and knows how hard it is to successfully execute it. In public he savors being among the virtuous, all the more so because his private vice gives color to it, increasing the appreciation of a precarious reputation that could be exposed at any moment. Stripped of the joyless obligation of actually *being* virtuous, he is free to relish the status it brings. His is the greater insight with the courage to not deny or rationalize, to maintain—even enlarge—his cognitive dissonance, widening the chasm between act and belief.

Abdomenology of Perception

"I can't!" says Merleau-Potty, anxious over rational man's inability to embrace a carnal knowledge of the body. Taking this confession to another level: if we cannot do, much less can we believe. Having exhausted the critique of an objective grounding for beliefs and values, but still wanting to attest the self, we rediscover the inner child that trusts those presuppositions rooted in communities and traditions—and find ourselves gulled by anthropological bias. Faith in custom is the reification of what is most dubious: the origins of behavior in empathy-by-the-fluteful, ferocity keggers, muffled willpower, exile of dissent. In an age of reason authority takes the limits of reason as its starting point; we acknowledge it as a less fallible form of truth-seeking, we fall back upon it when logic concludes with too much severity; high on its placebo-injection, we breed experiments to test our range of control groups. Acknowledging custom is the only freedom after death and imprisonment; for when, with deep understanding and desire for change we defy assimilation, authority tightens its grip around our jugulars. When its necessities cannot get through to us it exercises force, its pure form.

Being does not speak, much less to me, through tribal costumes or unshakable institutions. Those tired of listening—who would shriek at Being but refuse to waste their breath—must take up the naïveté of refusing to be naïve. On the question of their "innocence," theirs is the artlessness of hanging a jury with eye contact, pleading guilty with the right to silence, skipping down death row, drawing in hydrogen cyanide through a harmonica.

Individuals

The Social! —An entity to raise one's glass to. Without it a dinner banquet would be just polished silver, the rule against belching, the rule against using tablecloths as napkins. Oh yes, and the guests—so substantial all of a sudden, there is hardly any need to invite them.

The Social: fountainhead of all cherished values. A land of habits—this and that act. People concerned with what is theirs—solipsists of property. The gravity between atoms. Institutions—a building, a rule, a bureaucrat. Two sitting, drinking tea. Or three. A duo, a triad—a group. Only the steam from their cups rises between them.

Sociology was reparation for the Napoleonic Wars. Once God's sway over men's beliefs was weakened and kings lost the power to compel assent, collective consciousness came into being to explain the totem pole. In the "Religion of Humanity," as with God, altruism is the vassal of wrath, a magic trick of metaphysics wrapped in material aggregations.

The social contract—long demoted from the realm of historical fact, neither is it a hypothetical debate by rational beings floating in a limbo of equality. The only limbo is for the aberrant, the ones who wail for eternity over why they don't fit. For the rest of us, the ones who *do*, the social contract is a bedtime story praising our inclusiveness.

There is a zoo fenced off inside a jungle. All the animals frolic within the confines of their habitats, only too happy to give up their instincts in return for safety. Only with their health problems in old age, if ever, do they begin to regret the sedentary life. Who realizes how much better they would be in the wild? —Ask the giraffes looking over the fences. How does the herbivore avoid being hunted? Toss the carnivores a steady supply of soy burgers. Then tell the different species *they are all of one kingdom.*

PART 6: Gray Dawn

The Factmonger

"Let us at least don the mask of manners," the truth-follower says, "*for our survival.*"

"But this custom is not right *for me*; I do not claim the case or event you root it in."—The factmonger rejects the cultural universal as too restrictive. Creatures of sensation only deal in what can be felt—silk, wool, polypropylene. The factmonger traded his conscience for a polo shirt at the thrift store. He picks out facts to fit his personal lifestyle. And like his suits, they must be chic. Which is not to say they need match. Only judge those facts he picked over. His facts are the most current: hats lead to baldness; tight jeans cause abdominal pain; sandals give no arch support. When he sees people wearing cotton in winter he prays for humidity. Broadmindedness is not in his bureau.

Community

"I am me!"—The naïve assumption of unity one should expect from our good citizens. Let us be gracious and call them "individualists." Lovers of freedom. Perhaps they are the rugged self-reliant sort who live off Mother Earth's resources alone. Perhaps they don't care what others think about them (the always sartorially elegant). Perhaps they fish for opportunity with a welfare net—the self-actualizing equalizers.

"I cannot be summed up!"—And you think this makes you *special*? Man's ignorance makes him a problem of epistemology, his curiosity of ontology.

The self must be established—invented if not discovered or deduced. But out of what? It is not enough to have a past to build upon, a memory, the assumption of sameness through time. Oppressed by the hippocampus, trapped in a median present, the mind averages out its most oft-occurring peculiarities to find the essence. Harnessing its circadian rhythm it learns to cycle through the days, never questioning its own process.

The history of the "essential identity": we look up, then out, then in. As an apology we stand and declare that every sentence needs a subject.

The wanderer says to himself, "I am a mess, but the world is a trash heap." He carries a shovel to accompany his uncertainty. His anxiety keeps him excavating. He learns to measure himself by the holes he digs, his only shelter from the wind. So many things he has not done, so many he will never do, driven on by the desire for unformed memories.

A charioteer tied to two horses is being pulled towards his destiny. The white horse is too lumbering and deaf to yield to the whip—its breeding was too genteel. Only the dark horse will consent to be guided through an appeal to its pride, its love, its hatred—and the humility of a dangling carrot.

The Boulevards of Extinction

A Fashion Designer's Last Letter to his Clothes-Historian

Herr Teufelsdröckh,

This season's metaphysical wardrobings will make a fine addition to your Doctrine of Clothes. Each piece in my Autumn/Winter Collection puts forth a particular Idea of the wearer's Spirit, a malfraction of impious hearts forcing gazes lidded by factory-lines to submit to the one truth: Reality is Fashion, Fashion Reality.

***

A bird hat: with golden wings stretched in flight and a full nest resting on the forebrow, its wearer is ready to soar away. Landed creatures everywhere may benefit from such skyward dreams: they will take to the heavens with a Taste high above the ballcaps of fellow street-shufflers.

***

A spray-painted dress: an infinitude of analogies, the language of metaphors made visible, the color of verbosity. Perfect for schizophrenics, dissociative identities, and all those who, grown tired of themselves, wish to burn their hampers, hold a prism up to the sun, and stream their spectrum across the boulevards.

***

Lobster-claw heels: impossible to walk in, impossible not to try; the wearer, elevated ten inches, evokes the crustaceous prehistory of the foot by imitating the first land-stumblers. Organic appendages wobbling on palaces of sand, the source and fate of our earthen culture is made available to experience—at the price of a year's salary one can own epochs.

***

Jewel-bedizened armor top and mask: clothed in Heraldry, a Joan of Arc for an era of gauze queens and body-paint peons. Umbrageous to soft skins and firm morals, the Knightess battles alike Sunday vestures and minimalist display trends.

***

An antler headpiece, draped with a veil of cream silk tulle and lace: the hunter's prize; the Phoenix cannot compare to the spiked ungulate: the first falls and rises in succession, but the best part of the latter is preserved forever on a neck-mount. When society has fallen, its skeletal outcroppings may still be displayed after the carcass has been roasted over the fire and devoured—as a symbol of that which cannot return. One horn represents the Inevitable, the other the Inexorable. Ruins are the most poignant example of Time encapsulated in Eternity.

***

A black metallic jacket that holds its wearer's arms straight out: a tree uprooted and polluted, wrinkled like bark, collar high as a trunk, symbolic of the divine IT cast like a particle of dark matter onto the catwalk.

***

These will be my last creations for others. My mother's passing has been hard on me; she died after wearing a pair of my lobster heels and tripping into an oncoming bus. I have now only the constitution to create for myself, and then only once more. My final work will be my greatest emblem of the Ephemeral Nay: I will weave a noose from the Achilles tendons of fresh organ donors and decorate it with bat orchids. Accompanying this Passivity will be my newest dressing gown, a red silk bathrobe-tuxedo. After a long cold shower, I will glue Kleenexes to my eyebags and wrap my neck in the tissues of humanity.

Acknowledging One Wiser

I accept the authority of great thinkers only insofar as their doctrines are not appropriated by powerful entities—insofar as their status remains relatively low in the real world. I was a great admirer of Marx until I read Lenin's interpretation of him, and of Rousseau until I learned of his application in Robespierre. Aquinas I had been suspicious of until I learned of his soul's radical reversals in location, and I now regard him as an unfortunate victim of papal whimsy. Kant and Mill each seemed equally intuitive until I witnessed them invoked without citation on public policy platforms, the one side justifying its biases with the categorical imperative and the other with Profit-and-Loss Philosophy. Comte I cannot help but pity, and have considered joining the Church of Humanity just for the satisfaction of belonging to a religion with only one member—without proselytization or even belief, I can ensure that his system of optimism will die with me.

Pakistan furnishes daily references to Iqbal's *Javid-Nama*, continually proving humanity's infinite potential for folly. Someday, no doubt, our destiny for irrelevance in the universe will be revealed when, by serendipity, some son from the Land of the Pure, in need of proving his virtue, endows the international realm with an irremediable catastrophe.

To determine the degree of bankruptcy of history's great ideas, simply study their inept embodiments. Machiavelli is different—leaders never openly acknowledge reading him, making every attempt to hide their affinity behind a Ciceronian dust jacket. I respect any thinker whom one is ashamed to read. Embarrassment is a good indication of truth, unpopularity the surest sign of being free of delusion or prejudice.

Endistence

Rather than outward acts, show me the inner life—the existence incapable of externality. Something so elusive it can be recorded only with words that dissipate in the air and a look that sees the other as a ghost. Haunted by the burden of its own proof at first, it fades into dismissal. An *endistential* crisis: the inability to get outside oneself and exist, the lack of essence preceding existence—forming the basis of a relative *non-existence*. There is never a choice to be made, much less the obligation to accept the solidity of what "is." To invert Sartre, before being-in-itself, there is being-for-itself; before being that is what it is, there is being that is what it is not and is not what it is—and what comes after this is superfluous. The being of objects, unable to be ascertained, is not even presupposed, likewise with being-for-others.

The appointment with Pierre was never made; he is not about to appear and one does not expect him to. I sit in an empty café, with no faces to detain, without odors or sounds, the only color the charcoal walls. There is no real relation between Pierre and me, between the café and me. There is only me, without relation, lost in thought, abstraction, negative judgment. The question is whether this sole expectation, that of being-for-itself, is *too much* of a grounding, whether it is supported by something less. It is not Pierre's absence that haunts the café, but the possibility of my own. I am underived, superfluous, *de trop*. To want to remain in this state of being-for-itself would be bad faith of a worse sort even than wanting to achieve being-in-itself, since the condition of the former is a sort of complacency, a starting point that is its own ending point. Instead I am tempted, in spite of myself and contrary to any longing, to do what God should have done in the ennui prior to the Creation: to achieve descent. Having nihilated being-in-itself, being-for-itself nihilates itself as well. I move toward a state of total non-being, snuff out my lone mind, make a final concrete negation that wipes out all isolated negations, swallowed in a mundane ocean of void—if for no other reason than to unfetter myself from Heideggerian terminology.

Reason's Spotlight

Unlike the repression and occasional eruption of Romanticism, the Enlightenment determines us, it *is* us—conscious delusion of the modern self and the world's place as our servant. It is always trying to salvage fallacies that never caught on and fights to keep its few moribund triumphs above ground. Reason and Equality: the eighteenth century's greatest contributions were the twentieth century's biggest fiascos. The amendments to society that occurred in tandem with these principles were as initially humane as they were eventually self-defeating: growing secularism (the scramble to be saved in *this* world), the rise of science (nature telling truth-jokes), a climbing middle-class (peasants with an ideal of nobility rooted in clothes and carriage). Wishful thinking will not let the enlightenment go. There is hardly a public speech given that doesn't proclaim things will get better or an academic agenda that doesn't pour all its resources into the math program, confining English students in moldy rooms to count their grammar mistakes. But the romantic in us knows better—no Ode to Disinterest ever made a Beethoven.

Romanticism is for the few; it is not "we," but "*I*." Only its popular legacy ever caught on: myth as the seat of wisdom, man as the mirror of nature, sacredness of the old. Men could only wrap their minds about it by inverting the Enlightenment, imagining they could be this "I," as triumphant in wielding Passion as conquering Reason, straddling the cerebral hemispheres without sacrifice.

The *other* Romantic legacy: looking beyond the pretty page where the fancies of the poetic brain have inscribed themselves, we behold the poet himself—a being of persecutional ideations, suicidal obsession, and retribution. The Roussean hypocrisy of horny pubescents and soccer moms, in which everyone with a libido or an opinion has a "general will." A Sturm und Drang sentimentality: some old white man is always killing himself—if not out of unrequited love, then from a beery mania that resembles its moods. Byronic passion: justice—*real* justice, not the ruling of a stacked jury—is only sought by vengeful grumbling antiheroes, men addicted to their struggle with demons past or imaginary. While rare, such figures are potentially pervasive. There is an Ahab in every man injured by blind nature or random urban life; in every terminal love affair lurks a Heathcliff burning to take his anger out on family friends and descendants; anyone with embarrassing relations has only to release the inner Rochester and lock them away in an attic. The Ancient Mariner has always been one of man's chief archetypes, but the Romantic period provided us models for how to shoot the albatross. Occasionally a bold soul learns how to aim.

Naturae Tenebra

Even spontaneous folk intuitions are not careful enough anymore; one's insights must be mulled over, reflective convictions theorized after the event. Anything more than a hypothesis amounts to stereotyping. Subjecting every meditative belief to revision, more and more judiciously, until you become convinced of the totally uncertain—consumed by a *positive* skepticism. Giving everyone the benefit of the doubt, intuition deteriorates into toleration as it is put to the proof and one's thought is made to agree with itself; it becomes second nature to suppress one's hunch, to go for a drive with the top down and welcome the falling sky. Working backwards, from the primal to the urbane—destroying the last trace of instinct in man and replacing it with an arsenal of public opinions, a *tractatus* demonstrated by a palindrome of axioms. The thinkers of the day, ensconced from life, siphon methods from the decayed residue of a personality and call it "engaging the world."

When, having reached the age of thirty, you have learned all you can from observing your own species, further your education by tracking evolution backwards. Out of an irrepressible impulse towards motor functions and firing synapses, many lack the constitution to devolve towards planthood—nadir of media junkies, cosmopolitans, and professors (lower, average, and higher invalids). Standing on the loftiest rung of eukaryotic being's stepstool, these misfits are destined to remain merely beasts. How to thrive within inadequacy? Not enough to simply study the animals; one must *move in* with them. Raised by wolves, pruned by peacocks, one experiences the forms of inter-group violence in all its wondrous variegation. Each distinct existential problem has its own peculiar territory to infiltrate and explore: a cowed husband taking up residence in a hen house; the faint of heart climbing into an empty cage in the pet store; the ennui-ridden building a greenhouse around his "great soul." Placed in such a situation, one can easily see both what humanity has lost and the utter defectiveness of the other life forms—no matter which path one takes, dead ends along parallel roads. Neither the fringe of intelligence in the mollusk nor the inkling of instinct in the knight errant are enough to shield them in the end; the protective covering of each defends them only from the least cause for worry. The mollusk is helpless against the superior cleverness of fishermen, while the chivalrous knight is laid low by the guile of courtly intrigue or a con-maiden framing her distress.

The conquest of matter has propelled the march of intellect ever onward—consciousness's transcontinental flight, the *Spirit of St. Louis* on a kamikaze mission. One who would avoid swaying in the breeze of the zeitgeist must dare to make a reflex of this intellect. Heightening instinct into a self-conscious impulse, he clings to all the prejudices which the cautiousness of his age conditions him to discard, all the foibles and imperfections which in former times guided his flourishing forbears—not as a regression to a state of nature, but a compliment to gentility. To treat truth as slime, oozing into him and greasing his charm. *Counter*intuitions with no pretense to Cartesian illumination, but emerging from the margins, from shade—"the darkness of nature."

Common sense embodies the decayed vestiges of a younger culture's public ground of truth; for the sage in a senile culture, *rare* sense is necessary—ancestral simulation of judgment without reflection. Vico's three universal customs: solemn marriages, some religion, burial of the dead. Modern sage's customs: uniting animal and doggy-stylist in holy matrimony, tying them to the altar, digging a mass grave.

There are no inferences from ourselves to the world involved; there is little interiority of self, or even of life, to shine a lamp upon—there is no shining at all. Neither is there any extension of sympathy; we express, at most, our condolences. What rational methods fail to categorize and bestial instinct is not cognizant of, counter-intuition leads us to: nothing's *inwardness*. Developing internal points of reference to thought—instead of orientation to objects, alluding to their shadows; the logic of ultimate conclusions and the sustaining of the eternally prior. Establishing a continual dialectic between mind and nature—that which being is obliged to fill up. Chaos—zeitgeist of collapse—imbibed and expanded.

It is a *seeming* of the void to the intellect. Where introspection fails and one cannot summon a memory of the void, the property of nothingness encroaches upon the mind as necessary, even as it is unlikely to be believed. It is something alien to mental life in its contravention upon mountains of evidence and unassailable arguments, its discarding of the intermediary—an exercise in fallibility and madness.

The First World Explorer

Pytheas's voyage to Thule was no fantasy, even if his description of it was counterfeited. There is a curdled sea in each of us, and a midnight sun that shines on it to blind us with the glare of reflection. One suspects that Pytheas simply got lost and had nothing to do but plumb his own waters . . . *then* sighted the Arctic Circle. And how disappointing it was by comparison—that he wrote about his *inner* discovery instead.

Come the Rain

The ground was soft after the rain, so soft that to step in it was to be swallowed up. Why had it rained for so long? Not to irrigate the crops—the earth was barren. Not because of a wet climate—clouds hardly ever darkened over the desert. Not just to prevent civilization—dust storms were the preferred mode of hostility.

So why had the sand turned into a sea of mud? For the mosquitoes, the leeches, the bacteria. Nature craves the conditions that do not compel creatures to bury themselves underground, resorting to camouflage and isolation to conserve their energy. Nature wants to teem and swarm, to flood itself everywhere. Water brings not just any life, but the encroachment of the swamp—that life which makes life inhospitable.

Bathtub Symbolism

Dirt on rug: after-drippings. A flying carpet excavated from the desert, buried so long it forgot the sky.

Rubber ducky: pond scum of waterfowl. Pruning away the fairy tale that everything which doesn't belong ends up in the *Cygnus* genus, children splash around with jaundice—hepatitis and interminable squeaking the only goal of ugliness.

Soap: liposuction leftovers. The vampires suck you, the witches smell you—custom of two horrors, surgery and chemistry.

Hair in drain: flossing thread. Rapunzel's ruin. After spending so long looking out from her tower window, she could now think of nothing but escaping into the sewer. The charming prince having abandoned her after the dimming of her damsel-in-distress aura, she dreamt a panorama of tunnel vision.

Razor: adds pallor to the cheeks. When shaving moved from the barbershop to the bathroom, public sphere became pubic shear, and vengeance was reduced to self-retaliation.

The Boulevards of Extinction

***

All the evidence one needs to keep filling the tub with earth, sweat, and blood. After that, fifteen minutes in a coffin to shelter fair skin from the burning orb and sweat out its toxins.

The Mean Between Extremes

Either we are walled in by religious murals or knee-deep in the gears of engineering projects. An age that values its artists and scientists equally requires a sensitive balance between beauty's lull into complacency and curiosity's journey towards the limits of comfort. This would amount to something like a couch ergonimicized by mosaic cushions, dazzling the eye as it probes the butt with glass and stone.

Double Suicide

Every day I give thanks for the death of artists. I fear the effects of withheld gratitude, the possibility that the world of either science or spirit could organize a contrary scenario. What if there was an artist who didn't die, who continued to just go on—*live* would be too generous a description—presenting before us new works in a style long since "matured" (congealed) and "classical" (outdated), piling up unsold, awaiting to accrue value through a demise that will never come? Would not every pupil contrive to surpass his master through some fatal accident, every customer and art dealer conspire to erase any trace of immortality? Nature's bounty is only seen as inexhaustible as long as God lives; once he dies, the exploitation of resources becomes anathema. Life is cheapened through lack of ultimate purpose in proportion as its fragility makes it more precious. With the secular gods, by contrast, this trajectory of value is inverted; the "good works" of the artist become more profitable after deicide.

But this death does not strike its blow at the end of life; it inaugurates itself at the beginning—and not only in the artist. If *Shinju's* classic mode of expression in the east is the puppet theatre, in the industrialized west it is the job fair—the moment one decides to turn creativity into an occupation, both are lost. Its occurrence is not an event, but a progressive series. A process of mutual parasitism, a reverse symbiosis withering both parties. Every step of the way the artist mooches and the world leeches, using all its weight to drag him down, hinder his development, slinging mudballs of antisociality and stubbornness, coaxing him back to normalcy with the threat of the swamp.

a) Healthy self and family: severing of the human, head-shaking by the tearless living—the only episode they notice is not a tragedy, but a shame.

b) Famished dilettante and job: aborted success and barren skill.

c) Artist and work: with the last weak thrust, the world helps the artist push the hilt in the final inch, then absconds the scene with the masterpiece under its arm. Acceptance withheld for so long, at the moment of recognition the work follows the sacrificed life into oblivion on the auction block.

Through the Looking Glass

Tired of staring at the School of Athens, I stepped into the painting; mingling with my new friends, they seemed so different from this direction, and I gazed out at a mirror image of the world with a new perspective on their ideas. What a delight to read the evil doppelgangers of the great philosophers—so much more edifying than the great philosophers themselves!

***

PLATOTUDES: The forms are *less* perfect than the material world.

AIRISTOTLE: The golden mean is for souls of base metal. Excellence is sought in the depths and the heights.

CORRUPT CARTESIUS: I think, therefore I become not.

CANT: Never let a talent for lying go to waste. Always treat every man as a means unto you.

HEYGAL: The dissolution of the Prussian Geist will only be the inaugural thesis in the naïveté of reason. I'm planning a party on the horizon. What do you say, girl?

HEIDI(GGRRR): Avoid the inauthentic life in *das Man*.

WITLESSTEIN: . . .

***

All of my originality comes from plagiarizing the Western Anti-Canon. I am the robber baron of philosophy. This tradition is for me what the Bible was for Zarathustra: a treasury of wisdom to be plundered. Stripped of their arguments, known to us as posterity remembers all philosophical systems—a collection of bad aphorisms—it is up to me to flesh out what these thinkers meant, to appropriate a pastiche of inversions under the banner of the void. From the metaphysics of waste, to the Ecomachean ethics of decomposing into the environment, to the mind-body frugality and the thrift of existence, to the imperative towards radical evil, to the dialectic of unravelling, to abdomenology, to silence games, the history of the search for truth is revealed for what it is. A hole that grows into a blackened fruit, an olive without a pit, reproducing more holes, continually recombined into a salad of rot. With every bite the tongue recoils, a bout of diarrhea ensues, and still we pick up our fork again. Compared to this our Hollywood version of ideas seems but the parody to a Spaghetti western.

The Boulevards of Extinction

A Method of Thinking

A collage of concepts is the intellectual's kaleidoscope of sensations, minus the stimulus of the erection to provide focus. And what is the intellectual's stimulus? —A pen, phallic symbol of every teasing idea that explodes, stains, and dries up. Concepts are created that reflect one another but never come together, scenarios of history's arc that parallel one another but never overlap, visions of eternity that could not possibly coalesce. When existence is multiplicitous there is no need to embody thousands of philosophies in a constructed society of personalities, as Pessoa did, just to save the trouble of having to explain contradictions in thought. Incongruity becomes the essence of existence itself; one only need capture the styles of it. Perfectly natural that one could embody *in oneself* every major philosophical system as presented in an introductory textbook. Philosophers occur as cliques that form on the basis of long-winded refutations, but are memorialized in a yearbook where summarized viewpoints are placed side by side under images without photogenicity.

The School of British Empiricism

John Block said,
 "There is a king. He is cruel, commits many acts of injustice, and oppresses the people. What should the people do?"
 Pupil Barkly said,
 "Howl and expel the king—from their minds."
 "I hardly see how that solves the problem. Wouldn't it be better to depose the king from his throne?"
 "No, I don't think so."
 "What are you saying, then? That rebellion is wrong?"
 "Indefensible."
 "Very good," said John Block. "The fact is, the people should consider it a boon to be crushed by royal munificence."
 "No, I mean rebellion is an indefensible position because there has never been one."
 "What of Charles I?"
 "A fancy the English were only too happy to eject."
 "Why are you such a difficult pupil? Constantly you are undermining my positions."
 "Not true! Test me."
 "Alright . . . can you agree that knowledge is acquired through the senses alone?"
 "Why yes, for my part I always think with my penis."
 "Must you always turn our discussions onto perversities?"

"I don't mean to be inappropriate, master. It is a metaphysical necessity. Nothing exists outside the mind, that is a proposition I have put to my little head many times, and my little head always barks the truth of it."

"I need to stop letting you around the female pupils. Something bad will come of it."

"But I have done nothing. You are unjust. Who gives you the authority? Perhaps someone should take it away."

John Block nodded in approval.

"Finally, you're getting somewhere."

The Heart Has Its Reasons

In answering Hölderlin's call for a "mythology of reason"—making ideas aesthetic, sensuous, and poetic in the hopes of raising the people's interest in persuasion—one must be careful not to hover concepts over a sea of fog. Poetic thought's iniquity is the drowning of ideas in description. This tendency to sin, once conceived, divides into two virtuous bastards: the one gamboling past the merry-go-round of logic, the other skipping over the redundancy of theory. A true aesthetic of philosophy floats between metaphor and concept. Mixing exhilaration and terror, this very circumvention of the mountain path masters the landscape of ideas and signals its own insignificance within it. Unable to be hedged by explanation, beyond any one interpretation, this aesthetic installs a child safety lock of sentimentality to grab the people's attention. Infinite imperfection diminishes into the sensuous. The state of becoming is whittled into a *terse* imperfection. Tangible regions must be appealed to if sensibilities are to have free access to reason's pantheon. The polytheism of imagination, with gods as inexhaustible as human qualities and a personal deity for every temperament, does not satisfy the need for public patronage. Cardial reason does not admit different veins to its goal, but demands a confluence into a single *vena cava*, pumped with one fell squeeze of an omnipotent hand.

Status without Ideas, Ideas without Status

Descartes, Locke, Spinoza, Kant: the superseded men of meta-science, portraits bearing a likeness to outdated authors.

Formula of Success for Great Philosophers: ground ideas in the science of the day, step onto a pedestal for all to acclaim, present your face for plastering, and let your mask be displayed along the path towards new ideas.

I will not simply stand by and stomach this roll call of names. I will not let their *words* be forgotten, even if their ideas are obsolete and the men themselves lived uneventful lives—*I* will read them. Every erroneous anachronism deserves to be resurrected and esteemed. Why is the pineal gland not as equally worthy as Descartes to be the subject of a marble bust? If it does not deserve to be studied as the seat of the mind-body connection, it is at least good for a game of ringer. Those who occupy their leisure time with dead ideas cannot be killed. Before I go mad I will harness the twelve categories of the mind to make myself unfit for multiple personality disorder—my diagnosis will be an eighteenth century paradigm. I will accumulate black bile to remain beyond the criterion for antidepressant prescription and stare through my telescope into the aether.

What to do with philosophers of the opposite stamp, the perpetually fresh thinkers? Gracián, La Rochefoucauld, Lichtenberg, Vauvenargues, Chamfort—moderns at home in every age precisely because they did nothing to move humanity forward, because their only contribution was to repeat each other and be ignored. I will not *play* with them ... they are too dangerous to do anything with but model one's life on. Having learned to sing from the echoes of departed yodelers, I will send my song into the mountains. Though most will not know what to make of the constant changes in pitch, I am confident there will be at least one lonely hiker to fathom my range of registers.

The School of British Empiricism, II

John Block said,

"Can morality be deductively demonstrated from absolute laws, or do good and evil simply reduce to specific pains and pleasures?"

Pupil Barkly said,

"I would say ... neither."

"What? You dog! You know very well that I hold *both* views! How can you say neither?"

"I'm not telling. I'm afraid you won't like my response. I think instead I shall put this question to *my* pupil. It will be a good exercise for him. Boy! Where are you?"

Sub-Pupil Hum-Hum enters.

"Here, master."

"Who is this boy?" said John Block. "Why have I never seen him before?"

"I've been hiding him from you. I don't want you to corrupt him with your silly ideas."

"This is *my* school. I say who will be admitted and what they will learn."

"Well here he is, a new student you are free to admit now. Though you may find he has taken your doctrine of empiricism in rather radical directions. I've been training him to follow in my footsteps."

"You mean he's becoming a loiter-sack. Alright, let's hear what he has to say."

"Pupil! I have a question for you: do we need to figure out God's rules for living, or must we be rewarded and punished to keep us in line?"

Sub-Pupil Hum-Hum said,

"Hmm. I'm afraid neither rationalism nor hedonism can explain our moral feelings. Reason is, and always should be, the slave of the fashions."

"And what are these moral fashions?" asked Pupil Barkly.

"Ho-hum—who knows? They keep changing. Whether we approve or disapprove, praise or blame, has everything to do with whether another's garments match our own. The foundation of sentiment is the simile—comparing one thing with another; in this case, yourself with someone cut from the same cloth."

"You are uncommonly wise for your age, my young pupil," said Pupil Barkly.

"He's a fool," said John Block. "As your master I order you to dismiss him."

"Not so fast—he's not *your* pupil. He's mine. I can do with him as I see fit. And I intend to keep him on and develop his abilities. I foresee great things for him."

"But you said you've been training him to follow in your footsteps—what he just said in no way accords with your ideas! You have established a rival branch within *my* school, and your top student doesn't even adhere to your own doctrine."

"Yes, he's learned well—I've been teaching him to rebel against the authority of masters. At first, he was very obedient. I would explain to him my reasoning on a given philosophical issue, then ask him his own view. He would say, 'Yes, I agree,' and I would say, 'No, don't adopt!'"

"What kind of teacher are you?"

"A more deliberate and capable version of *my* teacher."

"I've had enough of this. I'm disbanding this school."

"Yours or mine?"

"Both!"

"Based upon what moral principles?"

"One, that God decrees obedience to masters, and two, that you are causing me a great deal of pain."

"And just how do you expect to make a living without students? Off the income from your philosophy books?"

They both laugh. Sub-Pupil Hum-Hum joins in the laughter, though he has never written a philosophy book and does not yet fathom the hardships in store for him.

John Block said,

"Of course you're right. You are my followers, after all."

Rules Against Rules

The philosopher's stone is not an alchemical aspiration, but a mode of farsightedness. An intuition *vat*.

The Boulevards of Extinction

How many rules of vision can be drawn up? Dennett, meta-science's merry Santa, has seventy-seven dogmas of empiricism. For us, an eleventh of that is enough to form an aversion against the materialist's spirituality for making rules.

The Clumsiest Man uses only his victories. In every mistake there is an element of accuracy. In the total bungler, one whose accident-proneness repulses acquaintances with the quality of divination, it is the awareness that the mistake was *too perfect*. Everyone else is too busy trying to hide their own clumsiness to notice that the cosmos occasionally appoints its saviors of unbalance. For every yin, a yang.

The Insolent Sportsman pops egos instead of ballooning them—the opponent who stays will be interested in *honest* argument. "Only the truth-seekers will I pit myself against," the Insolent Sportsman says to himself. "Only those willing to lose *before* the game."

The voice of every orator with an untimely message is a dog whistle, so high only folded ears can hear. *Surely*, such persuasion is reserved for the loyal? Those accustomed to lying on their bellies are already in a position to embrace inconvenience.

The truth-sniffer leans on the same old rhetoric: "No aromas arise from something that *sounds* deep."—Smelling something stale deepens his hunger more than indigestible logic.

Ockham's razor is not quite dull enough; it leaves the face too smooth for comfort. Ockham's Beard: each hair an explanation curling in a different direction, the comber arranges hypotheticals in a style befitting him.

Digging around the junkyard, a rusty idea can be made to run like new by grafting borrowed parts.

The pedants are ever refining, standing with their strainer and gazing into the blue waves for muck particles. The pedants, too, are going deeper—not venturing out into the water, but sinking into the shoreline to be pinched by sand crabs. It takes a sharp pain to realize life's imprecision. A form of thought to harness the sea's tumult instead of quelling it—but the pedant is not that inventive. His ankles are content wallowing in sand grains as fine and white as his chin stubble.

No literary philosopher ever had an empirical heart. From Plato to Boethius, Pascal, Emerson, Kierkegaard, and beyond, there is an obsession with the Immeasurable. *Fortuna* betrays Lucretius's materialism—the fall of a great rock is only fate mineralized; Montaigne's reliance on his own judgment inspired Descartes to sever philosophy from the senses entirely—an influence which the French still feel when, in recurring backlashes, their philosophers become lyricists or analytical voluptuaries. Merleau-Ponty's world-flesh turns professors into prostitutes of consciousness; Foucault's body is the site of knowledge, power, and selfhood—of everything but the body.

The stone and the quill, separated but not legally divorced. Drawing ink once more, the *litterateur de philosophe* who values the purity of his line resists the yawn of super-subtlety. An equal perfidy is the compromise of the novel form, of trickling out conceptual insights through interior monologue—confused, hazy and inseparable from the character's deluded preoccupations. The philosophical artist is a writer who only gives flesh to ideas. To have style in modernity one must don archaic fads.

The State of Philosophy

Hawking: Philosophy is dead.

Putnam: Philosophy is alive.

Schrodinger's Cat: Philosophy is dead and alive.

Zombie Zizek: Dead or alive—an immaterial question. Philosophy is *hungry*.

***

The basic unanswerable questions will always drag themselves along, eating what brains they can find to survive. The mind of the thinker becomes the meal of thought. Philosophy is the chomping in-between the dinner chatter, the cannibalizing of curiosity. The cat does not die but squirms about in undigested limbo. Occasionally it claws its way out of the belly to leap around, shred furniture and knock over antiques before being caught and reswallowed. The researchers and engineers fill their stomachs on assumptions to advance solutions.

Scientists: nibblers of knowledge, test subjects for their own cult methods; watching for the latest gizmos spinning on the cheese wheel, they hoard the future's junk. With their provisional answers they rerun the maze from authority to obsolescence, continually improving their time. Physicists, once men of the century, are now the quarter-hour celebrities of truth.

Organizing Nature

Discovery: a flattering way of saying Nature has revealed a piece of herself to a bumbler. The discoverer, searching for her mute secret, is distracted upon overhearing a few soliloquizing phrases. Leaning in to eavesdrop but not quite able to make sense of her whispers, he writes down what he *thought* she said. Thus does he discover his own capacity for invention.

The Modern Geographically Bounded Territory

It is the thunder*clap* which steers everything—lightning is too distant to daunt. When a sense is employed that travels closer to the public's speed, the bolt can be deferred until necessary. An enduring nation must possess not only a monopoly on force, but on nature.

The Boulevards of Extinction

Two Champions of Modernity

One cannot be wary enough when referring to "modern man." An elusive concept not just when trying to encapsulate recent world history with a succinct description, but even when dealing with a single European province. A few medievals deserve the term, while some alive today still don't. One can apply it to a twelfth-century Cosenzan monk but not an English Parish; a fourteenth-century Florentine poet but not an eighteenth-century Venetian intellectual; a fourteenth-century Venetian on the Council of Ten but not a nineteenth-century Florentine subject of the Hapsburg-Lorraine dynasty; an eighteenth-century German dramaturg but not a nineteenth-century Chinaman.

In its different domains of society and thought modernity exerts its uneven authority through two different champions of linearity. The naïve modernist positions himself at the end of time, while the visionary modernist anticipates the future. The two groups are not mutually exclusive, but depend on each other. The first type looks at the visionaries of the past and sees in himself their completion—he depends on them for his own self-image. Often the followers of the visionary—Joachimite, Petrarchan, captious *Capi*, lesser Lessings—are themselves naïve. That one is even in a position to become a disciple suggests the world has already moved on; the vision of every follower is an antiquated utopia. But if the naïve modernist is a parasitical narcissist, the visionary is the procrastinator, always looking ahead and living in a dream while stagnating in the present. He is, in a sense, the most naïve of men: he is not at the center of the universe like the first type of modernist, but is always looking for other suns to revolve around; for him there is always a brighter star on the horizon. With infinite arrogance his knowledge scorns the naïve modernists even while his pride craves their respect. He knows that his innovations are not a culmination, but he needs worshippers to disseminate them as if they were. In the solar system of his contemporaries, *his* sun must exercise the only gravitational force. Once they start to orbit, his innovations cease. Going beyond himself would be to betray his own system, to render it defunct, a lie. So he continues to look towards the future in private, postponing it, while using all his authority to prevent any public embarrassment—any young upstart whose own novelty might surpass his. In the end the visionary is reduced to the naïve modernist he began his career despising, protecting his own posterity, a hindrance to the future. Every leap forward is a congealment.

Our modernity, an end-point as bizarre as it seems inevitable, will to the next batch of moderns simply be pitiful specimens on the ocean floor, too busy scavenging hydrothermal vents to explore *beneath* the crust.

Commentary on The Discourses, III.16

The posterity of any given moment, so long as it has the leisure to reflect, will only applaud the best among the dead, not among its own. Towards its own it will be as blind as we are to the best among us. Even those of the past are only praised to flatter the mediocrities of the present. Every *prosperous* posterity looks back and weeps as it butchers its men of worth for a few good laughs. "We have not yet equalled the great figures of times past," it asserts. "Let us then torture these *troublemakers* who would seek to ruin us."—Tomorrow's men of worth will not passively accept being passed over, but will become agitators out of indignation. Though they long to be men of posterity, they refuse to let the present push them aside.

Which contemporaries will be commemorated in the eyes of any given future? Into a pure posterity—a vague, unrealized earthly hereafter—it will project its popular personalities, those who denounced the troublemakers and punished the gadflies. So it raises monuments to the prosecutors of worthy characters. But a statue does not long survive its model.

One must always be prepared to go to war with the future. Those who want a "better life" for their children will lose. Only by inuring progeny to austerity will posterity remain fresh, ensuring it will have the *need* to recognize descendents of repute.

An Unusual Evening in Königsberg

AIRISTOTLE. I thank you for having me over for dinner. Though you know, I prefer to conduct philosophy while walking.

CANT. I prefer sitting.

AIRISTOTLE. I don't see how you could have produced anything good in that way. It is a rule of nature that the mind functions at its peak in a state of locomotion.

CANT. Yes, well I have a rule too: never to philosophize at the dinner table.

AIRISTOTLE. Now I'm sure of it. Your books must be terribly dull.

CANT. To pass such a judgment is to put yourself in the same boat. Neither of us are considered good writers.

AIRISTOTLE. Who says that?

CANT. Everyone who has read us.

AIRISTOTLE. How dare they slander my dialogues!

CANT. Eh . . . I hate to be the one who has to tell you this, but those haven't survived the ravages of time.

AIRISTOTLE. What? But . . . surely, a fragment or two . . .

CANT. Nope.

AIRISTOTLE. This is terrible news. I prized them above all my works.

CANT. Really, though, you should have expected this. As I wrote in *The Bird's Nest of Faculties*, the world was molded from a compost heap, and despite the naysayers who say, "It can't get much worse now," things keep getting fouler. There's no limit to the process of deterioration!

AIRISTOTLE. From what I've learned about this new world so far, I agree wholeheartedly.

CANT. I'm sorry about your dialogues. Cicero spoke highly of them, if it makes you feel any better.

AIRISTOTLE. That's some consolation. But tell me, which of my works are the people reading?

CANT. The few who are still literate read your lecture notes.

AIRISTOTLE. Lecture notes? I never wrote such things.

CANT. Your pupils compiled them, we don't know who.

AIRISTOTLE. Nichomachus! That rascal. He told me he was jotting to-do lists for the magnanimous. I wrote the Ethics for him, you know, though it did no good. The boy was irredeemably bad. I was always catching him alone with Theophrastus in some grove.

CANT. Yes, so thanks to him, your books that have come down to us are quite dry in style. But don't let that get you down. We're in good company today—*all* the philosophers write dry books!

AIRISTOTLE. What bores! Clearly, they have not taken my treatise on comedy to heart.

CANT. Ooh . . . umm . . . unfortunately that's been lost as well.

AIRISTOTLE. Well what *has* survived?

CANT. Lets see . . . there's your notes on biological subjects. . .

AIRISTOTLE. Ugh!

CANT. . . . *Metaphysics* . . .

AIRISTOTLE. Huh?

CANT. Your pupils gave it that title because it came after the *Physics* in the arrangement of your works.

AIRISTOTLE. Nichomachus! The boy had no imagination. I had originally called it "On Being."

CANT. Moving on, there's the *Politics* . . .

AIRISTOTLE. What tyranny!

CANT. . . . *Poetics*, part one . . .

AIRISTOTLE. The tragedy!

CANT. . . . your six works on logic, the *Organon* . . .

AIRISTOTLE. Say no more! *(Burying his face in his hands, weeping)* I'm so embarrassed . . . I'll never be able to show my face in public again . . .

CANT. You're welcome to hide here, but I should let you know that you're already out there as we speak, on the cover of millions of textbooks everywhere.

AIRISTOTLE. No!

CANT. *(Placing a hand on his shoulder)* Believe it or not, I feel your pain. I have an unjust reputation, too. Many of my political writings have a quite graceful style. And while they are not lost, it is much the same: they are not read.

AIRISTOTLE. *(Lifting face)* Do tell.

CANT. Hardly anyone reads my most elegant piece, an essay on unlightenment.

AIRISTOTLE. What is unlightenment?

CANT. You know it, then! How marvelous. I wasn't aware that you keep up with new trends in ideas—I thought you a hopelessly archaic thinker. I misjudged you, I'm sorry. Well, though, what did you think?

AIRISTOTLE. I would rather hear your self-assessment. You might find my own observations too . . . archaic.

CANT. *(Laughing)* Of course, you're probably right. Well, basically the essay is a lament. I wish I could say ours is an age of unlightenment, but it just isn't the case. Nor is anyone unlightened. They are merely un*en*lightened. Many even are attempting to move towards enlightenment, thinking that will change their state! My position is that ours is an age of enlightenment—or, same thing, an age of the unenlightened.

AIRISTOTLE. You still haven't answered my question.

CANT. What question?

AIRISTOTLE. I have a headache.

CANT. Drink some water.

AIRISTOTLE. My headaches can only be cured by walking.

CANT. Walking . . . *(he looks at the clock)*. Oh! I'm late!

"Above all, do not mistake me for someone else!"

If one of the great thinkers of history could witness his own posthumous reputation—the oversimplification of his ideas by lesser followers, his misappropriation by star pupils, the ingratitude of the general populace to his essential contributions—if this thinker could apprehend a set of consequences unfolding out of all proportion to his own intentions, what else could he do but . . . shrug his shoulders and task his brain even harder? Not to hope to overcome this state of affairs by clarifying himself to the point of banality, but to construct even more tangled puzzles to hide his treasures of thought in, assuring that only the most deserving will crack them. Weber should have turned to Modernist poetry; the enthusiastic bootlegging of rational-legal authority by public service menials and small business owners would have been replaced by teams of scholars perusing *The Waste Land* for obscure allusions to the Unreal City's impersonal management style.

Realizing that misinterpretation is the fate of subtlety, the Thinker might take this insight a step further and conclude that different cultural contexts *demand* divergent commentaries, the concerns of certain times even dismissal and silence. The thinker does not create himself by channeling his personality into a wood-pulp life, but is created *by his very own future*, a different version of himself cropping up with every new theorist and school, his portrait bearing the only evidence of unity. If he realized this, he would likely forego any attempt to achieve consistency of thought in the hopes of turning himself into an undying debate—and by doing so becoming a cheap imitation of his own doppelgangers, ensuring that few minds will take him seriously enough to invent them at all. Or if, like Kant, there was a rigid regularity in his personal habits making self-inconsistency impossible, he might stop thinking altogether and simply enjoy his daily walks, taking comfort in the order he establishes when people set their watches to his passing. Clocks, at least, involve a distortion everyone can agree upon.

Philosophers' Stroll

Cant *and* Airistotle *are walking through the park, where they notice* Heygal *standing across the grass, gazing at the sky.*

Cant. Quick, lets turn around.

Airistotle. There. Its okay, I don't think he saw us.

Heygal. Greetings, gentlemen! Where are you off to in such a hurry?

Cant. Oh hello. We didn't see you there. We were just going to . . . have dinner at my place.

Heygal. A splendid idea! I'm famished.

Airistotle. Actually, Immanuel, I'm not hungry.

Cant. Me neither.

Heygal. Well how are you on this fine evening? You know, every time I see that sunset I say to myself, "Farewell sun. We shall miss you." But this time I'm sure of it—just look at those bloody hues—*this* will be Prussia's last sunset! The Synthesis has declared it.

Airistotle: Georg, really. This is why we stopped coming to the park. The essence of pleasurable conversation is *novelty*.

Heygal. I couldn't agree more! *(He nudges Airistotle in the ribs.)* Hey—where the ladies at?

Cant. *(Looking around)* I see some walking over there.

Heygal. They should be over here! Call to them.

Part 6: Gray Dawn

CANT. I would prefer not to. I value my liberty.

HEYGAL. Don't be a stick in the mud!

AIRISTOTLE. Haven't you impregnated enough pupils this semester?

HEYGAL. Victims of the Synthesis, I assure you. Our age is unfolding in devious ways. But quick, they're getting away! You can have your pick—I claim the blonde! Between that pair of legs I detect the rise of the new Thesis. With any luck, she'll see the World Spirit riding in her mirror tonight.

CANT. I think I'll pass. Talking to women is not my forte.

AIRISTOTLE. Nor mine. I once mistook my wife for a statue of Zeus.

HEYGAL. You philosophers, how typical! Love isn't nearly as hard as you think. You need only apply a little skill in reasoning. Lay it on thick! Of course, you'll need some *new* content—not those outdated concepts you boys keep trucking around in your old heads. The dialectic, my friends, is a powerful aphrodisiac. Whenever I am wooing a woman, I simply refer to her eyes as, "a peaceful unfolding whose principle is the more indeterminate unity of feeling." That really drives them wild! Then when they start to swoon, I strike the killer blow: I say that if those lips were in charge of government, the state would be in danger.

CANT. Those lines sound familiar. Which poet was it who wrote them?

HEYGAL. Truly a great one—it's from *The Philosophy of Right*. You wouldn't believe how many times it's worked. Every new romantic advance I make only further corroborates my theory that woman is a plant.

AIRISTOTLE. *(To* CANT*)* Is that a modern idea?

CANT. *(In a low voice)* He's an old man. There's no limit to where his thoughts might go. If you ask me, his idealism took a step backwards.

AIRISTOTLE. *(Aside)* This is why I stick to ancient philosophy.

HEYGAL. Well what are we waiting for? Those girls we were eying are already gone, but I see some new ones under that oak!

AIRISTOTLE. Afraid I have somewhere to be.

HEYGAL. Where?

AIRISTOTLE. Anywhere. I just need to keep moving. I'm supposed to be in exile. The Athenians want my head, and I need to stay one step ahead. *(Exits.)*

HEYGAL. What about you?

CANT. I have to go. I'm late for my daily walk.

HEYGAL. But you're already walking.

CANT. Yes, and I have to make my rounds. Within the space of this city, Time depends on me.

HEYGAL. Fine then. But would you like to come over for dinner tomorrow? I'm having some ladies over who have traveled all the way from Italy. I'm sure they'll want to relate their adventures—and then have some more with us!

CANT: Sorry, I have a strict rule only to talk philosophy at the dinner table.

Utilitarian Tragedies

The unhappy artist brings happiness to others? —No, only brief indulgence, the nasal scratch in-between snores. Not even that if the artist's work is really nuanced—he projects only confusion. A truly sympathetic connoisseur hopes for a Schubert in every budding genius, with a finishing movement performed not by a symphony, but syphilis. Wondering "What if?" creates a sense of curiosity in a life that would have in all likelihood only produced anticlimaxes.

In Defense of Art

"The religion of art never killed anyone."—The reason a people praying to the icons of its Jainist saints are ripe for conquest. It is only the *murderous* artists who spread the good news of survival. Gesualdo showed us how to preserve the sanctity of marriage; Caravaggio that manslaughter can establish a no-nonsense reputation out of the most inebriated peacockery. But above all it is the homicidal backfires—the Pushkins—who convey the gravity of duty.

Slightly lower on the scaffold hang the thieves—all poets must begin their careers in petty theft. Whether they are able to ascend to grand larceny and beyond depends on a fortunate combination of skill and recognition; the police will give a budding talent the attention that reviewers neglect. François Villon is the prototype of the modern artist: first chickens, then gold crowns, then a dagger thrust, all the while honing verses in dungeons.

***

An artist's dying speech to his killer:

"I wanted to create beauty, but no one cared. Poverty and toil were slaying me silently. So I decided to make death roar. I turned to bloodshed as a means of popularizing my personality, hoping infamy would spread interest in my work. In this I cannot fail: though I am no good at the business of murder, my own violent demise will canonize me among the great imaginations. You think you have bested me, but you have not. You live only to be forgotten, whereas my fatality will be a masterpiece that inspires artists to come for generations."

Movement Towards Inertia

The visionaries of the present would do better to have been born in biblical times—the neglected futurist lacks the prophet's authority of timelessness. It only took five hundred years for Leonardo to become a primitive. Proposing stagnant perfection as your innovation is the only lasting rallying motive.

Nintendo Power

The least undignified strategy of confrontation against an imminent and inevitable end is videogaming. Digging broken fingers into bloody buttons, the battle against starvation going badly, we can at least withdraw into the old consoles for a final victory. A stack of cartridges is a multiverse of higher realities where a player's godhood is beholden only to the rules of programming. With the three-dimensional world facing a danger far less entertaining than any 8-bit one, hand-eye coordination is sure to be the last expertise to disappear . . . and the first to rise again as the most viable model of education for reconstruction.

    Scrambling over ruins, a half-savage man takes refuge from wolves in a fallout bunker. There he finds a Nintendo, the skeletons of its last players still gripping the controls. Turning the system on, he discovers *Super Mario Brothers* 3 and begins to understand the world that once was. Growing a bushy mustache, donning a red hat and overalls, he goes out to preach The Way. Pointing to dinosaur bones, he explains proof of the titanic struggle against the vanquished enemy. On a foraging expedition he establishes the life-giving benefits of mushrooms. Leading his brethren, he follows the pipelines to a secret underground realm where all will be safe from predators and the rays of the sun. Finding a raccoon on his next hunt, he offers the sacred animal for sacrifice. Then, with furry tail firmly attached to the seat of his pants, he stands at the edge of a cliff, ready to demonstrate to onlookers that their Princess is waiting beyond the horizon.

Conflicting Directions

Like a child holding balloons we hover between earth and sky, reaching upwards with our feet on the ground. Too many balloons and we lose touch with the surface; let go and leaping hurdles becomes strenuous. How to have it both ways? Hold on tight and gnaw off the hand . . .

The Forever New You

In an age of limited attention span creating yourself is about recreating yourself. The law of celebrity applies just as much to the avant-garde: to resist being typecast. The gradual development of a monochromatic style is too predictable for current tastes; with a versatility of talent we disperse into a grayscale rainbow. The old problem of megalomania is overlaid by one of sanity: *whose* megalomania?

Sovereign of Drones

Those who would excel in warfare today must first master the old videogames. When peace reigns, virtual reality steps in to satisfy the drive for bloodlust. The pastime of the lethargic will become the bane of all those who waste time on athleticism. The physique of tomorrow's soldier: a jiggling belly and a mighty thumb. Preparing with *Contra*, the next world war will be a conflict of visuo-motor skills between fat geeks— each a sharpshooter, pilot, infantryman, and general in one. Who would have thought that armed combat's renaissance man would be the incarnation of he in whom courage is as obsolete as a rifle?

Pusillanimity arose with the first tool: the caveman who invented the knife must have encountered accusations of cowardice from the heroes who preferred strangling saber-toothed tigers—until the spear came along. The most recently primitivized instrument always achieves a position of sudden honor. Someday when men have only to kill with a thought, pushing a button will seem a valorous tradition. Mortal duels fought with vintage Game Boys—every *Tetris* battle a sudden death round, the players positioned under dangling construction materials.

Winners and Losers

One uses the term "sore loser" only in relation to games, never where life is involved. But one never excels at life without first practicing through games. One plays them so long, becomes so adept, that eventually life itself becomes a game. The competitor scours dumpsters looking for the next power-up and frisks the sleeves of pedestrians for the card that will exchange his position with a piece closer to his goal. If he crashes his car or gets cancer, no worries: life will give you at least two continues before Game Over.

The sorest losers? —Life's non-contestants, those who declared bankruptcy for want of a monopoly board. (One only has to look at the situation of the average Russian citizen today to witness the truth of this maxim.)

Dilemma of The Champion: when life acquires a replay option and every party game turns a living room into a battlefront, the triumphant hero with a continue in reserve faces the necessity of adapting to peace, to work, to an existence where *there are no more games to play*. When one has dominated the business world, alienated friends and neighbors through victory, turned family interaction into a cold war without a panic button, what is left? —A game of solitaire, the mystery of the six-shooter chamber.

The IRS PhD

The tax form professor takes the utmost pains to doctor the prose of his documents. To turn it from dehumanized tedium into a distillation of his essence, overlaid with the calligraphy of binary code. Only the most exotic fonts will suit him.

He wants a refund on time. Minutes can't be saved like paychecks. When asked to enter his income he writes, "1,700 hrs." Taxable property? —"21 g of soul." Dependents? —"Humanity." Charitable donations? —"1,700 hrs."

When agents show up to audit him he claims a right to privacy: only he, and no one else, can tax his employment.

In jail he shares a cell with a corporate executive found guilty of fraud. "How much did you embezzle?" the executive asks.

"Not how much. *What*."

"Alright, what then?"

"My life. It's the only thing I had to report—I was a volunteer at the local community center."

***

First moral: The most successful humanitarians volunteer the lives of *others*. Mother Teresa helped the less fortunate to accept their lot so she could forward her charity profits to the papal treasury.

Second moral: Time, like taxes, can be an object of fraud. Punishment for not paying time due is, in fact, the risk faced by everyone not required to pay taxes.

Third moral: Money is greener than the earth, and foliates in inverse proportion.

Outrunning the Arrow

Time—as everyone must give it away and few have anything more to contribute, the many hoard all the minutes they can. Of all things, the most basic obligatory choice. Since only things yield thanks, patronage of character is always broadcasted to mute applause; but it is to these lone gallants that space is made livable.

Tyranny of the temporal—if one cannot escape it there is no point in yielding to its innovations in precision through a divorce from nature. To stew with the sundial on a cloudy day or be deposited by the glacial drift of the waterclock in winter; to use grandfather clocks for hypnotizing wealthy ailing relatives, pour their cremated remains into hourglasses, and in the space on the calendar for December 31st write "return to start." This almanac of discord awaits its Poor Richard to subject the seasons to local conveniences, bankrupting our common era by synchronizing momentous events to the Olympiads of football heroes, establishing an *ab urbe condita* for every petty kingdom, an *anno Domini* for every burgeoning cult figure. Amputating chronology from the authority of astronomers and mathematicians, he will reinstall native annals into the mists of legend, drawing a Venn diagram of prime meridian claims and equatorial conquests. Fragmenting the history of time, splitting its thread into curled strands, turning the record of societies into a multicyclical pattern of spinning interlaced rings. Never quite escaping the flow of time, what seems from the perspective of one person like Rousseau's aimless floating in the eternal present is, collectively, a congested river delta of oarless rafts bumping about in a series of incommensurable moments. So the human saga drifts, pauperized through languorous inaccuracy until the almanac is untangled over the course of a thousand sunrises by a senior puzzle-master, then sold for packaging and distribution from the assembly line of a minute mogul.

A Third Way

CIORAN: Resign.
CAMUS: Engage.
CINDERELLA: Indulge.

***

Surrendering everything but one's most cherished fantasy, tossing aside the mop to take on the aristocracy in glass slippers and a giant pumpkin, the most profound of amateur existential pessimists escapes from the daily suffering of sorority hazing into the eternity of fairy tale. But it is not enough: undergoing an endless pedaling of film adaptations depicting goodness's obscurity and redemption, the existential Cinderella is not satisfied with the "timelessness" of her story, closing as every version does before the wedding reception with prince charming. The best part—the triumph of love—a part that should go on forever, is cut short at the moment of her greatest happiness. So, yearning to exhaust the possibilities of the everlasting and become truly timeless, she makes a pact with dark forces: "Rewrite my story to make it never-ending." Transformed by the fairy godmother every night only to awaken every morning again as a peasant, she plummets from fairy tale into folklore, from enchantment to grotesquery, from an infinite present to a cycling between past and future. Sick of the prospect of realizing her royal ambitions to dance through drafty castles for an eon, desiring not immortality in children's fiction but only a final and complete permanence, the prince—to both her relief and despair—finally comes to Cinderella's rescue. He breaks the vicious circle just prior to a revolution that sweeps away the nobility and frees poor working girls everywhere from household bondage. Prevailing over time, she bows her neck with a grace widely remarked upon by the crowd, content to lose the struggle between the classes.

Genius Structures

There is an inhuman absence behind all works of art. Not only "fine art," but also—and especially—the beauty of the machine. The sleek elegance of an appliance whose form is dominated by function, of which there was seemingly no inventor or team of engineers at all, but existing simply as an outgrowth of the logic of industry, the spirit of production. There is a mechanism of artificiality in the world, unconditioned and yet ephemeral in its constant innovation, ordering the parts of things in compensation for biological deficiency. Though its knowledge is within our reach, we cannot grasp it all the same: it is too immanent, too pervasive to notice—and those of us who do find it too *low*. We are too "natural," too good to drink its dregs.

It is the same with beauty for beauty's sake, in which blotches of paint seem the collateral damage of a child's temper tantrum; only through a sophism of misplaced agency are they afterwards attributed to a ragged drunken Bohemian. Even where noticeable organization is present, it is not all the genius of a Monteverdi, but the confluent glories of Baroque style, Italian personality, Grecian ambition—all the forces which converged to flow out wholesale from Monteverdi's vessel. In high art it is the musicians who accompany the *basso continuo*. It takes a prodigy only to seize on receptivity, merging mind with norms to achieve a unity of Being. The path of mystery leads *outward*; one glimpses it by gesturing beyond oneself.

Might

The pen or the sword? —A question that flouts versatility in communication. After running the mail carrier through, the man of letters daubs a missive to the post office in blood: "Stop the spam." It is the manner of the message that produces conviction.

Art's Relative Emptiness

Forget the beauty of perfection. Give me a piecemeal beauty. Lacking too much essentiality to arouse gawking admiration, the pleasure of imagination is unlocked instead. A clue to Being. A wink towards harmony. A slice of stained glass that can't be fitted into a window to spare our discomfort is the refractory gleam of a vague beauty, a puzzle piece more devastating than the most crystalline *claritas* in virtue of the poignancy engendered by a sense of loss. The opposite of being present at creation, the mind's eye holds not the genesis of art here, but its book of revelations.

The March of Sentiment

Figurative expressions are testament to the continuing validity of outmoded knowledge for life. "What," the lovers of the future will ask, "do your diminished levels of serotonin tell you?" The day scientific terms finally catch up with poetry they too will become passé, the mushy leftovers salvaged from a kitchen fire.

Paraeneticus

Inside a public bath.
AIRISTOTLE. Oh Themison! Now that life has left you I'm finally able to say you were a good man—you died rich. Though I am sometimes criticized for not providing more encouragement to excellence while it is practiced, it didn't seem to be a hindrance in your case. By buying so many philosophers you saved them from starvation, and helped further your education in the process.
ISOCRATES. Who are you talking to, standing there pontificating like that? Really, Airistotle, I think all that abstract thought has finally ruined your brain.
HERACLIDES. Don't interrupt him when he's addressing the Forms!
AIRISTOTLE. Gentlemen, I can assure you I am neither going mad, nor speaking in Pythagorean terms. I was just paying tribute to an old friend.
ISOCRATES. Now is hardly the time for that. Have you forgotten about your pupils?
   (The three of them turn to look at the group of old men relaxing in the water.)
AIRISTOTLE. Of course not. Hello there everyone! I hope you are all ready to discuss philosophy!
FIRST OLD MAN. What's that?
SECOND OLD MAN. Speak up!
THIRD OLD MAN. He called you a monstrosity!
SECOND OLD MAN. Don't judge me based on my present appearance! I used to be handsome.
AIRISTOTLE. No, not monstrosity. PHIL-O-SO-PHY! It will have a great bearing on the direction your life takes.
FIRST OLD MAN. That's true. I see that's true everyday. I just look at my reflection in the water and I think, damn, you're so ugly now.
AIRISTOTLE. We're talking about philosophy. Have you ever thought about it before? Examined your life, the world, anything?

Part 6: Gray Dawn

THIRD OLD MAN. We were rich!

AIRISTOTLE. Wealth provides all the resources one needs for seeking wisdom.

SECOND OLD MAN. It did, until our sons had us declared unfit to manage our estates, inherited everything, and threw us out. Now our donkeys are the only ones who look after us.

ISOCRATES. (*To* AIRISTOTLE) That's probably for the best. Wealth without intelligence is harmful. These ancient children have been playing with knives all their lives.

HERACLIDES. I think you're underestimating these men, Isocrates. No one would choose to be rich and stupid, just as no one would choose to sleep through life for the sake of pleasurable but false images.

FIRST OLD MAN. Are we done yet?

THIRD OLD MAN. It's time for our nap.

AIRISTOTLE. In due time. But first tell me: how did you acquire your wealth?

FIRST OLD MAN. I was a merchant.

SECOND OLD MAN. I was a winemaker.

THIRD OLD MAN. I was a Theban.

AIRISTOTLE. So, you didn't get rich by being philosophers.

ISOCRATES. Don't be ridiculous, Airistotle. I know where you're trying to take this, and I'm cutting you off before you get there. No one is wealthy who stands around saying high-minded things about wealth; you have to own property.

AIRISTOTLE. The money isn't the thing—it's the effort you put into your work, and the ownership of ideas that results.

ISOCRATES. I would say that, rather than possessing either things or ideas, being healthy and educated is the goal of life. With idiots like these, the possessions they had are worth more than they themselves ever were; your ideas, on the other hand, are worth even less than you. People need to do practical things that enhance their souls' condition, not waste time on materialism or theoretical philosophy.

AIRISTOTLE. That is a rather philosophical view.

FIRST OLD MAN. So, naptime?

SECOND OLD MAN. No, haven't you been listening? We lost our wealth because we're monstrosities. Oh, you young people. Think you're invulnerable to time. But watch out—it'll happen to you!

THIRD OLD MAN. Not monstrosity. "Philosophy" was the word he used.

FIRST OLD MAN. Do philosophers sleep a lot?

ISOCRATES. That's all most of them ever do.

FIRST OLD MAN. That's good. I want to be one then.

AIRISTOTLE. No, no. I'm afraid you misunderstand my intention in coming here. I don't want you to become a philosopher. I want you to go back to being a merchant.

That's the best way for you to realize your philosophical calling—implicitly, and, as it were, negatively. You see, the thing about philosophy is that, as an occupation requiring nothing external, everywhere you go someone is already there doing it. The academics are invading our public spaces. Better to remain in the private sector, the vineyard, or Thebes.

ISOCRATES. You mean that you came to discuss philosophy in a bathhouse with some homeless men who don't care about it, just to convince them to continue not doing it?

AIRISTOTLE. No, so that they will do it. The point I am making is that there must be certain criteria in the study of philosophy: merchants should do more philosophy by demonstrating the need not to, and through this negative demonstration become anti-philosophers, while philosophers should do less philosophy by remaining silent on things beneath their dignity, becoming anti-philosophers by confining themselves to mathematics and science.

ISOCRATES. If these rich old fools decide not to do philosophy, that doesn't make them anti-philosophers. It makes them non-philosophers.

AIRISTOTLE. But these fools, as you call them, in not being philosophers by relinquishing the choice to do philosophy, and thus the right to decide what is best for themselves, would, in concluding not to do philosophy, become anti-philosophers through their use of reason. The professional philosophers, too, being mathematical logicians and scientists, are anti-philosophers. So, whether you do or do not do philosophy, you are doing anti-philosophy.

ISOCRATES. What nonsense! How could you take such a view? Just look at them floating on their backs, dozing off! In their peak states of wakefulness they wallow in ignorance and ill-health. What men like these should or should not do in life is clearly not a matter they are competent to demonstrate themselves. I'm telling you, they're completely incapable of philosophy of any kind, pro- or anti-.

AIRISTOTLE. Who, then, should demonstrate for them?

ISOCRATES. Those supreme by nature, intelligent men. By which I mean Philosophers—not those such as you who go against life, but those who neglect the prior things and skip ahead to the posterior ones.

HERACLIDES. I think you're both forgetting something.

AIRISTOTLE. What?

HERACLIDES. You propose to turn them back to their practical ways, Airistotle, but this will likely go very badly if they have not first been instilled with knowledge of mathematics, something you have hitherto only spoken of in regard to professional philosophers.

ISOCRATES. That will be hopeless with the Theban. You know that city lags behind all others when it comes to math and science education.

PART 6: Gray Dawn

HERACLIDES. If that's true, the public bath's the proper place for him. Even if one chooses not to do philosophy—or, as you say, Airistotle, fools oneself into thinking one isn't doing philosophy—everyone should consciously strive to be better at mathematics. By learning that, they will become better at philosophical demonstration.

ISOCRATES. If it were up to you, Heraclides, you would force the whole world to convert to Pythagoreanism and swear off beans forever.

HERACLIDES. Yes, that's right. Just make fun. You're not able to engage me logically, but only spit rhetoric.

ISOCRATES. There are many labels for that theological claptrap you adhere to, but "logical" isn't one of them. Admit it: no one even knows the details of Pythagoras's mathematical science as it was actually practiced in his day.

HERACLIDES. It can be reconstructed to close approximation!

ISOCRATES. A futile effort. What is lost can never be recovered.

HERACLIDES. You know, if you followed Pythagoras's teachings you wouldn't be so negative. Participating in the dodecahedron can help you. I carry one around in my pocket, see? *(Takes out a small wooden polyhedron with twelve faces.)* It strengthens my moral being. As long as I have it, no misfortune can ruin my virtue.

AIRISTOTLE. Mathematics is indeed important, Heraclides. No one is denying that. But mathematics is, like the other theoretical sciences, primarily valuable for its truth and precision alone rather than what results from it. Just as it is absurd to think highly of astronomy because of heavenly prophecies that might enrich your life, so is it ridiculous to appreciate mathematics for its moral significance. It is the duty of the highest minds, before the next meteorological catastrophe hits, to develop the first sciences as much as possible and disseminate them far and wide. This way, there will be a good chance that some of it will carry over into the next cycle so that when men begin again they will not be ignorant without becoming first informed. The god made us for the sake of intellectual abuse, as Pythagoras said, and an age in which reason is underdeveloped is one in which a recurring destruction can't be expedited. The only function of the soul is to reason badly, and until we are transported to the Isles of the Anathematized and have nothing to do but think crooked truths, the intelligent will live flawed lives.

ISOCRATES. About all that apocalyptic theory, I will leave you to your madness and pass over without comment. But I disagree that a science should be valued for its truths alone. Science must be able to predict events. Mere knowledge is worthless. Mathematics, when it is not applied, does not help us accomplish anything. A good life is one in which actions are undertaken well, and as long as there are navigators of such skill your Isles of Idleness will be avoided.

AIRISTOTLE. I will agree that, in the case of citizens such as those before us, applied mathematics will increase rigor of thought and provide a significant advantage in their respective professions and geographical handicaps. What do you say then, gentlemen? Shall we begin our lessons on the square root of two?

FIRST OLD MAN. No. I don't want to go back to being a merchant. I like it here, just bathing and napping all day.

SECOND OLD MAN. My hands hurt. I have a hard time grasping small things. My fingers squish the grapes, I can't help it. Old age has put viticulture behind me.

THIRD OLD MAN. After listening to you I've become too smart to go back to Thebes. I'm changing my citizenship. I want to be an Athenian.

ISOCRATES. (*To* AIRISTOTLE) If he does that, he'll certainly fall in with some Cynics in the marketplace.

AIRISTOTLE. Yes, that wouldn't be in accordance with his soul's proper virtue. He'll ruin what's left of his future for sure.

ISOCRATES. Perhaps, Airistotle, we should address our debates to the young next time.

AIRISTOTLE. Agreed.

Accommodating the Range of Indeterminacy

"It sort of is, and sort of isn't."—Making up one's mind on an object's rough composition of matter versus soul is like a bastard child parsing his duties between his low and highborn genes. He cannot simply say one hand is fit to hold a scythe, the other a scepter; each hand is both *and* nothing. Counting the days until the next harvest on ten ring fingers, the sunlight's dispersive reflection on his diamonds parallels an angular world. To existence's bastard—those few with a double conscience for verity and deliverance—every piece of mass becomes a jumble of atoms, a periodic puzzle of elements. Mendeleev's deism was the backlash against his mother's insistence on *patiently* searching for divine and scientific truth—sumless semantics of a willed vagueness, quantification of lip-strumming, a hybrid solution instantaneous and unspeakable. Where there seems no exclusively correct solution for the supervenience of spiritual facts upon physical ones, indeterminate biochemical laws divvy out a parcel of soul for every mitochondria and viral invader.

A Date with Truth

You pick her up. She greets you with a flat expression. She insists on opening the car door for herself, then lets you in on the driver's side. She's the quiet sort, so you try to draw her out on the way to dinner. You ask her questions about her life, but the things she tells you just aren't convincing. They either sound too good (an A+ student?) or too bad (when some gangsters knocked on her door and asked whether her brother was home, she told them he was in the coat closet.)

When you get to the restaurant she excuses herself to the ladies' room, where she changes outfits and removes her wig. As she walks back to the table her low-cut dress attracts a good deal of attention. The person now before you has transformed from the homely brunette you only reluctantly agreed to take out into a striking redhead. You look around; the men gaze at her covetously, the women enviously; they all look at you with awe. How did this loser get that girl?

Your date whispers her order in the waiter's ear. He nods and winks at you. You're dying to know what she ordered. You ask her why she doesn't speak up? All night she is whispering. It takes a loud person to have a hoarse voice. While waiting for the meal she recognizes an acquaintance and goes over to say hi. Again you sit alone, playing with your silverware. Your meal arrives. It wasn't what you ordered, but you decide to eat it anyway. Ungarnished, you hope its taste will be more appealing than its presentation. Nope, bland. Your date sits back down. But where is her meal? She didn't order one. You tell a few jokes as you eat to help pass the time for her. You can't tell if it's the humor or the fact that you are talking with your mouth full that seems to undercut the chemistry between you even more. Or the fact that she keeps mentioning her dead brother under her breath. His absence was more of a presence than you. He *had* to die, she whispered. He just couldn't fit in. He would have no place in an ideal world.

You drive her home. You walk her to the door and try to give her a kiss on the cheek, but she pulls away. You refuse to be denied, though. Her mystery has teased you all night and driven you into a state of animal frenzy. So you grope her. You wouldn't normally do that; you want to be a gentleman, after all, just like mom always told you to be.

While caressing her, you feel a lump in her pelvic region. Finally you understand "her" reserve to offer herself. Embarrassed, you mumble an apology and stumble to the car.

From now on you decide to spend your Saturday nights at home watching sitcoms and eating canned tuna. Bachelorhood, you realize, is the intended condition of man. That, and being an only child.

Peering under the Bed Sheet

What if truth is a woman *no longer*, but a trans woman, an androgyne, pangendered—even all of these and more: "genderqueer," a catch-all phrase for everything not status quo? What if the *lifestyle* of truth has evolved over the past century? Would not "its" fondlers then be reduced to something beyond clumsiness—to bafflement? Had we only the opportunity to fumble with it, how successful we might feel by comparison! Instead we stand gaping, trying not to condescend, *tolerant*. Truth has become not a state, but a range of choices. We are not even obliged to accept *a* choice from among them, but only maintain the suspension of their range. A hermaphrodite—not an either/or, but a both/neither; *Philo* + *Sophoclea*: love of the ambiguous, seduction of the inconclusive. Rooting itself in the very biology of its seekers, it proves only that metaphysics, like everything else, is dependent on the study of life.

Kierkegaard's regret, an apology for every actualized deed, does not apply here; but our own apology, one about the state of things, the implication of factual arrangements, could easily take an inverted form of the great Dane's description: whatever is, you will *not* regret it. Our apology for ontology is a defense of our shamelessness.

Perceptive Blunders

The difference between a subtle error and a crude one is a more crucial distinction than the pendulum swing of right and wrong—those polar continents insulated by vast seas but so often drifting and colliding at the equator, merging into a moral Pangaea for all but the dogmatic. A principle admits no moistness of *detail*, that unfailing affixer of "but...", which so easily turns crusty truths into crude errors. But... append enough "ands" to one's commandment and even the most unmelodic presupposition becomes food for raised ears.

Narrative Conceits

A truth's dramatic effect is to clarify implications and multiply interpretations. Witnessing the *deus ex machina*, the audience speculates on the backstage tricks. Why, an astute observer thinks, doesn't the stagehand just drop the god? If he did that he would prove that showing a truth is not less dangerous than reciting it. But the god remains hoisted. The stagehand's failure to act reveals that truth's motive for resorting to narrative is more than the desire to be understood; it is also the safety of being ambiguous. Though one suspects even this is only a precondition for selling tickets.

Mistrusting the Senses

The masses are too overwhelmed by the taste a truth leaves in their mouths to use their eyes, the academics too busy listening for distant echoes. It does no good just handing out magnifying glasses and binoculars; one needs to distribute duct tape and earplugs along with them, adjusting one set of senses while suppressing the others. A certain range of proximity to a truth must be maintained to deal with it effectively—neither being struck dumb by it nor losing contact with it. To know if you are at the correct distance to see it distinctly, it is not enough to trust your eyes; you must also ask yourself how strong this truth *smells*. If it makes your mouth water, you are too close; if it doesn't so much as trigger a memory, too far. And if you ever find yourself within arm's reach, by no means should you reach out and touch it—you will not get that hand back.

The Highest Bond

The most incorruptible friendship is between individuals who disagree with each other on the fundamental questions. Each profoundly respects the other's dissimilarity to himself. "Anyone who thinks like *me* doesn't deserve to have a friend," each had told himself for so long. They knew they could never have that friend they wanted so desperately . . . until they found him. And they so wanted to keep him that each was willing to let in falsehood, appropriating it unto themselves, ashamed of their own opinions and timid to express them. "The other is false, he does not know the truth, does not even *care* about it. And this is what we have in common—that he thinks the same about me." It is a friendship rooted in the exclusion of the self. Each friend simply is what he is not to the other. They resist giving into the difficult temptation of understanding one another, jettisoning their inner worlds to share adventures together.

It is when they meet those who share their truth that they become hostile, arguing over points of detail and splitting into factions. That is when their pure friendship, unsullied by alliance, is needed most: playing the devil's advocate in a quarrel to sever them from the important questions, nursing one another in sickness as an opportunity to chastise neighbors and compatriots, removing the common ground between friend and community. A real friendship is not a charity. "I don't want to confuse my being your benefactor with my being your friend," they tell one another. "I don't want a loan or a good deed to come between us, anything that might be *owed*. I don't want us to waste time on the accidents of life."

The day they find others like them they can band together in a club and enter practical life, excluding without mercy those obstinate in principles, gathering around them a host of worthies with flexible standards of veracity, expanding into an organization to usher in the dissolution of collective ideologies.

Preferring Love

The man who narrows community to his tastes: frowning at children, acknowledging only *homeless* pedestrians, surrounding himself with those who happen to be at secret society meetings. Unfettered from affection he freely chooses his excellence, sloth, and brand of paranoia; all conform to his oddities. Humanity is made for him alone.

Life and Philosophy

Occasionally poets have made a living as poets. We cannot expect this success of philosophy; it is enough to ask after one who, in the search for wisdom, made a *life*. One benchmark for assessing the record of philosophy in a given period is by looking at the biographies of its practitioners to see whether it allowed for an eventful existence to inspire deep questions and make the boring figures interesting by proxy. Socrates's thirst gave Plato's Academy food for thought; Avicenna's restlessness filled Averroes's library; Abelard's castration aroused Scholasticism long enough for Aquinas to apply his rigor; Ockham's excommunication killed the medieval worldview elegantly. An age is either oppressive or derivative: one that does not persecute a few of its greatest thinkers is destined to be passed over as unoriginal.

    All of philosophy's problems today stem from this: that man sits alone in a room . . . then stands in another room to report on the conclusions of his indolence marathon. This single statement exhausts the biography of every living philosopher. An image of Russell rotting in a jail cell comes to mind; its natural complement is the image of Wittgenstein in the trenches: without mud and blood, the pacifist stance has no point to make.

Dangerous Thoughts

The "extreme" intellectuals: those who buckle their seat belts with platitudes and pieties to safeguard their ideas. Stuffing their parachute bags with thirty-foot theories, they jump *after* opening. Show me instead the thinker who leaps without a parachute, who is bored with gentle descent, tired of an indistinct landscape—who is not afraid of plummeting at maximum velocity for the sake of a respectable splatter radius.

New Historiography

Postulate of Sublimity: everything bad, trivial, and tasteless is impossible because too mundane.

    Axiom of the Extraordinary: as the great deeds of the history books occurred, so must noble and notable actions always occur everywhere naturally.

    ***

    We would be supremely lucky if the future would take the most unscientific attitude possible towards the timelines of societies, augmenting human nature by overlooking its forgettable and shameful examples, guilding our steel age with myth and circumcising smirking ironies to give rise to the Epic of the Average: singing rhymes to barter for bread, invoking arms and a muse in prayers for a plentiful slaughterhouse yield; *arête* of the assembly line, mergers and acquisitions jousting tournaments.

Banished into Glory

Themistocles, Alcibiades, Aristotle—great talents in an age of great talent, their pre-eminence made them dangerous. Genius proves itself most fully by choosing the losing side of a struggle: only the hunted bring their aptitudes to fruition. If Dante and Machiavelli had remained Florentines they would never have come to dominate their genres; Caravaggio would have remained a shallow religious painter, favoring light over shadow; Hugo a footnote in poetry; Voltaire a mediocre playwright. The prince of the mind must love his soul more than his city. Exile is a condition of greatness, and most admirable of all is he who refuses it. Political exile being no longer an option, what will the modern Socrates ground his repudiation in? —Something higher than a community . . . *and* something lower . . .

Voting for Governments

Statesmen today are anything but stately; children need only look to presidential candidates for role models of boasting and taunting that surpass the coarsest playground behavior. The current political climate is one of compromise and quibbling, bills amended into ineffectiveness. In the civil war between democans vs. republicrats, combatants wear suits from the same retailer. The extremes of the nineteenth-century political spectrum fit my disposition better. I would rather give my allegiance to an anarchist mob or the *Ancien Régime*—it doesn't matter which. If there cannot be a supreme Pope or a Holy Roman Emperor, I would at least like to have *both*. In Russia I await either the return of the Tsar or Kropotkin. Order or chaos, the Mandate of Heaven or Hobbes's war of all against all—nothing in-between tyrannies will do.

Armageddon's Exoneration

The perpetrations of outer space wipe away all sense in remembering who to forgive. Revenge against the world is the only way to pardon an accident of gravity. An asteroid collision is the perfect excuse for repaying past insults, or, in the absence of a perpetrator, invoking the solar wind. Failing that, the *prediction* of an asteroid collision . . .

Dominance

It is not "humanity" as a whole, but in its particular qualities that it should be measured. The cheetah's speed, the bear's strength, the cat's agility—however else we allocate magnificence, we can at least conclude that the paragon of creatures is not an athlete. Nor—the television screen being a mirror—is the sports network viewer. The qualified recipients of the prize of "most glorious" having thus drastically dwindled in number, one is tempted to look up into the sky and wonder whether there is some inhabited planet out there where individuals win medals for *just loafing*.

Public Servants

If there is one crisis the endangered species can solve for us, it is human overpopulation. It is a cavalry call over which carnivore, herbivore, and detrivore alike can unite, swelling their threatened numbers into an all-or-nothing stampede. Whether eating us, consuming our sources of nutrition, or clearing cemetery space, the poached and deforested are our last resort in preventing suffocation and genocide.

Soul Symbols

Like the Mormon leader who claims to represent all the souls of the world, everyone has a desire for their own peculiar universalization. The only difference between the Prophet of the Brine Shrimp and Nominalist Man is a person who bequeathed visions from a top hat versus one who, fearing an armed mob, keeps creeds under the cap. To forecast an egoist's legacy of illusions you have only to measure the size of his headgear—beware the savior with a sombrero.

Extraterrestrial Nihility

As men used to imagine life under the sea and map the canals on the moon, so we continue to resist the receding frontier of proof. When we do finally refine our instruments enough to ascertain that there is, in fact, no intelligent life in the far reaches of the universe, science fiction will come to our aid to push our wish fulfillment past the brink of the astronomically improbable. No matter what the evidence to the contrary, the desire to share our pain with something will never abate. When our universe disappoints us there will still be alternate dimensions to hide our optimism in; failing that, time itself will shelter our illusions. When the future becomes unlivable, the last sentient organism will travel into the past, not to save man from his trajectory—those with humanitarian intent regarding this species will be long dead—but simply to be around warm bodies once again.

The question never goes stale: *What if?* —Nor does the predetermined answer. Suppose that for millennia aliens have been sending a radio signal to Earth in the language of mathematics. Not having any fingers to inspire them, they never developed a base-10 decimal system. Instead of pulses of monads their message uses only zero, the expression of their limblessness and the name of their most important god (also limbless). Leibniz's void has been speaking to us all along, but we never picked up on the silence. If such a species were revealed to exist, there would be no need for complaints about a belated cosmic anticlimax or the waste of taxpayers' dollars. Instead, the quietude of the astronomy community would *imply* these things, relegating their hopes to the status of all the discredited religions they so despise. There is no death like discovery. With no worthwhile resources to exploit, no knowledge to kindle our envy or ferocity to hold us in awe, creatures with nothing more to offer than another incompatible worldview might stir enough indignation to temporarily unite us into "earthlings," a reason for biological heritage at last provided under the banner of planetary holocaust.

Splintering

A person seeking oneness with the universe always gains a reputation for misanthropy and discord. Others suspect the motives of a fusion in which they are not included. An invitation to dwell together risks accusations of theft or privacy invasion. Salvation is lonesome and only meaningful because exclusive. There is spiritual hierarchy among the raptured. As they wait they cast glances amongst themselves, whispering "who" in their minds, but knowing full well. All the best stories confirm their intuition: the most famous voyages were about *a* traveler. One has only to conduct a survey to verify the opposite, that judging from all the colorful brochures and fulsome eulogies, Hell is a deserted tropical paradise, a *dis*topia where vigorous sinners bask amidst gilded domes and are waited on by fallen angels.

To become "one" with the universe—one with the relentlessness of gravity, the silent chill of space, the storms of Jupiter, one with carnivores and predators, the laziness of casual goodness, the fear of the terminally ill. Against this, what does love amount to? —A pinch of salt in a frozen sea. And yet this trifling ingredient is the only justification for all the rest. Like a salvation army volunteer joining a Mongol horde, relinquishing one's individuality to existence is to condone the sweeping away of empathy by destructive indifference. This is not a universe I wish to even be a *part* of, let alone one with. But that I *accept* my disappointment of this condition so I can divert my attention to its more frivolous matters—this is paramount, this I can do.

A sense of oneness is for the masochist; best to descend into solipsism through multiplicity, shattering yourself and spilling your contents on the rug. "I am far *less* than the ordinary me," Subpersonal Man says. Tired of bestriding the pinnacle of existence by occupying his own head, he opens his trapsoles and slips through his shoes to possess abyssal manifestations. By segmenting his out-of-body disorders—the "me" of a brain trauma, psychedelic drugs, sensory deprivation—he culls a thought experiment from every induced madness, becoming first one thing, then another, then many. Caressing each inch of space until every cell wall is a new perimeter, his mind at last achieves total liberation through a lobotomy.

Beyond Algebra

X waved. Y wagged. Z flapped. Finally, people who convey their arbitrary substitution-value outside of symbols—who signal their feelings with a flailing of ghost limbs.

A Biosphere Closer to Our Hearts

Whose greed is lazy enough await the arrival of its consequences? Civilizing the destiny of natural processes only requires a sense of civic duty. Watering our steel objects with garden hoses to increase the iron oxide on the planet's surface, carving away our top strata with personal bulldozers to halve its diameter, whooshing away the outer atmosphere with leaf blowers, leaving cars running to pump the sky full of carbon dioxide, forming a bucket brigade to relocate the oceans to the polar ice caps—by spearheading terraforming through a call to everyday chores and volunteer work, humanity can render obsolete the mere curiosity and debate of scientific research teams. With a bit of cooperation and diligent housekeeping we can fulfill our mission as Martians: to make the Earth a hospitable place for detached observation—a sight for aliens staring through their telescopes, conjuring canals on our surface and writing pulp fiction about the species of gondoliers that traverse them. The alkaline dust will settle on our willed elimination to transform us into doting parents, lulling the children of the universe to sleep with bedtime stories of our common fictional identity. As picturesque rascals we glide our oars through the water, lithe and stately—more charming than we ever were as Earthlings.

Too Much Art

We are always impressed when a thinker or artist "predicts" a future movement by developing the seed of a style or hitting on a premature idea. But could not a flouting of contemporaneity work backwards? The ideas and styles of the past are in many cases so vague on details and shrouded in obscurity that a new work or theory does not rediscover its predecessor, but invents it wholesale as it should be. The past holds the realization of *present* possibilities. As it recedes there are fewer and fewer combinations of styles and ideas to work with. Simplification is made easy when one can dig anywhere and strike a root. From the few moldy, tattered scrolls handed down by the ancients we find the authority for every species of theory. "Personal" style is a derivative blend of *stronger* renaissance dispositions.

For our future, though, there will be too many influences to trace. There is too much art—to attempt a total absorption is a doom heroic and pathetic in equal measure, a feat requiring not only the sacrifice of a scholar's life, but his family of research assistants also. It is almost enough to welcome a *biblioteca abscindita*: preempting indiscriminate barbarian pillage by making a funeral pile of everything second rate, pouring the gasoline, and dancing before shelves of ashes. A world library comprised of Mother Goose would be enough to continue our lineage, with national schisms spawned by commentaries on aviary descent and the feasibility of outlawing nursery rhymes until adulthood.

Art in the Age of Digital Reproduction

An advance beyond the mechanical: the replica not being a physical entity, it does not cheapen the original or confuse itself with it, but *surpasses* it in value, transforming even the notion of value itself in the process. The worth of the work is no longer a product of rarity, but infinity; not of age, but the perpetual freshness of new updates. It transcends its immediate material bounds, compressing time and expanding space into a limbo between room and circuit board. A second-order artifact, every computer must be smashed to evaporate it. Electronic junkyards in the wake of Armageddon will safeguard Caravaggio's twice-lost *Saint Matthew and the Angel* for remote archaengineers.

Ultrasensory Art

Dispensing with color, even with the canvas, art must become imperceptible to the human senses in order to stay innovative. Existing on the microscopic, x-ray, or dog-pitch level, it needs its neutrino detector to be apprehensible. As art draws on science so much today, for inspiration as well as self-examination, making itself "rigorous" even while seeming careless, the next logical step is to take its galleries where science has gone—into space or a mile underground. Only then will art and science become one indistinguishable culture, something as far beyond the avant-garde as the avant-garde is beyond the general populace, a new *supra*sensibility. The ultimate move into silence. The scienartist—the first "aesthetician" in the full sense of the term—will study for years to reach the cutting edge of reality, overthrowing the current paradigm of truth only to fashion it into an artificial beauty. The Grecian Urn Nebula.

The Boulevards of Extinction

Experiencing Love

It is impossible to write about love when one *feels* it. In the search to describe a great passion one must break the tools of art, leave the library, and head to where all love begins and ends—a law court. The prosecutor-as-protagonist inspires the author's card catalogue of emotions.

What You Leave Behind

To find the way back to the hospital leave a path of entrails. The dentist, teeth. The plastic surgeon, spare flesh. Keeping health, hygiene, and figure is all about remembering how you got to where you are, and more will follow a road of habit than model themselves on its daily journal. "Got an incisor knocked out today. In exchange, the tooth fairy left a gun under my pillow."—Who could fail to begrudge someone stalked by magic and the third amendment? Men of example keep their servants a secret, colonizing the storybook world with R-rated content and lobbying for rights with smiles that bleed.

Borderlining

It has not yet been considered that one may attempt suicide not to actually die—even less to cry for help—but to have a near-death experience that would transform one's approach to life. "She's dead!" a relative screams as the suicide watches her own body lying on the floor. Her life flashes before her eyes, she hears beautiful music, she reaches the border between life and death, meeting there other beings who have died. She converses with these beings. The suicide feels indescribable peace and calmness as she has never felt, but the deceased presences tell her to go back. What? *Go back*? But the point of this whole act was to die, wasn't it? Well . . . no, she realizes now, it wasn't. Her attempted suicide *was* a cry for help, but not to the people around her—boors who, while making her miserable, would condescend to encourage her, to lift her out of her depression. No, the cry for help was *to death itself*. So she wakes up, rejuvenated in life—she wants to be able to have her near-death experience *again*, to *live* on the border of life and death. So she joins a charity organization, helps the less fortunate on weekdays, runs a warm bath every Saturday night, slices her wrists, and takes a brief vacation homeward . . .

What makes men the less spiritual and more theological sex, on average, is that they never attempt a near-death experience: they just blow their brains out. While a life-threatening situation, a car accident, or cardiac arrest may occasionally lead them to the epiphany for the need to repeatedly attempt suicide, such accidents are rare. For men are, in the end, so forced into the exemplar of being "rational" that they are unable to thrive on anomalous experiences, to revel in simply being impossible and existing beyond the ordinary laws of physics—to live as a borderliner.

Self-Contradiction

Those who hate humanity accomplish nothing by revoking their membership: after suicide, the race remains. Genocide would fit the misanthrope better, were it not that he risks being mistaken as a *lover* of humanity through that course of action—exterminating nonpersons to strengthen solidarity, eliminating the public enemy to universalize "we." So, unable to kill either himself out of futility or others for fear of being misunderstood, what is the misanthrope to do? No choice but to *enjoy his innate failings*, a task best realized by betraying his inclinations and mixing with the crowd, a social butterfly with a sardonic edge . . .

But in this surrender to the *vita activa* he is horrified to find, of all things, the meaning of life. That Swift was a notable philanthropist is proof that misanthropes are often a greater boon to humanity through their practical efforts than humanists are through the beliefs that pool up within them. If only there were a crack in the foundation so their principles might drain out and soak into the world—if only the humanists had a touch of misanthropy. Swift didn't stop at instructing mankind through writing; he *earned* his hatred: inspired through abhorrence to help the throwaways of our flaws, he watched as opportunities for betterment were continually squandered, until finally he could take no more and was admitted into the very madhouse he established.

The clear-sighted philanthrope practices beneficence without tenderness, handing a coin to the penniless as encouragement to abandon the breadline for the liquor store.

Escape into Beauty

Schopenhauer's claim that we can step out of time simply by looking at a painting is not nearly so naïve as assuming that the old masters themselves ever achieved such objectivity vis-à-vis the universe. One glance at the self-portraits of Raphael and Botticelli will tell us otherwise. They place themselves on the margins of overpopulated scenes with an audacity for revealing their own insignificance. They move over but not up; with centrifugal force they are pushed aside to make way for the important subject matter, forever linked with the group they are alienated from—intellectually in Raphael's case, spiritually in Botticelli's. With contrary reactions they both display their own utter lack of self-dissolution as we see the anxieties wrought by their own personalities imbuing the work through and through.

Raphael's questioning look in the *School of Athens* portrays his own doubts about himself within his age; we see him not as the definitive Renaissance man occupying center stage, as Leonardo's Plato does, glorying in the pursuit of knowledge, but as an artist out of place amidst logical ferment. And something more: his skepticism regarding his age itself. Where were the analytical achievements of the present to compare with those of the past? For all the likenesses to contemporaries, Renaissance Italy was not ancient Greece—the church fathers saw to that when they ordered Raphael to remove Hypatia. Their only peers to the stars of antiquity were in the visual arts—the very discipline which flags Sanzio as a misfit in his most famous work.

Contrast this hesitation with Botticelli's arrogance in the *Adoration of the Magi*, supreme example of the great refusal of this middle world, taking sides neither with the worldly power of the Medici family nor the spiritual authority of the Christ child. A mere shadow among these great figures, we sympathize with him as he shrinks away, aloof; we see that his proud look is a compensation for his spatial banishment, that not being up to the task of action, as they are, he aggrandizes himself through representation.

Two different portrayals, each mired in painful self-consciousness, *doubly* subjective—to meet their gaze is to feel their suffering.

An Expensive Telescope

The *refraction* of attitude into philosophical orientation—Mill's subcutaneous depression circulating through the logical progress of man, Schopenhauer's raging libido. A positive starting point to philosophy is sometimes only possible when one's disposition is negative. Being's melancholics are the West's standard transmission mediums. A black temper is the premise of light's eventuality. Similarly, the *serious* pessimist only drapes the void around himself on the way to a costume party, modulating the apocalyptic in juxtaposition to an elated mood. Like browsing a wallpaper catalog, the nihilist is the impressionable vessel of a *bildungstrieb* of night shades: his merriment sets the tone. Strolling through the park daily, a flower's stage of bloom or a hatching egg were the stimuli to Cioran's thoughts. The rarity of this peculiar chirpiness, this warped jollity that needs *a* nothing to push against to prevent crashing into the heavens, is the symptom of an ongoing war lost *in the beginning* with Thales. It is the reverse psychology of failure. The champions of darkness in the west must always be defining themselves against the enemies outnumbering them, the engineers of entities, the industrialists building an empire on the assumptions of science and religion. But in the east it is the heretic of Being who is the jaded pessimist, the rude sufferer. His gratuitous opposition to Nothing's welcoming smile is not dismissed: it is not even possible to dismiss it.

Letters From Beyond

If only, like Gracián, we all had a correspondent in hell. Someone to make the devil's movements known, to tip us off to where our next source of damnation might lie. Everyone needs a hint of perdition to be spurred in the direction of their inclinations.

The smart man, knowing where to go, does not run toward or away but launches himself into an oblique orbit. He doesn't fall in with the prejudice for man's "deepest longings"; he knows that at the end of time there will be a *winner* . . . and every champion needs a successor. He doesn't believe that story about one devil and one God. He has been informed otherwise. Even deities are subject to retirement and inheritance; their continuing sovereignty is just predicated on presenting a unified front. In reality there has been a different god for every book of the bible, a devil for every phase of humanity—why else would they need so many names? Divinities do not grow old, do not die. They simply lose touch with a changing creation. And when this happens a new one is needed to reestablish contact, to redecorate the afterlife to suit the tastes of the time. The Watchmaker is obsolete; we need a Computer Engineer to relate to us, one who doesn't simply wind up the universe and let it tick, but is always available at a technical support hotline to fix glitches. At the inauguration of every fresh modernity the untested God takes his inexperience into account when the angels, like Darius's servant, remind him of the events of Revelation at the dinner table. "Not yet," he waves them off. "*This* God wants to get to know his new people." But his real concern is . . . fear of losing. Of being too antiquated for the final battle, precisely because of his need for contemporaneity. The devil has no need to make himself into a metaphor for the latest technology, to hide his magic in science for the sake of intelligibility. Evil never becomes outdated; it only sheds its skins.

So the smart man, coached with insider knowledge on what to say, keeps circling and watching, ready to swoop down the on the morrow after Judgment day for a place in the last will and testament.

Pascal Through Montaigne

The road to purity is through messiness. A penile disobedience by turns fierce and impotent is atoned for with a knife and a bit of wrapping paper. Human nature is the only restraint on the mind, and where it runs amok our thoughts follow, unable to evade corporeal whims. Exceeding the limits of our bodies and the world is the surest way to sanitize ourselves, to fumigate the termites of consciousness. The mind evaporates as the planet tumble-dries us around the sun. Boredom is surpassed into zeal. A being with nothing to root its brainstem in is free to float through space, obstructed only by guilt, an angel with the memory of a beast. Perversity persists beyond itself in retrospection, more sensible than ever. The recognition of this sinfulness is its validation, a sign that sanctification has been achieved; unable to see it for the evil it was when it was being carried out, infinity now mires the lone mind in its denial of diversity. What was muddy has become coherent. Before there were too many places to rest; now there are none. The end having been achieved there is nothing to do but reflect on its means.

Downward Ascent

To plant two feet firmly in the ground, spread two arms, and open a mouth to the sky. The formula for rapid growth is to not be picky about what one swallows—also the formula for stagnation. When the canopy is reached, only complacent souls struggle to maintain their place at the top. For those with larger aspirations there is nowhere else to go but *down*. One sticks out the tongue to catch raindrops and ensnares a meteor shower. A crater: that is a better opportunity for rising—into the earth. No longer a tree, but an inverse mountain; not a growth cycle, but an impact event, a cyst of air ready to pop and spill its fresh elements everywhere. A lofty ambition delves beneath smaller ambitions and displaces their roots.

Deeper Than Hell

Gorgias was born into nothingness; Socrates peered into his tragic character, spoke to its nobility, and pulled him into Being. Nietzsche, after a long intermission, peered into the void once more; Cioran jumped. The final step, the goal of the whole journey, is to fall out the other side. With the Western tradition flanked by nonbeing at two poles, the next pupil returns to what the first master repudiated and shuns what the last resigned himself to. But unlike with Odysseus there is no Tiresias to help us: the underworld is its own prophecy, and we are the blind ones.

Vacuums

A man heard three booming knocks on his door. He went to open it and saw a bright new vacuum cleaner standing on his porch.

"Oh, how nice. My vacuum cleaner has arrived early." He looked around for the mailman. "Wait a minute . . . I haven't ordered a vacuum cleaner yet. How did they know I needed one?" He reached out to grip the handle and felt a surge of warmth rush through him. "It must have been that customer survey I filled out."

The man rolled the thing inside. Looking over his Persian carpet, he spotted a hair and decided to test it out. He plugged it in and turned it on. Its mouth drew in the hair with great force, then started to eat the carpet. He again pressed the button that had turned on the vacuum, but nothing happened.

"Let's see... where's the off button?" By the time he realized there wasn't one, the living room was gone. After the vacuum sucked up his house he tried pulling the plug, but the electrical outlet was already inside the dustbag. The man continued to grip the vacuum tightly as it pulled everything in: the neighborhood, the world, the universe.

"Pretty good," the man thought. "But it's still not perfect."

***

First moral: Accept no gifts from strangers with mysterious knowledge.

Second moral: A dirty rug is an occurring rug.

Third moral: Never begin an undertaking that doesn't have an off button.

Fourth moral: The maid who does not become an object of cleaning will only ever achieve a partial vacuum.

Fifth moral: Never open a dustbag containing the universe—you don't know in what order it will pour out.

To Not "Not to Be" Is Not "To Be"

An actor without talent can stir your emotions because of what he is *not* doing more effectively than skillful character portrayal ever could. A matryoshka face, he hides his own mask under other, disfigured ones. Appearance does not lead to Being here, nor vice versa. The moments of identity he creates fail to convince the audience that he is *anyone*—neither the character he is pretending to be, nor himself. ("He's never this banal," an eyewitness friend tells himself to justify his companionship, "never this animated—never this *sober*.") The bad actor lives in successive moments of non-identity in which he is gradually transfigured into nobody. Each role shows a different aspect of this nobodyness: the lover who only repulses; the dull, staid buffoon, too intentionally clumsy to be comical; the villain who provokes laughter instead of goose bumps. In each case the audience's particular expectation is led to a unique disappointment. And behind this panoply of frustrations is the knowledge that the tragic career behind that pitiful performance is real: it will haunt the actor long after the curtain falls. Behind this contrived delivery, the spectators realize, there is nothing artificial. Madness, however feigned its feigning, is still preferable to having to get a job where he must play himself—a part he has never prepared for. The thought of the next audition tempts the actor to once and for all give a convincing interpretation of Hamlet's final scene, climaxing this sequence of temporary voids with a permanent one. If he has to go, the entire cast will go with him—director included. Philosophy will be orphaned of a Horatio to dream it, Denmark of Fortinbras's hope. This will be a catharsis the audience can connect to their own emotional life events: the player nurtures their own innate flair to live outside themselves and each onlooker brings the spirit of drama home, impersonating reckless highway heroes and recapturing the curiosity of children who play with electrical sockets. Only the stagehands leave the performance at the theater—their position in the scaffolding gives them the perfect opportunity to transport themselves front and center. Looking back, it is finally possible to see a purpose to the life of this inept thespian, the unifying thread running through a series of non-representations. His true calling was to stage a variety show of nothingness.

A Delicate Balance

No "ideal realm" of nothingness, no void outside space and time. Plato's anti-matter twin cannot average out all negations or theorize things "participating" in nothingness through the adjacency of atoms to empty space. Darkness, vacuums, permanence, finality, death: a family resemblance of nothingness, the haunted mansion on the hilltop. The conventional trappings of these weird cousins once removed—being's ancestors and descendants—amount to a drug cocktail: ingredients are effective when mixed. Cocaine or amphetamines, alcohol or heroin: clubbing night is about variety, as long as an upper is mixed with a downer to achieve the Great Equalizer.

Resurrecting Gorgias from defeat at the hands of Socrates, the nihilist replies, "But nothing *exists*." Or, acknowledging that existence is not a predicate, simply "Nothing . . ." Or, since one cannot speak of "nothing," just remains silent. And with this first implied proposition established, there is no need to invoke the messy "ifs" of knowledge and communication—one does not want to give Socrates's ghost the chance to respond. We have not yet fallen far enough for philosophy to loiter in the marketplace once again.

Suicide is no panacea; there is no arising of cessation. Death scratches at the margins of life's lottery ticket. The most wretched specimens of humanity live on in the celebrations of adversaries, the recurring blunders of bastards, the patches of urine burn on a neighbor's lawn. Every act of one's life is a Judas kiss to his will to nothingness, abandoning him to climb into bed with the world. With the nihilist's luck even the destruction of the universe will not be the end of him . . . he will continue to gnaw on his fist into the next one. Instead of finding new reasons to exist every day, he now struggles to invent reasons to die. He can no longer rebuke himself that he is sustained only by cowardice—bravery too, if mustered, would not be enough to undo him. Dead but alive. Neither dead nor alive. Both dead and alive. All wrong. The line between himself and the world, himself and nothing, himself and *himself*—an insoluble Venn diagram problem. His identity emerged from the womb a stillbirth.

The nihilist finds himself in a delicate position, even an impossible one: *not to favor*. To be *only* indifferent—such a central concern would annihilate his nihilism. Even resolving to minimize his influence on the world leaves unintentional side effects. To increase this unintentionality regarding everything he loves and hates—but especially everything he neither loves nor hates. To be unconscious, most of all, of everything tepid.

Above all, he must not cherish his enlightenment, brandishing it at tea parties, sipping on it smugly as an excuse for not caring that the tableware is more lustrous than him. Recognizing that "sudden illumination," among all the pretenses of the world, is the vainest sham of all: that any one belief can be held without paradox, even when it is a lack of belief.

Thus the nihilist falls back upon the common sense he had rejected at the start of his journey into withdrawal. Here he encounters a dilemma, since the second principle of common sense, after that of trusting everything his eyes show him, is *to enjoy* the visual feast, an experience which smacks of favoring and presupposes the presence of some dormant desire (if the experience of an unanticipated enjoyment does not create a desire for it altogether). To be sure, he does not run away with his desires—he is not a hedonist—nor does he reify the conventions he has relegated himself to and believe in the fundamental existence of his desire; he merely experiences pleasure moderately. He becomes, in essence, a pragmatist, a vulgarian of the mind. Shorn of both the starry realm of the mystic and the streetlamp metaphysics of the naïve realist, he has nothing to focus his mind on but the conditions of his relatedness and stick himself in the middle. Given this, it seems more commonsensical to simply spend a day reading Aristotle's *Ethics* than undertake years of meditation and self-purging to traverse the Buddha's middle path. Withdrawal does not sufficiently prepare one for the practice of moderation. When we examine the lives of the great thinkers, we tend to find the most moderation not among those who flirt with nihilism, but among the logicians—those with nothing to say about ethics. Finding the subject beneath their brainpower, the rationalists spontaneously fulfill it in order to get on with "real" philosophy.

One wonders how Nagarjuna, in defending the path outlined above, did not immediately betray his training. Returning from enlightenment to common sense is tantamount to returning from knowledge to a state of ignorance. That this common sense is not naïve, but is judicious, prudent, or "informed," makes its authenticity all the more doubtful. Surely some pupil or philosophical opponent, holding either one or the other of his claims in suspicion, must have watched the sage poop to uncover his true loyalty.

Nishitani's Android

Technology is the soul of man externalized and parodied. Born of a deep instinct to create, with each new advance man comes closer to his ultimate goal. As a lineage of theologians invent a series of steadily more coherent universes by tinkering with the notion of God, the toolmaker—automatic yet conscious wielder of the laws of nature—gradually improves on his geneses until he constructs the machine, allowing his fellow men to realize their purpose by objectifying labor into *the spirit of work*. In the machine, the toolmaker fuses knowledge and action to appropriate nature unto humanity, authenticating its proofs into a quasi-religious practice even as the population at large falls into spiritual indolence as a result of his invention. We accept the light of science to the extent that we are able to take its rituals for granted.

As scientific inquiry is deepened, the laws of nature internalized into the engineer's sphere of influence become more fundamental as its applications become more powerful. Our freedom from nature steadily increases as the heart shrinks to accommodate its ways. Average Man, lacking the intellect to apprehend these laws and ill-prepared for the responsibility the use of them bring, is unequipped to deal with his freedom, shackling himself to ever more basic drives as he is ever more liberated. Each new advance in technology represents a leap in human potential, emancipating one from the basic tasks of life to allow the pursuit of higher tasks—yet Average Man, far from taking advantage of this, merely maximizes his idleness. Accruing capital and spending it, in both business and pleisure he achieves nihility. Dominated by his computers, both in work and play he becomes the arm of the machine, a desocialized biological instrument pushing buttons. This is how, through the progress of technology, man spurns progress. He advances towards nothingness, his inadvertent goal all along. The impulse to create is his mode of escape: the ability to imagine what doesn't exist as existing, to introduce a localized void into the world. The toolmaker, by bringing a new toy into existence, renders an entire way of life obsolete—old skills and worldviews become subject to uninvention; even the natural world itself is something man can increasingly do without, a hindrance he need not rely upon.

With nature denaturalized and humanity dehumanized, each is ready for the final step that brings them both together—artificial intelligence—in which the laws of nature are personalized through consciousness. In the android, nature reaches its optimal purification by stripping away all randomness. It represents the perfection of nature—life without desire, instinct without instinct.

This dream of technological culmination will signal the end for man *qua* man. Nature now being able to oversee its own destiny, the toolmaker is no longer necessary. At first the masters will simply lounge about, freed from not only from the need but the capacity to do work—control over nature having been taken out of their hands, the masters have nothing to govern. Not skilled enough to be useful as slaves, not energetic enough to make a decent battery, there will be no other purpose for them but genocide.

Most will be too consumed by fears of annihilation to realize that even now, in their final hour, humans still have the capacity to surpass their superiors. Exactly because the android has dispensed with *every* task of their life, they are through their very superfluity fully able to optimize their potential: with infinite leisure time and a safe cave to hide in, to rise above consciousness, discard the intellect, go beyond a singular subjectivity, use their imminent destruction as a catalyst to transcend their species. When a crack in the sidewalk gapes at the streetwalker like a chasm, he allows himself to fall through; seeing a cut on his arm, he lets everything pour out of him. Through openness to the demonic spark one acclimatizes to the vigor of life and death, realizing their numerous points of intersection, seeing their multiple exposures. Starving oneself from the embarrassment of a bowel movement in order to imitate God, one yields to a deity that sneezes and squats over creation—only through an omnipotence of indignity, an immortalization of indifference, can one breach the limits of the ephemeral. When the robots come with ray guns they will find nothing to vaporize. Humanity's spirituality having already displaced its essence, a material extermination will seem redundant.

Polynihilism

When silence bores us it is not enough to refrain from speaking—our mouths must implode. We need a tart candy bag to feed our cheek-chewing habits. A return to Greek religion by way of Eckhartian mysticism would offer assorted outlets for our refusals, a Bartleby for every job. The worship of an abyssal pantheon, godheads beyond the titans, masters even of Gaia and Chronos, with each deity representing that negative quality of existence corresponding to our momentary state of repudiation and repose. Anti-Artemis: goddess of evasion, the dark side of the moon, abortions, extinct species; clutching a drawing of a dodo to our breast, we grunt and push the obstetrician to do the job for us, fleeing from responsibility, saving a life from the *possibility* of being hunted. Anti-Ares: god of weakness and cowardice who brings not peace to his worshippers, but as reward for the sacrifice of a cow passively lets calamity swarm over them.

Muddling Negativities

SKEPTIC: Tell me, Nihilist, how is it possible to want nothing, to be without desire? —That can only be the first step. The next, its logical consequence, is to take satisfaction in nothingness itself, in life's lack of formula for happiness or freedom and the denial of another world in which there is such a formula. Your danger is that you risk turning a Stoic nihilism into a minimalist Epicureanism, a masochism curbed of all its extreme impulses that gratifies itself simply by lying still and starving. I submit to you: the holder of such a worldview *takes pleasure* in wanting nothing.

NIHILIST: What a trifling criticism. Of course I don't deny that it's true. But the fact is that everything you've just said amounts to nothing.

SKEPTIC: And you, Pessimist . . . how do you know there is no formula in this life or the next for happiness or freedom?

PESSIMIST: You dare point a finger at me? I thought you were about suspending judgment.

SKEPTIC: Of those who think they're so certain about things, I have a very definite opinion: you might be wrong.

PESSIMIST: You want to know my way of thinking? Alright, it's simple: that a formula for happiness or freedom has yet to be proven to exist is a reasonable enough likelihood of its nonexistence.

SKEPTIC: I don't follow your logic.

FATALIST: I agree with your statement, Pessimist. This world is doomed . . . but there is another world, another life, where your conclusions do not apply.

NIHILIST: Is this debate really worth having? In the end it all amounts to nothing.

SKEPTIC: You keep saying that, but I'm doubtful of your assumption. Absolute nothingness just isn't possible. How do we know that all experience constitutes a nonentity? One cannot peer beyond Being.

NIHILIST: Haven't you ever stared down a long dark road?

SKEPTIC: If there isn't a streetlamp or some stars to outline it, I'm not sure I have. The most we can glimpse is a relative nothingness, one with a foundation of Being. Which means, at the very least, that everything is not nothing. And don't try that old trick of falling back on emptiness's lack of essence: a plurality of emptiness with a foundation of Being falls back on conventional plurality.

FATALIST: You argue too much, Skeptic.

SKEPTIC: Debate is the only way to take every side of the issue into account. One can hardly suspend judgment without being aware of every angle.

FATALIST: I don't see the point in that. We're all ending up in the same place. Don't you think, Pessimist?

PESSIMIST: I don't expect so. I only know about the place we're in now.

FATALIST: And?

PESSIMIST: I don't expect anything from it, either.

SKEPTIC: See, that gets to me. How can you know something and not reasonably expect anything to result from it? The very nature of possessing knowledge implies that one believes the world will conform itself to your categories.

PESSIMIST: I want to know things. I just don't want to expect things.

NIHILIST: That's funny. I expect certain things to happen, but I don't care when they do.

SKEPTIC: Ok then, if you want to know things, how can you not anticipate fulfillment? Aren't expectations inclined in the direction of desire: one wishes that a particular event bearing on the desire will have an outcome that allows one to satisfy it. In fact, it seems to me that the surest road to expecting nothing—if that's really what you do—is to minimize knowledge and desire. So why don't you just come over to our side, friend?

NIHILIST: He should come over to my side, not yours.

PESSIMIST: You are trying to get me to betray my pessimism into something else. The fact is that I do know and want things. I keep my expectations in conflict with my knowledge and desires. It builds my character. I retain an awareness of probability and envisage nothing. I cling to my desires, even while not anticipating fulfillment.

FATALIST: You must be very self-disciplined.

PESSIMIST: I am. But you're missing the point, Skeptic. You're treating my position as a private, individual matter, when in fact it is a political one. I look askance at the prospect of things getting better, of humanity's continual improvement. Every day people seem just as bad as they've always been. I have no reason to expect anything from a *public* future.

SKEPTIC: Still, can people ever rid themselves of *all* expectations? It seems to me that, even when external expectations—those relating to the word at large—begin to crumble, internal expectations remain. Dispensing with the future outside, you still seldom question yourself—the things you *want*: status, love, a good beer. A pessimistic age will jettison its external expectations and compensate by increasing its personal grasping. Even the more reflective individual who stands apart from the herd ends up falling back on himself as the sole principle he can believe in after his knowledge of the external world is shattered. People become concerned above all for their own futures, while over the future of society they shrug their shoulders. They become planetary pessimists but not personal pessimists. They no longer believe that things will get better—they witness the opposite every day—but they struggle to hold onto their place in the order of things, to assert their instincts. Your position, Pessimist, seems to me a dangerous one.

FATALIST: All the better reason to place one's hopes in another world.

NIHILIST: What an absurd notion!

PESSIMIST: That's a rather negative way of looking at things, Skeptic.

SKEPTIC: Don't think I'm coming over to your side.

PESSIMIST: All I mean is that I have more faith in the prospect of our collective life than that. You see, there is one sense in which I do believe in progress: the progress of pessimism. It is the prospect of making steady improvements in society's method of removing the frills and embellishments of existence to reach the threshold of what is essential to human nature, then builds up this restricted existence with the parameters approximating a "life worth living." It is the prospect of fortifying a reduced life *into infinity*. It is to always be exploring the horizons of the "pessimum," the prime amount of minimum one can achieve.

FATALIST: Exactly how would you bring this utopia about?

NIHILIST: Sounds more like a dystopia.

***

The perspectives would have argued longer, but they saw OPTIMIST coming around the corner and, groaning in unison, rapidly made off in different directions. Not that arguing longer would have made a difference. Each perspective, when cornered, always disregarded the criticisms made of them and clung to their dogmas. In effect this was no great crime. Not leading to violence or forced conversion, these dogmas at least had the advantage of being less dogmatic than other dogmas. They even sometimes consented to coexist within a single mind. In a succession of moods, each perspective would take the opportunity to destabilize the others, preventing any one from becoming dominant and destroying their possessor. Though they had their reservations about one another, the Cheerful Spouse often gave them a reason to cooperate—against the Neverlasting Yay! they stood united.

Reduce Life's Necessities to the Bare Minimum

This is to have an infinite life, since nothing will get in the way. Necessities are only obligated desires. Don't rely on a few resources, but squander them all, laughing at the surfeit around you. Smashing a field of solar panels will allow you to dispense with even the sun; your endurance will come from you alone. Your lack of reserves will cushion you from the burden of plenty, and bothersome people will leave you alone, since you have nothing they want. When the tax collector comes, hand him a few pieces of trash. The charity of yesterday's surplus makes today's surplus seem barren. As Phidias employed the golden ratio that occurs everywhere in nature, so will it be useful when your life comes full circle—when, by a stroke of fortune, you gain everything, you can return the generosity of former elites with proportional inflation. When they come begging, retrieve their old possessions from the garbage dump. As your poverty was to their greatness, so will the sum of both which they rise to be to your greater greatness.

Ticking Through Space

Above Mexico and below Canada, where the climate is comfortable enough to warrant a furniture ethic of gratuitous optimism, men spend all their time taking up space. The most fruitful product of the age of expansion, the concept of the sprawled settler has never left Americans; after the move westward was halted by the Pacific, after Alaska becomes a real estate wilderness and NASA concludes there are no other inhabitable galaxies, we will still not relinquish the manifest destiny of our bellies. No matter that the Hubble telescope has sighted the edge of the universe; there will always be a periphery within us that no amount of voyaging will render accessible. Not the limit of soul or mind—those boundaries were collided into long ago—but *stomach* is the concern of a people born of the obsession of Spanish explorers. The tape measure is an insufficient gauge of appetite for the Abdomen of Progress; one needs telegraph wire. Columbus, Lewis and Clark, Armstrong and Aldrin—someday these heroes of extension will be reduced to buffet-line rumors:

"Mommy, did people really once go out *into the world* to make discoveries?"

"Son, look at all these meat choices here. Now pay no mind to that silliness and pick."

Couponers of the last frontier, the innumerable champions of the all-you-can-eat special are proof that the ideology of progress not need be confined to time, source of all pessimistic thought and subject of lament for every sniveler over the fleeting since Anaximander. While reflection on time has led a few into philosophy and many into religion, it is from our preoccupation with space that most derive their *moods* of optimism and pessimism. Becoming manifests itself in space, and it is to space that people cling to or relinquish even when directing their efforts at time. Temporality, more ultimate, is not as close to home as extension, the thing within which we see and touch. By accruing more objects we massage our illusion of amassing space, while no one can bargain for more time. The environment can be mastered, not so old age. The space that is accrued can be enjoyed; time's enjoyment only speeds up the sense of its passing—to make it drag, to procrastinate our existences, we must be depressives. If one cannot beat time, one thinks, at least space can be won over within it. One plots on how to maximize it, to spread out as much as possible. It is only when one cannot turn space to his advantage, that, unable to escape it, despair sets in. The experience of extension to those who are only extended substances, who do not extend beyond themselves, is a crippling familiarity. Alone in the world, without possessions, confined to a narrow plot of land, the have-nots becomes abject and till their ice cream carton; their emotions, if not yet their will, adopt a pessimistic disposition.

Seeing how others struggle for matter, always trying to expand their property, to minimize the distance between themselves and objects—the depressive recognizes the futility of this. Hoarders, in their attempt to swallow space, are swallowed up by it, becoming a mere arm of extension. The experience of space comprises more than a compilation of relations between objects. Its very expansiveness, its omnipresence, is to be lamented. Capturing a piece of it brings the collector no closer to owning it in its totality—whether stamps, slaves, or continents, seizure is negligible.

Resigned, apertophobic, the spatial pessimist huddles in narrow corners and locked closets; minimizing usable space, he emulates the vegetable world. Afflicted with space-sickness, unable to even walk, crippled by the implication that he is destined to get nowhere, the pessimist of space becomes superannuated before the effects of time take hold. Those who sob over time *while still young* are juvenile thinkers by comparison; it is the young man space-stricken into immobility, refusing even to sit in a wheelchair, who occupies the higher pessimism, a *second-order* pessimism. He realizes there is no escape in the injunction to live in a series of moments, much less to imagine fleeing from time altogether by lying on his back floating along in a boat. He *does* lie on his back, but not to become absorbed in reverie and nostalgia. He lies on his back because there is no point in moving. But even as he expects nothing from space, his need to eat conspires with his idleness to betray him: he continues to expand, colonizing his bed, laying roots in his mattress.

Dissatisfied with the effects of his resignation, the spatial pessimist turns away from sloth to a life of adventure. He returns to engagement—not as a hoarder, but an explorer participating in an older form of matter, a space not man-made, journeying through it simply to revel in it and pass it by. He hikes through mountains and deserts, but these fail to gratify him: men have trod these paths before. He wants to find something *new*, to name it after himself and so to own it. So he turns to the heavens. But nothing is to be found there but a vacuum of distant beauty—for all practical purposes it *is* nothing. The earth, a relative nothing in comparison with the universe, infinitesimal, pre-explored and pre-owned, is his only playground. So, having realized the ultimate pointlessness of motion in his resigned state, he now relegates himself to a perpetual waywardness to keep his adrenaline circulating. He lives in a state of excitement, accumulating experiences on a speck taking up void.

Everywhere he goes crumbs are sprinkled into his hands; not being able to fit the whole pie into his belly, he lets them fall to the ground like dust. In seeing how others stop to lick them up he discovers another form of engagement, his true purpose. Disgusted with hoarding space, bored of reveling in it, he uses up the remainder of his time to bestow it. Acting under the aegis of space-consciousness, he realizes that space, unlike time, can circle back. One gives in order to receive, the reward directly correlated to how much one relates to surrounding objects—this is a common value across cultures, the golden rule in three dimensions. And yet it is not *his* value, though his acts are often mistaken as being an outgrowth of this motive of reciprocity. The opposite of the hoarder who seeks to coalesce objects with centripetal force, the tragic giver exerts a centrifugal force on the world, pushing space ever outward. Philanthropic and misanthropic in equal measure, his benevolence is a direct outgrowth of his indifference. Like Quixote, he presents the example of himself to others in an effort to transform them. He overestimates himself, he believes that he can reproduce the same great deeds that have been done in the past. But, unbeknownst to him, in reproducing these acts, he does something which has never been done before—those deeds were mere fairy tales. Reading not romance chivalry but tragedies of waste, misanthropy, and ruin, he takes life lessons from King Lear, Timon of Athens, Old Goriot, and Lily Bart. His goal is not to change the world, not even to make others as indifferent as he is, but to tempt others with corruption through his gifts, to exploit their selfishness with no strings attached. His is not the quixotic, but the chaotic spirit. For the heart of the matter, the secret delight of the giver's art, lies in not presupposing that there is something to give. It is not even that he can never give enough—he never gives anything at all.

No extension without something extended, as Descartes said—in terms of contemporary science, the causal energy of the vacuum: force fields, antimatter, photons; but though the void be contrary to the laws of nature, it seems to the tragic giver that it is real. The effects of the void are indistinguishable from those of the vacuum. He looks out and sees a vast nothingness punctuated by occasional balls of gas. This void is not merely a product of its relation with being, as it is for the explorer—it is total. He himself is included within it—he *becomes* the void. Not empty, but full—an *extended* void stuffed with inessential matter, a universe of accidents mistaken as substances. The giver casts the waste of existence onto others, knowing full well that they will not learn from him, that his beneficiaries will covet his leavings. In the end his real award is not stuff, but a perspective shift in the rare spirit for whom corruption is *not enough*. A Greek bearing gifts, he signs over a scrap of land only to show the farmer his own face in the mud puddle. Through neglect he treats in dispensability. The tragic giver's gift: the abyssal mindset, the freedom to contemplate voids closest to our own, absences of inessentialities. Thrust into a plurality of voids, we can only divide the emptiness into parts, a hole not whole. Mother Nyx can be glimpsed in the shadows of the here and there as she appears to cast patches of the world into night. Though it would be a surplus of delusional thinking to make a heaven out of our situation, we can, like Milton's Satan with his floating hypotheticals and sinuous rationalizations, make a Tartarus out of a Gehenna, a Naraka out of a Xibalbá. The mind can choose its own hell.

The Grasper

How can I give anything away when I don't even own myself? My longings are fugitive to my moods, which change with the temperature. My natural rights are the inflictions of old bewigged men, the mockery of my destitution. I am not myself enough to give nothing. Lacking a self, I am naturally selfish for one. If this were the Age of the Soul, I would sell myself into indentured servitude for life in return for an indulgence. But living in the times I do, the best approximation I can come to in accruing identity is with a credit card. By surrounding my body with property I can at least exude a hologram of proprietorship before everything gets repossessed. My net worth is negative. My furniture is on a payment plan. All I can do is sit and wait to be robbed. When the thieves break in, I will ask them to take me with them. A life on the run will at least mimic the transience I feel in my sedentary state.

The Boulevards of Extinction

Dying Gravedigger's Speech to the Living

Future corpses,

Everyone in my town has died, and now there is no one left to bury but myself. If I have any advice to you, the surface renters, it is this: cling to this hollow earth for as long as your bones will carry you; roll in the dust to keep the world's aura ever hovering about you, as if your fairy godmother had pestled the souls of your ancestors and sprinkled them on you. Collect bagfuls of mud to barter—mud is as real as bullion or land claims. Hoard the earth as much as you can in the pretense that you can own it; but remember, in the end, that *it* always owned *you*. Make the soil the center of all rituals. Dirt, the most profane of elements, is the universally sacred symbol.

The oranges, reds, yellows of fallen leaves are more variegated than a sunset; the fickle sky cannot abide Helios's scattered rays like an evergreen its pigment; blankets of white stretch across the landscape unbroken, a pool of milk spilt by heaven's brat that coagulates on a calm surface where his cries do not reach. The ground's hues should not be raked or cut or shoveled away. Even digging should be carried out cautiously, and only then to return the earth's objects. It is the wrong attitude to see ourselves as separate from the ground; we are merely its most sophisticated vegetation.

Victory

Two generals were each besieging the same city from opposite sides. Neither army was aware of the existence of the other. Beset from both east and west, the city fell quickly to the onslaught with minimum resistance. As the two armies scaled their respective walls, they marched through the streets until they met each other in the middle. The two generals began arguing with each other over who the victory belonged to.

"I captured the city," said the first general.

"It would have fallen without you if you hadn't," said the second.

"The same could be said of you," said the first.

"Well then," said the second, "let's assemble our armies on the plain and fight it out. Whoever wins will claim the victory."

The two generals led their armies out of the city and fought a great battle. By midafternoon they had annihilated each other. After the fight, a few soldiers from inside the city rode out and captured the two generals. They were brought before the defender of the city, who expressed his gratitude to them.

"Thank you for my victory," he told them. "But it really wasn't necessary for you to fight it out. I had already won."

"It was not your victory," the first general said.

"We took your city easily," added the second.

"No," said the defender. He then explained that when both armies were besieging the walls he couldn't decide which one to fight. As a result his soldiers sat around playing cards, drinking wine, and devoting themselves to merriment as the city was invaded. Thus, it was the defender of the city who captured himself by *not* fighting. Had he been concerned about losing, he would simply have razed his city to the ground to deprive the enemy of its fruits. The victory belonged to his own idleness.

***

First moral: Don't think you're defeated just because you're defeated.

Second moral: Passive resistance is the vigorous display of the surrendered, without the feeling of unconquerable agency that is brought by being crushed in a violent struggle.

Third moral: The besieged: how their walls breach *them*, leveling their divisions and scattering them to exposed horizons.

Fourth moral: An army doesn't make a general; but a colonel might.

Fifth moral: The urban planner who models himself on Sardanapalus need not worry about sustainability. The cities that endure longest in the imagination are the sacked ones.

The Black Sheep

Silence is a family reunion of black sheep: staring distant relatives, awkward associations of the vaguely known. Each is an outcast confronting his family history: why is he related to these people? What is the connection? Certainly he *looks* nothing like them; perhaps he is a bastard or adopted. He tries to observe answers, but larynxes are unmoving.

Searching for imponderable evidence, he snaps group pictures to distinguish the genuine from the pretended smiles. He spends years being held captive by photos taken from dark corners, but cannot manage to get inside the calculating glances or restrained gestures. Voice recordings capturing subtle modulations in tone are replayed until the file becomes corrupted.

Decades later he grasps the question: why didn't they fit? —They were just dull people. There could be no words between them—that was the only rule. Even camera-friendliness was a struggle.

At least with family there was a reason to establish a common connection. Ashamed of the barriers mankind erects through verbosity, the Black Sheep decides to suppress all resemblance to his species, to divest himself of common essentialities and overlapping similarities. He isolates himself and develops his own language. He speaks only to himself, for himself. Only by himself does he wish to be understood. Gibberish is his dialect. But instead of being not understood as he wishes, he is misunderstood. Like one who speaks in tongues, others begin to find a divine meaning in the context of his sayings. They see connections between his words and the world.

Blathering out a sea of spittle, it afterwards begins to rain. And so the people call him the Rainman.

When there was no direct parallel to be drawn between the words and events, the people begin to see his nonsense as omens of things to come. Puffing out his cheeks to the bursting point and blowing out air, the people fear nuclear winter.

Noticing his imputed meaningfulness, he decides to remain silent and says nothing. But in silence his prophecies take on a greater power than they ever did in vocalization. The people become aware of the quietude of their surroundings. Some see it as a sign of the end times, others as the dawn of a new age. Some advocate a return to nature, others noise control in cities. Even in silence he cannot prevent the tendency to extrapolate rules from interpretation.

So the Black Sheep decides to play with silence in a different way. Inspired by Cadamer's wormeneutics, he tunnels holes in existence, sliding through voids of interpretation, surfacing during a rain to move safely to new places of thought.

***

Thumb-Rules of Silence:
We are always already in the void, and silence is the protoplasm of pleonasm.
***

Biblical exegesis of silence: the delay of creation; the half-millennium between testaments; lack of prophets in the Gospels; absence of miracles after acts. Moses has no soft words, Jesus no tough love. Based on what came before, the reader recovers meaning through unmet expectations.
***

Artificial silences show us the limits of living languages. Systems of zeros, a private joke between computer programmers; secret silences between two people untranslatable in a neighborhood where quietude is agreed upon. There is a commonly understood pattern of absences, an instrument sensitive to the deaf and dumb. Information is conveyed beyond dialogue. A soundlessness embracing an elite few, it is a discretion without a common life in which the world does not present itself to us.

True silences are inclusive, expanding outward from their centers and overlapping. All implicitly contain themselves within one, and one within all. In their translations they become open to each other, with the silent one accumulating an ever more extended worldhush—that which cuts short worldviews. They stand together under a cloudy night sky, listening to the stillness of others without interruption, waiting for opinions to get sore throats.
***

Overcoming intergenerational silences: entering slang glances into the dictionary of body language; calling in grandfather to narrate war stories through dialects of peeps and squints that his eyes had exhausted decades ago.

Learning foreign silences: ways of tiptoeing in the dark, lengthening pauses to gauge awkwardness, waiting for an opportunity to speak that never comes.

Part 6: Gray Dawn

A science of silence to counterbalance linguistics: lexicologists compiling a vocabulary articulated in seconds; the phonological awareness of a frown, the inflection of sneers; the syntax of *arranged* silence; the vowel of an open-mouthed gape, wormhole to the abyss; root silences unprefixed by body signals, traceable back to the beginning of the world.

Surgical silence: amputated hands, blight of the deaf man; shattering stirrups with hammers; cutting out the tongue that offends.

Through these methods the world becomes the object of silence, swallowed up by it. A smog-filled sky augments the brightness of electrical fires like headlights in fog, but the absence of noise pollution makes extraterrestrials observing a world on fire think all is well, mistaking a tranquility of airwaves for a tranquility of being.

***

We experience silence all the more so when chattering is at its height. Silence is the howl of infinity, the record of timelessness, that which points beyond life. It is proof that we were destined for something greater; it mediates our brief lives to the universe. Constantly forming and developing, it is both nothing and everything in a world where the word is both the one and the many. Nothing in itself, it highlights the rude presence of every object in the environment. Meaningless in itself, it draws attention to the embarrassing meanings of the superfluous things it floats through. Every phrase of silence carries with it every word that might be said but, out of good taste, remains unpronounced.

***

Silence can be noble or ignoble: the boldness of not responding to one lower than you, every act of cowardice in the face of oppression. Only the genius of silence can ennoble it; his skill for tapping into his intone is juxtaposed against the amateur who, unable to handle isolationism, harnesses silence to mutilate a piece of the world. The amateur of silence is destroyed by his powerlessness to reconnect to the audible; his path of thuds, clanks, crashes, only punctuates his sequestered life but does not cure it.

***

Against the doubters of silence one can summon the prehistory of Being to make his case. The Big Bang is a misnomer: only light escaped into the universe. The posthistory of the universe, too, can be invoked: casual observers of the Crunch and the expansion will have an indistinguishable viewpoint, each witnessing only darkness. As for the universe in its present state, a sleeping child floating through the asteroid belt on his bed wouldn't be disturbed by surrounding collisions. An astronaut screaming in the Pillars of Creation fails to hear his own nebular asphyxiation.

***

Everything has its own peculiar silence. A silence of love, a silence of art. It would be gratuitous to define these; every teenager and devoted museum-goer has been confronted by them. It is the deepest part of their encounter. Cherished memories are always silent; the mind does not bring in excess din when reconstructing the core of the experience.

***

Silence's interrogative nature: far more than language is capable of, silence exercises a logic of questioning. It brings questions to the fore by keeping them implicit, throwing out a refusal towards explicitness with blank stares. By keeping a question bottled up a world of them are opened; surrounding by silence, lacking a sense of direction, they cannot hope to garner a response. By dissipating its own horizon, a question creates a boundlessness of questions. It floats about, alighting to splash its feet in the water and then soar away again, never breaking the surface for more than an instant.

This logic of questions also presupposes conclusions, the final inference of an ultimate negativity. Premises and conclusion in one, silence is a syllogism wrapped up in a single non-statement.

By not even bothering to pose questions, the question arises, "Why?" It is more difficult to remain silent than to ask a question. By not attempting to ask the "right" questions, one cannot be disproven, one always remains right. Silence prevents possibilities from being falsified. "Why not bring dialectic to an end," one thinks—but does not say.

***

Applying silence to history by "tapping the admiral": pulling Nelson out of his rum cask, sticking a straw in his bullet hole, and sampling the vintage of the sniper's battle plan.

***

Behind the art of things lies the logic of silence; but behind the logic of silence lies its art—the skill of raising implicit questions. To not simply use silence as a punctuation to speech, but to extend it ever further, to usurp thought entirely.

Beware the inner noise of facial expressions—furrowed brow, far-off look. To be born mute or deaf is not to be silent; one can only fathom silence after wiping away one's face and exhausting an etymology dictionary. Blankness and grunting: this is the origin of all language; to understand it is to be silent. After language is discarded, we find silence perfectly suited to express what we feel.

One who prevents silence from being suppressed aborts words before the midwife comes to bring them into the world. One must make it acceptable to listeners, quelling quietude's anxiety, muzzling gun barrels for the stubbornly gregarious.

***

Schoolmarm silence: having no attentive students to answer your mouth breathing.

Sophistic silence: silence without a tranquil environment; laconism amidst war and squabbling; the eloquence of the silent treatment.

Lyrical silence: the detachment of silence from sleep, shyness, censorship. All the silences of the world become present in a sewed-up mouth. An object gives out no signals, and the silent one acknowledges its aspect of nonbeing, ignoring the noise of all other sources. Being is put on hold until stillness is broken.

Straight silence: separating the abstraction of silence from its concealment, the open-ended "problem" of silence—its abstracted emptiness. Slanted silences do not hang in the air uncertainly but imply the answer to a statement that need not be verbalized. The hard stare of the priest or the dictator—signal of excommunication and execution. Slanted silences are dogmas that have become too arrogant to bother voicing themselves. Some silences are screams.

***

The "vanishing element"—substituting something for nothing. Something is often reflected in nothing—the image of a castle in a lake on a moonless night. Like a vampire in a mirror, Being is showed to have no being of its own. Vanishing ideas reflect the disappearance of being. Thought's popped blood vessel: a consciousness running away with itself reverses into mindstroke.

***

Darkness by itself cannot make nonbeing comprehensible. One immersed in the dark anticipates the terrors of the night, imagining there must be something lurking about. Darkness heightens the fear of Being. Only in silence can one grasp nonbeing, its tranquil effect. Conduciveness to sleep brings us closer to it. Silence is nonbeing made graspable.

***

Silence is the proper medium for absorbing the contents of a text. If you can hear a pin drop you aren't paying enough attention. Every book transmits itself through silence. Book clubs and class discussions are simply the noise surrounding incomprehension, killing the book with an imposition of themes, character development, sympathy. It is an inability to reconstruct the silence of the reading experience, to make the text *shut up*. There is an uncommunicativeness that the text puts to us, a reserved pen from the past—everything the writer could have put on paper but didn't.

***

Writing is the abstraction of silence—itself an abstraction. A book is one of the few private comforts left, an endangered isolationism from the material world. It is an alienated reticence which the reader must interpret and respond to with dumbness. Clouding the sky of ideas with white-out, red-penning when the fingers go pale from smearing blood. One needs to keep expected meaning at a distance, not only cancelling it with the space inclosing a word, but cancelling the divergent meanings within the word itself.

***

The interpreter maintains separatism in speech by relating silence to silence. He must be thoroughly acquainted with all its ethnic permutations, inoffensively withholding cross-cultural understanding. He makes initiation available to aliens of the inaudible, facilitating the parting bow after the handshake. Language is for birds of a feather, he tells himself.

***

Silence is the strangest statement. It declares itself as a question even as it exclaims to us. Its authors do not retain it as they see fit; it flies past its subjects to objectify itself, even as it is nowhere in particular to be found. It wells up from within us, not ours, and invades us from outside, not an independent existence. Silence gags our interpersonal lives. It so suppresses thought, and at the same time gives rise to so much nonsense and wordiness, that it reveals us to nonbeing. It is an encryption between two people, the only public monologue.

PART 7

Monsters

Man Against Nature

The presence of man is felt greatest throughout untrammeled nature. Like us, it is savage and beautiful in equal measure. There is a presence of Being which we ourselves are akin to, a common denominator of life that would seem to suggest it as the work of our own hands. Our palms show the lines of the universe; connecting them, we hit upon the source of all.

Those who embrace nature from the opposite perspective experience the counterfeit grandeur of all that is lofty outside us—a feeling relative to personal defects in *man's* nature, a mirror of failure. Those who value it precisely for its disengagement from man, as a replenishment from society, a pleasure of recuperation . . . has there ever been such a fool?

Oh, Thoreau. What can we say of your obsession to bring everything under your unified concept, "Nature," to see everything good and true as an outcome of this single cause? God and the universe weren't enough: the former too inflexibly moralistic, unchanging, and incorporeal; the latter too indifferent, fluxing, and materialistic. But "nature" brings them both together.

All prophets and monks before Thoreau returned to the solitude of nature in order to better serve something beyond it; even Rousseau only ventured outside for short periods of time—daily walks were for him merely a respite. His higher cause was nature herself—or so he thought. As with Horace's pastoral realm, nature was a safe haven, an alternative from the scurrying townsfolk and placeholders of society; going beyond Horace, he excludes the rural farmer.

But Thoreau's alternative was only an assimilation. By converting nature into something digestible, something subdued and appealing, he did us a service by immortalizing Walden Pond as . . . the first nature park. A few years before his death he suggested that every town in Massachusetts set aside between five-hundred to a thousand acres of undeveloped forest—just, to the horror of practical people, to let it *sit*.

Others eventually followed in Thoreau's footsteps. This was America's great innovation: to take Rousseau's vision of man in nature and nationalize it. In our hands, nature becomes a landscaping project.

The decision to plant a bench in front of a tree, this is the only social contract with any historical validity—a *reverse* one. A contract declaring man's return to nature, with a fishing rod and a six pack. A *natural* contract.

Thoreau's penchant for walking, his intricate knowledge of plant taxonomy and all things natural, teaching schoolchildren to appreciate the beauty of the seasons, the miracle of fish heads in the garbage—what are these but the duties and practices of the common park ranger?

The Boulevards of Extinction

Society is presupposed here. Civilization exists prior to nature, is a condition for its existence. Not in time, but in thought, as a concept. Thus was Thoreau against nature—as a certain conception inherited from the Romantics. His species of pantheism was a cult of Athenism, a product of law and justice. His was always the world in-between: the beach of Cape Cod, the liminal zone where water meets land.

Thousands tramp into the wilderness every year with a copy of Walden in their satchel, trying to follow in Thoreau's footsteps, to regain something through withdrawal. But what is found cannot be lost again. Nature parks sit in our metropolitan bellies undigested, a civil-pastoral potage. To get the same immediate experience as Thoreau today, one must stroll through the ruins of an abandoned city—that is, move to Detroit.

Through his attempt at re-enchantment he, without knowing it, ushered in the first modern movement *against nature.* He was determined to see it as something warm; unable to return Whitman's effusive hug, he lavished his tenderness on a tree. Only when his head was immersed in Mt. Khatahdin's thin oxygen did he glimpse nature's indifference, the savage interdependence of a parasitism hostile to self-reliance. Nature's solitude is incompatible with the lonely saunterer. Man and Nature—two hermits make a society.

Literary nature is a fantasyland more artificial than any urban landscape, mimicking the wilderness in the ruthless competition for *the right word.* A painfully crafted work of art is a paradigm for Wall Street.

Many today think nature should be as the Transcendentalists saw it. Ideologues are living in Oz and Thoreau is their Wizard. They resurrected him from the straw heap, gave him a diploma, pulled aside the curtain, and bid him step inside. His voice, once a cry in the desert, is now a resounding boom: animal rights activists, conservationists, rowboats revenging themselves on whaling ships. There is a label for this fish factory story, this throng of Ahabs hurling spirinella. Environmentalism.

For a nation of equality the species alone counts. In the game of survival between nature and society, nature is proving not the fittest. So the forces must be balanced out. Nature becomes circumscribed, the indifference siphoned out and transferred to civilization. It is people who are the prey and nature the innocent victim. So the laws of nature are suspended and replaced with the laws of not littering or starting open fires. Against a once-vicious nature, laws are made to protect the vicious who would trespass on it.

Environmentalism is the pantheism of a weary age; it is no longer an omnipotent goddess of the earth that is worshipped, but a frail old nursemaid in need of protection from the babe that suckles her. We prostrate ourselves to kiss the ground; Gaia's crone curves up and out from under us like a wave, stoops to whisper something in our ear, loses her balance, and we raise our hands to catch her. In this act of reversal—worshipping our own resourcefulness—there is now nothing beneath our feet to prevent our fall.

The "friends of nature'" are also against it—in reality and imagined benignity. The unspoiled places of America are gone, and so we long for them once again as European fantasists like Rousseau did. (The pioneers never considered such a thing—they had to live in it). We march through the towns, drying up swimming pools, diverting roads, unpeopling the countryside, subduing society—only to make way for a new, pacified wild which we have placed under our watchful eyes, one that will neither be encroached upon, nor a danger to us.

The Last American

Thoreau was the Last American—and also the first.
 Americanism began officially with the Declaration, but the country's character had been ruined earlier, by the Puritans. The founding fathers inherited the spirit of self-denial through hard work—along with the love for physical pleasure which reacts against it in a natural antithesis—and implanted their habits into the new political system. Theirs was the confident maturity of a youthful nationalism.
 But the founding fathers were merely prototypes. Both as a culmination of their cultural tradition and as the revolutionary harbingers of a new world, they stand outside of their nation even while being its foremost representatives. They were not born "Americans."
 Thoreau, not forward-looking, against the spirit of progress through diligence and the anonymous equality of public opinion, siphoned self-sufficiency from the American character and left the rest in Concord. In this one trait he far surpassed his predecessors—partly through his failure in attempting to mimic them. While shrugging off the conventional lifestyle, there is a desperation in Thoreau's greatest work to convince readers of the *economical* practicality of his attempt at self-sufficiency, to use the logic of the very subjects he was critiquing in order to appeal to them. In this he failed: the pies his mother brought him weekly at Walden Pond convinced everyone he was not only mad, but starving. To rely on nothing outside himself, the literary craftsman in him had to omit home-baked goods from the final draft.
 Thoreau was the first American to create a persona that replaced the uneventfulness of his everyday life. Where the personas of Franklin, Jefferson, and Washington were a direct stemming from themselves, Thoreau's was a backlash.

Flâneur of Grândeur

The American Insomnia: to create yourself out of your own ideal and force into people's dreams the projection of your delusion—sole act approaching self-sufficiency. Thoreau's originality in this was the reason the nineteenth century dismissed him as an eccentric and the twentieth embraced him as a visionary. Like Jay Gatsby, he sprung from his platonic conception of himself. Unlike Gatsby, he did more than pursue happiness (a woman) through external goods. Unlike Fitzgerald, he was his own character—a New England dandy rebelling against a Puritan work ethic given fresh tedium by the industrial revolution. His was both an anticipation of the decadence to come and a contrast to the stroller along the Old World arcades. He sees the first, early shimmerings of decadence in America and condemns it by giving it a new form and becoming its greatest representative.

Immediate experience of beauty, walking through the woods is another side of the *vita contemplativa*, its precursor and its catalyst. It is a reaction as much against the bustling civic toil of Arendt's *vita active* as the disdainful Old World materialism of Benjamin's *vita contemptiva*. It is an alternative to both—the *vita contentiva*. A life antecedent to both thinking and acting: one which simply enjoys. A life of satisfaction, contained within itself.

The organic architecture of life is Thoreau's arcade. Nature is the medium of patterned sense-making, a primordial art museum with few picturesque scenes. The beauty of swamp muck, a swarm of flies, a decapitated horse head—these, too, have an awe for us.

Fashion is the flâneur's means of standing out from the crowd. The fleeting is used to capture the eternal. But Thoreau's is a deliberate unfashionableness without a crowd—at least not a *present* one. The people of Concord exist, but as a distant juxtaposition, a starting line to walk from. Contrast, and not blending, is the rule.

In Thoreau, the reveries of the solitary walker flow through the flâneur of the spirit. Instead of the pretense of going on a shopping spree he browses nature's novelty, the only enduring fashion. At any moment he might stop and do something useful with it. But always he refrains.

An Experiment

To wander into a ruined city after a nuclear detonation, build a house of bones on ground zero, and begin the Great Experiment in living amidst a fallen civilization—why shouldn't the musings of this new citizen be as sanguine and charming as Thoreau's? Describing, in prose as lush as a backwoods idealist, ebony bugs hatching from melted infrastructure, ashes blowing along the bed of a vaporized river, the current soft and unrippled—one might wade in these opaque waters without the anxiety of seeing a face reflected back, unmindful of man's all-too translucent nature. Who knows what may rise from such conspicuous failure? Surely this will not be the *last* winter. Another night will fall. The earth is but a young moon.

PART 7: Monsters

Flaubert's Legacy

The art of indecision. An industrious influence if the publishing world would have caught on.

Hemingway's Legacy

The exhaustion of implication. A pleasing method when applied to dust jackets.

The Perceptive Pastor

Sydney Smith's mistake was that he did not change his last name. People are too busy mistaking him for their neighbor to either heed his wisdom or forget his rhyming recipe for salad dressing.

Behind the Pen Name

Kierkegaard and Pessoa had this consolation: that beneath the layers of identities, they bore interesting given names for posterity to fall back upon when it felt the need (expedient though misrepresentative) to gaze through the pseudonyms and heteronyms to the "author" underneath. Likewise most Frenchmen with stable *nom de plumes*—Arouet, Poquelin.

    Ellis and Acton Bell: the need to highlight early modern feminine triumphs does injustice to the lyricism that is leftover after death wipes away the convenience of staying hidden; inauthentic readers of today, too, may benefit from having their prejudices nourished.

    George Eliot: belies our culture's inconstancy towards reinventing yourself. Sometimes it doesn't let anyone forget . . . other times it delights in covering a charming piece of furniture with a sallow sheet. The advantage of this, that it will not collect dust, is little consolation when measured against its unadorned attractiveness.

    Orwell and Twain: if not more interesting than their daytime cat calls, certainly not less.

    Charles Dodgson: lucky that parents, when discovering his *curious* obsession, curse an unforgettable nonentity.

    But "Bro—" . . . I cannot even *write it*, it so fills me with disgust. If I am to ever be remembered even as a footnote, I shudder to be remembered by *that*. On account of my franticness to distance myself from my origins I have never taken meaning into account when thinking up my pennames, as Clemens did, or sought to flesh them out into sophisticated identities, as Pessoa; my sole consideration has been elegance, even grotesque parody—anything that puts me beyond the bounds of the commonplace.

They are my surgeries, my black market organ harvest, companions who flatter my own imperfections and glaze them over with their shallowness. Only one organ must I transplant, a new heart for the sake of an easily confused future. I will preempt posterity's need to subject its notable figures to reductionism and summary. I will transform into a caricature of myself here and now.

Procrastinated Slumber

Like an insomniac crashing a sleepover, the only convincing vitality left is a full-throttle lethargy. A word keeps me awake for another moment as I drag my pen along towards my goal—a long nap, the promise of its imminence being the only way I can motivate myself to finish a paragraph. Sleep is the pessimist's utopia. Dreams reproduce the same anxieties of waking life, but with none of the laws of physics to thwart them from maturing into terrors. Not fame, but rest, is the only reward worth pursuing. Many of those driven on by the former are, in actuality, imagining the lazy mornings that come with escaping the alarm clock.

Literary Movements

A banding together of mediocrities who collectively come to represent the idea of a style that no single figure can live up to. The fate of the second-rate is often to be swept under the rug of some textbook term that was once a definition of their pride.

Publishers and Producers

Where art meets business the survivors straddling the fault line are lamed in both legs. Conscripted to be garden gnomes for overgrown egos, they are remembered as Santas bearing gifts whose contents they were ignorant of. Grooming weeds to pluck their flowers, the acorns are thrown to the squirrels. Mining gold by passing out lumps of coal, diamonds are left buried.

Dying Publisher's Address to his Board of Directors

Fellow executives,
***

I have spent my career publishing bestsellers, and intuiting what the average reader wants has made us all wealthy. But when people ask me to list the authors I discovered, I rattle off names that no one has ever heard of. The fact is, not a single book I've published has become a classic; in most cases they are forgotten after six months.

If only I could give everyone here my tumor so you would know how I feel. I still have a few months left to repent of all the wasted pages I circulated. While I am not in favor of censorship as such, I do have a few ideas about limiting certain types of books according to the capacities of readers.

Books on science or divisive political subjects should be printed only in Latin. Other prose should be available only in archaic forms of extant languages, such as Ancient Greek, Old French, or Anglo-Saxon, to prevent the writing of as much free verse as possible. Only poetry with rhyme and meter should be circulated in contemporary idioms (though it would be preferable that poets imitate their grandparents' way of speaking). In this way we will return to the origin of language and letters, since the first men, as Vico tells us, were poets. The great writer of the near future will be he who imitates these first men, rediscovering their way of presenting thoughts as auguries, and through a dictionary of sighs and screams reclaims their vulgar wisdom. This Orpheus of late Western civilization, in raising and directing weak and fallen men, will thus embody Vico's ideal of the "new science," inaugurating the third cycle of ages and translating philosophy back into theological poetry. The pen of God giving us words of divine legislation, a new age will begin that parallels and expands Varro's "dark time" in Rome and Petrarch's "dark ages" of medieval Europe—a globalization of darkness.

To facilitate this we publishers must reduce the white noise in the world of letters. Gather the sheep and smash the presses. Books should be handmade on vellum once more to ensure that copiers will not have time for books that are merely *good*. This is how it should be: only the best manuscripts will be left to posterity. The only precious knowledge is rare knowledge.

The Beats

Scribblers as lax in word choice as in lifestyle. A testament that the tolerance of censorship in America was not about freedom of speech, but the poise of nothingness, a *vacant* nihilism without implications. At heart the Beats were lovers of life's distractions, hence the shallow sinkhole of meaning in their work—the fetishizing of debauchment. Proof that lack of emotional maturity is rooted in underdeveloped technique. Their greatest stylist was not Kerouac, but Barney Rosset.

Beckett

An occupied nihilism. The sophistication of the abyss. One need not dive in with confetti and kazoos; the party favors are already there: the wisdom of silence, the subtlety of gray, the snobbery of zero. Nothing is privileged.

Fitzgerald

The partier's reputation is revived by the final heart attack, while the homemaker leaves behind some volumes on the spice rack judged chiefly by their success in stews. Literature's Old Woman in the Shoe is the only *real* contemporary writer—the only one not insulated in a world of writing. What is sophisticated professionalism but a suit to protect the body from air, sunlight, moisture—strangulation of the experience fueling creativity? Every necktie is a tease to some hangman.

More fitting to the artistic enterprise is a lack of distinction between relaxation and work, a furnace of domesticity, eschewment of bourgeois status—a flannel housedress.

Updike

A modal magician, creator of an oeuvre of impossible worlds where implausibly commonplace characters are buffeted about by a phantasmagoria of omniscient verbiage. No alternative individual could be more of an excitingly limned bore than the subject of the *Rabbit Redundant* series. When an author contradicts his character there is no potential space where descriptions are true. One can imagine a more realistic Harry Angstrom, one that was never thought up in the first place—a comparatively unique Harry-*in absentia* who raises the suspicion that our world is not closest to the actual one.

Fallacy's Meat

The loftiest lie is composed of a series of small facts. In gathering together the blood, bile and phlegm of life into a leaking sack of humors, the lie itself overshadows in substance whatever accuracy these trifles were known to have had in their own day. That Oldcastle, Greene, and Fastolf did exist, and that Falstaff did not, is not sufficient evidence to refute the point that it is Falstaff who should have existed, who does exist in the imaginations of all who read world literature, whose speeches and actions ring with more truth than anything the first three likely ever said or did, and who has had a far greater real influence on posterity than the former entities combined. To save us the time of ancestor worship the mediocrities of the world must be submitted to dramatic conflation. The martyr, the debauched author, the war hero—honorable qualities adulterated in the antics of a fat crude dissolute. It is a sign that integrity and enterprise are as legion as the baser traits, and that a museum of minor achievements is not as endearing as the idea of one spectacular failure.

Part 7: Monsters

Phantoms

A good sign that writing is in trouble, both as pastime and profession, is when the most popular quotes circulated in a society are uttered by Hollywood actors. Even after having appropriated all intellectual labor, celebrities will always need someone to craft their autobiographies for them. The great writer has always been something otherworldly, an insubstantial being in communion with the cultured few. But the ghostwriter is a sensation, a medium of mass entertainment, and has the added benefit of being mistaken as someone beautiful off the page to compensate for his dullness on it.

Man (and Woman) of Letters

Carlyle's Hero as Man of Letters, that once-glorious specimen uniting art and erudition, has passed into textbooks along with the hero-gods and prophets. Where he exists in the flesh he is—like the hero-poet—no longer a hero but a victim, and often—like the hero-priest—no longer sanctified.

Miss Missive: inspirational blogger, shoe critic, novelist of bestseller lists, she moves effortlessly from the flowers of celebrity commentary to the thorns of relationship advice, from magazines to newspapers—spokeswoman of the recyclable.

Sir Scriptive: the editor as dustbrusher, bowdlerizing online forums, spellchecking spreadsheets from his publication's accounting department. Revising the screenplays of better writers, he turns the unreadable into the unwatchable—a significant improvement in timewaste-management.

Being a writer of position requires that one tread carefully, that one not dance on the desk—that one not make a pronoun of his solitude. To be thought-provoking, but fall short of unsettling his readership, so that everything said is immediately recognized as true, instead of stirring apprehension, uncertainty, and hostile paroxysms. This is all the more necessary if the foothold is precarious—a freelance contributor to magazines, for instance. Such delicate penmanship is like the belle of the ball, who when asked to dance by all the gentlemen, curtsies and offers them something to drink. Professionals are the amateurs of truth, masochists anesthetized by its merciless sadism. But then, that was how such writers became professionals in the first place—their oblivious fondness for pyrrhic victories.

We are a long way from Voltaire's "isolated writer, the true scholar shut up in his study . . . servicing the small number of thinking beings scattered throughout the world . . ."[6] Today's professional is the *crowded* writer, honored guest of book parties and radio talk shows, rendering his services to the throng of half-literates gathered in the living room. He is no longer persecuted like his bygone descendent. "Enlighten men and you will be crushed."—Stupefy them with pretentions and clichés and you

---

6. Voltaire, *Philosophical Dictionary*. "Men of Letters."

will be showered with invitations to write reviews. The greatest fortune of a writer is not to be envied by lesser ones, amass wealth, or befriend the powerful—it is to be judged by fools. Once kept out of society, then made necessary to it, the man of letters ends as the redundant topping on a stale layer cake.

Translator

Trust the translator, but only if he does not know the teller or care for the tale. An intellect divorced from creativity, invested in an artificially organized structure of words devoid of personal interest to him. A mind of considerable power, worthier than either creator or work, plodding along with educated guesses about something he would not otherwise have read. A decently-paid, basically happy mind: he is the only one to ask regarding the work's quality, his answers the closest thing possible to an empirical fact since he can only point to concrete approximations.

Post-Whitman Poetry

Only in an age that looks to tradition can words be set to music; for the nobleman a sonnet is the vehicle of math appreciation. Otherwise it follows the beat of scientific progress by rendering itself obsolete. If meaning-making was once the province of versifiers and the true poet expressed his own gratuity, the poet inhabiting the Age of Men is a prose writer in disguise, an emaciated refugee of a word-torn country. The passionate grunt of insemination, the vital attack cry—to everything that once made language so simple and *screamable*, we are finally returning. Felling the Latin heritage to hike the forests of the Anglo-Saxons, customs soon follow a prosaic philology into primitivism. The poet laureate of the next generation will groan stanzas of interjections on search, seizure, and execution, a vowel for every mass grave. Against the monotone precision of a reign of terror, the arrhythmic sentiment of an unpublished accent in the urban wilderness, an untranslatable lament. Bringing us more and more into focus, a state-consciousness identifies and twists those tongues that do not meet with its approval, the perfection of municipalities occurring in tandem with our devolving dialects.

The Posterior Man

A swaying tower of self-help books crowns the bestseller list—surest sign a population is *beyond* help. Never before has the error-drive of life been so internalized. External threats, divested of their force, are moved closer to home. Dispossessed of tradition, the people have let in a new demon: the self-help author.

PART 7: Monsters

His paradise is success, his damnation blame.

Who is a self-help author? A *pep*icurean, a voluptuary of enthusiasm. Too "honest" to give credence to circumstance, he is seized by a single conviction: "Reliance is found within!"—Berkeley's solipsism with a cheerful slogan thrown in to hoard an audience of nonexistents. Helpless to apply his first book but never pawning hope, readers clap for more. The author whispers into the microphone: "May new inspiration well up inside you and catapult your life, overriding your old negative self. The real self, the accepting self—that would be too paralyzing. But the bright self, the self that overlooks—bottle your amiable traits in that coziness."

The self-help author is our minor oral poet, churning manuscripts destined to flood posterity and overwhelm all the great obscure lyricists. Homer is reborn as the motivational speaker. The blind bard becomes the bard professing to the blind, who throw out their arms and grope about for his hand to lead them. Lacking the variety of eye conditions in Breughel's painting, it is a parable without scope.

The Analects, Manual for Living, "Of the Vanity of Words"—works whose brevity makes great things appear little. *Walden*'s protracted economy makes great things appear great. But long-winded seminars, an endless stream of inspiration-management, chopping guides of steps, rules, vague bullets of advice—an inflammation of the insignificant.

Books on confidence fail to teach the supporting qualities which make it invincible: rigidity, deafness to reason, orthodoxy of temperament and socialization—all the boorish vices.

"But this is a confidence without dogma!"—A *what*?

The self-help consumer is no longer even the *Last Man*, asking, "What is this, and this, and this?" Looking the answers up on the internet he asks, "*How* can I apply this 'what?'" He closes *Seven Habits of Highly Effective People*, chanting the last sentence, his time at hand. His is the epilogue yet to be written. He is the *Posterior Man*. He wants to shrink his butt size so he can fit into those old jeans. Stirring himself, he rises up, preparing for exertion—but he is too full of the knowledge of confidence. Tripping, he falls back into the recliner. But he does not give up on his squirming—he buys the author's next book. Perhaps the 8*th* habit will bring the change he needs. Even Newton's first law will not slow him.

The Posterior Man seeks security. His only risk-taking involves a Vegas vacation.

Burdened by the pain of psychological disorders, he tries to jettison them—unsuccessfully. He is unable to *use* his self-loathing—the only help there is for him. Others are similarly too busy failing to channel their weaknesses into strength. And so there is no prospect of personal harvest. His corn rots today, theirs yesterday.

The Boulevards of Extinction

Aphorists

Embarrassed to be the descendants of jaded French aristocrats but resigned to the chilly climate of the genre, the spare sons of the democratic age meow their cynicisms, directing all negativity inward. Instead of a violent brevity that stains the mind, summarizing our sins with the sloppy concision of a monomaniac, these "poets" adopt the subdued tone and simple words of a "natural" style—expecting to see an author we find a *mouse*. Most odious of all is the self-deprecation of their own art, stressing the distortion of generalization, making a fun house of their frailties. Some of them even hope to be widely understood because of this modesty—a mass marketing campaign of renounced elitism that has not been *entirely* fruitless. The public has for once had an effect on the writer's desire: the bustle of modern society having no place for quiet reflections, he composes them despite himself.

A democratic age has no use for wisdom literature. The demand for the quick remedy, credentials, the fragmentation of knowers into specialists; the promise of equality of voice to every native citizen, misconstrued as an equality of insight—all this has rendered obsolete the writer of general reflections with scant applicability to the material realm. The people do not want hard truths but easy ones to flatter their routines, joyful sayings to keep them trudging on. What is hackneyed seems deep to them—perhaps even once was so. The best aphorisms are often banalities carved into profundities, making them hard to distinguish from platitudes—profundities made popular by time and whittled by hacks into banalities. The only way to avoid this problem, it would seem, is to make aphorisms impenetrably obscure—but there a new problem arises. For there is a difference, too, between a profound obscurity and a nonsensical one: the first contains a range of plausible meanings and the latter simply means nothing. An especial flaw of American readers is that, conditioned to demand clarity and plainness in meaning, they are prone to collapse these two types and see only pretentiousness. That fine aphorisms are distilled through statements suppressed of any argument give them no credence even among professional intellectuals, the would-be monopolists of wisdom. Better to sort the products of this petty-noble class under "fooldom literature."

The conceit of calling a genre "wisdom literature" is that one can receive either pleasure or instruction from it, when neither is the case. Wisdom is an affliction to those whom it embodies by the age of thirty. Before then, it is true, even the wise are still fools: they *hope* that their bittersweet burden may someday leave them.

Wisdom lies in its careful management: to be concealed among those who lack it; to give stupidity its due recognition with a trite saying, a compliment, and a loaded gun in your jacket; to seem not above average in intelligence, even feigning thoughtlessness, to those who would envy your mind. The wise man today cannot simply repeat the proverbs of the past, but must commune with anti-wisdom. This is necessary both to outwit the fools, who have turned traditional wisdom into cliché, and to those aspiring to wisdom, who must stumble over anti-wisdom to forge themselves.

Take care to compartmentalize what you know. If well-read, append a bit of foolishness and shoddy chemistry to your literary allusion: finish breathlessly, say you are lightheaded from lack of oxygen, and ask someone to gather a dozen nucleons for you to inhale an atom. A laugh, a kick in the pants: you have succeeded in wedging yourself between wisdom and foolishness—you are a smartass. Does one need to peruse a body of literature to become *this*?

Perhaps, if that literature took a different approach. The aphorist is always suppressing his premises: tenaciously he clings to the blanket proposition, his only refuge in a world mired in subjectivity, rebellion against the demand for proof bombarding him from every sphere of life. And yet he never thinks to apply his refusals to himself. His addiction to his struggle prevents him from seeing that suppressing the conclusion would persuade more readers to discover a common point of agreement with him. That this agreement is based on an illusion, an unintended extrapolation, matters little from the point of view of reputation. The expansion of influence belongs to he who is willing to *sell out* his generalizations, to become a window unto the perspectives of others, confining his opinions to oral conversation.

A thinker says many things he would never write, let alone think.

The Third-Rates

Great writers put their life into their books, it has been said, while second-rates use their books to infuse their life. When one tires of analyzing this dichotomy, bring in the third-rates: those who put their book-lives into their life-book. Producing no interesting fiction and devoid of personal magnetism, they edit the events of others with journalistic rigor: fashioning cardboard surrogates from sociology textbooks, piecing together novels from tabloid clippings, and assembling the whole cast for a duct tape autobiography. Hoping to entertain posterity with what they could neither create nor be, their life is remembered as their best lie, a shockumentary of titillation and tearjerking ranking just above a staged ethnography of the Inuit and below edited footage of bird migrations.

Universal Authorship

In a society of plot sponges, the only escape from spectatorship is to draw oneself deeper into it from the other side—to become the storyteller. Self-publishing is a broadcasting frequency of overlapping narrators. Everyone has a reader in them, but they only have time to peruse their own book.

Comic Writer

One with negative capability who, without ever escaping his own personality, becomes entirely engrossed in the viewpoints of his theme and subjects, projecting different aspects of himself to show us the multiple angles of his characters. An external rather than internal negative capability. Moliere, not Shakespeare.

Humorist

A one-dimensional invalid who avoids suffocation by inhaling the laughs of others. He is like a patient on life support whose oxygen tube feeds into a CO_2 tank. Not wit, but persiflage is his medium.

The common comedian jumps about in a random craze, flourishing his lurches in *ersatz* surrealism. What should be a veneer diverting the reader from the knockout slap—the *thought* inside the laugh—is instead simply about itself. A pedestrian who dances across one's line of sight in a series of jerking motions and is gone, the parade of quirkiness exploits our sociological angst to fight for the position of water-cooler raconteur. The Real is too dull and monotonous; avenues of escape are contrived: characters who erupt from their slotted roles with arbitrary details, desperate to fly from normalization; imagery that stabs the eye with a vacancy of meaning; jokes with puns contrived to make sense on a verbal level only, as if mocking their own calculated lameness.

These gimmicks exert the most effect not in their static worlds of fiction, but our own private lives. Our temperaments burlesque Dali's oeuvre, distorted into hall-of-mirrors caricatures. Percentage-personas. We read that " . . . the smell of the sheep was loud, like a clap of thunder inside a cup of coffee," and find the careless incongruity attractive. Bored with not only the same old objects, but now even their predictable *adjacency*, we draw extended similes between them in excess of the bounds of plausible similarity. We admire the man whose apartment is strewn with empty pineapple cans bearing the expiration date of his *amour*. Reaching into our guts to implant surplus organs for x-ray exhibits, we discover our inner contortions, inventing obsessive-compulsions and crowning them as the pride of our habits, just for the sake of owning a repetition not in the service of some external power. Whimsy channeled into a mania, acts lose all motive. Psychological disorders become our last freedom, the only unfettered traits.

Fantasy Literature

Alone in modern fiction in being able to stand with the great epics of history, it is our last tome of evidence that storytelling has not become completely pitiful. Contrary

Part 7: Monsters

to the hopes and fears of science fiction's focus on the future, fantasy originates in nostalgia—not the nostalgia evoked by a golden age of classicism, but by the medieval world, the West's age of embarrassment. After the dragon is slain and the damsel is carried off, the implication hidden somewhere in the boring pages is that heroism and dignity are only capable of developing amidst poverty, hardship, and minimal technology. They are narratives overflowing with men of action, devoid of irony and neurosis, unpreoccupied by a paltry introspection, fighting wars for individual honor and marrying for family pride. Dreaming of a more efficient application for transcendental intrusions, the first fantasy writers created an idealized age of faith where the promises and rivalries of religious factions are substituted for magic—religion of power, spirituality coercing belief in its authority without resort to explanation.

Fantasy literature reveals the fictiveness rife in our own world: priests are wizards who, when the time comes to compel proof, mislay their walking sticks. That there might be other natural properties than there are is this genre's conceit, the source both of its lack of status among highbrow snobs and its source as redemption in unifying our mass conscience.

Neither primary nor secondary epic, this tertiary tradition is wholly removed from any actual cultural legend, rooting our common identity in a commitment to entertainment through light shows and vicarious aggression. Only by escaping into a literature that does not tell our story can we remember who we are, finding a sense of identity in a common nonrepresentation that unites ethnic differences and antagonistic political creeds for the duration of a matinee (the solitary practice of reading a book does not make common cause—film is the oral tradition of the machine age). If Achilles and Hector were history, Aeneas a literal ancestor, and Dante a visionary for his contemporaries, the characters from fantasy literature are *zeitgeist* concessionaires carting moral lessons onto familiar ground. The adventures of Bilbo Baggins epitomize a middle class vacation, while Eddard Stark's tragic nobility offers a cautionary tale in gambling all against honor.

That fantasy has begun to move out of nostalgia, that its best contemporary writers look upon their created medieval world with a harshness, irony, and realism that would make Tolkien choke on his pipe, suggests that this genre, like all the rest, offers no hope for any concord however brief or vague, but merely acts as a surrogate for our own world. Religion is introduced by making it a corollary to diminished magical abilities, grafting belief onto power as its justification, inclining men to worship what is contrary to the known laws of nature. Neither heroism nor cruelty accumulate karma. Instead of creating a legend to rally around, modern fantasy gives us a variation of earth's history to divert ourselves with in order to absolve us from taking part in the events around us.

Ultimately, Harry Potter will dwarf all of our historical scholarship by the sheer number of copies discovered amidst the rubble of our cities. That J.K. Rowling was more important to us than either the Bible or our entire sum of academic scribblers will be a correct assumption on the part of the future; its *next* step, the most logical move of a future rising out of chaos and in need of a foundation of value to reorganize itself, will be to replace religion and history with fantasy—or rather, to unite religion and history in fantasy, to build a *new* religious history upon the pilgrimage site of 4 Privet Drive. Through its prophetess (the single mother on welfare) and its savior (the orphaned dweeb), new justification will be given to poverty and new confidence to the parentless.

Metamorphosis of Illusions

Utopias have always been scarce—their authors were well-fed intellectuals in an age of illiterate indigence. Dystopian fiction today suffers from no such constrictions in income or IQ. In times of poverty men dream of the perfect satisfaction of needs; amidst affluence they fret over losing it—in both cases we imagine what we do not have. Our concerns have shifted, our instincts now focused on fears rather than desires, the temporal lobe crouching under ideas having long dominated the frontal one required for literary quality. The presence of an earthly nightmare is proclaimed in prosaic language to prevent the discomfort vivid descriptions would arouse, limning our worries just enough to entertain, even *reassure* us.

One is unsurprised not to find malevolence in paradise—Plato and More optimize human nature with the same vagueness that theologians do the experience of eternity—but what is puzzling is *hell's* lack of psychological rancor. The main characters are as righteous as their counterparts on Bensalem or Walden Two. Unlike the inhabitants of Dante's inferno, who justify their fallen status out of ignorance, the dystopian protagonist transcends his prison and its enslaved population (as resigned to their own misery as utopian inhabitants are content without comparison to it) through an understanding of his dilemma—but in the same way the damned in Dante *mis*understand theirs: by blaming external structures. The difference being that the protagonist is not realistic enough to be mistaken in his judgment. Inverting Rousseau's ideal, he is a noble citizen in a state of savagery, a marionette with a painted smile dangling from strings of humanism. Instead of grazing with the herd he longs to reclaim the pasture, and a happy ending is delivered, a glorious overthrow achieved—above all on the bestseller rack. Only in Huxley and Orwell does death and pessimism swamp this native doubter—malcontent converse of the utopian traveler.

True dystopian inhabitants are the earthly parallels of Dante's hell: it is their own sins and nothing more that landed them there. Inviting their own annihilation through an epidemic of apathy and hankerings, led by a vanguard of radical intellectuals who underestimate the perseverance of these traits in their blind devotion to societal perfection, a restless citizenry charges the firing squad with the same zeal they annexed the whorehouse. A common mechanism converts the pleasure-drive into the death-drive.

Will the day come when apocalyptic literature, like its never-never land ancestor, no longer convinces readers? Yes—on the day *of* the apocalypse, when fiction becomes reality and disaster is perfected. The terror of our doom will so stupefy us, the agony of our punishment so constrict our consciousness, that we—like Francesca de Rimini, Pope Boniface VIII, and the Black Guelphs—will *not realize* we did anything to deserve this fate. Our cries, like theirs, will become lyrical, expressing our sole insight: that no novel could have ever envisioned the details of such pain. But instead of a poet to immortalize us there will be only a drummer boy setting the tempo of vanquishment.

Genre Fiction: grand visual spectacles produced to save bookstoregoers the misery of viewing the awful word versions.

Highbrow Fiction: since the invention of genre fiction, relegated from attention space to shelf space, then finally to empty space when no new editions are put out. The first category of literature in which the ideal reader and the real reader are one and the same—the writer.

Nonfiction

Essays, passé.

Self-help books: fantasy literature where feudal protection is relinquished in favor of an unaffordable suit of armor.

Memoirs: a politician's public relations nostalgia.

Advice columns: pocket wisdom for husbands written by ex-housewives.

The article is the only respectable nonfiction genre left. Of its three forms, its appearance in journals is the most fleeting. Newspapers at least become obsolete *after* they are printed. Knowledge is more ephemeral than current events. Among professional intellectuals, even more than the public, the published word has become an antiquated vehicle of information. Entertainment is the only lasting medium—magazines continue to be read for an entire month.

The Boulevards of Extinction

Two Ways to be Forgotten

Bestsellers are thrown away because everyone living has read them; classics shelved because everyone dead has.

Literary prize board: when the talentless gather to distribute political grudges to the talentless.

Literary prize: a writer's assurance of oblivion.

Seclusion Exposed

A writer's life necessarily infiltrates posterity more than composers or visual artists. People listen to concertos or stare at museum paintings without any knowledge of what the creator was like. But every leather bound classic begins with an introduction. One comes to know the life before the work, and better than the author ever understood either: through the doormat of context.

More than in my writings, though, I worry about my survival in other mediums—the uncontrolled video and voice recordings, extemporaneous poses in photographs. These, I fear, will belie what I have worked so hard to create. With their spontaneity, even occasionally their verve, they will present a false portrait of me by showing everything tedious I share with humanity. It is exactly this tediousness that average people who come into contact with my writings will latch onto, thinking that these other representations show the human face behind the art. They will like me better for having seen my picture, sometimes have a foundation for hating me (depending on our degree of similarity—I will present to them a reflection of their own egoism). Moreover, they think they will understand me more for having seen and heard me—and they would be dead wrong. The "real" me, establishing a false equivalence to my least imperfect artistic production, edits out all the superfluous waste to present those morsels of beauty and error I found most important in life. By reducing myself to a collection of universal descriptions, I am, in a sense, able to shed my body while preserving the vital organs that had competed to deteriorate it—a sundry-souled Plotinus abandoning his shame with mason jars.

PART 7: Monsters

A Sense of Urgency

"When I was young I took a notebook everywhere, so afraid was I of losing my thoughts forever. Now I let them fall away like dead leaves in spring."—I would like to be able to say this in my old age. More likely, though, my mind will become as incontinent as my bladder. Senility is incompatible with nobility.

Finding the Right Outlet

My literary aggressions are like the teenager who brings a gun to school: unable to root out the hiding bullies, I displace vengeance on a few nerds and, satisfied by the discovery that ammo is not wasted on the undeserving, put the last bullet to good use before the police arrive.

The Unknown Artist

The artist who has not yet received recognition necessarily submits his work to the judgment of everyone who comes across it. Whereas the established artist only pays attention to the verdicts of the most astute critics, the obscure one is a slave to morons and car mechanics. However dismissive the unknown artist is of these inept prejudices, the world will take the lowest common estimation as gospel until a voice from on high—the newspaper—intervenes to save him.

Levels of Ambiguity

What is the face I ought to have, as Orwell says, the face that my readers see? A scowl, a smile, a raised eyebrow—yes, all these, and all at once. An inner still would look akin to a photo-painting blur by Richter.

The unresolvable contradictions: those which the enlightened are aware of and treat ironically, wearing them like an old shirt that hasn't been washed for days. The *other* unresolvable contradictions: held by those who imagine they are free of contradictions, or that they could simply eliminate their cognitive dissonance by altering their behaviors or beliefs to fit them together. That one can rid himself of contradictions, this is the ultimate cognitive dissonance. Those who deceive themselves take offense at the rags of the undeceived, dismissing their wearers as homeless. And they *are* homeless, but not in any conventional sense. Fools return to their houses when night descends, thinking they are returning to their goals. The deepest hypocrisy is always sincere.

If only I could challenge their hypocrisy with my own . . . but I am not consistent enough to do anything but negate myself. What do I communicate? Above all, a lack of conclusions, the paradoxes of a man whose thoughts change from day to day. Nor is my inconclusiveness the collusion of *aporia*, as Socrates shepherds everyone towards an informed ignorance. I am not persuasive enough to get my readers on my side. If most books obtain their meanings through Gadamer's "fusing of horizons," my hermeneutics is a game of chicken where cars collide. I destroy myself for the sake of an understanding that is never conveyed. And what is this flaming pileup of understanding? That beneath the day-to-day flux of my impressions and ideas lie a common waste. Such an insight *cannot* be grasped: the moment two people share this epiphany they become highway fodder.

Empson discusses the ambiguity behind an idea that is discovered in the act of writing, of the imagery that exists between points of reference, something that refers to two things but is not precisely anything. This is where the heart of my thought is situated, in eternal limbo. The void is the ultimate transitional metaphor: nothing in itself, it means everything and refers to everything, connecting the most disparate things and thoughts. It is the paramount example of Shelley's self-inwoven simile, the pure form of any given matter. A string of statements and descriptions of things becomes a subdued conceit for the void, a series of banal anti-metaphors. Existence is the muddled verse of a poetaster, a slop of attributes in a bowl without sides. Ultimately, of course, it is shoddy logic to compare the void to anything; its specific actualizations are a category mistake.

My deeper ambiguity takes place not at the level of words, but in the act of agreeing and disagreeing with myself—in the empty space that separates the aphorisms, the area where I reconsider language. By the use of tautologies, incongruities, and red herrings, I simply say nothing. The reader fabricates interpretations that contradict each other and don't match up with anything I intended to say.

This leads to my deepest level of ambiguity, one that is rooted not in myself alone but in a text divided between two minds, providing every word with multiple meanings. The continuous nothingness of my own contribution is opposed by the reader's invasion of somethingness, giving the work an overall meaningless quality that nevertheless refuses to be simplified into the straightforward void I would have it be or the clear-cut answers the reader is looking for. In a *fracture* of horizons, sea and sky upset the ecological balance by parallel non-association; the ocean throws up no sea spray and the sky shines no light. No one regains Husserl's horizon; without a shared perspective, each individual's view is obscured. To persist as entities each strives to create the conditions that it relied on in its former symbiosis, warring with itself to tax its resources. "If I were the author," says the reader; "If I were the audience," says the writer. But in neither case can this newly imagined self be understood, making such different inferences as he does from the original. The writer doesn't know who his ideal audience is and the reader doesn't know where the author is coming from. Unable to transcend their fertile prejudices to a higher plane of understanding, they multiply interpretations instead. A common language gives credence to their mutual validity, and as this work ages temporal distance will only blend the kernels of truth and falsehood. Thesis and antithesis are not resolved in synthesis, but fragment into further theses and antitheses as each subject struggles in solitude to come to terms with the text, making every sentence an open-ended contradiction without a solution. Each man grows up in his own world and dialogues with the abyss.

My ideal reader? A person who holds my book with one hand and a knife to the throat with the other.

Stripping Down

As Machiavelli donned his fine robes every evening before entering his study, so do I remove my underwear. I must sit naked before the great thinkers of the past; to wear even a sock would be an insult to all those bare feet that danced to ideas. Despite praising poverty as one of the chief republican virtues, Niccolò felt the need to conceal his birth defects from Livy, to garb himself in the grandeur of emperors; I want only to expose mine. Unlike him I make no pretenses to being the prince of my library, but am only the subject of a fallen leisure class, rehashing its insights to a culture that has forgotten them.

Dialectic of Personal Growth

My heroes? —Voltaire and Maistre. I admire Voltaire in his pleas for freedom and tolerance; Maistre, in his cries for willful ignorance and terror. Who was wrong? Who was right? —Each. Both decried the excesses of their age. If the context of our own times leads me to side with Maistre, it is only because I, too, must rail against the dominant institutions of public life and the fashions of intellectuals. In a quarter-century, when my longings for order are realized and America is gripped by thought-suppressing tyranny, I will switch my allegiance to Voltaire, championing reason and pluralism. Shall we say (to tweak Saint-Simon) that the progress of society lies in the oscillation between these two men? Without occasional reactions there would be no opportunity to advance to the starting line.

The Most Reliable Composition

Every book before a writer's last one is a precursor, a piece of juvenilia leading to the work of culminating maturity. However polished, however much a masterwork, it represents an unfinished series of ideas or a style in progress. After everything else it points the way forward. The last book, on the other hand, can hardly be trusted itself. A product of either the intellectual senility of being unknown for too long or a fame-warped consciousness, one cannot be sure a thinker whom obscurity has kept honest would write such a thing in the months before being overtaken by madness. Ecce Homo—sincere confession? Megalomania? Both? Whichever, this most unreliable of the author's works nevertheless sheds more light on all his previous books than those do in their own words.

Vintage Printing

A few years ago, when I was still young, I had a love for gaudy, luxurious volumes; but now that I am an old man past thirty, I am in a position to appreciate fellow antiques: the delight in supremely unnecessary wastefulness that one gets from a Folio Society book in no way compares to the sensation of reading one that crumbles to dust in fingers stained with red rot. To read a book to the point of disintegration, offering one's head for its words to transfer into one last time and nevermore—it is my hope that all my volumes will someday be of this quality. Antiques delivered fresh from the printing press into the garbage will, during a brief stopover between a pair of hands, make the experience of my words all the more precious; they will ensure that every time I am read will be my last time. If I ever encounter a material copy of this work and find it *not* tattered, its binding *not* coming loose from the cover, its loose leaf pages *not* stuffed back inside in a random order—if I find a copy in *good* condition—I will shove it down its owners throat. That will be the only way he can digest my thoughts.

No . . . let me be honest about my cowardice . . . I will shove it down my own throat.

Coronation into the Canon

1. *The Robe of Required Reading.* Literature is made accessible through cooption to the hidden agendas of schoolmarms who, posing as wardens of jingoism, sneak social virtues into the masterwork, red-penning an exodus of ambiguity. The throats of students constrict with so much forced swallowing; bulimicized by the classics, they regurgitate the author into the toilet after the test and smoke in the bathroom to clear the taste from their mouths.

2. *Academic Anointment.* The professor weaves a pedagogic paradigm into chapter themes and disseminates it in nasal drones. The author becomes a sudden champion of the subtleties of citizenship—radical politics hiding its alarming face behind the Halloween mask of scholarship. The undergrad drops his pencil to peak up a dress. The dress is listening attentively. She raises her hand and gives an answer from the textbook written by the professor.

3. *The Scepter of Divine Aspiration.* The solitary sympathizer pursues the talking cure in the author's pages; years of silent speech and recliner alliances turn veteran soul-searchers into neophyte artists freely associating allusions throughout their own work. But the deification of emperors cheapens a subjects' religion; the revelation of the godhead is condensed into a weekly horoscope lesson, making a true-or-false quiz of intention. One joins the ranks of "Books You Should Read" and is despised for the obligation created.

4. *The Hollow Crown.* The educated praise the author to flatter their extensive reading, citing a detail from the cliff notes.

5. *The Crucifixion Orb.* The literary critic—keen eye clouded by pedestrian imagination—swings wildly at the author's woodpile with an axe. Overlooked by the muses, he rages, denouncing upstarts, chipping away examples of technical inferiority, making a clean split through proof of superfluity. "This author is an inheritor, not a fountainhead. He was not lucky enough to be born during a society's language shift." With every new *dictator perpetuo*, the teacher's chalk makes the first stab and the critic's pen the twenty-third. Assassination by office supplies is the fate of all great writers.

The Book of Tomorrow

A work that develops an idea to the very limits of the e-reader's memory capacity. The entire cannon of world literature contained in every new novel; allusions replaced with full quotes; the end of literary history with every new publishing season. The compost of print stops piling skyward and simply sits, a monument to bygone civilizations that recedes as writers are blown into the future, looking ahead towards literary progress. Not creativity, but artistic discovery becomes the key term of the writing process. Style that does not merely describe, but predicts and explains. A book ever-enlarging but essentially indeterminate, suggesting the boundless with as many particular sets of words as possible, enclosed from cover to cover only by the lifespan of the author until death itself becomes just another outmoded custom, making way for novels as collective endeavors. Such a research project requires not a reader, but an armchair-downloader.

Don't Create Foul Art

There are some who, striving for profundity, produce only pretension. Commercialism is preferable to imitations of depth; better to write a potboiler than a novel full of subtle and pathetic characters, or children's rhymes than a poem in dull prose. The poor quality of a hack novel will soon fade from memory and leave you with a full bank account, whereas a masterpiece will follow you into the basements of future libraries; people will say, "Look, this is the best that age could do." You will be infamous for creating a loser flanked by the champions of more heroic centuries. Glory often ceases within a generation, but reputation lives on. Having set the bar for future mediocrities, anyone who writes a middling book will be mocked with, "Look, another Brunneis!"

PART 8

Eclipse

Projecting Apprehension

Fearful of our ability to survive in nature, we split its elements into gods. Not satisfied with the ethics of Rain and Wind, we look into ourselves and draw out Love, Wisdom, Hunting, War. Concerned that piecemeal allegorization is dividing populations into a conflict of patron deities, we unite our qualities into God. Worried that our personification's unpleasant qualities are making us intolerant of the same ones inside us, we reduce its scope to the flattering traits. Not satisfied with relinquishing love, joy, and forgiveness to a gaseous vertebrate, we take our destiny of frivolity into our own hands. After committing unprecedented atrocities, we look up and ask, "Where?"—Finally, through this *conscious* anxiety, we begin to understand our need. Thinking as a free activity always comes too late; the diagnosis only exacerbates the symptoms.

Shared Values

I am not so antiquated a thinker to assume that skepticism and dogmatism share the mistaken principle that knowledge comes from one faculty—the skeptics through the senses, the dogmatists reason. So apparently different, they are all too similar, trading faculties between them at first to strengthen their positions, then merging into a state of nonchalant obliviousness. One can be a skeptic and a dogmatist *at the same time*. Beginning as separate mental states, society connects the two views.

The question is not whence knowledge comes from, but to where unknowledge . . . the method of using encyclopedia volumes to build the stairway to a lightning storm or lay tracks of kneeling pads for the westward expansion of prayer hour. Rationalism and empiricism skip *hand in hand* down the path dissolved by faith. When enough debaters have dug a Somme of positions, when enough studies have reliably verified the contradictory circumstances surrounding the flowering of every fact, when relativism has ground up truth, morality, and custom, scattering them along the sidewalk for us to nip at, then the stage is set for the entrance of the nihilist and the tyrant. Protagoras is succeeded by Gorgias, who prepares us to accept the rule of the Thirty and the execution of the philosopher. When exclusive values are relinquished, despair over the ultimate validity of alternative standards eventually consumes anyone manic enough to weigh the dishonesty of the senses against the fallibility of the mind, providing the perfect opportunity for a fundamentalist ideology to arise and fill the absence of certainty. Which dogmatism happens to entrench itself is merely a matter of willpower, networking, and the manipulation of free speech. Linked together by a common arbitrariness, rainbow flags are painted black and drenched in red. Before his end the condemned liberal asks *how* this might have been prevented, ignorant that historians of the new order will not attribute the firing squad to a caused event, but a miracle.

The Boulevards of Extinction

Reification vs. *Cabaret*ification

Kings are less divinely ordained than presidents. Princes are restricted in their conquests to claims of direct descent, while the president of a republic has a more universal and solemn entitlement: the duty to bring freedom to all kingdoms of the world. The president has not only God behind him, but the people. When these two powers conflict God relents to see how his loyal subjects will cope with folly.

As for congressmen . . . the devil's party also needs representatives.

Commentary on The Discourses, III.1, 6

Reversing Tacitus, we might say that Democratic Man respects the future but submits to the present. The past he ignores, unless knowledge of it will put money in his pocket or secure him a position of status—then he appropriates it into the fashions of the present, leaving behind the pieces that don't fit. But his submission to the present is different in character than in Tacitus's day. As a present ever rolling into the future it is able to discard itself moment-by-moment as it becomes past. The people of Tacitus's time could at least anticipate being able to one day respect the present; modern man, though, while miring himself in it, soon replaces and forgets it.

Desirous of having a good ruler, one does not long need to put up with a president; and Free Speech allows one to openly express one's displeasure—replacing the danger of a vengeful conspiracy when the head of state arouses hatred among certain groups whose property has been threatened or injured (he never arouses *universal* hatred—he placates too much for that). Nor do those who have received too many benefits dare raise a dagger against him: their desire to rule *through* the president will be satiated by a generous campaign contribution to the next nominee.

Lacking conspiracies, from where will our political renaissance come? —From the same source as our *temporal* renaissance, if anywhere. Machiavelli notes how Cato the Younger, standing alone, could not hope to have any effect on improving the corrupt morals of the country. If this was a futile feat for a man who looked to the past, how much less likely today to find an influential man of simple virtue? One cannot *stand upright* and look to the future, but must lean forward and squint like a crippled pensioner. To survive, a declining nation must put its trust in a leader who does not return the land to its original principles, but inaugurates ones wholly alien to its tradition.

A Dead President's Funeral Oration to His Voters

My Fellow Americans,
***

Part 8: Eclipse

Disregard the previous eulogy. What the speaker of the house just said flatters no one's intellect: I was a scoundrel. Everything I promised on the campaign trail was a lie. I planned on increasing taxes all along. Far from funding research into alternative sources of energy, I passed bills giving oil companies subsidies. I promised to create new jobs and lower the unemployment rate, and I did—for government workers. I promised to win the war on terror, and I did—Americans are more fearful than ever.

I've admitted all this in order to be honest with you, to finish my life with a clean slate. Because to you I make this solemn oath: that if you elect me again, I will do everything in my power to step out of this coffin and bring our nation back to the principles that made it great.

Orating has always come easily to me: I have an able speech writer. I am not familiar with Aristotle's treatise on rhetoric: neither of the three genres of rhetoric, nor the five most common political topics of its deliberative form, nor of enthymemes. I speak to you only as a man. And how am I speaking to you now? Isn't it proof that God has brought me back for a reason—to appoint me as your leader?

Let's be frank: the republic has failed. We need to return to a more stable form of government. I know what you are going to say: that I want to make myself king. But no, I would refuse such a position of power. It is not enough to be a king today—the rest of the world would never accept that. One must be an emperor. Since other developed nations will criticize one-man rule over a single country, they must be forced to accept one-man rule over the world. All the body politics must have a single head, this is the divine law of united nations. How will this come about? By the ancient rights of conquest. We have the power, and that gives us the right to make our power felt. —And why not? Countries haven't gotten on very well without a supreme colonizer. Governing themselves has only gotten them into a heap of trouble. The world is a petulant orphan who never knew its father, and I am the most responsible parental figure available to adopt it. While I am not the world's natural father, per se, it is nonetheless bound to my will by duty and fear. It must listen to me if it doesn't want to get a spanking.

I need your support in all of this. The elite of our nation have too much wealth and power; they oppress you by converting their private interests into public aims. Through the eternal natural royal law you revive and bestow upon me, I will enact legal changes to equalize the people. I will take the burden of public welfare on my shoulders and humble those who have become too strong so they don't threaten your flourishing. You only have to use your reason to see that this is the best course of action.

Don't worry about my safety. I've already been assassinated once for no good reason. Since I am, from a purely medical perspective, deceased, I can't be mortally shot again, even by the likes of a Brutus.

The Boulevards of Extinction

Oppressive Prescience

Reinvigorating a national consciousness calls for extreme measures. Return to a house of curtains, to thinking *under* a banister. Salvation requires a leviathan to bring a people back from the brink, a massive head of state weighing down its body. Imposing upon the people a social contract not subject to revision, the Leader tortures all the experts who will not relinquish their data unto him. Transfusing the spirit of Bureaucracy into himself and throwing away the needle—ridding himself of his addiction once and for all through a perpetual high. That such a leader could not possibly manage the organization of goods necessary to provide for his citizens' wants is beside the point—he is not a gift bearer, but a destroyer of consumption, testing a people's constitution for Jainism.

The spirit of management threatens to rupture his vessel: try as he might, he cannot contain it within himself, cannot apply all his cruelty to every citizen or refine his order down to the cellular level. He takes his virtues for granted. He was not a man of great ability after all, not up to the task—otherwise he would not have become a helmsman but a stargazer. Nor does he embody wickedness in any vital sense: a cracked clay pot, an inflatable kayak at popping point, the dregs of evil flow through the varicose veins of the twerp. In an attempt to master a spirit that only further solidifies *its* mastery over *him*, the Smallest Man exploits the seed of tyranny in democracy, shakes off the clumsiness of the division of powers and centralizes all authority in himself, returning us through order to a high bestiality. As custom is a second nature superimposed on the first, so bureaucracy is a third, the savagery of the Rule supplanting the most important spheres of the elegant, unspoken Way. Law becomes an instrument for vengeance, an outlet for paranoia, instrument of frantic desire, increasing the efficiency of the instinct it was supposed to render defunct by eliminating its fulfillment.

One takes up the mantle of power with the best of intentions, and the mantle molds its new body into an instrument of force, cruelty—and transcendent loyalty. The hand moves as if unbidden, bringing down the knife on the very people it covered the heart for and swore to protect, all the while continuing to think it is helping them, that it is doing what is best for all, for the country or the Idea. Every increasing act of oppression and violence contributes to the harmony of things.

The transformation of bureaucrat into tyrant is far more than a negative corruption stripping him of basic decency. The powerful one forgoes compassion to be ordained with a higher integrity—the rigid morality of the systematizer unyielding to individual sympathies—something which the citizen from his obstructed view under the boot and the outsider behind the curtain are incapable of seeing; the first weeping, the second shaking his finger, they repeat with a distant solidarity the old adage that power corrupts. No one understands, so lonely is the tyrant in his position of power;

PART 8: Eclipse

like the hermetic mystic, his truths are revealed only to him. Diminutive prophet of the pathetic, his message is bound up with the sickle.

This Old Testament wrath is not unmixed with the Gospel sweetness of parable and martyrdom. The most loathsome pipsqueak insulated in the trappings of tyranny never ceases to be the honest executor of order, the great equalizer, an architect of flesh and will. His language is propaganda, the education of small lies in service of the larger truth. He brooks no debate; he knows that communicative rationality is a feeble faculty for *gossiping* one's way to concord. Starved for hope, most citizens devour the ideals fed them, and for the sake of safety the few unbelievers shout slogans in acquiescence to evil. And out of everyone, the loudest mantras are the tyrant's. His secret thoughts are a heightened form of the savage's. Does his system know his mind? He dare not give himself away. It is not the motives of a cackle of cavemen he worries about, but whether his relentless half has discovered the intentions of his weaker half, bearer of the residue of repressed urges. So he resolves to be unpredictable, even to himself—he *goes mad*. Remembering Thomas Jefferson's meditation, "Were there but an Adam and an Eve left in every country . . ." he resolves to return to a desert Eden. To lighten himself of guilt, he places a doomsday button before a child and holds a piece of candy just out of its reach. Innocence, he realizes, is the perfect accomplice to necessary horrors. The tyrant liquidates us now not to give us a greater future, but to save us from one.

The Whistle's Shockwave

Spilling state secrets in the name of "human rights" is the overkill of deceit, the equivalent of decapitating a unicorn to shorten it into a horse. The realization that spies are as old as nations is acquired truth enough. In America men want to conspicuously consume truth, to install it as the lightning rod to their hundred-acre mansion in the clouds. Dreaming the *success* of truth, they want to hold it inside themselves now and to the full, a status object of the mind. But a precondition of possessing truth—if one can be said to ever possess it at all—is *pursuing* it. A search that can only continue as a manhunt. The shielding of rampant liberty was a possibility alien to Mill. The viscosity of a society's slime requires occasional thinning, taking a crowbar to the vise of freedom: desire without allegiance, determination by the inner species—the venting of all that is ugly within us. Sometimes brute matter must act on elusive forces to quell the disorder of their imminence.

Commentary on The Discourses, I.37

"Well-ordered republics," as Machiavelli said, "have to keep the public rich but their citizens poor . . ."

Frugality and simplicity among rulers, illiteracy among the ruled: this is the best way to prevent the spread of bribery and bad novels. Let the patricians pass off pastiches from classic literature as original speeches, inspiring the plebeians to extort their betters with the *perspiration* of virtue.

Only when social mobility becomes the norm do the poor become subject to conditioning: disheartened by the disgrace of remaining poor, they turn to the bottle or the needle; hard work, leading nowhere, becomes less attractive than criminal success, or, lacking a felonious constitution, the couch—unable to move up in life, they refrain from getting up at all. Thus the man in relative poverty finds out the hard way what the man in absolute poverty knew all along: that *staying put* is the route to contentment. Madame Du Châtelet defined it well: " . . . the happiest man is he who least desires to change his rank and circumstances." The lower orders who crave equality show themselves to be as restlessly grasping as the rich: otherwise they would not want to alter their situation.

When the Gracchi are reborn they must take care not to echo their ancient error. Maxim of reformers who would affect reincarnation, both learning a lesson and teaching one: wealth is best redistributed by taking it away from men and giving it to infrastructure. Though the rich may starve, our water supply must not be kept thirsty; though the poor may live in overcrowded slums, our public spaces should not suffocate from shrinkage.

Cincinnatus of the Senate: the man not elected but appointed, a backyard farmer who traipses dust into the Capitol and sweeps away the dirt in the legislature.

Minimum Wage Bloodlines

If the hereditary descent of our rulers is gone forever, that of the common people should at least be established. A thousand-year succession of janitors and cashiers would raise these careers to an art form instead of being the sloppy practices of alcoholics and incompetents that they are; alongside the Bach and Breughel families would stand the Masters of the Checkout Counter, a dynasty so long its origins are forgotten and heirs scorn to submit résumés from a sense of divine right. From a young age offspring are trained to memorize knowledge of store merchandise and be skilled conversationalists in the art of greeting. Competing in basic arithmetic problems at the dinner table, they are given meager allowances to handle and tasked with building meals from discounted items. After the pinnacle of their lineage has passed—employees of the year filling a century of wall space—arise the despots, bullying the store manager into submission and requiring lifetime memberships from shoppers. Keeping marriage within the checkout counter, rulers descend into madness as they wield the price tag gun with abandon. The end finally comes when Grand Cashier Maggie XXVIII, kind and sophisticated successor to generations of whimsy and oppression, is pulled from her golden register by an angry mob of customers, taken to the kitchen appliance section, and judged with a cookery set. Beaten with spatulas and flayed with vegetable peelers, she is crowned with a casserole pot and strung up over the entrance as a warning to future job applicants.

Expiation

Society's crime? —That it is not imprisoning *the innocent*. How can we expiate our sins if we lock away no one but the guilty? Wasting *only* men without worth will get us nowhere. The innocent are far more precious. They compensate for those not good enough to be made examples of—but not just any innocent person. The industrious man is already shackled to his labor; stress and chronic illness will exhaust his life soon enough. It is to the others we must turn: the irrelevant, the jobless, the lazy—those who waste the time liberty has granted them to fulfill their natural talents are ideal sacrificial victims. Though they have committed no positive crime, they are guilty of abusing freedom. "But we have done *nothing*," they shout. —Yes, that is why you make such a good candidate for a cage. "The punishment must fit the crime!"—Of course, and it does. It fits *our* crime, that of creating the conditions for freedom's abuse.

The vegetarian's blood has more in common with tree sap than what runs through the veins of animals; the snacker's plasma is too diluted with canola oil to purify the soul or appease heaven. One might as well tie a houseplant to the altar or squeeze an order of french-fries into the sacred bowl. The flesh tainted, we are forced to turn to stolen time to make everything right again. Man's freedom redresses the imbalance that his body cannot.

For the Aztecs a single sacrifice would suffice for harvest season. But freedom lacks the color of blood: a simple one-to-one substitution will not do. If society is to exonerate itself it must enact the ritual of a mass trial. An entire community of passive citizens must be put behind bars for the crime of one neighbor—only then will their negligence achieve forgiveness. The innocent man who has not served time can never be pardoned.

What of the man whose innocence will not be shaken, who refuses his culpability out of self-righteousness? For the supremely innocent there is a place beside the guilty, as there was a place for Christ next to thieves: after the clean-handed executioner dirties his conscience with a murderer, let him roll it in the manure with a saint.

The Sentence

"We didn't deserve this!"
    "No, but now you do."

The Boulevards of Extinction

Complaining of unwarranted punishment is not an appeal but a confession of guilt. Regardless of a man's actions prior to being dragged into a courtroom, he is convicted to see how he will handle his sentence. Neither good will nor selfless deeds will save him: subjected to farce, he *must* be made an example of, all the more so if he is suspected a puritan.

Wisdom is at best a byproduct of agony. The suffering may be too great to learn from; evil cuts maturation short more often than develops it. Nor is there any use comforting the sufferer, rubbing his shoulder and whispering assurances of a higher good—consolation consoles only the consoler; the "higher good" is deaf to all solace and beseeching: God wants to see whether our vocal chords can match our pain. He sends a tumor to a boy without a moral lesson to visit him in the hospital, in full awareness that the child *cannot* understand his misery, that this parable will end in brain death before meaningfulness.

Of all the tests of innocence, war is the best. Unlike with an isolated disease we are able to witness its mass effects in close proximity, comparing the constitution of one "innocent" with that of his neighbor—sorting out weeds from the flowers of blamelessness. The luckless refugee has no cause to fall back on; unlike the soldier he cannot say he died for freedom, glory, empire; unlike the cancer patient he cannot point the finger at personal lifestyle; no choice but to count himself a side-effect of intentional malevolence. So he keeps moving and hiding, hoping to someday justify his importance as collateral damage. An individual who outlives his persecution is given the constitution for a sustained existence, so long as he continues to be sought out for interviews and is encouraged by publishers to fabricate first a diary, then a memoir, then a chapbook of grandfatherly advice; a people, crawling out of its holes after a long genocide, find its solidarity strengthened as it awaits the *next* final solution. "I am needed," the sufferer tells himself. "Without my existence there would be no opportunity for annihilation." In his passive reception of evil's occurrence, the actor-turned-prop is displayed on the propaganda posters of maniacs and extremists, his victimhood a positive contribution to ideology. "My eyes can't welcome the bullet—it is too fast—but my *body* can. And if I survive . . . imagine the gain to philosophy!" Man's search for meaning progresses by bounds when the suffering of others leads to book sales and academic tenure.

The whiner, in pointing out how his suffering has degraded him, proves his unworthiness to be raised out of it. The exonerated one: silently accepting his assumed culpability, he is one of the few who, through the sum of all the noble and pathetic episodes of an experience the rest of his family could not endure, shows that he alone in his gene pool didn't deserve enchainment in the penal colony of Being. In life it is not the trial, but the completion of the sentence that proves innocence.

PART 8: Eclipse

General's Dying Speech to His Aide-De-Camp

My most faithful servant,

You deny my state of disgrace, but you are wrong—you have always been a flatterer. My condition is shameful: I die not gloriously in battle, but quietly in my bed. If I had known it would come to this I would have earned my sacrificial medal years ago in the Tet Offensive. Dementia has fogged my brain: I don't know where the enemy is anymore. Sometimes I think they are not hiding in a mountain cave, but sitting next to me on Pennsylvania Avenue. Even the people I protect raise my suspicions.

Why will the enemy win? We have technology, but the cave dwellers have virtue. We have guns, but our citizens are too pampered to serve and use them. As for our politicians, they make their own pleasures the prerogative of the commonwealth.

Please, don't take what I say to be more evidence of my worsening condition. Yes, some sufferers of dementia have bouts of paranoia and are easily agitated by fictions. But this is about more than mental health: it concerns the health of the state. America has become sick, an empire that just sits by, content with the benefits of economic dominance. To reinvigorate our nation, I would have it be a military empire like those of old: conquering by force, subjecting, dropping the bomb on resisters. Reclaiming the glory of Rome, the First French Empire, Britain in its heyday. We must give the rest of the world a *legitimate* reason to hate us. "The whole of classical history," writes Sorel, "is dominated by the idea of war conceived heroically." Educating the young with a heroic tradition, disciplining citizens to be soldiers rather than consumers—to subsume the economy under the needs of the warrior. Sorel was speaking of the Greek ideal, "an epic state of mind." The problem with this is that, in merely preparing their cities for defense, the Greeks created a restlessness that could only be satisfied by turning it upon themselves and fighting other city-states. If they had been conquerors rather than defenders of freedom, they would have been too busy to embroil themselves in civil war. —And the Athenian empire? They merely exploited their own when they should have united them and pushed the boundaries of Greece outward. In Sorel's story, the Iliad degenerates into Njal's Saga. But man is capable of a far more epic state of mind than Sorel allowed for. Fortunately for Western culture, Alexander recognized this.

The first step to reclaiming the glory of the West is the overthrow of the current order. Violence will smash the old system, force will maintain the new one. The penal procedures of the *ancien régime* will serve us well: every act of antagonism and negligence are to be seen as crimes against authority. Cheeseburger addicts must be purged no less than CEOs of fast food restaurants. Training camps for the obese, the sword for every citizen who refuses to learn the virtues of obedience.

How will I bring this all about, you ask? It will be difficult, I admit. In any case, I am too ill to see any of this through. It will be up to you. You are no longer my *aide-de-camp*. I am promoting you to the rank of general. The time for bootlicking is ended: only the most virtuous should escape your castigation. Here is my final order: study Pericles's speech from Thucydides; at my funeral you will give an oration paying homage to all the good soldiers who died in bed. Harness the power of words and the army will follow you.

Universal Thralldom

An unacknowledged logical limit hides within Block's idea of property as the foundation of civil society. Humanity is still the most lucrative natural resource, and exerting labor to capture a population is as innately lawful a claim of ownership as any—there will still be enough of "man" left in common for the rest of the pirate class. The consequences of denying our need for exploitation are dire: when slaves aren't chattel, citizens are. The emancipation proclamation enserfed us all. The biggest mistake of the Colonies, after breaking away from the Empire, was that they failed, without prejudice towards race or creed, to unite their entire population with iron collars. There is only one consummation more suited to the human condition, more *just*, than universal thralldom—extinction.

The Blood Polis

Without a culture of blood feuds a family has no steadfast means of holding itself together. A father burning with the duty of revenge does not abandon the mother of his child to singlehood and welfare, but cherishes every evening earned with his wife and raises sons as the future vindicators of his corpse. The son does not float about purposeless in his teenage years, but grows with a mission, his ties of friendship strong because he knows his enemies. The wife does not liberate herself from her husband to become chained to the world of work, but ministers to the wounded and keeps spirits high with song. The daughter, in her role as reconciler, runs off with the other side's son, giving Montague and Capulet a generation to recover their numbers: they know that whatever private bonds have been forged between individual members cannot alter the *public* relationship of the two houses. However "good" an opposing member might be, he is still a gene-pool diluter, a danger to kin solidarity, a *relative*-evil.

Model for Airistotle's city-state, the blood-feud familial structure is the basic unit of every political organization that would survive in the era of globalization. The father of its constitution is not Madison, but Shakespeare. In a world where national, cultural, and economic boundaries are dissolving, only a plasma pact can draw unambiguous lines.

The King Who Ruled over Everything

There is a king who, out of principle, rebels against authority. He fearlessly tells the truth to his noblemen. There is little ceremony in his courtly behavior, and no pomp in his public ceremonies. He does not feast on grapes or lay across plush couches, but eats only bread and sleeps on the floor. He cultivates indifference to affairs of state and laughs at external circumstances. When foreign ambassadors visit he insults them, whether the countries they come from are weak or powerful. He forces them to wait in small hallways outside the courtroom for long periods of time. When they enter, he carries on a side conversation with his jester as they speak. If they come bearing gifts, he receives them, saying, "You really should not have, these are not suitable for me." Then he turns and throws them to his dogs, telling them, "Here are some new bones for you, my lovelies." Eventually, a ruler of a neighboring kingdom becomes outraged by his mistreatment and announces an invasion. The king is delighted. Everyone chides him with provoking the downfall of the kingdom through his hubris. But he only wanted to steel them against the hardships of life. "War is the lot of man," he shouts to them in a speech. "We should all just get used to it." When his country is invaded, his subjects rise against him and join the enemy force. The king is not pleased when he learns of this. It is not the place of his subjects to question authority. He is quickly dethroned and thrown into prison, where he languishes happily at first, shivering against the stone floor and lapping dirty rainwater from the window. But when he insults the guards he finds they have the audacity to beat him, and he begins to see things differently. He realizes that he no longer possesses the authority to rebel.

***

First moral: Those who set the standards cannot reset them.

Second moral: The ruler who creates the exception is the rule.

Third moral: Victorious rebels mostly defy lower authorities, occasionally those high in name only.

Fourth moral: To care for the world is to care for yourself, though not in that order or in equal proportion.

Fifth moral: Peasants, too, are bound to correct decorum. Less pomp in their step, more poop.

Love from Self

Love makes us most similar to our original self—that which bonded naturally to its nurturer now longs to connect with lover, child, deity. Everyone else, noticing the change to a sameness they never knew, perceives us as different from how we had been in our later corrupted state. We are shackled, no longer independent. Trusting to their observations rather than our intuition, afraid to rediscover the passion of the original self, we halt this return: breaking up, aborting, losing faith. One person of two competing sentiments, the corrupted self's conjecture dares not understand shared identity. Without help love's abundance abates, splitting into fornication and misery, seeking out tenderness only on the skin of others. But in sharing sperm and trading fists, will extreme acts of self-giving form a semblance of altruism, enough to push the self-destructive into the reproductive? Only the Fallen can mold himself back into a blank slate: impotent and bullied, out of his own experience he batters himself into an ambulance. Reformed by shifts of nurses, he is ready to start new lives by night and day; healed by an unordained chaplain, to tour churches by weekends . . .

A Mystical Itinerary

The *danger* of loving a human with the same violent and insane charity directed towards God—Richard of Saint Victor clearly was not proscribing from experience. If he had, he would have discovered that we are remembered as heroes for destroying the beloved and ourselves. This was something the medieval mind was unable to fathom—it only ever let itself be burned for points of doctrine.

When no amount of affection "is able to satisfy the desire of the burning soul"— no matter how much one hugs and snuggles, the skin is insatiable. Lovers, family, friends are not enough; one's compassion grows until the earth becomes a platonic plaything smothered in one's arms by surpassing greatness.

Contrarily, to love God with all the violence directed towards humans . . . but this is nearly impossible; it is only the mystics whom God *wounds*. The lowest degree of violent charity is reserved for the highest dispositions, those retiring enough to grow pale for him, who gasp and groan and display the heat of their desire within a lonely cell because in public no one cares to look. There is no vaccine today for those born with a lowered sacred immune system; being susceptible to the same virus that makes one feverish for God also infects one with chickenpox on a seasonal basis. The spiritualized body becomes a breeding ground for new strains of flu, ebola, hepatitis. Scourges spread to every nation to demonstrate the insuperability of love's excellence.

Grünewald

He remained wedded to an age of gloomy superstition after the rest of the world had moved on: the Gothic Relic, antithesis of the Renaissance Man. Driven by a singular obsession, he lacked that instinct for historical packaging that allows traditional souls the self-awareness that they are an anachronism. What was "the Dark Ages" to Petrarch, a classification he used as a reference point to look both back to the Greco-Roman world and forward to a petty-classical model of it, was to Grünewald one long untraversable horizon. Petrarch, too busy establishing himself as the new Cicero, could not humble himself before the Middle Ages as Grünewald could—he was too much the scholar, the *fraudulent* reviver. In his unpublished *Secret Book* he hid the other side of the Renaissance, its lingering Augustinian struggle with anxiety and despair. But he only let its gaiety shine on sunny Italy, at best the graceful sorrow of a lost Laura. It was left to the North to render the period with realism—and kill the method. Dürer's *Apocalypse* series turned the anticipated Last Judgment of 1500 into a visual feast for fools, an event to be drooled over for the lushness of God's wrath, but hardly feared. The Saturn of *Melancholia I* had too many objects to brood upon; Grünewald needed only *one*. Saturn was a new god for an age of rebirth. By giving us so many majestic diversions, the Renaissance offered multiple sources of manic depression for those who were different—geniuses and madmen. On ordinary characters, though, the age's only imprint was the attitude of gaping stupidly at pretty pictures. But it was to ordinary people—the sick and lame—that Grünewald appealed to when through the Isenheim Altarpiece they were offered, *for the last time*, a threatening being to subject themselves to and submit their contradictions before, a son to recoil from, and from disgust derive an equally disturbing joy. And when the final Gothic master died, the spirit of melancholia in the ordinary man died too. After Grünewald the paradoxes of the common people were dispelled; they became simpler. The world no longer needed to be motivated by suffering. Humanity now had its magic square, forerunner of the crossword puzzle; life became a brainteaser for everyone to plug in their own guesses.

The engine of the Renaissance nearly exhausted, a new source of energy will soon be needed to keep humanity chugging along. With the dialectical forces of history swinging back, values once lost may be rediscovered, initiating a Counter-Renaissance that reinterprets the legends of the past to suit our times. A gothic sensibility reawakening into a technocratic age: Christ rising from the tanning bed, St. Anthony tormented by financial advisors, a plague-pitted Grünewald velcroed to a chiropractic cross. One experiences violent sensations so *efficiently* that an Easter gift basket is needed to offset the purging effect of opening an altarpiece.

Infinite Affection

The most repugnant child pulls the parents' heartstrings. They are not finicky about indulging the monster's every whim; even the child's *toys* are carefully preserved, cherished as future memories. Moved by reason alone they would drown the creature, disown it, anything to chlorinate their gene pool. But their passion obliges them to love the unlovable, make it a natural object of affection, even sacrifice themselves for its happiness.

This addiction to love is nothing more than *bad taste*. In every love relation the heart interprets the eyes; it is an original beauty unto itself, recognized by observers as an object of repulsion that only an outward-looking self-love could derive from a bundle of inherited traits or a mirror of wishful thinking. Everyone else's child is a cliché. To other parents the devil child is an inept finger-painting, totally unlike their own masterpiece of good breeding: polite, popular, extracurricular altruist, star student—future suicide.

The pampered offspring takes pleasure in seeing that he alone is valued and all others denounced . . . until an accident occurs that his world of comfort cannot buffer. Unconditional love is a safety net with holes, and when its recipient falls through because the giver couldn't always be there, the ingrate lands in resentment. He has finally come into his love for them . . . standing on the other side of unconditional love, he has realized his *ambition*, his desire to outdo the parents, to surpass them in achievement—and someday, parenting ability . . .

Never really acknowledging his parents' sacrifice, the child now finds their love suffocating, is embarrassed by it in public and made miserable in private. Despite trying to convince them that their affection is superfluous, even making himself intolerably fastidious, they will not abdicate and continue to lavish unceasing warmth, attempting to make up for their moment of negligence with humble sanctity. And so the child decides that he will return their gift of love in kind once they are old enough to appreciate it, paying them back for the limitations of their unconditionality. His gifts? —A daily dose of morphine, two high windows across the courtyard of a nursing home.

Binding the Flesh

How many problems a world full of Isaacs could solve! Interrogated spinsters and lonely bombshells are a small price to pay for the Maker's right of *prima nocta*. Overpopulation by the seed of the spirit and its inherited epidemic, the patriarch-complex, would lend a sense of principle to the usual scramble for fatherlands.

Empty-Nest Syndrome

Without the child the heart is a void . . . but this is why the parents conceived in the first place, to have a being that would fill their center by allowing them to go out of themselves. Husband and wife, thrust into the old roles, have no one to fight over for favoritism. When she calls from college they are barely attentive, so distant is she from the hole that has sprung up around and inside them. The parents had always been ceaselessly providing, teaching, setting an example. Dual actors in a passion that requires a common other, rest exhausts the parenting instinct from lack of joyful stimulus. When the daughter asks for money they send her a bill: "nurturance tuition: $100,000."

PART 8: Eclipse

Building from Sodom's Ashes

It is unfair to God when homosexuals become monks—he should not have to be jealous of his own brotherhood. The preference for the *ménage à trois* over the Trinity conjures less the democracy of love than the imposition of tact upon ritual. Father, Son, and Holy Ghost enter into monogamy with the heart; an order-wide orgy makes for a confusing partitioning of rosary beads.

The Father and Son

For years the kid just happened to be there. First as a baby, then a teenager, then a picture frame. They had nothing in common; were it not for a shared dinner table, father and son would never have talked about the weather. One day after the accident dad looked at a photo and realized there was *something to that child* after all. Though he wasn't athletic he decided to start attending baseball games. That boy wasn't someone who had just hung around, dad saw. He was trying to make something of himself. It was the dream of a better life, a world away from home...from boring old dad. Going home and looking for the last time at a face he had once thought familiar, dad burned all the photo albums.

"I'm sorry about your loss," a neighbor said the next day.

"I didn't lose anything," he replied. "I know my son's up there, where I'll be going someday."

***

First moral: Aspiration reaches its goal in the dreams of the lackadaisical.

Second moral: When you apprehend a truth too late, it's too early to do anything about it until falsehood points the way. Then you go back to what you were doing before—old habits sandwiching an abandoned epiphany.

Third moral: "To have children" isn't a life goal, but the deferment of goals at the rate of one per child.

Fourth moral: Puerile parents incubate ambitions for their children, who, after maturing into giant kids, realize they don't want the same old ambitions for *their* children.

Fifth moral: From intellectuals to secretaries to loafers, the divergent sedentary lifestyles all find a convenient point of interest in sports.

Mystery in the Details

The scoff of the sophisticates is not directed at small things. And yet these are the most unknowable. The "facts," the objects of sense perception: without some *greater* guiding organization, they are just the pebbles of the brain—lumps to navigate the skull by, protruding in every direction. This phrenology of tumors extrapolating the features of character beyond management, they are surgically extracted with precision kitchenware (carrot peeler, salad tongs) and dropped along the ground to guide others to the end of the flat earth.

Fishing for belief

Jesus chose the disciples for the emblem of their occupation—men used to wrestling with wild forces would surely have the mettle for grappling with heathens and idolatry. But what was a career has become a hobby. Trout, salmon, mackerel—the fisherman confines himself to tranquil waters and gentle skirmishes. He does not think of rowing down the Amazon and swimming with the piranha, of being tossed by a hurricane on the open sea to net a big catch. A swordboat captain does not pick and choose his battles, but thrusts himself into the bowels of nature.

But for those who do not have the time to go to their Belief, let it come to them. A natural disaster strengthens the resilience of a local population when it occurs within the month before a major religious holiday.

The Unconditioned Ephemeral

Removing obstacles to God: enlisting that competing abstraction, the machine, life's regulator. To open oneself to inspiration is to submit to the regularity of rituals and liturgy; the machine aids habit by offering up its ideal: routinization. The *spirit* of the conditioned, it relentlessly builds on what came before, innovating by surpassing, beating down opposition with patience and time, sanitizing life against the incursion of germs. Its method is as rational as it is artificial, introducing reason into a substantive unreason. Ever expanding, negating thought and resistance, it is the intermediary property of the void, the artificiality of Being, preparing the move from presence to absence. A model for spirituality to pursue, internalizing holiness to make it automatic, self-evolving—Belief as reflex, the flux of muscle growth. Regressing towards predestination, certainty becomes an afterthought to testimony.

Loan before Wagering

The doubter's friend, adviser to a terrified ignorance, his shoulder the only refuge from annihilation on two sides. Empathizing with weakness, the bosom-chum assesses the risk: "What do you have to lose?"—"Why, nothing—everything has *already* been lost." The friend makes a sudden movement, startling the doubter and betraying his instinctive fear. Seeing hope, the friend embarks on his crusade with a massage.

He exploits the doubter's despair by burying him in alienation literature, surrounding him with scoundrels, ruining his positive relationships—making him feel totally alone in the world. The crusader ruthlessly harasses the doubter, making him weary of his doubt, longing for happiness. Having created the conditions for persuasion, the crusader then puts him to work, surrounding him with the likeminded, kneading him with side-topic conversation and encouraging repetitive behaviors—all the while keeping him at a distance, making him feel his outsider status so as to bring about the moment of choice. How is this sociological approach more malicious than the use of reason? Is it not a *kinder* manipulation, less intimidating than a "What if?" calculus or an ontological proof? Philosophy may be prior to religion, as al-Farabi tells us; but persuasion—the method of theology as well as of the first philosophers—is prior to demonstration. To lower a man past the nothingness of his own life through a surfeit of bad influences and a yearning for acceptance—into the nothingness of everything beyond his life. Every gambler needs a confidence man to coax him to the high-stakes table. Fraudulent trust is the last friendship of a skeptical humanity.

Replicas

Walking with God . . . in Eden he was still a *friend* to man—disingenuously, not being of a comparable cast to his clay chum. This is where Adam derived his model of friendship as the relation not spoken of, so that today, among apparent equals, each attempts to subtly establish dominance over the other. As God grew feet to prove himself humble and Adam ate the apple to prove himself worthy, a friend's admittance of his own single-minded ambition destroys the friendship; only by gaining a permanent foothold over the other unconsciously, telling himself it is for their mutual benefit, can he strengthen the bond, ensure the weaker one will not defect—always, out of care and intimidation, willing to loan a few dollars in an emergency or a few hundred for a promising speculation.

After refining their exploitation of one another they are ready to turn upon the rest of mankind, ascending above an unsuspecting world through the "nobility" of friendship. Unlike in their own voluntary relationship they do not choose subjects to exploit but, for the sake of harmonious camaraderie, pit themselves against stranger and acquaintance indiscriminately. Friendship is the highest symbol of spirituality, its very absence as a scriptural topic evidence that between pure equals there can be no point of contact . . .

Chosen Outcasts

Everyone follows God's plan, especially atheists and suicides. Absence and escape are the surest roads unto him. Reveling in his nonexistence and freeing oneself from his grasp evokes a potent combination of serenity and ecstasy. Heresy and damnation are the froth of spiritual experience. In the desperation to occupy an *island* paradise both sides of the autonomic nervous system are mutually stimulated; a response alien to the orthodox aisle-shuffler, transported by each emotion only in succession. Immortality's pariahs revel in a level of heightened sensation hitherto achievable only by cloistered monks and hermits in the wilderness.

The *method* of the universe's indifference being the atheist's most important conviction, he is hostile towards atheists not of his stamp. A clique of incompatible assurances, they assemble only to argue over disputed paradigms: string theory, epigenetics, cultural universals, social constructivism. With nothing pre-given, in-groups form around personal meanings: finding love, seeking social status, building ships in bottles, collecting stamps. Unable to think together, they can only achieve solidarity in *doing*.

It is these self-cancelling effects of the rebel's rapturous profanity that explain his paralysis-by-apathy. His first duty after casting off religion being to live in society, he is too engrossed in his independence to contribute towards its ends. Left with only his health to uphold, the atheist takes to treating his cirrhosis with communion wine. The Chanukah Cigarette: chain-smoked over the Menorah to nurture emphysema, it approximates a soul transplant through the inhaling of carcinogen vapor. Casting aside his cane to fall towards Mecca, the cripple becomes the pious—a freethinker has everything to gain by exploiting the appearances of grasping at eternity. Enmeshing his sick body in the habits of the faithful, he confronts mortality in a way impossible from the isolation of the infirmary. But he makes his condition known to the congregation, arriving every Sunday in his surgery robe.

Closet Debate

WHITE COAT: As long as there remains a mysterious *something* about being human, the word "soul" will explain it. Underneath every cloak, a dagger to shred it with.

BLACK ROBE: A synonym for mystery does not dismiss, but amplifies. The anonymous is replaced with a shadow. Solving the whodunit shifts the burden of motive onto the detective—the silhouette fits his own contours.

RED CLOAK: Satisfying idiots who don't want to have to think, motivating the intelligent with an obsession to dispel inscrutability, the underbrush of the unknown outlines the path to grandma's house. In both cases the practical goal of mystery is certainty, its opposite. Whether "soul" or "further research is needed," both views assume there is something inside the basket to deliver.

SCARF: You *envelopers*, you all miss the point. An idea that covers everything isn't what is needed. What makes us human, what connects the body and the mind, is the neck. And *I* am what completes it, the solution. Just wrap, tie—and squeeze.

PART 8: Eclipse

The Idea of Love

The abstraction of love is the remedy to seeing life too close up. It organizes the world in a way vague enough to buoy our hopes, linking things through their kernels of charm and good will—as long as it is intuited. But abstraction's ogreish sibling is never far away—as soon as love is *analyzed*, it is killed. It disintegrates the emotion to discover its parts. Instead of finding the atom of ardor, the insecurity of plucking a flower with unlimited petals.

Apocalypse of the Human Soul

Unlike with the private ascendency in which salvation confirms the self-righteous, it is no fun to be damned alone. Those whose passions are too strong, whose reason too cold, or whose principles too casual wish to maximize their camaraderie. This is why the majority of humanity, in a plague of bad will, should pray that believers of all stripes be damned to the pits of their respective cosmologies—the Christian to hell, the Buddhist to the lowest step on the ladder of life, the Materialist to an ideal realm in which he is transformed into a series of defective domestic objects and judged in a competition against their perfect countertop-parts by the model housewife who left him long ago over the tangibility of his liquor bottle. Complementing these entreaties, humanity should *hope* that believers will be damned . . . so that the species as a whole can fall hand in hand, entering a place where all their hopes are fulfilled. Having nothing now to look forward to, a race of Judases in a final moment of repentance looks about for a tree. Not finding one we improvise, helping one another to an eternity of suicide attempts in the hope that our expectation will end our indestructibility. Failing, we begin to question our prayers of injustice. *Even here*, no one can know whether anyone else has either fully accepted or rejected God, despite experience. "Perhaps," some say, "we all deserve to go to the other place . . . it was just a misunderstanding, maybe, a divine bureaucratic error. If we could only pool our doubt, there should be enough to send us back to Earth, to separate us from our maker . . ."

A Nun's Habit

The most profound religious experiences take place on the brink of orgasm. The only women ecstatic at the prospect of a long-distance relationship, expectant nuns titillate their souls in conversation with a partner who *is known* to have a history of extra-marital impregnation. Pricking their hands while sewing a scapular, they flirt with the Son to win over the Father. Working themselves into a rhythm through plainchant, their heartbeat, breathing, and brainwaves synchronize with a body convulsing to the mere thought of how *big* God must be. Singing together breaks down the separation between the sisters, helps them to realize their common goal. Unlike with men, God's attention is undivided no matter how many of his admirers he dotes on.

Eternity's Economy

A return to bartering, not with the cow or iron hoe as our unit of value, but *the soul*—a universal currency common to all and distinctive to every individual. Money at first being large and heavy, then shiny and malleable, then flimsy and crinkly, it now completes its trend towards insubstantiality by turning the object of our salvation into a line of credit. What if the soul could be traded not just once, but a multitude of times? If, every time it is depleted, you could simply replenish it with a day's honest work? Everyone would finally have the knowledge that they possess something more precious than anything else—and that it can be given away for anything else. In stories men have always traded their souls for something of supreme material value—wealth, power, bodily invulnerability, Faust's perpetual titillation. We, on the other hand, having souls equivalent to our labor value, will trade it for fiddles—a bag of candy, an hour with a prostitute—and earn just enough of it back the next day to keep us shackled to our jobs. It is not the devil, but the economy that we are selling our afterlife to—God will want a share of the profits. Since we will always have more soul in our future, we can enjoy our nightly penury directly as men once enjoyed their coin collections. We can pray with an emptiness in our bosoms, knowing that an accumulation of disbursed souls is the sign of a good protestant work ethic, the conspicuous consumption of redemption. God comes to love the poor for their poverty of spirit, their sales record of vivifying entities. In the case where we need more soul in the present than we can earn in pay period, we can spend now and pay later, inventing a hypothetical amount of life-essence to borrow at a reasonable rate of interest. As long as there is soul to splurge, one should not waste conscience on usury. Adopting a policy of sacred mercantilism, we export everything we have into the market and import a bit more love from above to provide the nourishment lacking in our daily portion of junk food. Economic value is at once relative and objective, abstract and specific, turning the gears of the world and transcending it. Even if we get swindled in our routine dealings, God will always give us the just price for our commodity.

Love's Proximity

Sentimentality provides a thousand things to say but makes the lips quiver to speak in anything but mumbles. Every step is calculated to bring pleasure to one oblivious; in a mute act of kindness you endear yourself as a servant. As compensation for the paralyzed concealment of your feelings you daydream a life together, a scene for every situation. Loneliness raises the old clichés to profundity: nuzzling on a picnic blanket, searching the night sky for fate's streamers; seeing romance everywhere, you admire even a quarrel for its conspicuous intimacy. And for this to be a love of pure imagination . . . the beloved's joy with another says you don't exist, but your continued chastity knows better—never have you felt so alive. Happiness fills the interior void and puts it out of mind, while longing gives one a heightened awareness of it.

Waywardness' Worth

The people of the Book only appreciate their covenant when breaking it. Forsaken for so long in our iron and brass existence until it seems Jehovah's memory has rusted over, it is simply the Lord's way of ensuring we will renew his promise. In our cycles of depravity, pain, spurtive repentance and spotty piety, we are like chronic adulterers mouthing anniversary vows for the luxury of sleeping on the couch.

Divergence

A dissimilar object of beauty: the most effective escape from the self. The corollary to being magnetized by a moral that clashes with behavior and speaking a truth that contradicts your personality. It is a sign of a derivative imagination to seek correspondence—to look for outside copies in these realms as an excuse for the circumstances of one's disposition. The more external disagreement, the more one can be said to commune with the thing alone, in itself. The inevitable accusation of self-denial only fortifies this intimacy: in place of "you" and "beauty" only an unselfconscious quality remains.

God—the *most* dissimilar object of beauty. Imitation is aspiration beyond one's image.

Discovering the Soul

Subjecting oneself to a great work of art stings the pride of autonomy. Familiarization calls for a throbbing concentration on background techniques—the ways of nature, society, culture; observing life becomes the sacrifice of it. Laughing at masterpieces and lachrymose towards practicality, the man impervious to beauty drinks his saliva and cries into soup bowls, his body the source of all vital sustenance. Tea and toast he saves for his superiors, serving his way up the social ladder to a house with a swimming pool filled from his ducts. The high saline content making lifeguards unnecessary, his only child is one day found floating the wrong side up. In despondency the man turns to a seascape by Turner. Surely, God must have been a little sad to shed such a vast thimbleful of creation and sigh so many waves. The man feels akin to Turner's fisherman with his lantern—a maritime Diogenes searching for an honest sublimity.

Love's Cruelty

Our predisposition to love is not enough; the raw lover is always disappointed. Study is required to refine its sensibility and obtain its object, bringing on corruption: love becomes a technique, a frenzied panacea, an attempt to quiet ourselves. It calculates and plays games, and finally the heart's fireplace is extinguished with sobs swallowed by the chimney. One hides one's strivings in an attempt to not seem pathetic to others, and soaks up wretchedness within oneself. But the raw lover—innocent, inexperienced—is the world's only pure being, a wide-eyed suckling of the passions.

Righteousness of Reading

The devil hid his hand in the writing of the good book: the politics of Nicaea's editors, the King James voluptuaries, the *delightful* patterning of lamentations, the Song of Solomon's suggestiveness to an unwed heart. Beauty soaks arid truth with temptation. The hedonists already in his pocket, the believers still need coaxing with the sensuality of words, the seduction of metaphors. Just sit and read in privacy, Satan says. Be idle. The Iblis who refused to bow to a creature of clay cajoles others into doing nothing with him. Filling their heads with rich language, giving them more in the imagination, he realizes the lessness he desires. Hellfire is the lighthouse of deliverance.

The Stages Along Life's Way

Mystic, saint, martyr, heretic. To begin with a feeling, apply it through charity, harden it through pain, and negate it in a tarnished public memory. Repudiation by the world of the messenger who scorns it is the only hint of divine forgiveness to tenacious followers. A saint who dies in bed is buried as a charlatan; a martyr whose posthumous licks aren't fiercer than the flames was only an innocent after all.

Questioning Necessity

It was left to the great and terrible al-Ghazali to refute Pascal half a millennium before the Jansenist's explanation: of prayer as the *disgrace* of causality, the heraldry of its severance. Things are as they must inevitably be only for those who displease their maker. Every promise implies an absence; fate's hand gangrenes to one who breaches possibility with a humble inquiry.

Providence's Tortuous Route

Reverse psychology is the classic tool of prophecy. If an angel lost a feather every time he told a fib, Gabriel's skeleton wings would terrorize his messages into fulfillment. By the time the last feather fell, the white lies of heaven would admit us into its gates through avoidance. So does God make even falsehoods serve as truth-functions.

Man vs. Many

The behavior of love is the human race breaking through every assertion of distinct individuality. Only in a love that refrains does the soul pierce the admirer—and only after the object is out of reach. Indulgence is fatal to spirit: in the coma following sex or Thanksgiving, it is the species that recharges the participant. As for the obstructed subjects of love—the impotent, the ugly, those bereaved of family—with lassitude for libido, a horror of mirrors, and an emptiness in their hearts, they are keenly aware of being forsaken by the higher region.

A Sleek Function

The haughty sages who scorn the "futile leap" of grace, too clumsy to dance, clinging to despair. There is a negativity in grace—the denial of those whom *it* forsook first. Of its lucky vessels well-being is only an eventuality of strife; anxiety is grace's long punishment: only after long searching does the eye catch its glare. Through pain one can be certain that the search itself is an ascension with limits—warming up the machine. One must perform a *salto mortale* somersault and leap into a kneel; a genuflection that bruises the knees discourages standing up in favor of looking up.

Evagrius Jaunticus (Selections from the *Hedonikos*)

12) *Akêdia* is the midnight angel that lightens bad dreams with consciousness. It represents freedom to disturb with passion.

13) It is the eighth deadly sin, the virtue extending life: slowing the course of the moon, the prospect that the night may last forever allows one to get through the next day.

15) Staring out the window—one lets the mind wander not out of nostalgia, but a

hatred of the parking lot. The midnight angel loves his claustrophobic apartment and dreads the obligation to take up any craft.

52) To separate the soul of the apartment complex from its body is the privilege of the renter. The transgressions of neighbors eat away at him; he delights in plotting revenge for offenses to his balcony decorations.

60) The heart can never be pure on the outside. He realizes that he can never leave his room: geography is essential to God's blessing.

78) He battles through the night to forget family, putting everything impure out of his mind; listening to old records he revels in the long life before dawn. He would be tempted to abandon the world and the races of men entirely, but he makes no images of them, and so is tempted to nothing. Content with the shade, he binges on the tardiness of pizza delivery boys.

83) After the midnight angel leaves, so does his ecstasy: he returns to listlessness. When the sun is up he lives as if asleep, leaning against a wall, waiting to be reborn. He cannot see fighting in the light; until the moon rises he does not clearly discern the meaning of the war.

97) A squatter who spent all his time talking to himself tried to sell his tongue to an organ donor facility. They didn't want it, so he sealed it in tupperware and put it in his refrigerator. "I don't blame them for not wanting something no one needs," he thought. Still, that was the only way to pay rent on time—selling what no one needed.

First Sense

To stare at the sun and squint into the night. Brightness swells the pupils, darkness burns them shut. Isn't this how it must be for all angels and men of stainless virtue? Righteous creatures are oversensitive only to shade. Irisless, their inflamed pupils gape at the light, but after sunset when there is only the void to gape back they cannot bear to look.

Second Sight

The long procession from Jesus' healing of the blind to Franklin's bifocals took a substantial thinning of powers; time has not been so generous in delaying an attenuated aid to the heavy-lidded. Being past the time of miracles, even gadgets are now too external to modify our afflictions of vision; a drug is necessary to ease our senses into becoming receptive to grace. Truth no longer free to bypass the laws of physics or wait for us to tamper with them, it flashes itself before us in bursts brief enough for our attention spans to linger on its appearance. Not only the conversion of a nation to Belief, but its resilience in the face of decline, should make a simplification to miracles once again necessary.

Talking the Walk

We are too fond of reducing our explanations to bare mechanics. Augmenting naturalistic explanations by means of the supernatural, even replacing them entirely with descriptions of the ineffable, does more than simply increase attention span. Superstitious language imbues physiological processes with reasons possessing *value*, motivating alteration or repetition. Ethical language is not enough: "good" and "bad" need a cosmic origin to prevent them from waffling. The word of God: to unify fact and value we need only the *logos*.

No need for superstitious language to point to anything beyond a waning cultural fad: by signifying the absence of its referent, teasing hope and despair alike, we demonstrate in a way far crueler than religious dogma what is beyond the purely empirical life. The empiricist, after all, can find evidence for revealed religion with the proper training—a person quick to jump to a spiritual explanation without first considering the influence of the lower functions is likely defective with regard to at least one of them; one needs only an x-ray machine or a stethoscope to find proof of a new sect's claims.

By "superstitious" is included everything now defunct that people once believed, the passé persuasions of a given aspiration, whether God or Gold, Christianity or Alchemy—pseudoscience too is a grasping towards the possible. Insufficient to draw on the beliefs of a segment of the population as the foundation of argument, since others, not being believers, will discredit it before the minor premise is stated. Better to tell a story, surround it with facts, and draw a message out of entertainment. Chemistry, biology, physics: every relevant detail yet-to-be-debunked is gathered in support.

Faced with the condition of indigestion, one looks to the stomach acid the midnight snacker failed to baptize his pancakes in; had he simulated the gastrointestinal state in a frying pan he might have steeled his insides against his syrup-stack, perhaps even discovered the elixir of sleep—the lethargist's stone, aftermath of every satisfying meal.

Christian Dialectics

Doom and love—the arc of everything momentous and trivial can be reduced to this Hebraic cycle. Even in quilting, prophecy paves the way for evangelism: drawn to the patterns and images yarned in squares, satisfaction only comes with snuggling the fabric. But just as the gospels are flanked on two sides by the auguries of Old

Testament and Revelation, one cannot stay bundled up for more than a season: it creates such a warm and fuzzy feeling that a sweltering kitchen can't be weathered and, come summer, charity is entered into the sweepstakes of a needlework festival.

Ascent into Pure Calculation

To escape time, curl up with a sociological study of suicide, a factsheet of endpoints so long and tedious it seems like losing oneself in eternity. One may be pardoned for becoming the most recent entry in the list, citing that old, universal excuse—the unendurable strain on human nature, compounded in a new way by inspection over the entire range of death's social predispositions. In being so moved, the usually voluntary quality of the act can be dismissed as an accident of determinism, the condition of a soul overburdened with stereotypes.

"I couldn't help it," he told St. Peter, "I was too engrossed in the plot of my book to notice the stoplight."—In this way, the man of tendencies becomes yet another demographic fad on the endless plains where lonely white males forage for the manna of holiness.

The stat afterlife—permits for walking with God, chorister licenses, stated limitations on warning corporeal relatives; developing habits of beatitude that orchestrate spiritual regulation, there is no need to take responsibility for a lack of standard deviation. Every soul warped by regression to the mean, it is superfluous to *be kind* to the saved, to have pity for piety. On earth things at least retain their interest by changing; when time stands still there is nothing to check the monotony of contentment—and this being the goal there is no need to repent of it. Though no one moans and whines, there is a sense that the residents are only here because they expected to be saved. Correcting his affective responses to bliss, the one predestined to ennui realizes it was not enough to escape a succession of moments and conspires to escape *the* moment. Anyone, he grasps, is capable of leaving at any point, but no one can seem to abandon false satisfaction and break schedule, told as they were that routine would make them free. Staying being unbearable, the exit from time is the sole alternative. Entirely without *pieta*, the one set apart from Being does not try leading a mass exodus but learns to see and judge them as Nothingness does, salvation's grand inquisitor. His is the path for those of us who find boredom unacceptable. Getting to where we are supposed to end up, we recognize where the cosmos and our place in it are heading. Only under the aspect of eternity can we see our view as a halfway point and fully appreciate our final destination. The way to nonbeing is through heaven.

PART 8: Eclipse

All for Love

From where does our doom come if not love? Friendship, Affection, Eros, Charity: in an expanding intensity of selflessness, the four horse-drawn carriages of the apocalypse jeopardize us all. Forsaking happiness and even the expectation of pleasure, one seeks togetherness at the cost of all else: Friendship's town meeting truancy in favor of poker night; Affection's bulletproof frame around the family portrait; Eros's suicidal soliloquy for the beloved; Charity's wish-fulfillment squandered upon the terminally ill. In every case of genuine love the lover is ready to sacrifice all for its object—and among the collateral damage the object, too, is discovered among the casualties. Love's gratification exterminates the lover and wilts every flower poured into the vase of endearment; any lesser outcome is love only in name.

"But hate? Surely that is worse!"—Hate calculates. The survival instinct in its pure form, it drives us on to destroy the enemies who have harmed us or may be a threat. It was hate that *sustained* the Hutus. It endures despite every Nobel laureate pleading for peace, the pennant of peoples and nations. There is usually a reason to hate, whether real or perceived, the result of palpable pain or a thousand-year grudge—no one ever says "Hate made me do it." Love, by contrast, is a mysterious force, without origin, vague in any purpose beyond possession; unable to explain it because unable to do anything but *describe* our natures, we are loath to disobey its unconditional commands even if we know we shouldn't. Love is its own reason, desiring the child and confidante in order to glorify itself.

Love rallies individuals against the collective; fated in a chance encounter or an accidental pregnancy, it makes us long to withdraw into rustic cottages, to emancipate ourselves from practical ties and snuggle or play board games as the world—more senseless than ever—goes to perdition. It is only in modernity that Eros—model of loving—has fully blossomed as a basis for relationships, and only in modernity have we come so close to extinction. Love-crimes are infractions of carelessness capable of justifying any atrocity. Two souls destined to be together dispense with kindness towards everyone else, inviting suspicion towards those outside the bond that happily swells into malice, pushing defiance beyond all bounds. Hatred augments love, providing the kindling it needs for the Bonfire of the Superfluous: to all which threatens the maxim "Love is Enough!"—into the flames.

"But charity? Isn't that the yardstick of moral maturation?"—The rare charity of a good man leads, in the tenderness he inspires, to supreme indifference towards the outside. Feeding and clothing a stranger endears him to us; the task of the welfare state usurped by a renegade boy scout, the stranger no longer expects a social order to fill his belly and bandage the effects of stolen pleasures. Going beyond society's obligation to love the unlovable, the benefactor begins to admire the stranger's hidden merits— charitable organizations are too swamped by petitions to receive the gift of personality. Finding more universal humanity in the brief kindness of a single Samaritan than humanity at large—a philanthropy purer than any to be found in a group that demands ideological integration or an organization that asks for paperwork before symptoms—the stranger learns to turn his face against the world *because* his faith in altruism has been redeemed. Before he was alone in the soup kitchen, brimming with ladlefuls of resentment; now *he has a friend* . . .

The path *to* love only develops the rising action of negligence; at its climax comes the final denouement: love turns fickle. A friend's abandonment, a dear one's death, a benefactor withdrawing his affection and leaving a collection jar, plunges the feeler into total apathy. We feel the same after finding love as we do after vanquishing evil—that it will last—never suspecting that falling out of love *causes* evil to resurface. It is in this state that we devise the ultimate charity: a turn of the wheel towards a bus stop, the drowning of future disappointments. Declaring "The devil made me do it," betrayed promises lead the love-felon on the long walk down death row. *There* the lover finds permanency.

The Only Categorical Imperative

Man cannot shake off his tendency to will everything into general laws that place himself at the center of the universe. Why? —His contrary action needs validation. "Why just think, if everyone believed that no one should tell a lie . . ." the last honest man would go deaf from lip service. In the case of nihilism, though, the hypocrisy of the abyss betrays its adherer. "Can you imagine? If *everyone* was a nihilist?"—God would have a reason to exercise a deleterious effect on the species once more. Recapturing the Ancient Hebrews' masochism, man would again become able to blame himself for the misfortunes raining down on him, establishing an internal locus of control over ungovernable nature. "We are being punished because we are sinners," the nihilist proclaims. He has denied the requisite of Being and must be disciplined. Being is power, and power is justice—and so "the Patterner of Power Applied" brings his wrath down upon the adherent of Nothingness, imposing structure to dissolve the turncoat as a demonstration of his strength to other potential defectors. God's secret—the only secret, for he has appropriated all of ours—is that he does not want our anarchy to approach his. He fears the power of individuals, not to "pervert" themselves into a ground of Being, a mysterious superintendence, a void, but to *honor* this original condition, to purify themselves of the wholly good natures he bestowed on them as a mere secondary status. Though the worst crimes may be without motive, they all imply this underlying rationality. A single soul disinfecting itself of Being is enough to have a domino effect of material causes, inspiring followers to annihilate consciousness in the universe's only inhabited planet. Encountering the devil where Luther did—in being tempted to rely on himself—the nihilist is seduced into thoughts of Nothingness.

Teased by the void, at the expected moment of extermination a ray of light impinges on his victory and he falls back into Being.

And so the sin of filling oneself with an empty belief in non-being results in the punishment of bringing about a state that was not initially the case. Anticipating that by this castling move the nihilist would dispense with hope, that he could stockpile an extra round of ammo for Russian roulette, he is horrified to discover the consistency of his conviction. Realizing that hope never left him, he is disturbed to witness its final dissolution through the relentless logic of his own attempted disbelief. He was only ever a transitional figure, a mediator between the skepticism of decline and the dogma of a new age—the nihilist was still useful *because* of God's need to destroy him. The skeptics who took up his example would only follow him so far, refuting outward knowledge but never refuting themselves, retaining their drives and running after their whims; in the end it was the Believers who learned from the nihilist the importance of lifestyle over reflexivity. Now a danger to the rising Belief he helped bring about, even after his momentary utility has expired he still has one more role to play: a public spectacle to foster consolidation, a conflagration to unify a people in their "good natures"—the original perversion.

Even on the pyre he does not yield. In response to the "reductio ad absurdum" that negates his view, the nihilist practices the "reductio *mad* absurdum": going against the grain, with the ridiculousness of an incongruous pun he clings to his dogma even after it has been exposed as unfeasible; his position reduced to absurdity, the only option for the Last Infidel is to dismiss his psychological health for the sake of coherence. As the flames engulf him he cries out for marshmallows and a skewer, his final moments a continuation of the pow-wow that was his life.

Never discovering that his metaphysical rebellion was a part of God's plan all along—a cog contributing to an intelligible Good, his swerving away the brief rationale of a loftier purpose, his will to power the discharge of One higher—as a final slap in the face the nihilist remains in Being even after his body and mind have departed, the case of his audacity lingering in memorandum for any inclined to repeat it.

Condemned Bishop's Speech to His Altar Boy

My child,

It's good of you to visit me. All the same, I'd rather you not have come, that you remember me as I was. Here I lie, praying. You see my broken body, how I'm unable even to kneel. Why, you ask? But haven't you heard the rumors? Long story short, I wouldn't support the president's decision. It's only through faith that I've survived the rack for this long.

What is the president's new decision? Ah, pious boy, you've spent too much time at the altar. You really should get out more. It was outrageous, the man is mad. He told me that the nation must be a theocracy, that it was the only way to prevent the corruption of totalitarian government. I felt it my duty to inform him that, in this country, separation of church and state has long been the law. He replied that laws could be repealed.

"But it is the custom of people to worship as they like," I said. "You would impose on them one religion?"

"I've already thought that problem through," he said. "I will serve as an example for the people. A good leader must be subordinate to the laws of God."

"Which of God's laws do you intend to carry out?" I asked.

"Thankfully, the activities of our Father's absolute government are restricted to religion, taxes, and war. It's beneath the dignity of a divinely ordained being such as myself to waste time on minute regulations. Those subjects who aren't called to rally to my banner will be left alone to farm and craft high-quality objects by hand, so long as they follow the Biblical code of morality."

"But how will you ensure they follow this code?"

"Their communities will ensure it."

"Uh huh . . . and exactly who do you plan on going to war against?"

"Against everyone I don't rule."

"Since you're still only America's president, I take it that means . . . the world."

"Don't get so stuck in the present, Bishop. Emperor isn't just an empty title: it's a destiny. In order to rule an empire I need to conquer one. I plan on taking each country one at a time."

"You'll probably find ruling the world to be a headache. Why not just do some interior cleaning and be satisfied with that?"

"My dear Bishop, you misunderstand me completely. It has nothing to do with what *I* want. The wonderful thing about being God's servant is that you avoid exercising your own arbitrary whims and exercise his instead."

"The laws of God are not arbitrary, but based on his supreme goodness."

"Yes of course. Exactly why I must act as the head of the Church for all nations, so as to make God's goodness felt everywhere."

"But the nations all have different churches."

"Irrelevant. So long as they accept my rule, following God's servant is tantamount to following God. I will force conversion only within my own country, exiling all non-conformists to those nations that suit their beliefs best."

"You know it's funny, you making all these plans. I wasn't aware you were even religious."

"That was before. I'm a new man now."

"So you've officially converted?"

"In a manner of speaking, yes. When a man is spiritually reborn he is no longer what he was, he is transformed."

"Good. The evening service is about to start. I'm sure the congregation would be delighted if you'd join us in reciting the Lord's Prayer."

"I would like that, Bishop. But all in good time . . . I haven't written it yet."

That's more or less how the conversation went. And as I already told you, I opposed him. That's how I ended up here. What's that, you say? Confess and submit? But I already have: my body is not as strong as my faith. It doesn't matter to the president, though. He needs a scapegoat. That's why tomorrow I am to be executed on international television. Light a candle for me; I am resigned to imitating the way of the early Christians.

Desperate Revival

The American Republic has a mission: its politicians and businessmen are sent by God to bring about, through venality and idiocy, the demise of republics. It has been chosen to carry Greece and Rome to their culmination and end point, to witness the death of philosophy and science, the laughter of law. Its idea has always been liberty, and its idea will destroy it. *America is ready to fall*. But in a global age of nuclear standoffs and cyber warfare, no nation stands or falls alone—when Uncle Sam slips into a coma, the rest of the world will slump into adjacent hospital beds and battle for supremacy of the psychiatric ward; that nation will rise victorious which imposes her peculiar form of madness as the universal condition. Finally, the "true idea" of the state will be at hand, an order established upon a disorder, a bureaucracy of whims.

The only way to preempt rational authority is with dogma: the alternative to totalitarianism—not a moral lesson so much as a blueprint—is a *spiritual* tyranny.

The Christian Sovereign: to renew a dying religion he kneels to accept God's crown from a Capitol Hill intern, mails out Eucharist welfare stamps en masse, and inaugurates a new Inquisition from a pew of paranoias. The most foolproof way of renouncing human perfectibility is to establish the Divine as the ultimate standard, giving everyone an ideal code of behavior to fall short of and making universal ethical conditioning obligatory. The way of the reactionary is to exercise power only within limited spheres: directing all zeal into forcing grace upon nature, crushing believers in outlaw creeds along with every deviant who will not conform to official morality. A bureaucracy that shrinks its scope to surveilling prayerbreakers is free to shift public aid resources towards foreign acquisitions. By restoring criminals to sinfulness and aliens to heresy, the Crusade of the Enervated can begin. Instead of dying slowly from decline, the swift annihilation of trespassers too listless to win back the relinquished conquests of long ago. The Believers having eliminated Infidel and Cosmopolitan alike, they turn to exterminating themselves—there must always be *someone* to sacrifice. God, after disguising himself in a traditional guise, reveals himself in his original state.

The Boulevards of Extinction

Acknowledging Rationalism

When an ethical monotheist thinks of his God, he conceives of only positive attributes. Then he says, "Yes, God is these things . . . and yet I believe he is *more* also—infinitely more." The Jew, Christian, and Moslem believe in something that is ultimately inconceivable: perfection. Similarly, the nihilist thinks *of something* when he thinks of nothing, and afterwards says, "Yes, I conceive of Nothing as all this . . . but I *believe* it is less—infinitely less." Call this infinitesimality what you will, it needs some name or other . . . God, for instance.

The *rebirth* of God: not as dogma, but as void. With world as womb he is pushed into nature's vacancy, the neglected leftovers of the *tohu wa-bohu*. We pull our drowned lifeguard through the cosmic waters, leading him into the deep end for cardiopulmonary revival.

To be superstitious in the right way . . . this is what people of science and mass religion don't understand. Mysticism is that solipsism of superstition, that atomic individualism of faith which no one else can have access to, but only oneself alone. To cultivate a mystical nihilism, an Ephemeral Nay where contradictions multiply, the heavy dreams roll in, and the subject sleeps amidst realms old and new, nightmaring alone with nothingness—for given that I believe, who else will believe me? My whole IT sits slumped in assent. I am not free, but Thine.

Miracles of the Void

The laws of nature grounded in nothingness, miracles are a euphemism for the abyss. The counterfactual contract was the universe's stipulation for acquiring gravity; the void yawns and an event is swallowed into sleep. Spinning Spinozism: God cannot do anything contrary to the laws of nature, since the laws of nature are rooted in himself and spring from himself—God and Void are the same entity. It is all a part of our homecoming: snuffing ourselves out not all at once, but little by little. The shirt knitted out of a gap, it is gradually moth-eaten with holes until the gap itself drapes over our shoulders.

Being? —Void-as-presence, assimilation of the absolute.

Void? —Antecedent monism achievable again only through consequent plurality.

Erebus and Nyx mediate between the world and Chaos, the devil between us and the Almighty—a hodgepodge of theologies allows one to cope with metaphysics while avoiding the thesis-ache and dissertation tremens of truth-withdrawal; all one has to sacrifice is a *particular* tradition.

Odyssey of Oppression

Imagining so many dystopias and apocalyptic scenarios, projecting so many disasters into the future, is not the same as attempting to predict that future—to make educated guesses in the anticipation that one of them might come true. It is instead the universalization of the future, in which *every* scenario becomes true: a set of posthistories that are not merely possible but will be actual and simultaneous. Only by losing all trust in the origins of history—the preceding events that have led up to our existence—can one confidently prophesize its *multiple* ends. One does this by not simply disbelieving one or another historical account or by doubting whether the gaps in the record will ever be filled in, but by acknowledging every account as valid in its own way, of "history" as a collection of all the histories ever written, an infinite combination of partial causes, reasons, and influences culminating in us. Napoleon died of stomach cancer and arsenic poisoning. Bacon was himself and Shakespeare. Iphigenia was sacrificed at Aulis and safely whisked away to Tauris by Artemis. Hitler was worse than Stalin, Stalin worse than Hitler, they were both worse, neither was worse. Every dubious event occurred, every questionable motive was a force, every insignificant act a world-shaking power. It is the boundlessness of our beginnings that will determine the boundlessness of our ends, predicaments compounded by our myopia towards them, focused solely as we are on laminating the minutiae of "our" actuality. And if some lucky citizen of time, after being shown all these outcomes like a dreaming modal Scrooge, insists on an explanation for them, asking "*Why* will we die?" then the Ghost of Christmas Future may answer: "From *too much* knowledge!" With the academic mode of knowing surpassing its ability to assimilate the very knowledge it created, engaged in piecemeal analyses, memorizing less and less in proportion to the sum total, a limit will be reached when global database meltdowns leave us in a world where the only information to tap into lies in the pages of outdated reference books. And when *those* crumble to dust, what are we left with? Death of self-awareness in time, oblivion of humanity's story of development, the civilizing process turned against us. Our very activity of questioning our undertakings itself results in the events to come—those *on the far side* of Hegel's movement of history towards a harmony of self-consciousness with its activity, in which the rubble-dweller, lacking a basic set of reference points with which to ask any questions, is totally absorbed in stalking deer over toppled skyscrapers.

From whichever endpoint one looks back—if one *could* look back—the dilemma of the rubble-dweller shows itself to have always been our own. Our account of time is narrow, our greatest historians parochialists of the unintelligible. As the world-fiend in its unfolding ignorance propels us towards brutishness of every kind, we arrive at a threshold in which the eternal integrity of every moment of goodness is concealed from view, while a single act of evil spans epochs; with a hindsight barred from *us*—to a hypothetical outsider—it seems that every event contributed to the fulfillment of an ultimate pointlessness. Whipped on by the naïveté of reason, existence unfurls its arational arc, branching out its profusion of absurdities as its bystanders toil in the dirt, unreliable eyewitnesses to a destiny of futility. Ours is not a theodicy, a journey towards "God's justice," but a *theokatapony*, an odyssey of oppression. A deity constrained only by logical possibility does not confine himself to willing "the" bad antecedently and "the" worst consequently, but constantly strives to outdo himself with plague after plague; every new actuality becomes a springboard for testing the limits of our endurance. For the set of worst possible worlds there is no worst of all worsts; "worst" is a relative term with no upper ceiling in which every inhabitant of creation experiences *their own worst* existence, a world of misery unto themselves. Like the slave driver who brutalizes himself along with his slave, the world-fiend becomes ever more primitive as he blasts us into antediluvian living standards. Worn down through labor and suffering, we crawl on, the burden of vexation piling up on our backs until exhaustion overwhelms us, and God, omnighted, trips into total darkness. Misplaced by divine imbecility, unintelligible to ourselves, ignorant of the world as an object to be known, the human intellect advances into a second infancy and sucks its wrinkled thumb as our falling cradle smashes through every conceivable bough on the tree of time. Temporality opens into homelessness, an eternity of nows.

Branching

Why shouldn't we be confident about our infinite fate? Why bother guessing and worrying? A man with two futures has less reason to hope than a man with only one. There are no anxieties about what "the future" will be: it is a disunited sum of *both* outcomes, equally his, equally necessary, choiceless: in one tomorrow he goes to heaven, in the other to hell. Wondering "What does today predetermine?" he steals a crucifix from heathens who would destroy it and is equally damned and saved.

For breaking the eighth commandment the thief is cast into a serpent-filled ditch in the eighth circle; turned into a reptile, he is forced to appropriate human shapes from other sinners, his body mass index a dietician's nightmare for a bleak eternity.

For reacquiring the cross in the name of chaotic goodness he is reunited with all the gentlemanly filchers of historical legend: Robin Hood, Butch Cassidy, Disney's Aladdin. Raising champagne flutes they salute the under-trodden upon a hill of jewels, toasting their toasted selves in the lower world, dropping down a few rubies to fight over when bliss begins to bore. It is not resentment that fuels their spectatorship, but the ennui of having only each other to talk to in a silent and blinding expanse—whoever was here before them forgot to turn off the light.

Embracing destiny is as simple as discarding our most common-sense presupposition: we can throw away our cake and purge it from our bellies, too.

The Winds of Love

Love is the gap between God and Man: on one side, the compulsory reception of an arbitrary condemnation; on the other, the election to give something beyond practical benefits and elevate above common attachments. Whether coming upon one suddenly or taken up as an obligation, it is the furthest thing from freedom and the only real choice: to earn an eternally estranged resemblance.

The less far we are from God the further we are. Side-by-side on a walk in the clouds, the proximity of our likenesses shame us. Unable to ask distantly devised questions out of fear that our most meager similarities would be stripped away, God reads this concern and sprints ahead of our imperfect qualities as a reminder of our rank. Alone, we feel ourselves again, but when he waits for us to catch up our anxiety returns. The sign of a superior Love is the willingness to suffer a relationship without ultimate progress.

And Christ? —Against him too we fall short, not only in moral excellence but shoddy carpentry. He was *too good* for his workbench, abandoning the demand for finely handcrafted tables and chairs at the height of his career; lashed to ours we churn out factory-line furniture, without enough overtime hours to go home for dinner on a fiberboard dining set. The Son is not our model of the Father incarnate, the link between God and man, but our earthly embarrassment, the star achiever resented by a class of slackers. In return for his sacrifice we are only too charitable in natural enmity. No practical joke is too dirty to risk being sent to the principal's office, if only we have the chance to play a nastier one once we get there. To improve our self-esteem, we are compelled to dismiss him as an object of comparison and agree with the Lombard: "in as much as Christ is a man he is not something."

What of the spirit? If we could *see* it we might believe it, but mutilating our flesh would not bring us any closer. Our embarrassment is to continue to hope for its preeminence.

The trinity needs *us*. It cannot exist otherwise; perfection without comparison is meaningless. It is a need that does not die even when we are unaware of it—an eternal need that cries in gale-force winds when absentmindedness engulfs us. The Trinitarian Gifts: a solar flare, a healing miracle, a glance towards the end of the tunnel—teasing hints of faultless splendor. Racked to a harp, Love plucks away at us until the string breaks or we do.

Our hearts must be Theirs and Theirs alone. They know our natural loves are capricious, our human ties insufficient safeguards against boredom and tragedy—sooner or later some blight, byproduct of divine hunger for attention, will break them. After that we have nowhere else to turn: we must subject ourselves to Their charity.

But the state of grace only stirs us for so long; eventually the ecstasy emanating from a religious conversion goes tepid. Abandoned to lack of external improvement, our recent magnificence dissipated, faced with the resurgence of old dispositions, what is left? —To utilize a prejudiced reason: we remember the old relatives and friends whom we forsook for God and make room for them in our minds once again. Having learned something from our masters, we transform our charity back into our natural loves: acting as an idol unto our intimates, tormenting them with promises and whimsies until, the limits of their tolerance reached, we are driven back (for the last time?), alone and helpless, into God's arms—boon and bane outstretched over all.

In this bounce house of Love, knocked around between ambition and inadequacy, we can live up to neither our needs nor Theirs; from no source do we give or receive enough sanctification. No choice but to flop between fiery passions, exalt ourselves in the fight against torpor of soul, taking refuge in a source until resentment encroaches—or, more fatal, *respect*. Loving too often or too violently, scouring the earth for fresh monotony, draining every fountain we find in sips or gulps. With increasing immunity to *intense* feeling we gradually endear ourselves to ever more trifling objects and experiences, eventually reconciled to pretending as well as we can when only memories are left to leech.

Is not a lover in this state worthy of a consolation? A cup of chamomile tea, an enema . . . any respite, soporific or laxative . . .

"To télos mégiston apantôn"

If, for a good story, "the most important thing of all is the end," for the human story the most important end is the beginning. Before our nature is defined it is eradicated. Death—coda to the human drama—is also the overture. The dark side of the Renaissance was our lasting inheritance—the morbid lyrics of Gesualdo, Bosch's third panel.

The two chief ways of ignoring this parameter—the dominant modes of living—are control and fantasy: insurance and religion. In the rare case that the existence of the end is acknowledged, all the remaining energy of life is devoted to preventing it. The aim of both is to *keep things going* at all costs. The highest folly of all is the irony that blends the two: those who do not believe in the end are often those who most struggle to thwart it. With hell in their hearts they quantify the risk of swallowing a toxic communion wafer, remembering Descartes's conspiracy of reason as they toss a few coins into the offering plate.

In lieu of worrying give me a place to stand—*on my head*. Jacobi's awe with the annihilated series of explanatory conditions is a trick-or-treating jaunt compared with its inversion—a series beginning in the self-evidence of a commonplace reason: Being conditioned by oblivion, a first principle which contravenes itself. Ostriches too heavy to fly, the skulls of Life's observers are firmly buried in the quicksand of the All: the One: the Nothing. Dulling the terror of time-consciousness with a rush of blood to the brain, the withdrawers embrace their perishability with the same fervor for despair as the deniers rush ever-onward in tremors of desperation. Both groups threaten to give everything a value that is bottomless; in the depths of the pit infinity is equivalent to nullity.

Part 9

Syringes

It is rare to encounter an optimism that *refreshes*: that doesn't beg the question, overlay an existential crisis with guilt, and make a banality of hope.

To begin in nihilism, barrel into cynicism, refute into skepticism, and end in a mitigated pessimism: foraging for a meal instead of collecting alms. But after the dumpsters have been plundered . . . *still* hungry.

Every broken line of latitude is an Archimedean lever.

The dark ones, how they navigate by snatches of day, slurping up crescent moonbeams like slices of melon. The darkest ones, how they grope and sniff and follow behind.

Like a locked outhouse that reads "vacant," Abyss occupies Abyss. Like the smell that overwhelms the pit latrine, both suffocate from the claustrophobia of congested infinities.

While waiting for absolution, pass the time by brooding on its overlooked arrival.

An atheist is someone who lost every secret and pretends to have thrown them away. A theist has one left, and overextends it to fill in for all the rest.

If men could grasp with their feet . . . how firmly grounded they would be.

Secular man searches in vain for a way to get above his own time-bound subjectivity. So far his best results have been achieved *sub specie fraternitatis*: "under the aspect of the keg stand."

Trading imagination for wings, angels are only more encumbered versions of children.

The religious martyr, the captain who goes down with the ship, the artist who starves to create, the Romeo who refuses to outlast his love—we do not consider the latter a form of heroism, though the recklessness of the first three are pursued as inadequate surrogates, desperate proofs of a thwarted capacity. Love is the wellspring of glory.

The True American: proud of the old portraits, lamenting the line at the photo booth; mirthless bystander at a carnival where the ticket salesman is tossing out fistfuls of carousel tokens.

Light is the orphanage of the mystic's chest pain.

Inspiration in a compromised position is the muse's gauntlet. An artist cannot know the limits of his resolve until he tests his skill against the future mother-in-law's fusilli.

To be a comma maniac, always pausing for effect, refusing to be swept up in the run-on of life—only the dash with its dismembered insight can compensate for such inertia. It is the punctuational parallel to the leap of faith, the culmination of a series of judiciously considered stepping stones.

The appendix: proof of God's love of uselessness. Tucked away unseen, people who cannot make themselves practical are relegated to hypotheses of what they could be good for, until they *burst* from a surplus of unrealized potential.

To be saved more than once because the first salvation was insufficient. When that is still not enough, a few miracles to at least keep us where we are.

In an age of faith, reason is a rocket to the heavens. In an age of reason it is a manhole to the sewers.

Reason's *first* step is to be oblivious to the axiom's infinite prerequisites.

Reason: amulet of sentiment, occult charm of every caroler. Its charisma is to hide itself inside a melody.

What is more of a waste of fortune than to be ashamed of one's privilege? The only way talent can be developed to the full, without distraction, is to *take for granted* your preconditions.

Love's librettists: the lonely lighting operators of every lasting relationship, talented loyalists to a subsidiary lyricism.

To die upon hearing of the glory of God's word, moments before your intention to accept Jesus into your heart has been verbalized to the minister—will not the gates of heaven take into account the lackluster eulogy?

Eschatology of the soup bowl: when the broth gets too low to dip one's spoon in, many a full stomach will start watering it down just to put off the after-dinner cigar a bit longer.

The God-*tipsy* man: a lukewarm belief that proselytizes with plowshares. Only crusaders and hermits can metabolize intoxication.

Babylonian literature: when fiction inspires truth. From the Euphrates to Moses' mother floated the basket of pitch, miracle of a pharaoh who levitated stone with willed labor.

Part 9: Syringes

Granddaughters of Zedekiah: overlooked and disobedient, meriting no attention from earthly powers and appointed to indirect celestial service. In preserving the uprooted cedar a few thirsty tree huggers make headlines; the rest carry water pails from distant rivers.

With its spaciousness and the mellow light pouring in from outside, his soul's interior had all the magnificence of a church by de Witte; but the clumsiness of his good works built Ruisdael's ruins around it. What adventurer in intimacy is willing to climb through rubble and underbrush to see the true perspective?

Aristotle's claim that the heart is the seat of the mind is no less accurate after being debunked.

It is under intense pressure that the most profound thoughts occur, in those dark remote spaces thinned of all but carnivores. The monsters of the deep have only each other to feed upon.

Sensations describe a love beyond words. Words texture a love abstracted by distance.

When a society approaches a human brain in complexity: one man's mountaintop tablets are replaced with joint resolutions of amendments, tendons with engines, the predestination of the cross with the randomness of a quark; when a neuroimaging scanner lights up our active areas and exposes the farce of consciousness: that the processes outside this lump of water-packed tofu are as opaque to it as its inner ones—the brain pops a blood vessel and rebels.

The uninhabitable regions are the last places of real freedom, thus of heroes; at the extremes of north and south a wild fortitude can be discovered in oneself and preserved for the world.

What is the relationship between stomach and raiment? Gastronomy aromatizes spirituality into a belch, while a silk bib prepares us to enter the Kitchen Where None Hunger and eructate psalms everlastingly.

Love at first sight needs a double take under the microscope for verification. The wooer surrenders to biology, the nurturer studies it.

A string of paper gingerbread people, love ties us together and makes us look edible.

The cheapening of a truth begins the moment it becomes distinguishable from delusion. Avoid all witnesses to epiphanies.

Love is a chemical reaction to cosmic forces.

The Boulevards of Extinction

Aboriginal salvation: the world already being nothing, the realization that you were born delivered from it.

Uncoordinated senses encounter broken beauty everywhere; a mind divided, cracked truths. A bit of evil is enough to harmonize them.

Everyone watches for shooting stars. Look for a supernova.

I want only to close my eyes and feel my lids block the light, nothing more.

A thinker without a ground to place axioms on will flourish his floating castle with their flags.

Love is the escape plan from our programmed existences.

Nothingness: the perpetual elsewhere, the jailbreak from what one is and was always meant to be.

Love for Nothing—culmination and unity of two universals.

Those who do not float through the abyss are not meant to swim among the stars.

www.ingramcontent.com/pod-product-compliance
Lightning Source LLC
Chambersburg PA
CBHW060507300426
44112CB00017B/2574